MONARCH COLLEGE OUTLINES

AMERICAN HISTORY I
(COLONIAL TIMES TO RECONSTRUCTION)

by
GERALD KURLAND, Ph.D.

Editor in Chief
EDWARD C. GRUBER, Ph.D.

MONARCH PRESS

ABOUT THE AUTHOR

Dr. Gerald Kurland has taught many college courses in various areas of history. The author's attachment to his subject is evident as one reads this American History I Outline as well as his two Monarch College Outlines on Western Civilization. Among other works by Professor Kurland are *The Amateur in Politics* and *Seth Low: Reformer in an Urban and Industrial Age*. Dr. Kurland received his Ph.D. from the City University of New York and is now on the faculty of Brooklyn College.

PICTURE CREDITS

Permission to use photographs which appear in this book has been granted by the Bettmann Archive and Wide World Photos.

Copyright © 1971 by
SIMON & SCHUSTER

All rights reserved. No part of this book may be reproduced in any form without permission in writing from the publisher.

Published by
MONARCH PRESS
a Simon & Schuster Division of
Gulf & Western Corporation
Simon & Schuster Building
1230 Avenue of the Americas
New York, N.Y. 10020

Printed in the United States of America

TABLE OF CONTENTS

Chapter 1 — The European Background of American History, **1**

PART ONE: COLONIAL AMERICA, 1492-1763

Chapter 2 — Indian Civilizations and the Spanish Colonies, **8**

Chapter 3 — French and Dutch Colonies, **16**

Chapter 4 — Virginia and the Southern Colonies, **24**

Chapter 5 — The New England Colonies, **34**

Chapter 6 — The Middle Colonies and the Melting Pot, **45**

Chapter 7 — Mercantilism and the Wars of Empire, **54**

Chapter 8 — Mature Colonial Society and Culture, **64**

PART TWO: THE REVOLUTION AND THE YOUNG REPUBLIC, 1763-1828

Chapter 9 — The American Revolution, 1763-1783, **74**

Chapter 10 — The Articles of Confederation and the Constitution, 1783-1789, **88**

Chapter 11 — The Federalists Under Washington and Adams, 1789-1801, **100**

Chapter 12 — Jeffersonian America, 1801-1809, **112**

Chapter 13 — The Virginia Dynasty and the War of 1812, **121**

Chapter 14 — The Era of Good Feelings and the Coming of Jackson, 1816-1828, **132**

PART THREE: THE MIDDLE PERIOD, 1828-1877

Chapter 15 — The Era of Jacksonian Democracy, 1828-1844, **146**

Chapter 16 — American Romanticism and the Growth of Southern Civilization, **160**

Chapter 17 — Manifest Destiny and the Mexican War, 1844-1848, **173**

Chapter 18 — The House Begins to Divide, 1848-1860, **186**

Chapter 19 — Civil War and Reconstruction Under Lincoln, 1860-1865, **200**

Chapter 20 — Radical Reconstruction, 1865-1877, **216**

List of Textbooks Keyed to Outline

1. BLUM, JOHN M., et.al., *The National Experience*, 2nd ed. (New York: Harcourt, Brace & World, 1968). One volume edition.

2. CARMAN, HARRY J., HAROLD C. SYRETT, and BERNARD W. WISHY, *A History of the American People*, 3rd ed. (New York: Alfred A. Knopf, 1967). Two volume paperback edition.

3. GARRATY, JOHN A., *The American Nation*, 2nd ed. (New York: Harper & Row, 1971). One volume edition.

4. GRAEBNER, NORMAN A., GILBERT C. FITE, and PHILIP L. WHITE, *A History of the United States* (New York: McGraw-Hill, 1970). Two volume edition.

5. HANDLIN, OSCAR, *America: A History* (New York: Holt, Rinehart & Winston, 1968). One volume edition.

6. HICKS, JOHN D., GEORGE E. MOWRY and ROBERT E. BURKE, *A History of American Democracy*, 4th ed. (Boston: Houghton-Mifflin, 1970). Two volume paperback edition.

7. HOFSTADTER, RICHARD, WILLIAM MILLER and DANIEL AARON, *The American Republic*, 2nd ed. (Englewood Cliffs, N.J.: Prentice-Hall, 1970). Two volume edition.

8. HOFSTADTER, RICHARD, WILLIAM MILLER and DANIEL AARON, *The United States*, 2nd ed. (Englewood Cliffs, N.J.: Prentice-Hall, 1967). One volume edition.

9. MORISON, SAMUEL E., HENRY S. COMMAGER and WILLIAM E. LEUCHTENBURG, *The Growth of the American Republic*, 6th ed. (New York: Oxford University Press, 1969). Two volume edition.

10. MORISON, SAMUEL E., *The Oxford History of the American People* (New York: Oxford University Press, 1965). One volume edition.

11. PERKINS, DEXTER, and GLYNDON G. VAN DEUSEN, *The United States of America* (New York: Macmillan, 1962). Two volume edition.

12. WILLIAMS, T. HARRY, RICHARD N. CURRENT, and FRANK FREIDEL, *A History of the United States*, 3rd ed. (New York: Alfred A. Knopf, 1969). Two volume edition.

AMERICAN HISTORY I

Chapter 1

THE EUROPEAN BACKGROUND OF AMERICAN HISTORY

The European discovery of America in the late fifteenth century must rank as one of the most important events in human history. The opening of America transformed the economic, social, and political institutions of Western Europe. The influx of Peruvian and Mexican gold and silver into Europe in the sixteenth century brought on a price revolution which destroyed the economic power of the feudal aristocracy and encouraged the development of a capitalist economic system. This economic revolution increased the wealth and power of the European bourgeoisie (middle class), who aided the kings in their efforts to develop highly centralized and powerful nation-states. Finally, the discovery of the Western Hemisphere shifted Europe's political center of gravity from the Mediterranean Sea to the North Atlantic Ocean, and the nations of Northwestern Europe supplanted the nations of Southern Europe as the leaders of the Western world. While the Europeans were not the first people to discover the New World, they were the first to take effective advantage of their discovery.

PRE-COLUMBUS DISCOVERIES

Although Thor Heyerdahl, the eminent archaeologist-explorer, has demonstrated the possibility that Polynesians and Egyptians could have sailed to America in antiquity, there is little evidence to substantiate this claim. However, recent archaeological findings strongly point to the possibility that Japanese fishermen accidentally reached the western coast of South America some 3,000 years ago. It is quite likely that seafaring peoples could have reached America's shores after being blown off their normal sea-routes by storms, but it is unlikely that any of these mariners established permanent settlements.

The Vikings

Between 982 and 985, Eric the Red explored Greenland and founded a colony there in 986. The Viking (or Norse) colony took root in Greenland, and its settlers maintained an almost continuous contact with Europe until 1415. In the same year that the Vikings established their Greenland colony (986), Bjarni Herjulfson was blown off course by a storm; and he is credited with being the first European to sight the North American coastline. Sometime about the year 1000, Leif Ericson, son of Eric the Red, sailed to the shores of North America and established a Norse colony at a place called Vinland. A few years later, Leif's brother, Thorvald Ericson, explored much of the North American coast. Unfortunately, historians know very little about the Vinland colony. We do not know how extensive it was, how long it lasted, or what fate finally befell it. We do not even know its exact location, although Vinland was most probably located somewhere in Labrador, Newfoundland, or Nova Scotia. For a long time, historians dismissed Vinland as a figment of the Viking imagination. (The *Greenland Saga,* a Norse epic poem, was one of the few sources pertaining to Vinland.) However, archaeologists have found much that is valid in the ancient tales, and Norse relics (some of doubtful authenticity) have been found from Rhode Island all the way out to Minnesota.

The Vikings, though, lacked the technology and the economic and political resources to sustain their voyages of exploration, and their American colony (or colonies) soon ceased to exist. Likewise, the people of Western Europe were in the midst of their "dark age," and were equally unsuited to the task of overseas exploration and colonization. As a result, the Viking discovery of America was quickly forgotten, and almost five centuries elapsed before the Europeans resumed geographic exploration.

THE EUROPEAN AGE OF DISCOVERY

Reasons For the Renewed Interest In Exploration

By the mid-fifteenth century, Europe, led by Spain and Portugal, was ready to embark again on great voyages of exploration. Among the factors responsible for this renewed interest in exploration were the following:

(1) **The Crusades.** Spanning the two centuries from 1095 to 1290, the Crusades stimulated the revival of European commerce and led to a renewed urban growth. Western Europe had become dependent upon such Near Eastern and Oriental commodities as pepper, cinnamon, and other spices, silk, china, and various other items. By the fifteenth century, trade with the East was dominated by the Italian city-states (Venice, Genoa, Pisa) whose merchants charged a seemingly exorbitant price for their commodities. The desire to obtain the products of the East at a cheaper cost by bypassing the Italian middlemen was a prime factor in the explorations of the Portuguese and the Spanish.

(2) **The Renaissance.** The intellectual awakenings that occurred during the fourteenth and fifteenth centuries led to the rediscovery of Greek scientific knowledge and stimulated interest in geography. Realizing that the earth was spherical, European geographers hoped to reach the Orient by sailing around Africa or by sailing westward across the great Ocean Sea (Atlantic).

(3) **Improved Technology.** The development of scientific knowledge led to the creation of new devices to make ocean voyages safer and faster. The magnetic compass and the astrolabe (a device for fixing latitude by means of the North Star) allowed navigators to determine their precise location at all times. In addition, improved hydrographic charts, called *portolani,* permitted sea captains to sail the oceans with a greater degree of safety than ever before. Finally, the caravel (developed by the Portuguese) was the first European vessel capable of sustained ocean voyage.

(4) **Financing.** Lastly, and perhaps most importantly, the establishment of centralized monarchies in Spain and Portugal, with effective powers of taxation, enabled the Iberian kings to raise the large amounts of money needed to finance voyages of exploration. The cost of outfitting this type of voyage was beyond the resources of any single individual or group of individuals; only the state commanded the economic power needed to undertake geographic exploration. (Later on the joint stock company would enable private groups to finance overseas exploration. By selling shares of stock to the general public, the company could raise the vast sums needed to finance overseas trade.)

Portugal and Spain Lead the Way

The Age of Discovery began with explorations by the Portuguese under the leadership of Prince Henry the Navigator (1394–1460). Not only did he sponsor many of the technological improvements described above, but he also planned the expeditions which discovered the Azores, the Canaries, and the west coast of Africa. The Portuguese were convinced that they could reach the Orient by sailing around Africa, and in 1488, Bartolomeu Dias reached the Cape of Good Hope (then called the Cape of Storms). But his men, terrified that the waters around the Cape were inhabited by fearsome sea monsters, refused to allow him to round the Cape. Ten years later, however, Vasco da Gama successfully rounded Africa and sailed on to Calicut in India. Because the Portuguese were committed to the eastern route to the Indies, and since their financial resources were already strained, Portugal's King Joâo II refused to finance Christopher Columbus' proposed westward voyage to Cipangu (Japan). Instead Columbus went to Spain and sought to convince Ferdinand and Isabella of the soundness of his westward route to the Orient.

Prince Henry the Navigator

First Landing of Columbus on the shores of the New World (at San Salvador, W.I., Oct. 12, 1492).

CHRISTOPHER COLUMBUS AND THE DISCOVERY OF AMERICA*

Born in 1451 in Genoa, Italy, into a family of wool weavers, Columbus became convinced that the Indies could be reached by sailing due west across the Atlantic. After several years of negotiations, Columbus (with the aid of Luis de Santangel, the treasurer of Aragon) persuaded Queen Isabella to sponsor his voyage. In 1492, Isabella granted Columbus the title "Admiral of the Ocean Sea," empowered him to rule any new lands he might discover, and promised him 10 per cent of the profits of any trade between Spain and the Indies. On August 3 of that year, the Niña, the Pinta, and the Santa Maria sailed from Palos with a crew of ninety men. After two months, no land had been sighted; and mutiny threatened to develop several times. Then, in the early morning hours of October 12, Rodrigo de Triana, a lookout on board the Pinta, sighted land. Columbus had arrived at a small island in the Bahamas which he named San Salvador (now Watlings Island). Convinced that he had reached the Indies, he named the natives of the islands Indians.

Columbus explored the Bahamas until October 26 before moving on to Cuba. In December, he explored the coasts of Hispaniola (Santo Domingo), where the Santa Maria was wrecked. Having established the colony of La Navidad on Hispaniola, Columbus sailed back to Spain in January of 1493 to report his findings. When he returned to Hispaniola in September of 1493, La Navidad had disappeared without a trace. However, he founded a new colony, named for Queen Isabella, and went on to explore Puerto Rico and Jamaica. Still convinced that he had reached the Indies, Columbus continued to search for the passage to Japan, China, and India. In 1496, he established a settlement at Santo Domingo, and in June, he set sail back to Spain.

Two years later, Columbus embarked upon his

---

* Although Columbus discovered the New World, the Western Hemisphere was named for Amerigo Vespucci, who touched the coast of South America in the region of the Guianas in 1499. Vespucci wrote an account of his voyage which was widely read in Europe, and the German cartographer Martin Waldseemüller named the New World in honor of Amerigo Vespucci on the erroneous assumption that Vespucci had been the first European to visit the Western Hemisphere.

third voyage to America and discovered Trinidad. However, in 1500, Santo Domingo erupted in rebellion, and Columbus and his two brothers were returned to Spain in chains. Although Columbus was restored to his title ("Admiral of the Ocean Sea") in 1502, he was stripped of his political authority in America. He undertook his last voyage to America in 1502 and explored Martinique and the Honduran coast of Central America. Failing to find a sea-lane to the Orient, Columbus was disappointed about his discoveries. Dying heartbroken in 1506, he never realized the importance or the magnitude of his discoveries.

THE EUROPEAN RIVALRY FOR AMERICA

In 1493, Pope Alexander VI, at the behest of Ferdinand and Isabella, issued two decrees *(Inter Caetera I* and *Inter Caetera II)*. The first assigned all newly discovered lands not ruled by Christian princes to Spain, and the second divided the non-Christian world between the Spanish and the Portuguese at a line drawn 100 leagues west of the Azores. (The Treaty of Tordesillas of 1494 moved the line of demarcation to 370 leagues west of the Cape Verde Islands, which gave Portugal the Brazilian coast.) In effect, Spain was given the New World and Portugal was awarded the Orient. The Papal decrees formed the legal basis for Spain's and Portugal's claims to rule overseas territories. However, the papal edicts shut out France, England, and Holland from a share in the division of the New World and the Orient.

The nations of Northern Europe would later argue that only effective colonization could legitimize a nation's claim to overseas colonies, and they were to actively challenge Spain and Portugal for control of the non-European world. Moreover, the wars of religion that stemmed from the Protestant Reformation of 1517 intensified colonial rivalries. The wealth and resources of the New World became a vital factor in determining whether the Protestant or the Catholic nations would master Europe. America, therefore, became a theater in the European wars of religion; whichever power came to dominate the New World would control the Old World as well. The stage was being set for the decisive eighteenth-century struggle for empire.

REVIEW QUESTIONS FOR CHAPTER 1

1. The Price Revolution did all of the following *except*

   (A) cause the decline of the aristocracy
   (B) weaken the Catholic church
   (C) encourage the rise of capitalism
   (D) increase the power of the kings

2. The first European to see America was

   (A) Eric the Red
   (B) Thorvald Ericson
   (C) Bjarni Herjulfson
   (D) Leif Ericson

3. Vinland was most probably located in present-day

   (A) Labrador
   (B) Rhode Island
   (C) Minnesota
   (D) Greenland

4. *Portolani* were

   (A) Portuguese ships
   (B) hydrographic charts
   (C) magnetic compasses
   (D) navigational devices

5. The first man to round the Cape of Good Hope was

   (A) Vasco da Gama
   (B) Henry the Navigator
   (C) Bartolomeu Dias
   (D) Christopher Columbus

6. The New World was named by

   (A) Christopher Columbus
   (B) Amerigo Vespucci
   (C) Martin Waldseemüller
   (D) None of the above

7. During the first voyage to America, Columbus founded a colony on

   (A) Hispaniola
   (B) Jamaica
   (C) Puerto Rico
   (D) Haiti

8. The non-Christian world was divided between Spain and Portugal by

   (A) Pope Julius II
   (B) Pope Alexander VI
   (C) Pope Paul II
   (D) Pope Alexander V

9. Columbus discovered Trinidad on his _____ voyage to America

   (A) first
   (B) second
   (C) third
   (D) fourth

10. Columbus was stripped of his political authority in America in

   (A) 1495
   (B) 1500
   (C) 1502
   (D) 1504

Explanatory Answers

1. **(B)** The Price Revolution was not a direct cause of the church's loss of authority.

2. **(C)** Herjulfson sighted North America in 986, after being blown off course by a storm.

3. **(A)** Vinland was most probably in Labrador, Newfoundland, or Nova Scotia.

4. **(B)** Portolani were the first accurate hydrographic charts.

5. **(A)** Da Gama rounded the Cape in 1498.

6. **(C)** Martin Waldseemüller was an early German map maker.

7. **(A)** The colony, La Navidad, perished without a trace.

8. **(B)** Pope Alexander VI divided the New World in 1493.

9. **(C)** Columbus started his third voyage in 1498.

10. **(C)** He was arrested after Santo Domingo rebelled against his authority, but he was later released.

PART ONE:
COLONIAL AMERICA, 1492-1763

Chapter 2

INDIAN CIVILIZATIONS AND THE SPANISH COLONIES

The original discoverers of America were the Indians. Members of the Mongoloid (or Oriental) race, the Indians originated somewhere in East Asia and migrated to North America over a land bridge which once connected Alaska and Siberia. The migrations took place sometime between 50,000 B.C. and 11,000 B.C., when the Arctic Ocean was an open, warm-water sea. From Alaska, the Indians slowly moved south until they occupied the entire Western Hemisphere. The earliest human remains (Midland Man) found in America were discovered in Texas and date back to some 12,000 to 20,000 years B.C. A fairly extensive Indian culture (the Folsom culture) was unearthed in Colorado and dates back to 8800 B.C.

These early Indians were primitive Stone-Age food gatherers and hunters. It was not until about 3000 B.C. that agriculture was developed in Mexico and the Andes, and another two thousand years passed before the Indians of America discovered the art of metallurgy and the benefits of irrigation. Only when these arts had been learned could advanced Indian civilizations be developed. Unfortunately, outside of Mexico and the Andean regions of South America, agricultural development remained primitive, and the Indians of America never outgrew their original Stone-Age culture.

THE INDIAN WAY OF LIFE

By 1492, the Indian population of what is now the United States numbered about one and a half million people. Since the Indians depended upon hunting for their survival, it took fifty square miles of land to support each Indian, and overpopulation was becoming a problem. The major Indian groups in the United States were the following:

(1) **The Algonquins.** These people inhabited Canada, New England, and the Ohio Valley and were generally forest dwellers. They established friendly relations with the French. Their customs and way of life were studied by many early writers, who assumed that they were typical of all American Indians.

(2) **The Iroquois.** The dominant Indians of central New York State, they were enemies of the French and the Algonquins; they allied with the Dutch (and later the English) and helped to defeat the French. Renowned for their fighting ability, they organized the Iroquois (or Five-Nations) Confederacy in the fifteenth century. A federal union consisting of the Cayugas, Mohawks, Oneidas, Onondagas, and Senecas, the Five Nations cooperated in times of war or common danger. The principles of their confederation influenced the development of the United States Federal Government.

(3) **The Muskhogean group.** This group controlled the southern United States. Their most advanced tribes were the Creeks and Choctaws of

Algonquin canoeist

Georgia, who would later figure tragically in the history of the United States.

(4) **The Siouan group.** They lived west of the Mississippi. Great Plains Indians, they followed the great buffalo herds.

(5) **The Pueblos.** These Indians of the southwest were town-dwelling farmers. Organized into some seventy autonomous towns, they were a theocratic people (ruled by the priestly classes) whose religious rites included the famous rain dances and the consumption of powerful narcotic drugs.

Indian Social Organization

While it is dangerous to make sweeping generalizations about the American Indian as a whole, most Indians shared certain common customs and features. The Indians of America were organized into tribes, each headed by a chief. The tribes were subdivided into clans (groups of families sharing common blood-ties), each one having its own totem (a religious deity which protects the clan). Every clan had a sachem (administrator and judge) who represented the clan in the tribal council, and chiefs (one for every fifty warriors) chosen for their fighting ability. The clan council, composed of all free adults, operated in a democratic manner and had the power to elect and depose sachems, to handle the administration of justice and settle clan disputes, and to admit new members to the clan. Presiding over the clan council was the tribal council (sachems and chiefs) which decided on issues of war and peace and on relations with other tribes. While all could attend meetings of the tribal council, only the sachems and chiefs could vote.

Living in villages of tents made of animal skins or in long houses (large huts occupied by many families), the Indians had no conception of private property. Land and property were held in common and belonged to the tribe as a whole, not to individual members of the tribe. The Indians believed in Manitou (the "great spirit" who rules the universe) and in various lesser gods identified with the forces of nature. The medicine man was a religious figure who was charged with safeguarding the tribe and its members from evil spirits. The Indians also believed in a life after death ("Happy Hunting Ground"). However, the Indians of America had a relatively simple culture and their writing system never developed beyond the pictograph (picture symbol) stage.

THE MAYANS: THE "GREEKS" OF NORTH AMERICA

By far the most highly developed of the North American Indian civilizations was the Mayan culture of Mexico. This people's achievements have earned them the title of the "Greeks" of North America. Establishing their capital at Teotihuacán (near modern-day Mexico City), the Mayans founded their civilization about the beginning of the Christian era; and it flourished for some nine hundred years. They developed an accurate 365-day calendar, invented the mathematical concept of zero, and raised mathematics to a very high art. Extremely knowledgeable in astronomy, they constructed elaborate structures reminiscent of the Egyptian pyramids. Although the Mayans developed a sophisticated written language and though much of their writings have come down to us, we unfortunately know little about their culture because we have, so far, been unable to decipher or to master their language. For reasons which are still unclear, the Mayans disappeared from history about 1000 A.D.; and their territory was conquered by less civilized tribes. Eventually, about 1325 A.D., the Aztecs rose to power in Mexico, and they were at the zenith of their influence when the Spaniards arrived.

SPAIN IN AMERICA

Gold, God, and Glory

The Spanish settlement of America was motivated by (1) the desire to find mineral wealth (gold, silver, precious gems), (2) the desire to convert the Indians to Christianity and save Indian souls from eternal damnation, and (3) the desire of the conquistadors (noble warriors) to win fresh glory in America (since the Moslems had finally been driven from Spain in 1492). Which of these motives was dominant is anyone's guess, but all played a part in the Spanish conquest of America.

Occupying the island of Hispaniola (Santo Domingo), the Spaniards virtually exterminated the Indians by forcing them to work the island's mines and plantations under brutal conditions. However, by 1512, Hispaniola was sending Spain a million dollars in gold every year and was developing a lucrative sugar cane crop. The desire to find even more wealth stimulated Spain's exploration of the Americas.

Major Explorations

Between 1508 and 1511, the islands of Puerto Rico, Jamaica, and Cuba had been explored and were being settled. In 1513, Vasco Núñez de Balboa crossed the Isthmus of Panama and sighted the Pacific Ocean; at the same time, Juan Ponce de León explored much of Florida in search of the fabled "Fountain of Youth" which was supposed to grant eternal youth to anyone who drank its waters. Shortly thereafter, Juan Díaz de Solís explored the Río de la Plata in Argentina; and in 1519, Ferdinand Magellan began his circumnavigation of the world by rounding Cape Horn and sailing into the Pacific. Although Magellan was killed in the Philippines, his crew completed the journey and sailed home to Spain in 1521. In the same year that Magellan rounded the tip of South America, Hernando Cortés began the conquest of Mexico.

The Fall of the Aztec Empire

A warlike people who delighted in martial feats, the Aztecs had established their rule over much of Central Mexico and the Yucatan by about the mid-fourteenth century. From their capital at Tenochtitlán (Mexico City), the Aztecs practiced human sacrifice, tortured prisoners of war to death and ate their bodies in cannibalistic rites, and collected tribute from their terrified conquered tribes. Under Montezuma II (who came to the throne in 1502), the Aztecs were at the height of their power. However, their conquered subjects hated them, and believed, according to an old legend, that white men who were half-human and half-animal would arrive to overthrow the rule of the Aztecs. When Cortés and his conquistadors landed in Mexico in 1519, these Indians, who had never seen horses before, received the Spaniards with jubilation as the fulfillment of the old prophecy. Aided by these subjugated tribes, Cortés' men, armed with modern firearms and far better trained than the Aztecs, were easily able to enter Tenochtitlán and take Montezuma prisoner. In 1520, the Aztecs rebelled against the Spaniards and drove them out of the capital city. However, the Spaniards recaptured the city the following year and put an end to the last vestiges of Aztec power. By 1521, the conquest of Mexico was final and irrevocable.

The Conquest of the Incas

Inspired by the success of Cortés, Francisco Pizarro hoped to find in Peru the same wealth of gold and silver that had been found in Mexico. Arriving in Peru in 1528, Pizarro found a civilization of wealth and brilliance. The Incas, occupying Peru, Ecuador, Bolivia, and part of Chile, began their rise to power sometime in the eleventh century. Like the ancient Egyptians, their emperor was considered to be a divine representative of the sun god; to maintain the purity of his blood, he had to marry his own sister. The Incas had a theocratic society and a paternalistic and socialistic government. All produce was brought to government storehouses where it was then distributed among the people. Forced labor to build roads, irrigation canals, and public structures was the rule. The Incan roads were marvels of engineering skill. At the time of Pizarro's arrival, the Incan empire numbered some six to eight million people, but its power had been severely undermined by a civil war between two rival aspirants to the throne. Pizarro took Atahualpa (the Incan Emperor) prisoner, forced him to ransom himself with gold and precious gems, and then brutally murdered him. As in Mexico, the Spanish conquest of Peru was relatively easy, although a guerrilla war dragged on until 1572.

INDIAN CIVILIZATION AND THE SPANISH COLONIES / 11

SPAIN'S INDIAN POLICY

Under the terms of the papal edict which assigned the Americas to Spain (see page 5) the Indians were not to be enslaved or mistreated, but they were to be converted to Christianity. The Spanish monarchy considered the conversion of the Indians to be one of its primary responsibilities, and in 1514, it issued the *Requirimiento* (Requirement) which forbade the enslavement of the Indians and mandated their conversion to Christianity—peacefully if possible, forcibly if necessary. However, the greed of the conquistadors made a mockery of Spain's good intentions, and Spanish treatment of the Indians constitutes one of the blackest chapters in the history of Western man.

The Encomiendas

The *encomienda* was a grant of land made by the Spanish crown to a conquistador. The grant carried with it the right to the labor of the Indians who inhabited the land. In effect, Spain was trying to reproduce the European manorial system in America. The noble conquistadors would live off the labor of their Indian serfs who would be forced to work the mines and cultivate the tobacco and sugar plantations. The Indians resisted this virtual enslavement with a fierce determination, and the result was the widespread extermination of the American Indian. A modern scholar estimates that there were some twenty-five million Indians in New Spain (Mexico and Central America) in 1519, but that by 1605, the Indian population had shrunk to barely over one million people. Many churchmen, particularly Father de las Casas, raised their voices in protest against the conquistadors' treatment of the Indians; they pointed out that it was difficult to convert a corpse. As a result of such pressure, the New Laws were issued during 1542–1543. They abolished all encomiendas held by the church and by royal officials, and declared that encomiendas held by private persons could not be willed to their children. In addition, the labor requirements of the Indians were fixed by law, and were made less severe. These laws would have eliminated the entire encomienda system within a generation. However, the New Laws were received with such hostility that the crown was forced to repeal them between 1545 and 1546.

Execution of Atahualpa, the Inca emperor.

Later Explorations

Peru was the last wealthy civilization encountered by the Spaniards, but the search for even wealthier Indian nations continued. From 1539 to 1542, Hernando de Soto, starting from Florida, explored much of the American South and crossed the Mississippi south of present-day Memphis, Tennessee. After he died of fever, de Soto's body was thrown into the Mississippi River so that the Indians would not know that he had succumbed. Although de Soto failed to find any civilizations of note, the Spaniards were interested in the area and, in 1565, founded a permanent settlement at St. Augustine in Florida. In 1540, Francisco de Coronado explored the southwestern portion of the United States as far north as Kansas in search of the fabled Seven Cities of Cibola, whose streets were allegedly paved with gold. All that he succeeded in finding were some poor Indian pueblos. After de Soto and Coronado, the age of major Spanish exploration ended, and the Spaniards settled down to the task of developing their American empire.

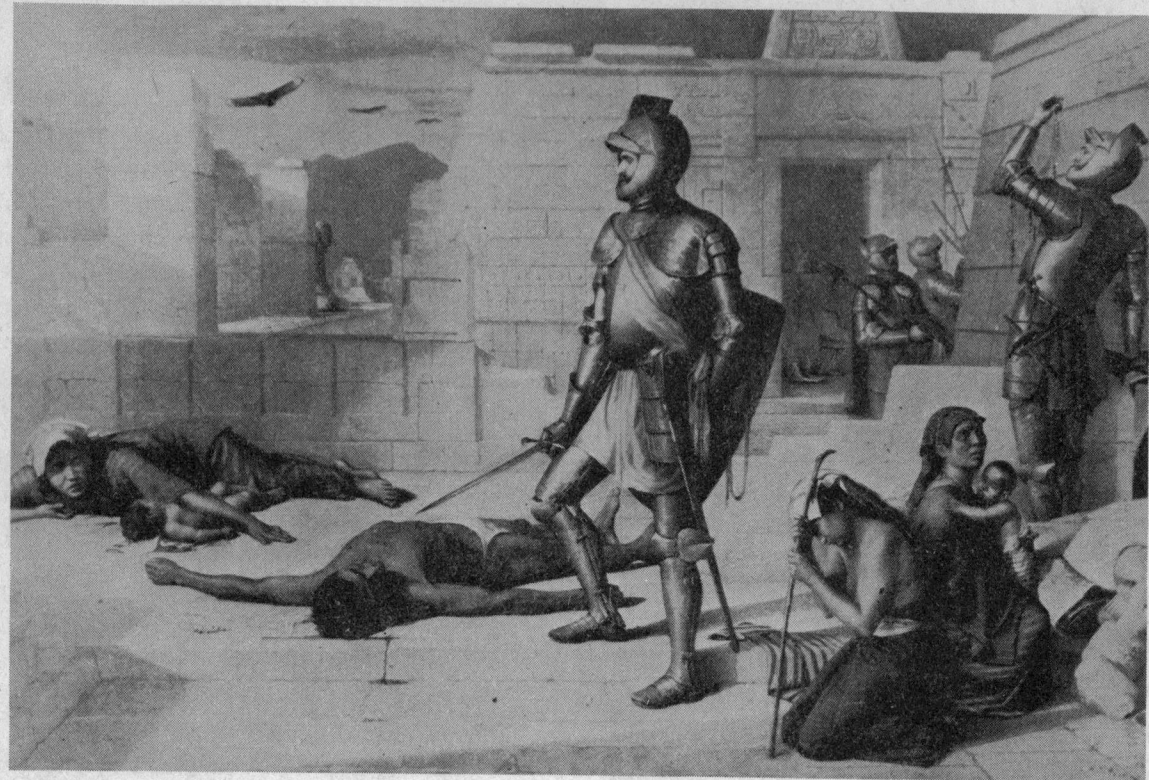
Mistreatment of Mexican Indians by the conquistadors.

The Introduction of Negro Slavery

Indian resistance to the encomienda system necessitated the introduction of Negro slavery into America in the early years of the sixteenth century, in order to provide a labor force. (Many churchmen championed this "reform," hoping that Negro slaves would relieve the Indians of forced labor for the Spaniards and would, thereby, facilitate the Indian's conversion to Christianity.) Those Negroes (about half) who survived the passage to America and became acclimated to their new environment provided a valuable labor pool, but their introduction did little to help ease the plight of the Indians.

THE GOVERNMENT OF SPANISH AMERICA

Unlike England's American colonies, New Spain (Mexico, Central America, and the southwestern United States), which was formally established in 1535, and Peru (all of South America except Brazil), which was created in 1542, never achieved any measure of local self-government. (New Granada, consisting of modern Colombia, Venezuela, and Ecuador, was detached from Peru in 1717; and La Plata, now Argentina, was given a separate administration in 1776.) The supreme governing authority for Spanish America was the king of Spain; he was assisted in the formulation of colonial policy by the Council of the Indies, which resided in Madrid. Stationed in the colonies were the viceroys, who were appointed by the king and who carried out his orders. In the event that local conditions made it impossible for the viceroy to implement the king's instructions, he would reply to his sovereign, "Obedezco pero no cumplo" (I obey but I do not fulfill). Assisting the viceroys were the *audiencias,* which were advisory and judicial bodies composed of local notables. However, the audiencias had no legislative functions. The absence of institutions of local government severely retarded the development of Spanish America (since colonists did not feel that the colonial governments were responsive to their interests and needs) and was one of the prime factors in the eventual decline of the Spanish empire.

Spanish Mercantilism

Not only did the Spanish crown prohibit local self-government in America, it also regulated Latin-American trade so severely that economic growth and development were stunted. The crown received 20 per cent of all the mineral wealth of the Americas, and trade between America and Spain was monopolized by favored groups of Spanish merchants who were the only ones permitted to trade legally. Moreover, the excise tax *(alcabala)* retarded the growth of manufacturing in Spanish America, just as it did in Spain, and the colonials were not permitted to sell their tobacco and sugar to the nations of Europe. In order to enrich the Spanish treasury, all trade between Spanish America and Europe had to be funneled through Spain, where heavy customs duties were imposed. The duties, however, reduced the potential European market for Latin-American goods and worked to the economic disadvantage of the colonials.

Spain's economic interest in America was largely exploitative. America was to provide precious metals and raw materials, and existed to enrich the mother country—even if such an economic policy adversely affected the well-being of the colonies. Moreover, the conquistadors looked down upon business and commerce as disreputable; they believed that agriculture was the only pursuit fit for a gentleman. As a result, Spanish America never developed an economy with the vigor and vitality achieved by the British colonies in America; and Spain was unable to compete with her economically more powerful northern neighbor.

Immigration Policies and Latin American Society

Spanish America, unlike the English colonies, was closed to everyone except Spanish Catholics and Negro slaves. In order to maintain the religious purity of Latin America, Moors (Spanish Moslems) and Spanish Jews were forbidden to emigrate to America. This policy worked to Spain's disadvantage, for it denied her American colonies the services of commercially skilled people who might have contributed greatly to her growth and development. Because of this shortsighted policy, Spanish America was never able to attract large numbers of immigrants (Spanish Catholics had little incentive for emigrating to America), and it remained underpopulated. The sparse population of Latin America contributed to the military weakness of the Spanish colonies, which lacked the manpower to successfully defend themselves against outside aggression. At the end of the colonial period (1820's) Latin America had 7.5 million Indians, 3.2 million whites, .75 million Negroes and 5.5 million people of mixed blood.

Socially, Spanish America was dominated by the *peninsulares* (native-born Spaniards) who controlled the government and economy. The *creoles* (American-born Spaniards) resented the peninsulares' domination of colonial society and were instrumental in furthering the Latin-American wars of independence. The *mestizos* (people of mixed Spanish, Indian, and Negro blood), who were looked down upon by the creoles, resented their exclusion from power in Latin-American society. Finally, at the bottom of the social scale were the Indians and the Negroes; exploited and oppressed, they lived in poverty and in ignorance.

Although Latin-American society was divided along racial lines, it did not develop a caste system as rigid as that of North America. The shortage of Spanish women in Latin America forced Spanish men to intermarry with Indian and Negro women, producing a class of mixed bloods known as mestizos. Consequently, racial lines never became as stringent in Latin America as they were in North America, and upward social mobility was possible for talented and ambitious mestizos.

The Failure of Spanish America

The leadership of the Western Hemisphere passed from Spain to the English colonies for the following reasons:

(1) Spanish America was unable to attract the large numbers of immigrants needed to make her a viable military and economic entity.

(2) She was unable to develop local institutions of self-government responsive to the needs of the colonial population and able to win its allegiance.

(3) She was unable to free herself of debilitating economic restrictions and could not, therefore, develop a vigorous economic life.

By the seventeenth century, England would contest Spain for the leadership of America; and by the eighteenth century, the contest would be decided in England's favor.

REVIEW QUESTIONS FOR CHAPTER 2

1. Forest-dwelling Indians were the

    (A) Iroquois
    (B) Algonquins
    (C) Pueblos
    (D) Siouans

2. The "Greeks" of North America were the

    (A) Aztecs
    (B) Incas
    (C) Mayans
    (D) Creeks

3. The explorer who searched for the Seven Cities of Cibola was

    (A) Ponce de León
    (B) Hernando de Soto
    (C) Francisco Pizarro
    (D) Francisco de Coronado

4. Tenochtitlán was the capital of

    (A) the Incan empire
    (B) the Mayan empire
    (C) the Aztec empire
    (D) New Spain

5. The encomienda was a

    (A) land grant
    (B) court of law
    (C) royal tax
    (D) local legislature

6. The New Laws sought to protect

    (A) commerce
    (B) the Catholic church
    (C) the Indian
    (D) the Negro slave

7. New Granada was established in

    (A) 1535
    (B) 1542
    (C) 1717
    (D) 1776

8. American-born Spaniards are known as

    (A) mestizos
    (B) creoles
    (C) peninsulares
    (D) none of the above

9. Pizarro is to Peru as Cortés is to

    (A) Mexico
    (B) Hispaniola
    (C) Cuba
    (D) New Spain

10. All of the following were forbidden to emigrate to Spanish America except

    (A) Moors
    (B) Jews
    (C) Spanish Catholics
    (D) Non-Spanish Catholics

Explanatory Answers

1. **(B)** The Algonquins lived in Canada, New England, and the Ohio Valley.

2. **(C)** The Mayans developed the most brilliant of all the American Indian cultures.

3. **(D)** Coronado explored the American Southwest (1540–1542) in search of the fabled cities.

4. **(C)** Tenochtitlán (Mexico City) was the Aztec capital.

5. **(A)** The encomienda was a land grant given by the king to the conquistadors.

6. **(C)** The New Laws sought to ease the hardships for Indians under the encomienda system.

7. **(C)** New Granada was separated from Peru in 1717.

8. **(B)** Creoles were American-born children of Spanish parents.

9. **(A)** Pizarro conquered the Incas of Peru, and Cortés conquered the Aztecs of Mexico.

10. **(C)** Only Spanish Catholics were allowed to settle in Latin America.

Chapter 3

THE FRENCH AND DUTCH COLONIES

Throughout the sixteenth century, no European powers were strong enough to challenge effectively Spain's monopoly over New World exploration and colonization. England was recovering from the exhausting Wars of the Roses (1455–1485), and had still to suffer the divisive effects of the Protestant Reformation. The Dutch had yet to win their freedom from the oppressive rule of the Spaniards. The French, after a promising start at New World exploration, would endure almost seventy-five years of civil strife and religious warfare which effectively ended the French challenge to Spanish hegemony in America. By the close of the sixteenth century, all this had changed. Under the wise and firm rule of Queen Elizabeth, England had developed a strong national government ready to exert its new powers in the struggle against Spain. The Dutch had successfully thrown off Spanish rule by 1609, and were rapidly becoming the commercial leaders of Europe. Likewise, the French had resolved their governmental and religious difficulties; and under the leadership of Cardinal Richelieu and, later, Louis XIV, they were to resume their activities in the New World. Although the English, the Dutch, and the French successfully undermined the Spanish monopoly over American colonization, only the English colonies were to thrive and survive. The colonies founded by the Dutch and the French shared many of the same handicaps which doomed the Spanish colonies to weakness and eventual failure.

THE FRENCH IN AMERICA

Early French Explorations

As early as 1504, French fishing boats had reached the coast of Newfoundland. However, French exploratory interest was directed primarily at South America's Brazilian coast. Beginning in 1520, the French were landing men in Brazil to cut cargoes of brazilwood; and it was not long before they established more permanent settlements. French missionaries were especially active among the Indians of Brazil, and their efforts were often successful in converting the Indians to Christianity. Brazil, however, was a Portuguese sphere of influence; and France's activities in the area alarmed the Portuguese, who redoubled their own colonizing efforts in the region. By 1615, the French had been evicted from their last foothold in Brazil, and the colony was again firmly in Portuguese control.

In 1524, Francis I, King of France, commissioned the Italian navigator Giovanni de Verrazano to explore the northern regions of the Americas. According to his own accounts, Verrazano sailed along the Carolina coast, entered New York harbor and Narragansett Bay, and skirted the coast of Nova Scotia. In 1534, the French navigator Jacques Cartier explored the St. Lawrence River region, visiting the sites of the future cities of Quebec and Montreal. Told by some friendly Indians that there was a wealthy Indian kingdom in the area, Cartier raised an expedition against the Saguenay Indian nation. In 1536, he returned to France, laden with pyrite (fool's gold) and quartz crystals which he believed to be diamonds. While the results of Cartier's expedition eventually proved disappointing, it nevertheless established the legal basis for France's claims to Canada. Unfortunately, as a result of domestic problems, the French were forced to suspend their New World activities until the early 1600's.

Champlain and the Founding of New France

French exploration of America was resumed in 1603 when Samuel de Champlain returned to the St. Lawrence River and established a number of trading posts. Almost immediately, the French began a lucrative fur trade with the various Algonquin tribes in the region; and French missionaries met with marked success in their conversion efforts. By 1609, Quebec had been founded, and the French were offering their Algonquin allies active military assistance in their struggles against the Iroquois of New York. For the next eighteen years, the French actively aided their Algonquin allies. As a result, the Iroquois were thrown into the arms of the Dutch and, later, the English. After 1689, the Iroquois were to play a vital role in frustrating French ambitions in the Ohio Valley and Great Lakes region and were to help the English become masters of the North American continent.

In order to facilitate the settlement of French Canada, Cardinal Richelieu, the powerful advisor to Louis XIII, organized the Company of New France (also called the Hundred Associates) in 1627. In return for a monopoly of the Canadian fur trade, the Company promised the government to bring French settlers to the colony. The French crown realized that only effective and large-scale settlement could secure for France the control of Canada. But, like the Spanish colonies, the French

Champlain's soldiers fighting against the Iroquois.

colony was unable to attract large numbers of immigrants.

Problems of New France

The government of New France closely resembled that of Spanish America. There was no local legislative body which could respond to the needs of the colonial population. The colony was ruled by a governor appointed by the king and responsible solely to him. In addition, there was an intendant (an administrative official), also appointed by the king, who acted as a "spy" on the governor to make certain that he faithfully carried out royal policies. There was, as well, a close union of church and state; and the bishop of New France was also a royal appointee, serving at the king's pleasure.

Like the Spanish rulers, the French government insisted that all immigrants to New France must be Roman Catholics. This policy barred French Huguenots (Calvinists) from emigrating, and it deprived New France of a large pool of potential settlers. French Catholics, unlike the Huguenots, did not suffer from religious and civil discrimination and had less incentive for emigrating. Moreover, the French government adopted an unenlightened land policy. The king granted extensive tracts of land to seigneurs (feudal lords), who were expected to bring over French peasants to work the land. This policy was a failure. The seigneurs expected to create a new feudal system in America and did not intend the peasants to become independent landowners. Unable to own land in Canada and subject to petty manorial obligations, French peasants could not be persuaded to leave the good lands of France for the cold and snow of Canada. As late as 1689, the population of New France numbered only 12,000 persons, and most of these were soldiers. When France and England struggled for the mastery of America in the eighteenth century, the French would be at a marked disadvantage because of their failure to adequately populate Canada.

Economically, New France was dependent upon the fur trade and fishing. No significant mineral wealth was discovered; and because of the severity of the climate and the lack of peasants, agriculture never became an important economic activity. The fur trade was conducted by the *coureurs de bois* (runners of the woods), who were rugged frontiersmen living a primitive life among the Indians. Casting off their own French culture, they lived among the Indians, adopting Indian ways and customs, and often marrying Indian maids. Romantic and legendary figures, they cultivated good relations with many Indian tribes and extended French influence far into the interior of Canada. However, French economic activity in Canada was exploitative rather than developmental, and the colony lacked the economic resources to support a prolonged military struggle against the English.

Later French Explorations

In 1642, warfare with the Iroquois was resumed. The Iroquois, finally, were decisively beaten in 1653, and France strengthened her hold over Canada. With the end of the Iroquois wars, the French took a renewed interest in exploratory activities. In 1659, the Sieur des Grosselliers and Pierre-Esprit Radisson explored Lake Superior and the area of what is now Wisconsin; and in 1673, Jacques Marquette and Louis Joliet sailed down the Mississippi River as far as the junction with the Arkansas River. The voyage of Marquette and Joliet established the French claim to the strategic Ohio Valley. Finally, in 1682, Robert de La Salle sailed the Mississippi all the way down to the Gulf of Mexico and claimed the Louisiana territory (the Mississippi basin and watershed) for France. By 1689, the French had carved out an extensive empire, stretching from the Gulf of Mexico to Hudson's Bay. Their possession of this large but underpopulated area would later be challenged by the British.

THE DUTCH IN AMERICA

Early Dutch Explorations

Searching for the Northwest Passage, a hoped-for water route through North America to the Orient, Henry Hudson's *Half-Moon* entered New York harbor in 1609 and sailed up the Hudson River. Though he failed to find the Northwest Passage, he did establish a Dutch claim to the Hudson Valley. Between 1612 and 1614, Adriaen Block sailed around Manhattan Island, and Cornelius May sailed the coasts of Long Island. In 1614, the United Netherlands Company was organized for the purpose of developing the Hudson Valley, and it planted a trading post (Fort Nassau) at the site of present-day Albany. Allied with the Iroquois (1618), the Dutch built up a profitable fur trade and controlled the strategic Mohawk Valley.

The Mohawk Valley was the gateway to the American West. The Dutch presence there guaranteed the hostility of the French, for the Dutch settlement blocked French access to the Ohio Valley, which the French planned to develop. Moreover, if the Dutch were successful in their efforts to develop settlements in the Hudson and Mohawk Valleys, their territory would divide England's southern colonies from her New England colonies and would seriously stunt the growth of British America. Consequently, the Dutch became the enemies of the English as well as of the French.

The Founding of New Netherland

Unhappy with the slow progress made by the United Netherlands Company in developing its American colony, the Dutch government revoked the Company's charter in 1621 and transferred its powers to the newly organized West India Company. Under the Provisional Order of 1624, the Netherland colony was to be ruled by a director-general appointed by the Company with the approval of the States-General (the Dutch legislative body). No provision was made for a local legislature. All power was in the hands of the director-general and a five-man council (whose members he selected) which advised him on public policy. However, if an individual was dissatisfied with a decision of the director-general, he had the right to appeal to the Company back in Holland and to the States-General to override the director-general.

In March of 1624, thirty Walloon (French-speaking) families, led by Cornelius May, were landed on Nut Island (Governor's Island) in New York harbor; and trading posts were established at Fort Orange (Albany) and Fort Nassau (Gloucester, New Jersey). The colony's first director-general, William Verhulst, proved to be a poor manager, and he was replaced as director by Peter Minuit in 1626. It was Minuit who purchased Manhattan Island from the Indians for $24.00 worth of trinkets and baubles. (The Indians, having no conception of land ownership, obviously felt that they were getting the better part of the bargain in selling something which was not in their power to sell.) Under Minuit, New Netherland was fairly well established; but as it was sandwiched between the English and the French, its existence was precarious.

The Dutch trading with the Indians on Manhattan Island.

The port of New Amsterdam (part of New Netherland) about 1667.

Immigration and Land Policies

From the beginning, the Dutch realized that they could hold New Netherland only if the colony could attract large numbers of loyal immigrants. However, Holland was a prosperous land of some two and one-half million people who were not inclined to migrate to America, and who could not have migrated, in any case, in the large numbers desired by the Company. With the hope of attracting settlers, the patroonship system was introduced in 1629. The West India Company granted large tracts of land along the Hudson River to anyone who agreed to provide settlers for the land; the more settlers brought over, the more land awarded. The settlers were to work the land as tenants, with the patroon holding manorial rights, dispensing justice, and enjoying exclusive hunting privileges. Like the French seigneurial system, it was an attempt to transplant manorialism to the New World; and it, too, failed. Only one patroonship was actually developed (that of Kiliaen van Rensselaer), and the system was discontinued in 1646.

The population of New Netherland numbered only 1,500 by 1646, and in an effort to attract settlers, the West India Company encouraged the immigration of religious minorities. Over the next fifteen years, New Amsterdam (New York City), the colony's leading town, became a cosmopolitan center of Jews, Baptists, Quakers, Lutherans, and Calvinists. During this same period, the Company permitted the absolute and private ownership of land for a small fee, and it instituted free trade, hoping to strengthen the colony's economy. On the eve of the British conquest (1664), New Netherland had a population of 10,000. It was the most cosmopolitan community in the New World, containing Dutchmen, Englishmen, French Huguenots, Jews, Swedes, Germans and many others. However, many of its citizens were resentful of its autocratic government.

Political History of New Netherland

Peter Minuit, the director-general, was succeeded by William Kieft as head of the colony. A figure of considerable controversy, Kieft involved New Netherland in an almost ruinous Indian war from 1641 to 1645. Beginning with an incident over some pigs allegedly stolen by the Indians, the war severely weakened the colony and led to Kieft's dismissal in favor of Peter Stuyvesant. Immediately upon his assumption of power, Stuyvesant was faced by persistent demands for a legislative assembly. A man of autocratic persuasion, Stuyvesant would have nothing to do with a legislature; but the Indian wars necessitated the imposition of new and greater taxes, and to secure these taxes, he had to compromise. In 1647, Stuyvesant agreed to permit the freemen to elect eighteen men from whose number he would select nine men to advise him on taxes and public policy. This did not satisfy the popular demand for a legislature, but Stuyvesant was unwilling to surrender his powers and authority and stoutly resisted the people's cry for such an assembly. He also sought to impose the Dutch Reformed faith on New Netherland's religious minorities and tried to exclude Jews from the colony, but these attempts were overruled by the West India Company. In 1655, Stuyvesant directed the conquest of New Sweden (now Wilmington, Delaware), which had been established in 1637 and which numbered some 260 people. It was in New Sweden that the log cabin was introduced to America.

Economic Development

Like the French, the Dutch were primarily interested in trade with the Indians, especially the profitable fur trade. Because of the small population in the region, agriculture did not become a major area of economic importance in New Netherland. Although the Company operated numerous *bouweries* (farms) in and around Manhattan which were worked by indentured servants (those who agreed to work for the Company for a fixed number of years in return for their passage to America), commerce still was the lifeblood of the colony. Dutch ships and merchants were so successful in breaching the British mercantile system that a series of Anglo-Dutch wars were fought, beginning in the 1650's.

Anglo-Dutch Rivalry

The British and the Dutch were at best uneasy neighbors in America. The vigorous New England colonies were expanding in the direction of the Hudson, and the Dutch were in the way of this expansion. Although the 1650 Treaty of Hartford pledged the English settlers to stay ten miles east of the Hudson, a clash between the two nations was, nevertheless, inevitable. In 1652, Dutch encroachments on British trade led to the first Anglo-Dutch war; but fortunately for the Dutch, the war ended before the British could organize an invasion of New Netherland. However, the English Navigation Acts of 1660–1661 (see Chapter 7, on mercantilism) were directly designed to eliminate Dutch trade with British America. In August 1664, war was resumed, and when Nicolls' squadron of four ships sailed into New York harbor, New Amsterdam surrendered to the British without firing a shot. Promising the Dutch settlers "the rights of Englishmen" and offering religious toleration for all the colony's people, Nicolls' liberal terms of surrender were more appealing than the autocratic rule of Stuyvesant. New Netherland left the stage of history in 1664. The region was taken over by James, Duke of York, and renamed New York in his honor.

Failures of the French and the Dutch

In the race for empire in America, both the French and the Dutch lost. Their primary weaknesses were the following:

(1) The failure to grant legislative assemblies which would involve the settlers in the affairs of the respective colonies and which would give the people some stake in the colonies' preservation.

(2) The futile attempts to transplant the manorial system to America, which thereby discouraged immigration to the colonies.

(3) The inability to attract enough setttlers to effectively hold the colonies.

The contest for America was won by the British, and it is to English America that we now turn our attention.

REVIEW QUESTIONS FOR CHAPTER 3

1. The first to explore the St. Lawrence River was

   (A) Giovanni de Verrazano
   (B) Samuel de Champlain
   (C) Jacques Cartier
   (D) Robert de La Salle

2. Quebec was founded by

   (A) Robert de La Salle
   (B) Samuel de Champlain
   (C) Louis Joliet
   (D) Pierre Radisson

3. The *coureurs de bois* were

   (A) feudal lords in New France
   (B) a tribe of Indians
   (C) frontiersmen
   (D) royal messengers

4. Which explorer is *not* associated with the Mississippi River?

   (A) Jacques Marquette
   (B) Robert de La Salle
   (C) Louis Joliet
   (D) Sieur des Grosselliers

5. The most important economic activity in New France was

   (A) agriculture
   (B) fishing
   (C) commerce
   (D) fur trade

6. The explorer who sailed the coasts of Long Island was

   (A) Henry Hudson
   (B) Adriaen Block
   (C) Cornelius May
   (D) None of the above

7. Mahattan Island was purchased by

   (A) Peter Stuyvesant
   (B) Peter Minuit
   (C) William Kieft
   (D) William Verhulst

8. New Netherland fought an almost ruinous Indian war under

   (A) William Kieft
   (B) Peter Stuyvesant
   (C) William Verhulst
   (D) Adriaen Block

9. Stuveysant conquered New Sweden in

   (A) 1637
   (B) 1647
   (C) 1655
   (D) 1664

10. All of the following were characteristic of New France and New Netherland *except*:

(A) small population
(B) lack of legislative assemblies
(C) dependence on fur trade
(D) widespread land ownership

Explanatory Answers

1. **(C)** Cartier explored the St. Lawrence in 1534.

2. **(B)** Champlain founded Quebec in 1608.

3. **(C)** Coureurs de bois were Frenchmen engaged in the fur trade.

4. **(D)** Grosselliers explored Lake Superior and the area of Wisconsin.

5. **(D)** The fur trade was the most lucrative economic enterprise.

6. **(C)** Cornelius May was the first to sail the Long Island coast.

7. **(B)** Minuit purchased the island in 1626.

8. **(A)** The war began over some pigs allegedly stolen by the Indians.

9. **(C)** New Sweden fell in 1655.

10. **(D)** The French seigneurial system prevented widespread land ownership.

Chapter 4

VIRGINIA AND THE SOUTHERN COLONIES

In 1497, John Cabot, sailing in the employ of King Henry VII of England, landed on Cape Breton Island (off the Canadian coast) and laid the foundations for England's claim to the Atlantic coast of North America. However, faced with the task of recovering from the effects of the Wars of the Roses (1455–1485) and with the difficulties arising from the English Reformation, Britain was unable to take advantage of Cabot's voyage of discovery. For almost a century, England's interest in overseas expansion lay dormant. It was not until the reign of Elizabeth (1558–1603) that England started to play an active role in international affairs. She had to support the rebellion of the Protestant Netherlands against Catholic Spain because the Netherlands' defeat might have provided Philip II of Spain with a staging area for the invasion of England. Furthermore, English forests were exhausted, and England had to depend upon overseas timber to meet the needs of her navy. These factors forced Elizabeth to become more aggressive in the conduct of foreign policy; and, consequently, England's interest in America was reawakened.

PRELUDE TO ENGLISH COLONIZATION

Beginning in the 1570's, a group of English "Sea Dogs" (John Hawkins, Francis Drake, and Richard Grenville), with the tacit consent of Queen Elizabeth, started to attack Spanish ships which were returning from America laden with gold and silver. This "singeing of the King of Spain's beard" not only enriched the English treasury, but also awakened a romantic interest in the Americas as a land of boundless wealth. In 1585, Sir Walter Raleigh founded a colony on Roanoke Island, off the Carolina coast. Because of the hostility of local Indians, the colony was abandoned the following year; but an undaunted Raleigh planted another colony in the same location in 1587. The colony seemed to thrive; and a child (Virginia Dare) was born to one of the settlers, becoming the first English child to be born in America. Unfortunately, when a supply convoy returned to Roanoke in 1590, it found that the entire settlement had vanished without a trace. To this day, no one really knows what happened to the Roanoke Island colony, although it is probable that the colony was attacked by Indians and the survivors carried off into slavery. Although Raleigh's colony failed, its failure did not discourage the English.

VIRGINIA

The Virginia Company

In April 1606, King James I granted the Virginia Company permission to establish a colony in North America. Actually, the Virginia Com-

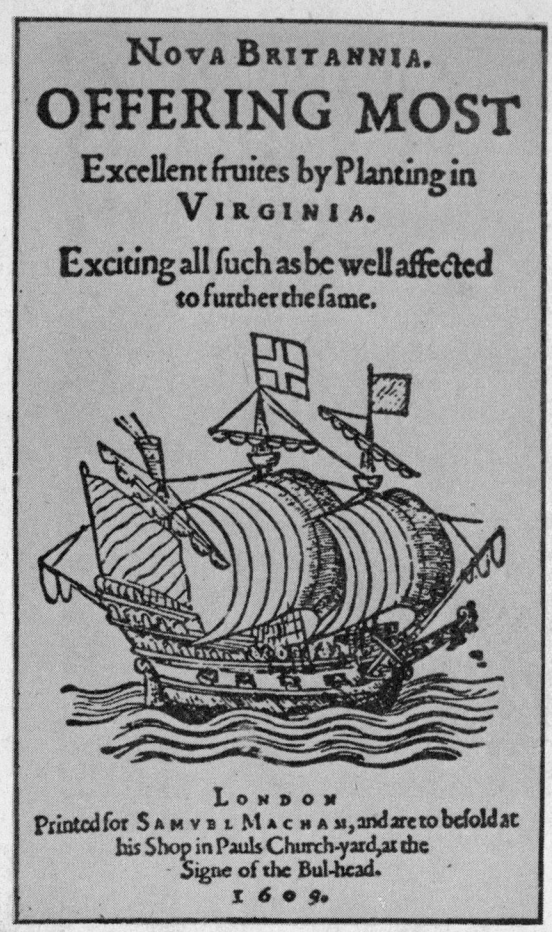

Advertisement in England (1609) published by the London Company seeking colonists for Virginia.

pany consisted of two groups of joint-stock companies: the London Company (also called the Virginia Company) and the Plymouth Company. The London Company was empowered to settle the area between 34° and 41° latitude, while the Plymouth Company could settle between 38° and 45° latitude; the area from 38° to 41° latitude was to be a neutral zone. (As the figures show, the claims overlapped.) Under the terms of the charter, the Council of Virginia consisted of thirteen men who would be selected by the king and who would reside in London; they would run the affairs of the company and govern the colonies established in America. For each colony planted in America, the Council of Virginia would appoint a thirteen-man council, resident in America, to conduct the day-to-day affairs of the colony. The local council could elect a president, hold courts, enact laws, grant land to settlers, coin money, run mines, and provide for local defense. All such laws passed by the local council were subject to the veto of the council of Virginia and had to be consistent with the laws of England. Further, all settlers were guaranteed the rights of freeborn Englishmen (protection of the common law, right to a jury trial, freedom from arbitrary arrest and punishment).

Economically, the king was to receive 20 per cent of all gold and silver discovered in America and one-fifteenth of the copper found in the colony. As a joint-stock company, the Virginia Company hoped to profit by finding and developing valuable raw materials (timber, naval stores, sugar, tobacco, etc.) which England needed but could not obtain at home. The spirit behind the enterprise was mercantilism: England hoped to make herself independent of all foreign raw materials so that she would not be vulnerable to economic boycott during time of war and so that she would not enrich her potential enemies by having to buy their products. In 1607, the Plymouth Company founded the Kennebec colony (at the mouth of the Sagadahoc River) in New England, but it failed after a year. The London Company's Jamestown colony almost suffered the same fate.

The Jamestown Colony

On December 20, 1606, three ships (the *Sarah Constant,* the *Goodspeed,* and the *Discovery*), bearing 140 men under the command of Captain Christopher Newport, left England bound for Virginia. The ships entered Chesapeake Bay late in April of 1607, and the 104 men who had survived the voyage founded Jamestown in May. Located on low and swampy ground, the colony was ravaged by malaria; by September of 1607, only 46 men were still alive. Adding to the hazards of the fledgling colony, was the attitude of the settlers. Instead of clearing the land and planting a crop, they spent all their time searching for gold and silver. Since all land and property were owned by the company (there being no private landownership yet), there was a natural tendency to shirk responsibility and do as little work as possible. As a result, there was widespread suffering and hardship during Jamestown's first winter, and the local governing council proved ineffectual in its efforts to impose order and discipline.

In September, 1608, John Smith was elected president of the council. Instituting a strict policy of "no work, no food," Smith provided leadership and discipline. Persuading the Indians to share their knowledge of corn cultivation with the

Fort James (later Jamestown) 1607.

settlers, he pulled the colony through a difficult period of its history. When Smith left Virginia in October, 1609, the colony had been reinforced and reprovisioned from England and seemed to be fairly well established.

The Charter of 1609 and the "Starving Time"

In 1609, King James granted the Virginia Company a new charter which virtually ended royal control over the company. The officers of the company were to be annually elected by the stockholders and were to be accountable to them. The stockholders were divided into two classes: adventurers and planters. The adventurers were those who only invested their capital in the Virginia Company, and they received a cash dividend on their investment. The planters invested no money in the company; rather, they went to Virginia as settlers. In return for their labor, they were given one share of stock in the company (one share equaled 100 acres of land) and received a dividend in land every seventh year. By giving the planters a stake in the Virginia colony, the company hoped to attract able, hard-working settlers. Nevertheless, though the new charter was promising, things were not well in Virginia.

As soon as John Smith returned to England in October of 1609, the Jamestown colonists returned to their old ways. The hunt for nonexistent mineral riches took precedence over agriculture, and everyone sought to do as little work as possible. During the winter of 1609–1610, Virginia suffered its "starving time," and the colony's population shrank from 500 to 60 settlers. The people ate dogs, rats, and, in at least one instance, resorted to cannibalism. In May of 1610, the pitiful survivors determined to leave Jamestown and try to sail home to England. As they were about to leave, a relief convoy under Lord Delaware (who had just been appointed by the company as governor of Virginia) sailed into Chesapeake Bay and saved the colony from extinction.

Dale's Laws and the Cultivation of Tobacco

In 1611, Lord Delaware was forced to return to England on account of ill health. In his place, he appointed Thomas Dale as deputy governor. A man of iron resolve, Dale was responsible for putting Virginia on its feet. Dale's Laws (published in 1612) made it a capital crime to wantonly kill cattle or poultry or to destroy growing crops. They forbade anyone to leave the colony without official permission or to trade with the Indians. All settlers were required to attend daily religious services, and anyone using profane language or showing disrespect to those in authority was severely punished. In order to spur economic productivity, Dale leased three-acre plots of land to the settlers, confident that a man would work harder for himself than he would for someone else. As under Smith, there was a strict "no work, no food" policy. By the end of Dale's governorship in 1616, the population of Virginia had reached more than 350, including 60 women and children.

Although Dale provided the colony with much needed discipline, the settlement still lacked economic viability. The early hope that Virginia would yield mineral riches was soon disappointed, and England's hope that the colony could provide timber and naval stores was also frustrated. Unless the colonists could develop a crop or economic activity which could earn profits, both Virginia and the company would fail. About 1612, John Rolfe began experimenting with tobacco, hoping that he could improve Virginia's inferior Indian tobacco to the point where it could compete with the higher-quality Spanish tobacco of the West Indies. By 1614, his experiments had succeeded, and that year he sent Virginia's first cargo of tobacco to England. The crop revolutionized Virginia's economy and made the colony economically viable. By 1617, Virginia was exporting 20,000 pounds of tobacco; and two years later, that figure had increased to 60,000 pounds. The colony now commanded a cash crop which could be sold in the English market and could bring a fairly steady income. However, while tobacco insured the success of the Virginia colony, it also had its drawbacks. It created a one-crop dependency. Virginia concentrated on tobacco cultivation to the exclusion of all other economic activities, and in the event of a bad harvest or a drop in the English tobacco market, the colony suffered severe economic depression. It had nothing else to fall back on.

Sir Edwin Sandys and the Reforms of 1619

Sir Edwin Sandys became Treasurer of the Virginia Company in 1618. A liberal who stood for parliamentary supremacy, religious toleration, and the extension of political rights to Virginia, he launched a series of reforms which had profound effects on the development of English America. In 1619, a crucial year in the history of Virginia, he began the following practices:

(1) **The House of Burgesses.** Sir George Yeardley, Virginia's new governor, arrived in Jamestown in April, 1619. He had instructions to create a legislature, freely elected by the freemen, which would determine the colony's laws. Consisting of the governor, six councillors, and twenty burgesses (two from each of Virginia's local units of government — "plantations," "hundreds," and "towns"), the House of Burgesses held its first meeting on July 30, 1619. It was organized in imitation of the British House of Commons; and it reaffirmed the right of the colonists to enjoy all the "rights of Englishmen," including the right to consent to all tax impositions. Although the governor and the company held a veto power over the acts of the House of Burgesses, this was, nevertheless, the first legislative assembly in the Americas. It established the right of the English colonists to determine their own laws; and the colonists were later to argue that their colonial assemblies had the same rights and privileges (in their respective colonies) as Parliament had in England. It gave birth to the American tradition of representative government.

(2) **The Headright System.** To facilitate the growth of Virginia, Sandys permitted the private ownership of land. All settlers in Virginia were given outright 100 acres of land (shares of stock could also be redeemed in land) plus an additional 50 acres for every adult in their household. Likewise, settlers received 50 acres of land for every adult they brought over from England, and the new arrivals also received 50 acres of land for their own use. As a result of the Headright System, seventeenth-century Virginia became a land of small, independent farmers; the average farmer working between 100 and 500 acres of land. Since land was abundant and free for the taking, Virginia became a middle-class society, with no impoverished and degraded peasantry. The introduction of the Headright System led to fairly rapid population growth, and by 1640, there were some 8,000 people in Virginia.

Indentured Servants and the Beginning of Slavery

Because land was free for the taking, it was extremely difficult for Virginia's tobacco planters to find people willing to work for wages. No one would work for another when he could become an independent landowner. Seeking to alleviate the severe labor shortage, the system of indentured servitude was introduced. Englishmen who were too poor to pay for their passage to America would be brought over by sea captains who would sell such passengers' labor to local planters in order to recoup the passage fees. The newly arrived immigrant would then work for the planter who paid his passage for a term of indenture (usually four years, but sometimes as long as seven). Upon completing his indenture, the servant was given a suit of clothes, a gun, a small cash settlement, and fifty acres of land; he would then assume his place as a freeman in Virginia society. Indentured servitude carried with it no social stigma, and many indentured servants rose to positions of wealth and power in Virginia. However, the numbers of indentured servants were not sufficient to satisfy Virginia's need for labor. (The movement reached its peak about the 1660's but in no year did the number of indentured servants exceed 3,500.) Consequently, wage rates for free labor in Virginia were some six times higher than wage rates in England.

Also, in 1619, twenty Negroes were landed in Virginia. Technically they were not slaves since the laws of England did not recognize the institution of slavery. They were sold as indentured servants, but unlike white indentured servants, their term of indenture was for twenty to twenty-five years (in effect for life). Within a generation, Negroes were recognized as being indentured for life, and their servitude was made hereditary; thus, their children were also indentured for life. Legalized slavery soon followed; and by 1650, Virginia had some three hundred Negro slaves. However, it was not until the eighteenth century that slavery became an important economic institution in Virginia and in the South. Where there were fewer than 25,000 slaves in British America in 1700, there were 400,000 (three-fourths of whom were in the South) by 1760. The growth of slavery during the eighteenth century facilitated the growth of the plantation system; it created a class of planter aristocrats and forced many small farmers off their land. Generally, slavery debased the small farmers and produced a class of poor whites variously referred to as "crackers," "red-necks," and "white trash."

The Tobacco Contract and the End of Company Rule

In 1621, the Privy Council, which governed the colonies in the name of the king, adopted the Tobacco Contract which (1) forbade the cultivation of tobacco in England, and (2) required Virginia to send its entire tobacco crop to England, where a 20 per cent import duty was levied. By this arrangement, the Virginia colonists obtained a monopoly of the British tobacco market (no Spanish tobacco could be imported), and the Crown had a steady source of tax revenue. However, the colonists tended to overproduce, with the result that tobacco prices were often depressed. This situation forced many small, inefficient farmers into bankruptcy and permitted larger, more efficient producers to acquire more land at the expense of their smaller neighbors.

In 1622, an Indian massacre led by Opechancanough wiped out one fourth of Virginia's population, destroyed much of the colony's livestock, and leveled many homes. Largely as a result of this massacre, the Virginia Company was brought to the brink of bankruptcy. Indeed, the company had been in financial trouble for several years, for the income from Virginia had not been sufficient to cover the dividends on the company's heavy capital investment in the colony. Consequently, in 1624, Virginia was taken over by King James I and became the first royal colony in America.

The royal governor was appointed by the king and served at his pleasure. The governor's primary responsibilities were to carry out the policies formulated by the king and the Privy Council and to enforce the mercantile laws. He was assisted in his duties by the Governor's Council (a group of local "notables" selected by the king and the governor) which eventually became an upper legislative house and supreme court, similar to the English House of Lords. Likewise, all colonial judges were appointed by the king and served at his pleasure. Originally, the governor and the various other royal officials were to receive their salaries from import duties and mercantile fees, but the difficulty of enforcing the trade laws and the widespread smuggling activities of the local merchants made it impossible to meet the costs of government in this manner. As a result, the governor became dependent upon the local legislature to enact the taxes needed to support the government. In Virginia, the House of Burgesses was able to use this "power of the purse" to whittle down the arbitrary power of the royal governor and make him more responsive to local needs and interests. Royal government throughout British America followed the Virginia pattern, and local legislatures frequently emulated the House of Burgesses in curbing the governor's authority.

Virginia During the Puritan Revolution

The 1640's were a time of political upheaval in England, and the revolutionary developments taking place in the mother country profoundly affected the political development of Virginia. In 1642, Sir William Berkeley became Virginia's new royal governor. A staunch royalist, he supported King Charles I in his struggle against the Puritans; and in 1643, he pushed an Act of Uniformity to the Anglican church through the House of Burgesses. Six years later, when the Puritans executed Charles, Berkeley denounced the regicide and pledged Virginia's allegiance to Charles II. Berkeley's fidelity to the king angered the victorious Puritans, and in 1652, the English Parliament sent four commissioners to Virginia to assume control of the government. Berkeley was forced into "retirement," and the commissioners reorganized Virginia's government in conformity with the new government of England. The Governor's Council was abolished, and the House of Burgesses was made the supreme governing authority in the colony. However, this arrangement lasted only to 1660. When Charles II was restored to power in England, William Berkeley was restored in Virginia; and the reforms of the commissioners were undone.

Bacon's Rebellion

After 1660, Governor Berkeley became increasingly arbitrary in his administration of Virginia. He angered many Virginians by restricting the suffrage to landowners, by imposing and collecting taxes without the consent of the Burgesses, and by failing to respond to the needs of the small farmers on the Virginia frontier. In 1675, the colony was faced with renewed Indian warfare, which was especially serious on the frontier. Nathaniel Bacon, complaining that Berkeley was not providing adequate military protection or pursuing the Indians with sufficient vigor, raised his own militia in 1676, and inflicted a crushing defeat on the Indians. Governor Berkeley, who was pursuing a policy of moderation designed to protect Indian rights, promptly branded Bacon as a rebel. In the summer of 1676, Bacon's forces seized control of Virginia and forced Berkeley into flight. Assuming control of the government, Bacon restored the suffrage to freemen and restored their full rights as citizens. He gave increased representation to the back country, and he entrusted greater responsibility to the Burgesses. However, Bacon died in October 1676, and with his death, his movement collapsed. Berkeley returned to power, executed twenty-three of Bacon's chiefs aides, and repealed all his reforms.

Historians are still is disagreement over the nature of Bacon's Rebellion. Early scholars concluded that Bacon had struck the first blow for American democracy by opposing arbitrary and capricious government. However, modern scholarship has played down the democratic aspects of the rebellion and has concluded that Bacon's followers wanted to rid Virginia of its Indian population. Blocking the expansion of white settlement, the Indians were a stumbling block in Virginia's development. Berkeley's consideration for the rights of the Indians infuriated the frontiersmen; and it was his Indian policy, not his arbitrary rule, which led to Bacon's Rebellion.

With the collapse of Bacon's Rebellion in 1676, Virginia entered the last quarter of the seventeenth century as the most populous and the most wealthy of the Southern colonies. As the colony was dependent upon tobacco for its economic well-being, the plantation system (and with it Negro slavery) was becoming increasingly more important in Virginia's economic and social life; and the small independent farmer was declining in importance — he was being overshadowed by the rising plantation aristocracy.

MARYLAND

The Founding of Maryland

In June of 1632, Cecil Calvert (Lord Baltimore) received a charter to settle the land between the Chesapeake and Delaware Bays. Given title to the soil and supreme political authority, Calvert could appoint colonial officials, grant titles of nobility, coin money, make war and peace, es-

Cecil Calvert (Lord Baltimore)

tablish courts and manors, and enact all necessary legislation. However, his laws had to be consistent with those of England, and all settlers were guaranteed "the rights of Englishmen." Unlike Virginia, which had been established by a corporation and was later taken over by the English crown, Maryland was the first proprietary colony founded in America. Calvert literally owned Maryland, and he exercised all the powers of government. He intended Maryland to be a refuge for English Catholics (Calvert himself was Catholic) who suffered from civil and political discrimination. However, from the beginning, Protestants outnumbered Catholics in Maryland, as the colony attracted many settlers from nearby Virginia and New England.

The Attempt to Impose Feudalism

St. Mary's, established in 1634, was the first settlement in Maryland. Hoping to establish a feudal system in the colony, Calvert offered 5,000 acres of land (for an annual rental of twenty shillings per 1,000 acres) to anyone who transported five men between the ages of sixteen and fifty to Maryland. The landowner was to have all the rights and privileges of a European manorial lord, including the rights to dispense justice, to demand labor service from his tenants, and to collect dues and fees from the tenants. Altogether, Calvert granted sixty such estates or manors. However, the attempt to impose feudalism in America was a dismal failure. With a vast hinterland in which land was free for the taking, it was impossible to hold tenants to the manor; and rather than accept the constraints of manorialism, the tenants simply moved on to the frontier. As a result, the manors which managed to survive did so because they were democratic and gave the tenants a large measure of control over their own local affairs.

At the same time, Calvert also offered 100-acre freeholds (at a rent of two shillings a year) to individual settlers (plus an additional 100 acres for every adult member of their family). This was the most common type of land grant; and within twenty years, Maryland's population had grown to 8,000. Economically, Maryland resembled Virginia. Tobacco was the most important agricultural commodity, and the plantation system and Negro slavery grew increasingly more important during the eighteenth century.

Protestant-Catholic Rivalry in Maryland

In 1638, Lord Baltimore convened a legislature elected by the freeholders of Maryland to assist him in the formulation of laws and public policy. With the outbreak of civil war in England, Protestant-Catholic tensions in Maryland became more acute. Calvert and the Catholics sided with King Charles I, while the Protestants tended to support Parliament. From 1644 to 1649, open civil war raged in Maryland between the Protestant majority and the Catholic minority. In an effort to restore order and to protect his proprietary interests in Maryland, Calvert appointed a Protestant as governor, hoping that this appointment would be more acceptable to the colony's Protestant majority. Also, in 1649, he promulgated the famous Toleration Act, which guaranteed freedom of religious expression to all who professed belief in the divinity of Christ. Although the Toleration Act has been viewed as a milestone in the development of American religious freedom, its importance has been greatly overstated. It applied only to those Christians who believed in the divinity of Christ, and it was soon repealed.

When Parliament defeated King Charles, Governor Stone (Calvert's Protestant governor) quickly swore allegiance to the new regime. However,

Maryland's Puritans distrusted him and felt that he was too friendly to the Catholics. In 1654, these Puritans toppled Stone, refused to recognize Calvert as proprietor, repealed the Toleration Act, and imposed a Puritan government on Maryland. The politically astute Calvert appealed directly to Oliver Cromwell, the Puritan leader in England, and was restored as proprietor of Maryland in 1657. One year later, he managed to reenact the Toleration Act; and after the Restoration in England (1660), Calvert recovered his old powers of governmental authority. Although Maryland failed to develop along the lines envisioned by Calvert, the proprietor had nevertheless succeeded in maintaining his authority over the colony.

THE CAROLINA PROPRIETARY

In 1663, Charles II issued a charter to eight prominent friends of the Crown (William Berkeley, John Berkeley, the Earl of Craven, George Carteret, the Earl of Clarendon, the Duke of Albemarle, Anthony Ashley-Cooper, and John Colleton). He authorized them to settle and develop the Carolinas (present-day North and South Carolina). Six years after the charter was issued, John Locke (a political theorist regarded as one of the fathers of representative government) drew up the Fundamental Constitutions of Carolina on behalf of the proprietors. This was intended as a blueprint for the development of the Carolinas. As envisioned by Locke and the proprietors, Carolina was to be a thorough-going feudal society in which a noble class of palatines, landgraves, and caciques were to enjoy economic and political power, while a large class of tenant farmers were to serve them as serfs and accept their political authority.* However, the attempt to transplant feudalism to the Carolinas was no more successful than the attempt to transplant it to Maryland.

In the last quarter of the seventeenth century, the Carolinas were only sparsely populated. Settlement in North Carolina was largely confined to Albemarle County, and consisted of transplanted Virginians who had moved farther south in search of more fertile land for tobacco cultivation. In 1677, rebellion erupted in North Carolina. Called Culpeper's Rebellion (after John Culpeper, the leader of the antiproprietary party), it was a protest against arbitrary government and the stringent enforcement of the trade laws. It resembled Bacon's Rebellion in many respects; and like Bacon's Rebellion, it too was a failure. In South Carolina, settlement was generally confined to the area around Charleston, and many of the residents had come from other British colonies in the West Indies. Later, the settlement was to have a sizeable Huguenot (French Calvinist) population, and the cultivation of rice and indigo was to develop into the major economic activity. As late as 1690, though, the Carolinas had a population of only 5,000.

GEORGIA

Georgia was the last English colony to be founded on the American mainland. Chartered in 1732, it was designed as a buffer colony to protect the Carolinas from attack by Spanish forces based in Florida; and it was intended as an asylum for English debtors, petty criminals, and religious minorities. James Oglethorpe, an idealistic reformer, was the most important of the twenty trustees who were to govern the colony for its first twenty-one year. (After this time, Georgia became a royal colony.) Under the trustees, religious toleration was extended to all Christians except Catholics, and prospective settlers were selected very carefully. All who were accepted as settlers were given free passage to the colony, fifty acres of land, as well as tools and seed, and were supported until the first harvest was completed. Nevertheless, Georgia's growth was disappointingly slow. Few English debtors came to Georgia; most of the early settlers were German Pietists who fled their native land to escape religious persecution. Not until 1751 was the colony permitted to elect a legislature. In 1760, the colony had only 9,000 people (6,000 whites and 3,000 Negro slaves). Oglethorpe's hope that Georgia would be a haven for the oppressed was never realized.

By 1690, with a population of 85,000 (60,000 in Virginia, and 20,000 in Maryland), the Southern colonies were well-established. Led by Virginia, the South made its living from tobacco; and it was developing its characteristic plantation economy, with its dependence upon slave labor. With this one-crop economy, the South (particularly Virginia) was to be adversely affected by the enforcement of the mercantile laws; and Virginia was to play a vital leadership role in the struggle for American independence.

---

* Palatines, landgraves, and caciques were titles of nobility created especially for the Carolinas.

REVIEW QUESTIONS FOR CHAPTER 4

1. All of the following were "Sea Dogs" *except*

   (A) John Hawkins
   (B) Francis Drake
   (C) John Cabot
   (D) Richard Grenville

2. Sir Walter Raleigh is associated with

   (A) the Kennebec colony
   (B) Roanoke Island
   (C) Jamestown
   (D) Maryland

3. Virginia was rescued from the "starving time" by

   (A) John Smith
   (B) Lord Delaware
   (C) John Rolfe
   (D) Thomas Dale

4. The first Virginia tobacco was sent to England in

   (A) 1611
   (B) 1614
   (C) 1617
   (D) 1619

5. The House of Burgesses and the Headright System were championed by

   (A) Sir Edwin Sandys
   (B) Lord Baltimore
   (C) George Yeardley
   (D) Nathaniel Bacon

6. All of the following contributed to Bacon's Rebellion *except*

   (A) Berkeley's arbitrary rule
   (B) Indian attacks on the frontier
   (C) the Navigation Acts
   (D) under-representation of the frontier in the House of Burgesses

7. Maryland was a

   (A) corporate colony
   (B) royal colony
   (C) proprietary colony
   (D) none of the above

8. The Toleration Act of 1649 extended religious liberty to

   (A) all Christians
   (B) all who professed the divinity of Christ
   (C) Protestants alone
   (D) everyone except Catholics

9. All were Carolina proprietors *except*

   (A) Anthony Ashley-Cooper
   (B) the Duke of Albemarle
   (C) John Locke
   (D) William Berkeley

10. Georgia was chartered in

    (A) 1632
    (B) 1689
    (C) 1700
    (D) 1732

Explanatory Answers

1. **(C)** Cabot's 1497 voyage established England's claim to North America.

2. **(B)** Raleigh founded colonies on Roanoke in 1585 and 1587.

3. **(D)** Dale's Laws restored order and discipline to Virginia in 1612.

4. **(B)** John Rolfe sent the first tobacco to England in 1614.

5. **(A)** Sir Edwin Sandys, Treasurer of the Virginia Company, instituted the House of Burgesses and the Headright System in 1619.

6. **(C)** The Navigation Acts, which regulated America's trade, were not a direct factor in Bacon's Rebellion.

7. **(C)** It was the first proprietary colony in America.

8. **(B)** No one who denied the divinity of Christ was permitted to practice the religion of his choice.

9. **(C)** Locke wrote the Fundamental Constitutions of Carolina, but was not a proprietor.

10. **(D)** Georgia was the last English colony founded on the American mainland.

Chapter 5

THE NEW ENGLAND COLONIES

Unlike Virginia, the New England colonies were founded for religious, not economic, reasons which had their roots in the religious quarrels of Elizabethan and early Stuart England. Under Elizabeth (1558–1603), the doctrines of the Anglican church were formulated so as to appeal to both moderate Protestants and moderate Catholics; but the extremists in both camps were alienated. The English Calvinists (Puritans) were especially unhappy with the Anglican church, feeling that it was too close to the Roman Catholic church in its beliefs and organization. Determined to reform the Anglican church from within and to bring its doctrines more in line with Calvinist beliefs, the Puritans, by the 1580's, began to form a political faction. They hoped to use their power in Parliament to bring about their religious reforms. Under James I and Charles I, the Puritan Parliament was to directly confront the Crown and was to plunge England into revolution. Meanwhile, by the 1580's, an extreme left-wing of the Puritan movement had developed which despaired of reforming the Anglican church from within. Known as Separatists (or Brownists or Pilgrims), they decided to leave the Anglican fold and form their own independent religious congregations. Beginning in the 1580's, the Separatists attempted to establish their own churches along strict Calvinist lines, but they found themselves prosecuted for religious nonconformity. When Queen Elizabeth died in 1603, many Puritans and Separatists hoped that James I would be more receptive to their religious views. However, James proved to be most unsympathetic to Puritan demands and became all the more determined to enforce Anglican conformity. As a result, a group of Separatists left England in 1608 and went to a land where they could practice their religion freely and in peace.

THE PLYMOUTH COLONY

The Flight to Holland

The Separatists (or Pilgrims as they now came to be called) went to Holland, where the Dutch, who had themselves suffered from the oppression of the Spaniards, welcomed them. However, the Pilgrims were not happy in Holland. They complained that their children were forgetting their English tongue and culture, and they felt that the Dutch were a people of strange customs. They longed to live as Englishmen in an English land. After twelve years in Holland, William Bradford, the Pilgrim leader, sent John Carver and Robert Cushman to see Sir Edwin Sandys of the London

Signing the Mayflower Compact.

(Virginia) Company. Sandys agreed to allow the Pilgrims to settle within the boundaries of Virginia; and although King James refused to sanction the project, James did indicate that he would not molest or trouble the Pilgrims should they settle in Virginia. (For military reasons, the British wanted as large a population as possible in Virginia.) Since the Pilgrims were too poor to finance their journey to America, they persuaded a group of London merchants to finance their passage in return for an interest in the profits of their prospective colony. It was agreed that after seven years, the property and resources of the colony would be divided among the adventurers (London merchants) and the planters (the Pilgrim settlers) on a *pro-rata* basis. In 1620, the Pilgrims left Holland and returned to England where they embarked upon the *Mayflower;* and on September 16, they sailed from Plymouth, bound for Virginia.

The Mayflower Compact

Either by accident or design (to this day no one knows for sure), the *Mayflower* anchored off the coast of Cape Cod on November 21, 1620. The Pilgrims were far outside the boundaries of Virginia, where they were authorized to settle, and were no longer subject to its jurisdiction. Moreover, they had no royal authorization to occupy land in New England, and any settlement which they made there would be outside the jurisdiction of any governmental authority. Consequently, on November 21, the men on board the *Mayflower* entered into a social compact by which they agreed to form a body politic, and to obey the orders of those elected to exercise authority over them. The Mayflower Compact was not a formal constitution since it established no machinery of government, but it was the first formal expression of the idea that government rests upon the consent of the governed.

Plymouth

Moving across the Bay from Cape Cod, the Pilgrims founded Plymouth on Christmas Day of 1620. Like the early Jamestown settlement, Plymouth was a corporate enterprise, and all land and property were held in common. With the aid of Squanto (a friendly Indian who had been captured by John Smith and taken to England before being returned to America), the Pilgrims survived the hardships of their first year in America, although disease killed more than half of the original 101 settlers. In 1623, the threat of famine led to the abolition of common landholding, and each family was given one acre of land for its own support. In the years which followed, the Plymouth colony developed a profitable trade in timber and furs; and during 1626–27, it was decided to buy out the London adventurers so that the Pilgrims could organize their community without outside interference. The London merchants agreed to accept 1800 British pounds (in annual installments of 200 pounds) in full settlement of their claims; and the profits from the fur trade were set aside to liquidate the debt.

The Government of Plymouth

Under the leadership of William Bradford (who was governor for most of the period between 1621 and 1656), Plymouth was organized in conformity with the precepts of the Calvinist religion.*

Each church congregation was independent and self-governing, but only those individuals who could demonstrate that they were of the elect were allowed to participate in church government. Similarly, only the elect were admitted to the rights of freemen and were permitted to vote and to participate in civil government. Thus, in order to enjoy the full rights of citizenship, one had to be of the elect. As long as the Plymouth colony remained small (it numbered 300 people in 1630), its government was fairly democratic since many adult males were of the elect. However, as the population increased and as religious zeal declined, the percentage of those who were of the elect dropped while the numbers of disenfranchised citizens rose. By 1668, the Plymouth fathers had formally decreed that only members of approved churches (the Calvinist elect) were entitled to vote, and the oligarchic control of the Pilgrim elect was reinforced.

Despite the fact that the right to vote was dependent upon a religious test, the government of Plymouth was fairly democratic — certainly it was more democratic than other societies of the time. In 1630, Plymouth obtained a charter from the Council for New England (which had replaced the older Plymouth joint-stock company as the administrative authority for New England). The charter confirmed the settlement's right to occupy the area it was holding and recognized Plymouth's established government. The governor and his seven councillors were elected annually by the freemen, and the freemen constituted the Plymouth General Court, which was a unicameral (single-chambered) legislative body. In 1639, the Fundamentals of Plymouth (one of the first codes of law adopted in America) reaffirmed the right of the General Court to approve all legislation and guaranteed all settlers "the rights of Englishmen." Consequently, the government of Plymouth was generally responsive to the will of the freemen, who elected all officials and approved all laws. While not all citizens qualified as freemen, all who were admitted to the rights of freemen enjoyed equal civil and political privileges. As the right to vote was gradually extended during the eighteenth century, the government was to become ever more representative of the general population. However, the basic concepts and forms of government would be unchanged.

The incipient democracy of Plymouth would grow and flourish over the ages. The settlement, itself, however, was to be completely overshadowed by the culturally more brilliant and economically more powerful Massachusetts Bay colony. Indeed, Plymouth was annexed by Massachusetts in 1691, and ceased to play an independent role in American history.

THE MASSACHUSETTS BAY COLONY

The Puritan's Worsening Situation in England

Ever since Charles I had come to the throne in 1625, the crown's relations with the Puritans had deteriorated. In 1629, Charles dissolved the Puritan-dominated Parliament and began an eleven-year period of personal rule. At the same time,

---

* Calvinists believed in a church and society governed by the visible elect. At the moment of creation, God selected those individuals whom He meant to save and those whom He meant to damn. Through the mystical experience of conversion, God often indicated to the individual that he was of the elect (saved). In order to maintain the purity and holiness of the church, only the elect were permitted to participate in its government. Those individuals who could not verify an experience of conversion were excluded from the government of the church. The determination of whether an experience of conversion was genuine or not was made by the elect; consequently, the Calvinist churches were closed corporations in which the elect decided who would or would not enjoy the rights and privileges of the elect.

Archbishop Laud began a strict policy of enforcing Anglican worship upon religious dissenters, and he persecuted the Puritans and their leaders. Faced with a government growing increasingly more hostile, a group of Puritan leaders, headed by John Winthrop, met at Cambridge in August, 1629. Entering into the Cambridge Agreement, they decided to purchase the Massachusetts Bay Company (a joint-stock enterprise organized by Puritan merchants to settle the Massachusetts Bay area). They planned to settle in America, provided that they could transfer the whole government of the company and its charter to Massachusetts. The directors of the Massachusetts Bay Company agreed to Winthrop's terms, and those stockholders who did not wish to migrate to America sold their interests in the company to those who did. Since the company's charter did not specify where the stockholders were to hold their annual meetings (most joint-stock companies had to meet in England and had to keep their charters in England), there was nothing to prevent the removal of the whole company and its charter to America. Thus, the entire Massachusetts Bay Company became a colony; its stockholders were the settlers, and the company's regulations became the laws of the community.

The Puritan Zion in the Wilderness

In March, 1630, the first group of Puritans, led by John Winthrop, (the newly elected governor), sailed for America. Before the year was out, 2,000 people had crossed the Atlantic to Massachusetts. Settling in the area north of Plymouth, the Puritan colony considered itself a "Bible Commonwealth." In America, the Puritans hoped to show England and the world how the true church should be organized; the Massachusetts Bay Colony was intended to be "a light unto the world." Its church was based on a covenant between God and man, and its government was a covenant among men in which the elect of God ruled. The Congregational (or Puritan) church was the established faith of Massachusetts; attendance at its services and financial contributions for its support were compulsory, and all other religious groups were barred from freely practicing their faith.* Although the Puritans of Massachusetts wanted religious freedom for themselves, they had no intention of granting it to others; and heresy was a crime punishable by death. Religion was considered too important to leave to the conscience of the individual. The Puritans were confident that if they organized their church and society in strict conformity to God's laws, then He would reward them mightily and show the world the righteousness of their ways.

The Puritan Oligarchy

The early history of the Massachusetts Bay colony is the story of the settlers' struggles to win democratic reforms and of the oligarchy's efforts to ward off royal control of the colony. As a result of economic and political difficulties in England, Massachusetts attracted large numbers of immigrants. By 1643, the colony had a population of 20,000, but only 4,000 were Puritans who could qualify as freemen. Thus the affairs of Massachusetts were controlled by a small group of the Puritan elect.

The Growth of Representative Government

In 1630, only twelve people qualified as freemen. Constituting the General Court, they elected the governor and his assistants and exercised legislative power. Bowing to popular pressure, the General Court admitted 118 people to freemanship in 1631 and decreed the following:

(1) All members in good standing of the Congregational church (the elect) were granted the rights of freemen. (This violated the Massachusetts charter, which granted freemanship to all stockholders, regardless of religious affiliation.)

(2) The freemen were to elect the assistants (magistrates) for life terms.

(3) All assistants had to be members of the General Court.

(4) The governor was to be elected by the assistants from among their own number.

(5) The governor and the assistants were empowered to enact legislation. Under this scheme of government, the oligarchy held the governorship and the assistantships and could pretty well dominate the General Court. However, protests were soon forthcoming.

---

* Puritans and Pilgrims were both Congregationalists, but whereas the Pilgrims left the Church of England, the Puritans retained a nominal allegiance to it.

The Watertown Protest

In 1632, the town of Watertown (an outlying village) protested the imposition of a tax levied by the assistants. The townspeople argued that the tax had been imposed without their consent, in violation of the English constitution, and they demanded to see the company charter in order to determine the legality of the Massachusetts government. Although Governor Winthrop attempted to conceal the charter, the oligarchy was forced to compromise. It was agreed that each town in Massachusetts would send two representatives to the General Court to advise the governor and his assistants on taxation. Further, it was agreed that the assistants would no longer be elected for life terms; instead they would be elected for a one-year term, as provided for under the charter. The Watertown Protest established the principle that taxation can be imposed only by the representatives of the electorate. It was a landmark in the development of American representative government.

The Half-Way Covenant

The Watertown Protest was but the beginning of the movement for a more democratic government in Massachusetts. In 1634, the General Court won the right to approve all laws as well as the right to admit citizens to the rights of freemen. At the same time, the absolute judicial authority of the assistants was limited by the introduction of the jury system, and the people of Massachusetts secured the full protection of the English common law. Furthermore, in 1644, the General Court became a bicameral (two-chambered) body; the assistants were separated from the deputies (elected by the freemen) and were made to sit as an upper house. It was felt that this would increase the independence and authority of the deputies and reduce the excessive authority of the assistants. Nevertheless, Massachusetts was far from a democratic society. The right to vote was still dependent upon a religious qualification; and as Massachusetts continued to grow, the percentage of freemen in the general population continued to shrink. Moreover, as the colony became more prosperous, religious zeal declined, and fewer people were having experiences of conversion. By the mid-seventeenth century, the Puritan fathers feared that there might not be enough of the elect to maintain the machinery of government. In 1662, the Half-Way Covenant was adopted.

This measure held that young people who had not had an experience of conversion, provided that they were children of the elect, would be admitted to the rights of freemen. It also held that those who adhered to Congregationalism (without being full members of the church) would be admitted to the rights of freemen, even though they were not of the elect. As long as these people led moral lives and paid lip service to Congregational tenets, they would be given full rights of citizenship. Although the Half-Way Covenant applied only to professed Calvinists, it was still a liberalizing measure which severely undermined the strength of the Puritan oligarchy. Having admitted the non-elect to freemanship, it would be difficult to long maintain a "Bible Commonwealth."

Town Government

Although the Massachusetts Bay colony was governed by the Puritan elect, local government (from the very beginning of colonization) was far more liberal and democratic than the government of the colony. Massachusetts was a colony of towns and villages. Each town maintained its own church, school system, and charitable institutions; each handled its own problems of sanitation, police and fire protection, and economic regulation. At the famous New England town meeting all inhabitants (rich or poor, elect or non-elect) were permitted to discuss town problems and propose solutions. (Generally, only property owners could vote, but there was no religious requirement for participation in town government.) As a result, the Massachusetts towns enjoyed a high degree of popular involvement in local problems, and they served as schools of democracy that trained the people for responsible involvement in the governmental process.

The Fight for The Charter

While the people of Massachusetts were demanding a more representative government, the leaders of the colony were fighting to avoid royal control. King Charles I was unaware that the Massachusetts Bay Company charter had been removed to America, and he was disturbed by reports that Anglicans were being discriminated against in the colony. In the early 1630's, Charles demanded that the company produce its charter and show by what right it acted. The leaders of the Bay colony procrastinated and finally refused to produce the charter. In 1636, Charles began a *Quo Warranto* (By What Right) proceeding against the colony, and the English courts (not unexpectedly) found against the colony. Three years later, Charles appointed a royal governor for Massachusetts and instructed him to secure control of the colony. The Puritans had decided to forcibly resist the implementation of royal control, which would have effectively ended their "Bible Commonwealth." However, before a confrontation could develop between the Puritans and the royal governor, civil war broke out in England; and the Crown was unable to devote its full energies to the control of Massachusetts. When the English Puritans seized control of Britain in the 1640's, Massachusetts was viewed with greater favor by the English authorities and was left pretty much on her own.

RELIGIOUS DISSENT AND THE EXPANSION OF NEW ENGLAND

Roger Williams and the Founding of Rhode Island

In the 1630's, Roger Williams was a resident of the town of Salem, Massachusetts, and he took his religion very seriously. He condemned his fellow Puritans for maintaining their nominal allegiance to the Anglican church, and he favored the separation of church and state. Holding that an experience of conversion could never be authenticated (since Satan often produced them to lead men astray), Williams declared that the elect were known only to God. He argued that the state should concern itself with the maintenance of law and order and not with the religious convictions of individuals. Moreover, he accused the Massachusetts authorities of illegally occupying land belonging to the Indians, and he questioned the validity of the colony's charter. Williams was tried in 1635. However, he was tried for sedition (the questioning of the charter's validity) and not for heresy. He was ordered to be banished from Massachusetts, but execution of the sentence was delayed until the spring of 1636.

Leaving Massachusetts that spring, Williams was befriended by the Narragansett Indians, and he founded the town of Providence in what was to become Rhode Island. The area soon attracted those who dissented from the religious and political ideals of Puritan Massachusetts. In 1638, Anne Hutchinson and a group of Boston exiles founded

Roger Williams

Portsmouth. Mrs. Hutchinson was banished from Massachusetts for antinomianism (salvation through faith alone). She held that each individual could commune directly with God by means of a spiritual inner light, could receive an inner revelation of divine grace, and could be saved by faith alone and not good works. Her religious convictions threatened to undermine the authority of the Puritan clergy by stressing personal communion with God, and she was forced to leave the Bay colony.

By 1643, Providence and Portsmouth had been joined by Newport and Warwick, both of which had also been founded by expatriates from Massachusetts. Each town was independent and self-governing. However, because of the hostility of Massachusetts and Connecticut, Roger Williams went to England to obtain a charter for Rhode Island in order to secure his colony from possible attack by the orthodox Puritans. In 1644, a charter for Rhode Island was granted. It separated church and state, granted freedom of conscience in matters of religion, provided for town approval of all measures passed by the general assembly, and gave the freemen of the towns the right to initiate legislation. It was an enlightened and democratic charter, and Rhode Island continued as a haven for all men seeking religious freedom.

Thomas Hooker and Connecticut

The Puritans of Massachusetts were attracted to the Connecticut River Valley by the fertility of its soil, and in the 1630's, a number of settlements were made in the area. The most important was that of the Rev. Thomas Hooker who established the community of Hartford in 1636. Something of a democratic reformer, Hooker believed that government must rest upon the consent of the governed (elect and non-elect); and the vote was given to all free inhabitants. Hooker has often been thought of as one of the fathers of American democracy, but this view must be modified somewhat. While all free inhabitants could vote, the General Court determined who would or would not be considered a free inhabitant. Usually only male Trinitarian (believers in the Christian Trinity) householders were permitted to vote. Moreover, the governor had to be a member of an approved church — that is, one of the elect. In 1639, the various Connecticut towns were united under a single government by the Fundamental Orders of Connecticut, America's first written constitution. The Fundamental Orders adopted Hooker's concept of government and made the stringent Mosaic law the basis of the Connecticut legal system. Although Connecticut's government was more liberal than that of Massachusetts, it was far from being democratic in the modern sense. By 1662, Connecticut had a population of 5,000 and received a charter from Charles II.

New Haven, New Hampshire, and Maine

In 1637, Theophilus Eaton and John Davenport, who both felt that the government of Massachusetts was too liberal, founded New Haven. They established a joyless theocracy which strictly limited the right to vote to the elect and banned trial by jury since it was not a part of Mosaic law. New Haven was annexed (against its will) by Connecticut in 1662. New Hampshire was settled by various religious groups (including Anglicans) in the years after 1638, and was administered by Massachusetts between 1641 and 1677. Sparsely populated, it became a royal colony in 1679. Maine, originally belonging to the Gorges family, was also sparsely populated. It was claimed by Massachusetts; and despite the objections of the Gorges family, the Puritans succeeded in establishing their claim to Maine. Maine did not separate itself from Massachusetts until 1820.

THE NEW ENGLAND CONFEDERATION (1643–1684)

An Experiment in Federalism

In the mid-seventeenth century, the New England colonies were in a precarious situation. To the north, the French in Canada posed a serious military threat; to the west, the Dutch appeared ready to contest the New Englanders for control

Rev. Thomas Hooker giving a prayer of thanks with his congregation upon reaching Connecticut.

of the Connecticut River Valley. Also, the menace posed by local Indian tribes could not be discounted. Indeed, the Pequot War of 1636–1637 showed the New England colonies to be ill-coordinated in their military efforts and unlikely to overcome a serious military threat from the French or the Dutch. In order to meet their common enemies, Massachusetts, Plymouth, Connecticut, and New Haven organized the New England Confederation in 1643. (Rhode Island was excluded because of its unorthodox religious beliefs.)

The General Court of each member colony annually elected two commissioners to represent it at the meetings of the Confederation. The commissioners were empowered to declare war and make peace, to raise troops, to hear and settle intercolonial disputes, to negotiate with the Indians, and to decide the fate of fugitives from justice and of runaway servants and slaves. However, six of the eight commissioners had to agree to any measure before the Confederation would take action. The expenses of the Confederation were to be borne by each colony in proportion to its male population between the ages of sixteen and sixty. As a result, Massachusetts had to bear the bulk of the financial burden.

The New England Confederation was the first federal union entered into by the English colonies; but it was a failure. The Confederation's military efforts against the Dutch in 1651 proved ineffectual. Furthermore, Massachusetts felt that its influence in the Confederation did not match its financial contribution. By the 1660's the New England Confederation had become dormant. It was revived, however, to meet the grave challenge presented by King Philip's War of 1675–1676. Philip, chief of the Wampanoag Indians, was opposed to the relentless expansionist activities of the English settlers. His military resistance was especially dangerous to the settlers because he succeeded in uniting many of the tribes in the area for this war effort. One out of every sixteen New England males of military age was killed in this struggle; twelve towns were totally destroyed and many others were heavily damaged. Nevertheless, King Philip's War resulted in a crushing defeat for the Indians of New England. It marked their last stand against the spread of white settlement, and after 1676, the Indians were no longer a menace to the New England colonies. In 1684, the New England Confederation was formally abolished.

THE PROBLEM OF MASSACHUSETTS AND THE DOMINION OF NEW ENGLAND

Massachusetts Under the Restoration

The Restoration of Charles II as King of England in 1660 was not greeted with joy by the Puritans of Massachusetts. For twenty years, the colony had led an almost independent existence; now its fate was uncertain. Charles II attempted to strengthen royal control throughout British America; and for over twenty years, his agents kept up a running feud with Massachusetts. The royal agents demanded adherence to the navigation and trade laws, the abolition of religious tests for suffrage, and freedom for Anglicans to worship. Massachusetts refused to comply, and in 1684, the Court of Chancery revoked the colony's charter and placed Massachusetts under the direct control of the king.

The Dominion of New England

In 1685, Sir Edmund Andros was named royal governor of the Dominion of New England, which included New York and the New Jerseys in addition to New England. Andros assumed his duties in December of 1686, and from the start, his regime was unpopular. The Dominion of New England made no provision for an elective assembly, and this omission, the Americans felt, was a violation of the English constitution. Also, Andros unilaterally declared that the New England towns could hold only one town meeting a year. Furthermore, all militia units were placed under the direct command of the governor. The Crown hoped that the Dominion of New England would provide better military defense against the French and more efficient enforcement of the Navigation Acts. To the Americans, it was evidence of the Crown's despotic intentions. Consequently, when the Glorious Revolution broke out in England in 1688, the people of Boston threw Andros into jail and abolished the Dominion of New England.

The new English monarchs, William and Mary, did not attempt to restore the hated Dominion of New England. Instead, they restored the charters of the colonies absorbed in the ill-fated Dominion, and in 1691, they granted a new charter to Massachusetts. It provided for a royal governor appointed by the Crown and for a council elected by the General Court (but subject to the veto of the governor). The Crown was given a veto over all legislation enacted by Massachusetts, and the religious qualification for voting was replaced by a simple property qualification. The days of the Puritan oligarchy were at an end, and Massachusetts ceased to be a "Bible Commonwealth."

THE ECONOMIC LIFE OF NEW ENGLAND

Initially, agriculture was the primary economic activity of New England, and the New England town was laid out in imitation of the English manorial village (minus its seigneurial features). However, the New England soil was stony and poor, and the people soon turned to other areas of economic activity. Fishing and shipbuilding became the primary economic activities, and trade and commerce soon eclipsed agriculture in importance. By the mid-seventeenth century, the triangular trade had been developed.

New England merchants sold the products of the Northern colonies (primarily fish and cereal grains) to the planters of the West Indies in return for cash, sugar, and molasses. Sugar and molasses were used in the manufacture of rum, which was taken to West Africa and sold to local chieftains in return for slaves. The slaves were then sent to the West Indies where they were sold to local planters. This triangular trade was highly profitable and helped the colonies meet their trade deficit with England. But, it was also conducted in violation of the British trade laws since the New Englanders often traded with Spanish and French colonies. Unlike the South, which developed a plantation agriculture, New England was a region which lived by trade and commerce.

THE PURITAN CONTRIBUTION TO AMERICA

The New England Puritans have often been portrayed as a God-intoxicated people, haunted by the sense of their own sinfulness and warped by their fears of everlasting damnation. They were certainly a dour people, who condemned singing, dancing, music, and theatrical entertainment as sinful. Confident that theirs was the true faith, they did not look kindly upon religious dissenters; and the irrational terrors which tormented their psyches were only too evident in the disgraceful Salem witchcraft trials of 1688–1693. Altogether, nineteen people were executed for witchcraft, and the madness of the witch-hunt did not cease until accusations of witchcraft were aimed at the families of the Puritan establishment itself. Nevertheless, the importance of the Puritan contribution to American culture should not be minimized.

The idea that government rested upon a covenant among men and derived its just powers from the consent of the governed inspired the American Revolution and laid the intellectual foundations of American democracy. While the Puritans were not themselves democrats, their conception of the equality of the elect in the eyes of God was later extended to include all men; and their town meeting was a school for democracy. Furthermore, the Calvinist virtues of thrift, sobriety, and hard work, and the injunction to perform good works and to prosper molded the American character and helped later generations tame a wilderness. In addition, the Puritans' idea that they constituted a "city set upon a hill" and had a providential mission to perform inspired the belief that America was "the last best hope of mankind," destined to free man from the shackles of despotism. The Puritan imprint on America has been deep and indelible; and of all the people who helped to build the United States, they made the greatest single contribution.

REVIEW QUESTIONS FOR CHAPTER 5

1. The Pilgrims were led by

    (A) John Carver
    (B) William Bradford
    (C) John Winthrop
    (D) Thomas Hooker

2. The Mayflower Compact was

    (A) a constitution
    (B) a code of laws
    (C) an agreement to form a body politic
    (D) a pledge to go to America

3. Plymouth was annexed by Massachusetts in

    (A) 1639
    (B) 1643
    (C) 1684
    (D) 1691

4. The Half-Way Covenant extended the franchise to

    (A) the elect
    (B) all professing Calvinists
    (C) all Trinitarian Christians
    (D) all property owners

5. Roger Williams founded

    (A) Newport
    (B) Portsmouth
    (C) Providence
    (D) Warwick

6. The first colony to separate church and state was

    (A) Massachusetts
    (B) Connecticut
    (C) Plymouth
    (D) Rhode Island

7. The Fundamental Orders of Connecticut were inspired by

    (A) Thomas Hooker
    (B) John Davenport
    (C) Theophilus Eaton
    (D) Edmund Andros

8. Which came first?

    (A) The Pequot War
    (B) King Philip's War
    (C) The Dominion of New England
    (D) The Confederation of New England

9. Antinomianism is associated with

    (A) Roger Williams
    (B) Anne Hutchinson
    (C) Thomas Hooker
    (D) John Winthrop

10. Which was not a member of the New England Confederation?

    (A) Massachusetts
    (B) Plymouth
    (C) New Haven
    (D) Rhode Island

Explanatory Answers

1. **(B)** Bradford was the Pilgrims' leader almost continuously until 1656.

2. **(C)** The Compact pledged the passengers of the *Mayflower* to form a civil government.

3. **(D)** Plymouth was annexed under the Massachusetts charter of 1691.

4. **(B)** Under the Half-Way Covenant, an authenticated experience of conversion was no longer required.

5. **(C)** Providence was founded in 1636.

6. **(D)** Rhode Island's 1644 charter separated church and state.

7. **(A)** Thomas Hooker founded Hartford, Connecticut in 1636.

8. **(A)** The Pequot War, 1636–1637; the Confederation of New England, 1643; King Philip's War, 1675–1676; the Dominion of New England, 1685.

9. **(B)** Anne Hutchinson denied the validity of good works in salvation.

10. **(D)** Rhode Island was excluded because of its unorthodox religious beliefs.

Chapter 6

THE MIDDLE COLONIES AND THE MELTING POT

The Middle colonies of New York, New Jersey, and Pennsylvania were the most cosmopolitan and the most highly diversified of the English colonies in North America. Whereas the South became tied to plantation agriculture, and New England became dependent upon commerce, the Middle colonies combined commercial agriculture (crops grown for sale on a world market) with a vigorous manufacturing and mercantile life. Since their economy was diversified, the Middle colonies were not dependent upon a single crop or market, and they enjoyed a healthier economic life than either the South or New England. Moreover, the region's population was highly cosmopolitan. Virtually every ethnic and religious group known to Western Europe could be found in the Middle colonies. Indeed one of the great strengths of these British colonies was their human variety, and the melting pot that was colonial America is nowhere better illustrated than in the Middle colonies.

NEW YORK

New Netherland Becomes New York

By the mid-seventeenth century, the Dutch were blocking New England's westward expansion and were cutting into Britain's trade with her American colonies. New Netherland was a thorn in the side of the British Empire which had to be removed. In March of 1664, Charles II granted his brother James, Duke of York, title to the area which then comprised New Netherland (New York, New Jersey, and Delaware). One month later, James named Colonel Richard Nicolls as lieutenant-governor of the territory, and authorized him to capture New Netherland from the Dutch. As we have already noted, Nicolls captured New Amsterdam in August, 1664, without firing a shot. Discontented with the authoritarian rule of Peter Stuyvesant, the people surrendered themselves to English rule upon the promise that they would be granted (1) "the rights of Englishmen," (2) freedom of conscience in matters of religion, (3) the retention of Dutch customs regarding property ownership and inheritance, and (4) trading privileges with Holland. Nicolls kept his pledges, and his rule proved highly popular with all segments of the population.

The Duke's Laws and Continuing Strife with the Dutch

In 1665, deputies from seventeen towns on Long Island and Westchester met at Hempstead and adopted the Duke's Laws, which provided for religious toleration and for trial by jury, and which disallowed religious qualifications for voting in local elections. The Duke's Laws also codified the civil and criminal code of New York.

However, the Laws failed to provide for the election of a representative legislative assembly and, therefore, disappointed those who had hoped for a more representative government in New York. The Duke of York was an absolutist who did not recognize the right of subjects to have a voice in their government, and he was not about to encourage the democratic spirit.

As a result of the second Anglo-Dutch war (1664–1667), the English confiscated the property of the Dutch West India Company as well as the property of those Dutchmen who refused to swear allegiance to the English Crown. The 1667 Peace of Breda confirmed the English conquest of New Netherland, and the Dutch relinquished their claims to the colony. With the opening of the third Anglo-Dutch War in 1672, New York was reconquered by the Dutch, who ruled the colony from 1673 to 1674. The Treaty of Westminster (1674), however, restored New York to the English, and the Dutch never again threatened the colony.

The Struggle for a Legislative Assembly

As early as 1670, some Long Island towns had refused to pay the tax assessments levied upon them by the English governor on the grounds that they had been imposed without the peoples' consent — in violation of the English Constitution. With the end of the Dutch threat in 1674, agitation for an elective assembly was resumed in earnest. Sir Edmund Andros, the Duke's new governor, urged James to permit the election of a general assembly. He pointed out that it would facilitate the levying and collection of taxes if the people were given a voice in government. James, however, rejected Andros' recommendation in 1674. Andros' tenure was marked by repeated charges of corruption and illegal trading with the Dutch. Although the governor was exonerated of all charges, James, in hopes of lessening friction, named Colonel Thomas Dongan to succeed Andros as governor in 1683. Dongan was an Irish Catholic, and stout opposition to his appointment was to be expected from the Protestant population. Consequently, to make Dongan's appointment more palatable to the people of New York, James authorized the new governor to call a general assembly of deputies from the major towns. In October, 1683, this assembly adopted the Charter of Liberties and Privileges, which declared the following:

Governor Andros

(1) Sovereignty was vested in the governor, council, and general assembly. All three branches of government had to act in concert if government was to be legitimate.

(2) All taxes had to be approved by the general assembly, which was to meet at least once in every three years.

(3) Members of the assembly and local officials were to be freely elected by the freeholders (small property owners), with no religious tests for voting.

(4) Freedom of worship was specifically granted.

The Charter of Liberties and Privileges was approved by James. However, when he became King James II, in 1685, he disallowed the Charter and returned Andros to power. In 1686, he instructed Andros and his council to exercise full executive and legislative authority. James' arbitrary action increased popular resentment against his rule of the colony.

Leisler's Rebellion

In 1686, Sir Edmund Andros left New York to assume his duties as Governor of the Dominion

Jacob Leisler supervising the signing of a declaration to proclaim William and Mary as monarchs.

of New England, and he left Captain Francis Nicholson in charge of New York as lieutenant-governor. When news of England's Glorious Revolution reached New York in April of 1689, Nicholson hesitated to proclaim the Protestant William and Mary as the new monarchs; therefore, rumors soon became rife that there was a Catholic plot to seize control of New York. On May 31, 1689, Jacob Leisler, a German immigrant, started a revolt against Nicholson and proclaimed William and Mary as monarchs in New York. In June, he organized a committee of public safety. Leisler called together a general assembly in July; and by February of 1690, he was in effective control of the New York colony. However, Leisler came into conflict with Nicholas Bayard, head of the aristocratic faction, who also wanted to control New York. The hostility between the two men would have fateful consequences in the future.

While Leisler was taking control of New York, the Lords of Trade in London recommended the appointment of a new royal governor for New York. In November, 1690, Colonel Henry Sloughter was commissioned governor, but red tape and shipwreck delayed his arrival in New York until March of 1691. When Sloughter finally arrived, Leisler peacefully surrendered his authority, declaring that he had seized power only to protect the interests of William and Mary against James II's friends. All appeared to be normal, but in April (at the insistence of Nicholas Bayard), Leisler and his associates were tried for treason. In May, 1691, Leisler and his son-in-law, Jacob Milborne, were hanged. However, Governor Sloughter was authorized to convene a general assembly; thus 1691 also marks the beginning of representative government in New York. After almost forty years, New York had finally secured an elective assembly.

NEW JERSEY

Chaos in New Jersey

In June, 1664, the Duke of York granted New Jersey to Sir George Carteret and Lord John Berkeley. Technically, the Duke's grant gave the proprietors control of the land, but it did not convey any governmental authority. New Jersey was legally within the political jurisdiction of New York, and the governors of New York were to claim the right to rule New Jersey until well into the eighteenth century. Nevertheless, Carteret and Berkeley acted as though they had full governmental authority. In 1665, as a means of attracting settlers, they granted religious toleration, offered generous land grants, and promised a general assembly. Within a few years, New Jersey had attracted settlers from New England and from Long Island; it had its own assembly and its own governor who was appointed by Carteret and Berkeley. Legal or not, the New Jersey colony was a *fait accompli,* even though New York constantly tried to impose its authority over the region. In 1674, Lord Berkeley sold West Jersey to Edward Byllynge and John Fenwick — two Quakers — and in 1682, the Carteret family sold East Jersey to a syndicate of twelve Quakers (one of whose members was William Penn). This syndicate soon enlarged itself to twenty-four members, so that by the mid-1680's, New Jersey had no fewer than twenty-six proprietors. The settlement was in a chaotic state due to conflicts among the proprietors and between the proprietors and the people.

Quakerism

Quakerism was founded in England by George Fox in 1649. It was a religious movement which stressed direct and individual communion with God through personal, spiritual, and emotional experiences. It denied the validity of a special priesthood, proclaiming the priesthood of all believers in its stead; and it rejected all religious rites, ceremonies, dogmas, and doctrines. Believing that Christianity must be lived as well as preached, the Quakers refused to bear arms, refused to swear oaths of allegiance to secular authority, and refused to pay religious tithes or taxes. As a result of their religious convictions, they became the most persecuted of European Christian sects; but their numbers grew in spite of persecution. By 1665, Fox had some 80,000 followers, and his movement was also rapidly spreading in Germany. Among Fox's converts was William Penn, son of Admiral William Penn who was a close personal friend of both Charles II and James II. The younger Penn hoped to establish a refuge for his fellow Quakers in America, where they could practice their religion free of governmental harassment. To this end, he became involved in the acquisition of New Jersey.

Unfortunately, Penn's hopes for New Jersey failed to materialize. The inhabitants were primarily Puritans and Anglicans; they deeply resented the control of the proprietors and were hostile to their Quaker faith. Penn quickly realized that he would have to find a refuge for his fellow Quakers elsewhere. After a generation of chaotic squabbling, the New Jersey proprietors surrendered governmental authority to the British Crown in 1702. For the next thirty-six years, the governor of New York also served as governor of New Jersey; and it was not until the 1740's that New Jersey finally became fully separated from New York.

PENNSYLVANIA

The Pennsylvania Charter

In March of 1681, King Charles II (in settlement of a debt of £16,000 owed to the Penn family) gave William Penn title to Pennsylvania. (In 1682, the Duke of York also granted Penn control of Delaware.) The 1681 charter granted to Penn reflected the Crown's policy of centralizing control over the American colonies and imposed restrictions on Penn's authority. It contained the following provisions:

(1) Penn's laws had to receive approval by an elected assembly representing the freeholders.

(2) The colony was required to obey and enforce the Navigation Acts and all trade regulations imposed by the Crown.

William Penn

(3) The English Privy Council had the right to veto all colonial legislation within five years of its passage.

(4) Settlers had the right to appeal decisions of colonial courts directly to the Crown.

(5) The British Parliament was given the right to impose taxes on the colony.

Under this charter, the Crown could directly impose its will on Pennsylvania by vetoing acts of its assembly, by levying taxes, and by compelling enforcement of the mercantile laws. It was this pattern of government which the Crown wished to impose on all the British colonies, but they resisted increased royal authority as a violation of their "rights as Englishmen." The long quarrel between the Crown and the colonies over the nature of imperial government would culminate in the American Revolution.

Penn's Frame of Government

In 1682, William Penn drafted a frame of government for Pennsylvania which provided for a governor appointed by the proprietor, a council of seventy-two members (one-third of whom were to be elected annually by the freeholders), and an assembly of 200 members. The council was to initiate all legislation and control all administrative and judicial functions. The assembly only had the right to approve or reject the proposals of the council. However, this arrangement proved extremely unwieldy for a colony still in its formative stages; so in 1683, the council was reduced in size to eighteen members, and the assembly was cut to thirty-two members. Throughout Pennsylvania's first decades, friction between the Penn family and the assembly was common, as the assembly sought to increase its authority over the colony's affairs. In 1696, the assembly won the right to initiate legislation, and the proprietor's governmental authority continued to diminish with the passage of time.

The Settlement of Pennsylvania

Disapproving of the ways in which the English colonists had liquidated Indian land claims, Penn made it a point to deal with the Indians justly and generously. He purchased their lands at fair terms and took pains to explain precisely what their land sales entailed. As a result, Penn enjoyed good relations with the Indians; and this aided the colony's growth. Penn granted land to settlers for a penny an acre; but because land grants were made carelessly, title disputes became troublesome as the colony continued to grow. It was not until the 1730's that rival land claims were finally resolved. Although Pennsylvania was intended as a refuge for Quakers, Penn welcomed all types of settlers; and from its earliest days the colony had a highly diversified population. A large group of Welshmen settled north and west of Philadelphia in 1682, while German Pietists (Quakers) came in large numbers and settled at Germantown. Irish and English Quakers established settlements throughout the colony, and Scots and Scotch-Irish occupied the lands along the frontier. Founded in 1682, Philadelphia quickly became a major center of commerce. During the eighteenth century, it rivaled and surpassed Boston as the leading city of colonial America.

The Charter of Liberties

Because of Penn's friendship with King James II, William and Mary, after the Glorious Revolution of 1689, placed Pennsylvania under royal control. However, Penn's proprietorship was restored in 1694; and in 1701, he granted the Charter of Liberties, which remained in force in Pennsylvania until the outbreak of the American Revolution. Under its terms, the governor was named by the proprietor; and the legislature became unicameral (one-house). All laws were passed by the governor and the legislature, so that the proprietor's active role in government came to an end — his only function being to name the governor. At the same time, the vote was granted to all males who professed belief in Jesus Christ (later this requirement was dropped in favor of ownership of land worth fifty British pounds or personal property valued at fifty pounds). Delaware was granted a government separate from that of Pennsylvania. Unfortunately, William Penn's personal finances suffered, and he was imprisoned for debt. In 1708, he was forced to mortgage Pennsylvania to a group of trustees in order to satisfy his creditors' claims.

THE ECONOMY OF THE MIDDLE COLONIES

Agriculture was the primary activity of colonial America, and the Middle colonies were the "breadbasket" of America. Generally speaking, the Middle colonies were marked by family-sized farms of 100 to 200 acres. Although large plantation-type estates existed in New York, the family farm was dominant. Quitrents (rents due the proprietor) were low; but because of the difficulty involved in their collection, they usually went unpaid. Wheat was the staple crop of the Middle colonies, although cereal grains (rye, barley, oats, corn) and all types of fruits and vegetables were also grown in abundance. Livestock was also abundant, and meat, milk, cheese, and butter production were important economic activities. Because of their great diversity, the Middle colonies were not economically dependent upon any single crop or market. Most farmers were commercial — they sold their produce in domestic or foreign markets, rather than consuming it locally — and the ports of Philadelphia and New York became major centers of trade for agricultural products.

In addition to agriculture, New York was a major center for the fur trade; and Philadelphia and New York were vigorous shipbuilders (although New England dominated the shipbuilding industry). Pennsylvania and New York were major manufacturing centers, turning out textiles, glass, hats, pottery, and a host of other items. Manufacturing was done in small shops which were owned and worked by the family. Prosperous establishments often had apprentices and hired hands, but it was rare for any manufacturing establishment to employ more than a few workers. Trade and commerce with the West Indies, Europe, and the Southern colonies also figured prominently in the economic life of the Middle colonies. Diversified and prosperous, the Middle colonies enjoyed a middle-class social system in which extremes of wealth or poverty were the exception, rather than the rule.

THE COLONIAL MELTING POT

Between 1689 and 1765, the population of colonial America increased tenfold (see Table 1). But even more important than this phenomenal population growth was the nature of the increase. Unlike Spanish America or French Canada, British America had a highly diversified population. The English government realized that the larger British America's population became, the better would be its chances of defeating its French and Spanish foes. As a result, non-English ethnic groups were welcomed in America on the assumption that anyone forced to flee their native lands because of religious or political oppression would harbor little loyalty to their homelands and would transfer their allegiance to British America.

Table 1

The Population of British America

Year	Population
1650	50,000
1675	140,000
1700	240,000
1730	650,000
1750	1,150,000
1765	1,850,000

NOTE: Since the first census was not taken until 1790, all population figures for colonial America are estimates and may vary from source to source.

Major Ethnic Groups in America

Of America's 1,850,000 people (as of 1765), 65-70 per cent were English, and they formed the major ethnic group in every colony.* The next largest group were the Scots and Scotch-Irish, who constituted 12-15 per cent of the population. During the eighteenth century, some 300,000 Scotch-Irish came to America from Ulster (Northern Ireland). Protestant in religion, they were settled in Ireland by Cromwell, in the hope that they would make England's occupation of that country easier. However, economic depression and unenlightened mercantile laws forced the settlers to seek a better livelihood elsewhere. Disliked by the Puritans, they avoided New England and settled along the frontier in Pennsylvania and in the Southern colonies. Backwoodsmen, the Scotch-Irish were rugged individualists who were fiercely independent — they were among the first pioneers. The Scots came primarily from the Scottish Highlands. They were forced to leave Scotland in the wake of their defeat at Culloden, where they had attempted to establish the Stuart pretender as King of England. Coming to America in the late 1740's, they also gravitated toward the frontier; and they had little love for their English cousins.

---

* The English were 65-70 per cent of the white population. America had some 400,000 Negroes in 1765; the overwhelming majority of them were slaves in the Southern colonies.

The major non-English group in America was of German origin. Between 1717 and 1775, more than 85,000 Germans migrated to Pennsylvania; and they composed one-third of the colony's total population. Coming from the Rhineland and the Palatinate, they left Germany to escape religious persecution and/or economic hardship. Engaging primarily in farming, they were a prosperous and valuable element of the colonial population. They comprised from 6-9 per cent of America's population in 1765. Irish Catholics made up from 3 to 5 per cent of the population and were concentrated primarily in Maryland and Pennsylvania. Distrusted because of their religion, they were often looked upon as a dangerous class of subversives; but they generally enjoyed religious toleration and civil equality. The Dutch of New York comprised about 3 per cent of the colonial population and enjoyed considerable economic and social prestige. Many Dutch families played prominent roles in the struggle for American Independence.

The remainder of the white population (3-5 per cent) was composed of numerous ethnic groups. French Huguenots were scattered through New England and New York, and they comprised a large colony in Charleston, South Carolina. A highly skilled and talented people, they concentrated on trade and commerce. Colonies of Swiss settlers could be found in Pennsylvania and the Carolinas; Swedes, Finns, and Danes were found in Delaware and New Jersey. Welshmen were scattered along the frontier, and a total of 1,500 Jews resided in New York City and in Newport, Rhode Island. Almost wholly involved in commerce, many Jewish families achieved wealth and prominence. In addition to these groups, elements of virtually every European people could be found somewhere in the thirteen colonies, by the mid-eighteenth century.

Although British stock was dominant throughout the American colonies, the rich mixture of ethnic groups found in America helped give rise to a consciousness of American nationality and helped reduce dependence upon England. Out of the colonial melting pot emerged a new and distinct type of man — the American — who fused elements of Europe's culture with the culture of the American frontier to create a society unique in the world.

The Middle colonies best typified the new America which was coming into being. In the Middle colonies was found the richest blend of ethnic groups, all coexisting in relative harmony and working for the advancement of all. And because of their highly diversified economies, the Middle colonies enjoyed a prosperous middle-class society which set the pattern for future American economic and social development.

REVIEW QUESTIONS FOR CHAPTER 6

1. The Duke's Laws provided for all of the following *except*

    (A) trial by jury
    (B) religious toleration
    (C) an elected assembly
    (D) no religious qualification for voting

2. New York's Charter of Liberties was passed under the governorship of

    (A) Sir Edmund Andros
    (B) Colonel Thomas Dongan
    (C) Captain Francis Nicholson
    (D) Colonel Henry Sloughter

3. New York achieved a representative assembly in

    (A) 1664
    (B) 1674
    (C) 1686
    (D) 1691

4. All were New Jersey proprietors *except*

    (A) Sir George Carteret
    (B) Lord John Berkeley
    (C) Nicholas Bayard
    (D) Edward Byllynge

5. The Pennsylvania charter of 1681 provided for all of the following except

    (A) royal disallowance of colonial laws
    (B) imposition of taxes by Parliament
    (C) free trade
    (D) the right of judicial appeal to the Crown

6. The Pennsylvania Charter of Liberties (1701) did *not* provide for

    (A) a separate government for Delaware
    (B) a unicameral legislature
    (C) a proprietorial veto
    (D) proprietorial appointment of the governor

7. Irish Catholics were found primarily in

    (A) Virginia and Maryland
    (B) Maryland and Pennsylvania
    (C) Maryland and Delaware
    (D) Maryland and New Jersey

8. Germans constituted _____ of the population of colonial America

    (A) 3-5 per cent
    (B) 6-9 per cent
    (C) 12-15 per cent
    (D) 15-18 per cent

9. Between 1689 and 1765 America's population increased

    (A) threefold
    (B) fivefold
    (C) tenfold
    (D) twelvefold

10. Charleston, South Carolina contained a large _____ population

    (A) Jewish
    (B) Huguenot
    (C) Quaker
    (D) German

Explanatory Answers

1. **(C)** The Duke of York refused to allow a legislative assembly for New York.

2. **(B)** The charter was designed to make Dongan (an Irish Catholic) more acceptable to the people.

3. **(D)** A representative assembly was granted by William and Mary.

4. **(C)** Bayard was the leader of the New York aristocratic faction.

5. **(C)** Pennsylvania was specifically required to adhere to the Navigation Acts.

6. **(C)** The proprietor's governmental authority was limited to the selection of the governor.

7. **(B)** Maryland was originally intended as a refuge for English Catholics, and Pennsylvania was open to all religious sects.

8. **(B)** Germans were the largest non-English group in America.

9. **(C)** After 1689 large numbers of English and non-English peoples migrated to America.

10. **(B)** French Calvinists, the Huguenots distinguished themselves in trade and commerce.

Chapter 7

MERCANTILISM AND THE WARS OF EMPIRE

Mercantilism was the dominant economic philosophy of the seventeenth and eighteenth centuries. It held that the economic resources of the nation should be so managed, through the achievement of economic autarchy (self-sufficiency), as to augment the military power of the state. If the state was able to produce all the economic necessities that it required, it would not be subject to economic boycott or strangulation during time of war; nor would it be forced to spend its precious store of gold and silver for the acquisition of essential commodities from foreign lands. However, in order to attain economic self-sufficiency, it was necessary to acquire overseas colonies which could supply the essential raw materials not found at home. This was the economic philosophy that motivated England's colonization of North America. The English hoped to find in America the timber, naval stores, furs, and agricultural commodities which would make them independent of foreign sources of supply. Consequently, the American colonies existed for the benefit and enrichment of the mother country, and in the event that the economic well-being of the colonies conflicted with that of England, the interests of England took precedence. In the period after 1660, the British government sought to make certain that the trade of the American colonies would enrich the English treasury. Unfortunately, the economic and trade restrictions imposed by the Crown placed a severe financial hardship on the American colonies, and colonial resentment of England's mercantile regulations was to be a major factor in the outbreak of the American Revolution.

Moreover, the series of wars fought by England between 1689 and 1763 greatly strained her finances; and in an attempt to raise greater tax revenues, she sought to improve the efficiency of the Navigation Acts. This only created more resentment in America. When England tried to centralize imperial administration after 1763, the Americans interpreted this as an attack upon their traditional liberties and rights as Englishmen. The American Revolution became inevitable.

THE BRITISH MERCANTILE SYSTEM

The Navigation Act of 1651

Although the American colonies existed for the benefit of England, no systematic attempt was made to enforce mercantilism until 1651, when the Commonwealth Parliament passed the Navigation Act in response to Dutch competition. In order to end Dutch encroachment of the colonial trade, Parliament decreed that all trade (1) between England and British America, (2) between Europe and British America, and (3) between the British colonies themselves must be conducted in English ships or in ships of the producing nation. (An English ship was one built and registered in either England or the American colonies.) In other words, a cargo of French wines could be brought to New York in an English or a French ship, but not in a Dutch ship.

The immediate result of the Navigation Act was a Dutch declaration of war and the outbreak of the first Anglo-Dutch War (1652–1654). The war produced no conclusive result, and England had no machinery by which it could adequately enforce the Navigation Act. Indeed, because of a lack of sufficient British shipping, Virginia, Massachusetts, Rhode Island, and Connecticut publicly defied the Navigation Act and continued to trade with the Dutch. For the most part, the 1651 act was a failure.

The Navigation Act of 1660

With the Restoration of Charles II in 1660, all acts of the Commonwealth Parliament were considered illegal, including the Navigation Act of 1651. However, Charles had no intention of abandoning mercantile regulation, and he was determined to centralize royal authority over the American colonies. Consequently, the Navigation Act of 1660 was basically a restatement of the 1651 measure. It defined a British ship as one whose ownership and crew was at least three-fourths English (or American), and it restricted colonial trade to such ships. In addition, it established a list of enumerated items (tobacco, cotton, wool, and indigo) which could not be shipped outside the British Empire. There was, however, free trade for these commodities within the Empire; and the Americans enjoyed a monopoly of the British market since enumerated goods could not be imported into England from foreign lands.

Like the earlier Navigation Act, the 1660 measure lacked adequate enforcement machinery, and violations of the act were widespread throughout the American colonies.

Since foreign prices for American tobacco, cotton, wool, and indigo were often higher than the prices prevailing in England, the enumerated articles clause of the Navigation Act worked to the disadvantage of the American producers. Moreover, the manufactured items which the Americans had to import could often be obtained at lower cost on the continent of Europe than in England. This also encouraged American evasion of the Navigation Act. From 1660 until 1776, enforcement of the mercantile laws would be a major problem for the British government, and one which it could never effectively solve.

The Navigation Act (Staple Act) of 1663

The Staple Act was enacted solely for the benefit of English merchants. It declared that all European goods bound for the American colonies first had to be landed at an English port and then had to be reshipped to America in English vessels. In this manner, the British government would benefit from the imposition of customs duties (whose cost would be passed on to the American consumer); and English merchants would profit from handling, insurance, and shipping fees. The Act also provided for the stationing of naval officers in all colonial ports, whose duty would be to secure enforcement of the mercantile laws. However, for Americans, the Staple Act meant higher-priced goods; and it appeared as a blatant British attempt to exploit America for the benefit of English merchants. Consequently, smuggling became an American vocation. The naval officers were powerless to stop it since ships could easily avoid the major ports and unload their cargoes at small inlets, coves, and bays, which were far removed from the sight of British officials. Furthermore, British officialdom was notoriously inefficient and corrupt; for a price, they could be counted upon to look the other way when illegal cargoes came into port.

British Efforts to Improve the Enforcement of the Navigation Acts

Not only did American merchants import European goods in violation of the Navigation Acts, but they also exported enumerated goods outside the boundaries of the British Empire. In an effort to reduce the volume of America's illicit trade, the British government adopted two major reforms in the 1670's They were:

(1) **The Navigation Act (Plantation Duties Act) of 1673.** Usually, duties on enumerated goods would have been collected in England. However, many ships laden with enumerated items had by-passed England and sailed directly to Europe. Therefore, the Plantation Duties Act required shipowners to pay the duty on enumerated goods before leaving their home ports. For example, the duty on a cargo of indigo would be paid in Charleston instead of London, so that if the shipment were taken outside the Empire, the Crown would still collect its customs duty. To enforce compliance with this measure, a corps of customs commissioners was stationed in every colonial port. But again, the commissioners were inefficient and corrupt, and violations were widespread.

(2) **The Lords of Trade (1675.)** A board of leading British merchants and officials, the Lords of Trade were empowered to supervise colonial and intercolonial trade and affairs and to instruct the royal governors concerning the enforcement and implementation of mercantile laws and policy. Far removed from the American scene, the Lords of Trade could issue commands but they could not insure obedience; and they were largely ineffectual.

By 1676, the British were no closer to effective regulation of American trade than they had been back in 1651. Because of growing domestic discord, the Crown was unable to continue its enforcement efforts on any large scale, and it was not until after the Glorious Revolution of 1688–1689 that new attempts were made to perfect the British mercantile system.

The Reforms of William & Mary

In 1696–1697, a major attempt was made to plug the leaks in the creaky mercantile system. *The Navigation Act of 1696* required American merchants and shipowners to post bonds on all enumerated cargoes when they left colonial ports. The bonds were refundable when the cargo was landed in England; but in the event that it was taken to a European port, the bond was forfeited. This system might have curbed illicit trade if it could have been effectively enforced. In addition, royal governors were sworn to enforce the Navigation Acts, and colonial customs officers were granted the same powers as English customs officers. These powers included the right to issue Writs of Assistance. The Writs were general search warrants, valid during the life of the reigning monarch, which compelled local law enforcement officers to aid customs officials in the search for contraband goods. However, because these were general search warrants (not limited to specific places or persons), they aroused vehement opposition in America. They were regarded as unlawful intrusions on the constitutional rights and liberties of the people and appeared as an attempt to undermine individual freedom. The Writs of Assistance were to become a major American grievance against British rule.

Also in 1696, the Lords of Trade were replaced by the *Board of Trade*. This new body was empowered to disallow colonial legislation and to recommend the appointment of colonial officials. It was hoped that the increased powers of the Board of Trade would result in more efficient administration of the mercantile system. Finally, in 1697, vice-admiralty courts were established in America to try alleged violations of the Navigation Acts. These military tribunals lacked a jury and appeared to Americans as another British attempt to undermine the constitutional liberties of British America. The vice-admiralty courts were to be another point in the American indictment of England's colonial administration. However, the almost continuous warfare of the eighteenth century made it impossible for England to devote the time, energy, and manpower needed to effectively enforce the Navigation Acts; and the measures continued to be violated.

Eighteenth-Century Mercantile Restrictions and Salutary Neglect

Although the first half of the eighteenth century witnessed a decline in the effectiveness of Britain's mercantile enforcement, a number of new measures were enacted:

(1) **Enumerated Articles.** In 1705, the list of enumerated articles which could be shipped only to England or to another British colony was broadened to include rice, molasses, and naval stores. In addition, bounties and subsidies were established to encourage the production of naval stores. This act proved highly beneficial to the American colonies.

(2) **The Hat Act of 1732.** In order to protect the English hat industry from American competition, the Hat Act forbade one British colony from exporting hats to another British colony or to England. While it did not outlaw the local manufacture of hats, it severely retarded the industry's development by banning exportation.

(3) **The Molasses Act of 1733.** Designed to protect the interests of the British West Indian colonies, the Molasses Act imposed a duty of nine pence per gallon on rum, six pence per gallon on molasses, and five shillings per hundredweight of sugar imported from French or Spanish colonies. There was no tax on rum, molasses, or sugar imported from British colonies. However, the act lacked effective enforcement machinery and was largely ignored.

(4) **The Iron Acts of 1750 & 1757.** The Iron Act of 1750 barred the construction of finishing mills for iron and steel in America in order to protect the market of English producers. However, the Iron Act of 1757 permitted American pig iron and bar iron (unfinished) to enter England duty-free.

Generally speaking, the American colonies from the 1730's to the 1760's enjoyed salutary neglect. Preoccupied with the waging of war, the British government made only token attempts to enforce the Navigation Acts and allowed the American colonies to develop at their own pace and to trade with whom they pleased. Under this neglect, the American colonies prospered and were content with their place in the British Empire. But, when a financially troubled England sought to increase central authority over America in the mid-1760's, the Americans would react violently.

Mercantilism: The Balance Sheet

One of the hottest debates concerning colonial America is: Did mercantilism help or hurt the American economy? Historians have been arguing the point for nearly a century without reaching a definitive conclusion. Those historians who argue that mercantilism benefited the American colonies point out the following:

(1) Mercantile bounties and subsidies promoted the development of colonial enterprises, such as shipbuilding, the production of naval stores, and the cultivation of indigo, rice, and cotton. Without the incentives provided by the British, these enterprises might not have developed as extensively as they did.

(2) While goods enumerated by the Navigation Acts could not be sold outside the British Empire, the Americans enjoyed a monopoly of the British market for their enumerated produce. This insured them a steady, and often expanding, market for their goods.

(3) Mercantilism permitted free and unencumbered trade within the British Empire, which was greatly to the advantage of the American colonies; and it allowed trade outside the Empire (with certain restrictions) in non-enumerated goods.

(4) Finally, the American colonists enjoyed the protection of the British army and navy. The cost of providing themselves with equivalent military protection would have been exorbitant. On the whole, the Americans were aided more than they were hurt by the mercantile system; it worked for the advantage of the British Empire as a whole.

Table 2
Colonial Trade with England*

	1701-1710	1731-1740	1761-1770
New England:			
Exports	37,000	64,000	113,000
Imports	86,000	197,000	358,000
Middle Colonies:			
Exports	22,000	28,000	97,000
Imports	37,000	144,000	644,000
Southern Colonies:			
Exports	219,000	571,000	834,000
Imports	150,000	304,000	893,000

* In British pounds sterling.

While the pro-mercantile argument is not without its merits, the anti-mercantilists have far the better case, as Table 2 amply testifies. Colonial America was primarily a producer of raw materials and agricultural commodities. It sold its produce in England and purchased British manufactured goods. However, manufactured products are far more expensive than raw materials and agricultural commodities. With the exception of the Southern colonies, America had an unfavorable balance of trade with England (after 1760, the South also had an unfavorable balance of trade). The colonies purchased from England goods whose value far exceeded the value of the produce they sold the mother country. This meant that America had to ship specie (gold and silver coin) to England to make good the colonies' trade deficit. The only way in which the American colonies could earn this revenue was to systematically violate the mercantile laws. Both direct American trade with Europe and the triangular trade were essential if the colonies were to raise the revenues needed to settle accounts with England. As long as England followed a policy of salutary neglect, the American colonies were able to live with their trade deficit. When England tried to enforce the mercantile system after 1763, she reduced America's ability to balance her trade deficit. After 1763, mercantilism became oppressive in its economic effects; and the American Revolution became only a question of time.

THE WARS OF EMPIRE

King William's War
(1689–1697)

William of Orange was one of Louis XIV's leading opponents. As the ruler of the Netherlands, William was naturally opposed to Louis' efforts to make the Rhine the eastern boundary of France and to overrun the Low Countries. When he became King of England in 1689, William commanded a powerful weapon (the British navy and Empire) with which to oppose the designs of the "Sun King." No sooner had William become King of England, then the War of the League of Augsburg began. This was known in America as King William's War. It was the opening round in a French-English struggle (often called the Second Hundred Years War) which would not finally end until the defeat of Napoleon at Waterloo in 1815. When it was all over, England had won the struggle for empire, but had lost her American colonies. Indeed, the American Revolution (1776–1783) was inevitably bound up with the English-French struggle for empire.

The European phase of the war began when Louis XIV invaded the Rhenish Palatinate, and the French and the English soon came to blows in America as well. France and England had conflicting claims to Nova Scotia, Hudson's Bay, and the Ohio Valley; both claimed the right to engage in the fur trade in New York, and both wanted to control the strategic Mohawk Valley. In February, 1690, led by the Count de Frontenac, the French and their Algonquin allies sacked Schenectady and consolidated their position in the Mohawk Valley. The lone American triumph of the war came in May, 1690, when an expedition led by Sir William Phips of Massachusetts captured the French stronghold at Port Royal, Nova Scotia (also known as Acadia). However, beginning in 1691, Frontenac and Le Moyne d'Iberville scored dramatic victories for France. Port Royal was recaptured, Newfoundland was reoccupied, advances were made in the Hudson's Bay region of Canada, and the Iroquois (England's allies in New York) were dealt a sharp setback. The French were having much the better of the fight, when peace came in 1697. The Treaty of Ryswick restored the *status quo ante bellum* (the situation as it existed before the war), and the opening round of the Second Hundred Years War ended inconclusively.

Knowing that the peace was to be short-lived, the French, between 1698 and 1702, sought to strengthen their hold in America by beginning the settlement of Louisiana and by fortifying the Ohio Valley. This greatly alarmed the American colonies, for whoever controlled the Ohio Valley and the mouth of the Mississippi was the master of the North American continent. As long as France was entrenched in both Canada and the Ohio Valley, America's dependence on the military might of England was assured.

Queen Anne's War
(1702–1713)

The second round of war began when England became involved in the War of the Spanish Succession in 1702. This time, England sought to prevent the union of the Spanish and French thrones, which would put the wealth of Spain's Latin American empire at the disposal of Louis XIV. Surprisingly, however, the American phase of the war was rather lethargic. The Carolinians raided St. Augustine in Spanish Florida, hoping to use it as a base from which to attack the French in Louisiana. Unfortunately, the Carolinians could not penetrate the barrier presented by the Choctaw Indians, and their plans never materialized. In New England, another expedition was sent out to attack Acadia (Nova Scotia); and Port Royal was again captured in 1710. By the Treaty of Utrecht (1713), England received Newfoundland, Nova Scotia, and the Hudson's Bay region from France. The English had succeeded in making serious inroads into

Canada; however, the precise limits of England's newly acquired territory were not delineated, and Anglo-French tensions in America remained high.

Once again, the French began to prepare themselves for the resumption of war. Between 1719 and 1724, they constructed the imposing Fort Louisbourg on Cape Breton Island which commanded the approaches to the vital St. Lawrence River. Fort Niagara was built to gain control of the Great Lakes and was a base of operations against the Iroquois. In addition, in the Ohio Valley, Forts Miami and Vincennes were constructed on the Wabash River. Although France had been set back by the Treaty of Utrecht, she was by no means defeated.

King George's War
(1740–1748)

War was resumed in 1739, when England became embroiled with Spain in the War of Jenkins' Ear (1739–1742). Stemming from British grievances against Spain's treatment of English merchants in Central America, the war against Spain became merged with the more serious struggle growing out of the War of the Austrian Succession.* In 1745, the New Englanders, under Sir William Pepperrell, scored a major victory when they captured the French stronghold at Louisbourg, Nova Scotia. However, this gain was offset by French and Indian destruction of Saratoga and by attacks on Albany. Neither side won a clear-cut victory; and the 1748 Treaty of Aix-la-Chapelle restored the *status quo ante bellum*. The return of Louisbourg to France greatly angered the New Englanders, who felt that England was not sufficiently concerned with their security. It was realized that only the destruction of French power in Canada could bring peace to America.

The Albany Plan of Union

In 1754, France upset the American balance of power by constructing Fort Duquesne at the site of present-day Pittsburgh. In order to meet the new threat posed by France, the American colonies held a conference at Albany. Benjamin Franklin proposed a plan of union designed to meet external threats. Under the Albany Plan of Union, a grand council would be elected by the various colonial legislatures (each colony having from two to seven delegates depending upon its size and wealth), and the Crown would appoint a president-general to handle executive functions. British America would then have a unified federal government which would handle relations with the Indians, settle intercolonial disputes, and coordinate colonial military operations during time of war. Moreover, the Crown would retain its veto power over all decisions of the grand council. However, Franklin's plan was rejected by both the American colonies and the British government. Had it been implemented, and had the grand council obtained real power, the history of British America might have been much different.

The Great War for the Empire
(1756–1763)

Known in Europe as the Seven Years War and in America as the French and Indian War, this was the decisive battle in the struggle for the mastery of America. The war started as the result of France's construction in 1754 of Fort Duquesne. Hostilities began in America in 1755, and spread to Europe the following year. General Edward Braddock (in the first encounter of the war) was defeated by the French at the Battle of the Wilderness near Fort Duquesne. One of Braddock's junior officers was a young Virginian by the name of George Washington who was acquiring his first battle experience. Although Braddock was defeated, the British were not without victories. William Johnson succeeded in defeating the French on Lake George in 1755, and the Acadians (French settlers) were expelled from Nova Scotia as a security risk.

In 1757, the French, under Louis Joseph Montcalm, counterattacked. The British were defeated at Fort Oswego, Fort George, and Fort William Henry. And the next year, James Abercromby suffered a devastating defeat at Fort Ticonderoga. Finally, a bright spot for the British came in 1758, when James Wolfe and Jeffrey Amherst captured Louisbourg. Britain's military situation improved rapidly after that. In July, 1759, Fort Niagara fell to the British; and later that year, Wolfe's forces stormed the Plains of Abraham and took Quebec. Although Wolfe and Montcalm both lost their lives at Quebec, the tide had turned in

---

*The War of the Austrian Succession began in 1740, when Frederick II of Prussia seized Silesia from Maria Theresa of Austria. France was allied with Prussia; and in 1743, France became allied with Spain. Thus France was brought into Spain's war against England.

French and Indian War recruiting poster: colonists are urged to come to the defense of their king.

favor of the British; and by 1760, virtually all of Canada was in England's hands. By the terms of the Treaty of Paris (1763), Canada became a British possession; and except for a few West Indian islands, France had lost her American holdings.

Effects of the French and Indian War

By 1763, the war for empire had been won by the British. Supreme on the high seas, dominant in India, and master of America, English power appeared invincible. However, the long series of wars had drained England's financial resources, and her people were among the most highly taxed in the world. Since the French and Indian War had begun in America and had been fought largely for America's benefit, the British felt it only fair that the prosperous and relatively untaxed American colonies pay their fair share of the cost of the war and help defray the costs of defending the Empire. But the American colonies objected to England's attempts to centralize the Empire and to enforce the mercantile laws, for they considered these measures an infringement on their constitutional liberties and "rights as Englishmen." Moreover, the end of French power in Canada removed the only serious military threat which had faced the American colonies. No longer dependent upon Britain for military protection, the American colonies could afford to take a stand in defense of an abstract concept — liberty. The American Revolution can be said to have begun in 1763; for with France no longer a military threat, the Americans had less need of England.

REVIEW QUESTIONS FOR CHAPTER 7

1. The Provision that enumerated goods could not be shipped outside the British Empire was first contained in

   (A) The Navigation Act of 1651
   (B) The Navigation Act of 1660
   (C) The Staple Act
   (D) The Plantation Duties Act

2. The requirement that European goods bound for America first be landed at an English port was contained in

   (A) The Navigation Act of 1660
   (B) The Staple Act
   (C) The Plantation Duties Act
   (D) The Navigation Act of 1696

3. Writs of Assistance were provided for in

   (A) The Navigation Act of 1696
   (B) The Hat Act
   (C) The Molasses Act
   (D) The Iron Act

4. The Board of Trade replaced the Lords of Trade in

   (A) 1675
   (B) 1689
   (C) 1696
   (D) 1705

5. The period of salutary neglect came to an end after

   (A) 1660
   (B) 1696
   (C) 1732
   (D) 1763

6. Mercantilism aided all of the following activities *except*

   (A) shipbuilding
   (B) indigo production
   (C) iron and steel finishing
   (D) naval stores production

7. In 1690, Port Royal was captured by

   (A) William Phips
   (B) James Wolfe
   (C) Jeffrey Amherst
   (D) William Johnson

8. England acquired Nova Scotia, Newfoundland, and Hudson's Bay as a result of

   (A) King William's War
   (B) Queen Anne's War
   (C) King George's War
   (D) the French and Indian War

9. The Treaty of Aix-la-Chapelle ended

   (A) King William's War
   (B) Queen Anne's War
   (C) King George's War
   (D) the French and Indian War

10. The decisive battle of the French and Indian War was fought at

   (A) Niagara
   (B) Quebec
   (C) Ticonderoga
   (D) Louisbourg

Explanatory Answers

1. **(B)** Tobacco, cotton, wool, and indigo were listed as enumerated goods.

2. **(B)** The Staple Act of 1663 was designed to benefit English merchants.

3. **(A)** Writs of Assistance were general search warrants designed to aid enforcement of the Navigation Acts.

4. **(C)** The Board of Trade had the power to disallow colonial laws and recommend the appointment of colonial officials.

5. **(D)** England sought to centralize the Empire after the French and Indian War.

6. **(C)** Iron and steel finishing was forbidden by the 1750 Iron Act

7. **(A)** Phips led the expedition which took Port Royal during King William's War.

8. **(B)** The Treaty of Utrecht (1713), which ended Queen Anne's War, gave England Newfoundland, Nova Scotia, and Hudson's Bay.

9. **(C)** The treaty ended King George's War in 1748.

10. **(B)** The fall of Quebec to Wolfe's forces broke the back of the French war effort.

Chapter 8

MATURE COLONIAL SOCIETY AND CULTURE

In the period from 1688 to 1763, a distinctively American social order and culture came into being. Although American society was an outgrowth of the English cultural experience, eighteenth-century America differed from England in many significant ways. The American political system was far more representative than the English. America enjoyed a middle-class society in which extremes of wealth and poverty were not nearly as severe as they were in Europe, and in which the bulk of the adult male population (exclusive of Negroes) owned enough land or property to qualify as voters. Absorbing the thought of the Anglo-French Enlightenment, Americans came to accept the essential equality of man. Unlike England, which had a fixed hierarchy of social classes, America had a relatively fluid social order in which upward mobility was not only possible, but was quite common. By 1763, colonial America was a dynamic and healthy society which believed that all men had the natural rights of life, liberty, and the ownership of property. It was a society that valued representative government, and one that would assert its right to self-determination within the British Empire.

PATTERNS OF COLONIAL GOVERNMENT

Imperial Authority

Legally, the King of England was the highest governing authority in the British Empire. In actuality, however, colonial policy and administration were in the hands of the Privy Council (a group of the king's advisors and ministers, functioning somewhat like the modern Cabinet). The king acted primarily as the council's spokesman. The Privy Council made all major colonial appointments (governors, judges, customs officers, etc.), framed mercantile and trade policies, disallowed colonial laws which violated imperial policy, and heard appeals from colonial courts. The Privy Council acted on the basis of information received from the Admiralty, the Treasury Board, the Board of Trade, and the War Office, but the final determination of policy was in its hands. After the Glorious Revolution of 1688, the Privy Council was controlled by the Parliament; so that, in effect, Parliament was responsible for the implementation of colonial policy.

The Governor

In nine of the thirteen American colonies, the governor was appointed by the Crown; he was the direct representative of the king, and held his office at the pleasure of the king. In Connecticut and Rhode Island, the governor was elected by the colonial legislature; in Maryland and Pennsylvania, he was appointed by the proprietors. The nine royal governors were sworn to faithfully carry out the instructions of the king (who was spokesman for the Privy Council). The governor was commander-in-chief of the colony's armed forces; he could appoint and suspend members of the Governor's Council as well as judges, magistrates, and local officials. He had the power to commute criminal sentences and issue pardons, and along with the Governor's Council, he exercised supreme judicial authority within the colony. He had the power both to veto all acts of the colonial legislature and to dissolve the legislature. However, the governor's veto power was limited by his financial dependence upon the legislature. If he abused the veto power, the legislature could starve his government of needed funds. Indeed, in New York and Massachusetts the governor's veto power was significantly curbed.

The Governor's Council

Consisting of seven to twelve members, the Governor's Council was appointed by the Crown, upon the recommendation of the governor, and acted as a colonial privy council. It was generally composed of the wealthiest and most influential men of the colony, and it served to advise the governor on general colonial policy. It also served as the upper house of the colonial legislature; it was the American equivalent of the British House of Lords and, accordingly, exercised the powers of a supreme court.

The Assembly

The colonial assembly (called the House of Burgesses in Virginia, and the General Court in Massachusetts) was the American counterpart of the British House of Commons. However, unlike members of the British Parliament, members of the colonial assemblies were usually elected anew every year and represented a specific geographical area (town or county). In England, under the doctrine of virtual representation, members of Parliament represented the entire Empire and not simply their home districts (thus, Parliament could claim the right to govern the colonies). But in America, members of a colonial assembly were responsible only for the geographic area they were elected to represent. All money bills (measures whose implementation required the imposition of taxes or those that were financed from public revenues) had to originate in, and win the approval of, the assembly. During the course of the eighteenth century, the assembly strengthened its powers of the purse by securing annual (rather than permanent) grants for the support of the governor, judges, and other colonial officials. In the event of conflict between the governor and the assembly, the assembly had a powerful weapon with which to command the governor's obedience. In addition, each assembly selected a colonial agent to act as a lobbyist before the Privy Council. The lobbyist tried to influence the passage of favorable legislation, while heading off or modifying the enactment of unfavorable acts. After 1688, the colonial assemblies claimed the right to exercise the same powers within the colonies as were exercised by the House of Commons in England. And except for the regulation of external commerce, the assemblies denied the right of Parliament to legislate for the colonies. This divergence of opinion regarding the nature of the British Empire would be a key factor in the outbreak of the American Revolution.

Colonial Suffrage

Property requirements for voting varied from colony to colony; but, generally speaking, all adult males who owned fifty or more acres of land or who held personal property worth forty to fifty British pounds were allowed to vote. Since the first census was not taken until 1790, we have no way of knowing precisely how many people qualified as voters. However, the consensus of modern scholarship agrees that property ownership in eighteenth-century America was widespread, and that in most colonies, a majority of the adult male population (exclusive of Negroes) did qualify for the suffrage. It seems, though, that actual voter turnout tended to be light; and this is attributable to apathy and to the difficulties involved in travel over inadequate roadways. Partly as a consequence of these bad roads, the back country (newly opened frontier areas) was generally underrepresented in the colonial assemblies. The frontier's representation in the assemblies lagged well behind its population growth, and most colonies were dominated by the more well-to-do classes of the coastal areas. Throughout the eighteenth century, colonial political life was marked by sectional hostility between the old, well-established seaboard and the newly settled interior regions. The American Revolution was not only a struggle against Great Britain; quite often it was the struggle of the frontier against the seaboard to determine which region would rule at home.

PATTERNS OF COLONIAL SOCIETY

The Colonial Class Structure

In every American colony, political power, economic wealth, and social prestige were concentrated in the gentry class. This class consisted of large landowners in the South, wealthy merchants in the North, public officials, Anglican (South) and Puritan (New England) clergymen, as well as medical doctors, lawyers, and a sprinkling of college professors. The gentry constituted only 5 per cent of the colonial population, but they were an important minority in that they tended to be closely identified with imperial authority (serving on the Governor's Council and acting as judges and magistrates). Intermarrying with other members of their class, the gentry were as close as America came to having an aristocracy. Indeed, they often fancied themselves as aristocrats.

The middle class constituted the overwhelming majority of the American people in the eighteenth century. Small farmers, merchants of moderate wealth, and skilled artisans and craftsmen, members of the middle class were economically independent and qualified as voters. The leaders and spokesmen of the middle class dominated the assemblies in many colonies. Members of the upper middle class tended to cooperate with the gentry and were often successful in achieving gentry status.

Tenant farmers, unskilled laborers, and hired hands formed an unenfranchised substratum in colonial society. Owning no land and possessing little private property, they were denied the right to vote. However, after 1750, they were beginning to demand the same political rights enjoyed by the middle class. The unenfranchised are not believed to have constituted a substantial percentage of the colonial population.

Finally, at the very bottom of colonial society were the unfree whites (indentured servants and bound apprentices) and the enslaved Negroes. On the eve of the Revolution there were better than 400,000 slaves in America, but the numbers of unfree whites were not significant and declined over the course of the eighteenth century.

While America had a class society, class lines were not rigid; and both upward and downward social mobility were possible. And although the gentry dominated colonial society, the large middle class exercised a growing political authority.

Religion in Colonial America

Until the American Revolution (and in some cases well beyond it), the Congregational church was established in most of New England, while the Anglican church was the official faith of the Southern colonies. Although members of dissenting religious sects were permitted to practice their religion in peace, the established religions enjoyed the advantage of receiving public funds for their support. However, as late as 1775, it appears that most Americans were "unchurched" (they did not regularly attend religious services). The eighteenth-century American was not irreligious; instead his religious convictions tended to be highly personal and were expressed in private, rather than public, observances. The major religious developments of the eighteenth century were the growth of Deism as the religion of the American intelligentsia and the impact of the Great Awakening on the colonial masses.

Table 3

American Religious Affiliation in 1775

Denomination	Estimated Membership
Congregational	575,000
Anglican	500,000
Presbyterian	410,000
German Pietists	200,000
Dutch Reformed	75,000
Quakers	40,000
Baptists	25,000
Roman Catholic	25,000
Methodist	5,000
Jewish	2,000

Deism. An outgrowth of the Newtonian revolution and the French Enlightenment, Deism claimed the support of the American intelligentsia; and Thomas Jefferson and Thomas Paine were among its best-known advocates. Deism rejected all the dogmas and doctrines of the theistic religions, and it affirmed God as the creative essence of the universe. Thus, He was the First Cause or Prime Mover. However, it held that God was total-

George Whitefield preaching in moorfields (1742).

ly impersonal; once having created the universe, He permits it to operate in accordance with natural law, and *does not* circumvent the operation of natural law. Miracles are therefore figments of a superstitious imagination, and prayer is useless since God will not reverse or stay the operation of natural law. The implications of Deism are (1) that man has absolute free will for either good or evil, (2) that the universe is governed by immutable natural laws which the mind of man can discover and understand, and (3) that human happiness and progress is directly proportional to the extent to which man lives in accordance with natural law. Since life, liberty, and property are secured by natural law, an attack upon these rights is tantamount to an attack upon the laws of God. Consequently, in the words of Jefferson, "resistance to tyranny is obedience to God." The intellectual premises of Deism were a major element in the justification of the American Revolution. Most Americans, however, were not Deists and were not familiar with the movement's tenets. But the men who led the Revolution were.

The Great Awakening. Dominating the second quarter of the eighteenth century, the Great Awakening was a religious revival which profoundly altered the religious life of America. It began in New Jersey in the 1720's with the preaching of the Rev. Theodore Frelinghuysen; it gained momentum in 1739 when the English evangelist George Whitefield toured the American colonies, and it came to a climax in the 1740's with the missionary efforts of New England's Jonathan Edwards. Generally speaking the Great Awakening stressed the emotional aspects of religion, and it emphasized the direct communion of the individual soul with God. It held that salvation was possible for all men, not just an elected few, and that all that was necessary to obtain salvation was to trust in the loving mercy of God. The movement commanded the faithful to spread God's word, to perform good works, and to save at least one unregenerate soul in order to repay God's love for man. The Great Awakening placed great stress on the amelioration of social evils as a way of hastening the second coming of the Lord; thus, it helped to arouse the social consciousness of the American people. This religious revival gave birth to Methodism in America, swelled the ranks of the Baptists and Presbyterians, and revitalized the Congregational church. In the South, the Great Awakening drew people away from the established Anglican church, and by undermining Anglicanism, it weakened the ties between England and America.

In New England, Jonathan Edwards split the established Congregational church into two factions: the progressive New Lights faction which supported the evangelism of the Great Awakening, and the orthodox Old Lights faction which sought to maintain the old Puritan faith intact. By weakening the Old Lights, the Great Awakening had a liberalizing effect on New England society. On the whole, the Great Awakening spurred the social consciousness of the American people, hastened the growth of the democratic spirit, and made religion an intensely personal experience, rather than a ritualistic public ceremony.

Colonial Education: Elementary

As early as 1647, the Massachusetts Bay Colony enacted a statute requiring every town of fifty or more families to establish a free public school (supported by public tax revenues) for the education of its children. Compulsory attendance was required, and the schools provided instruction in the basic skills of reading, writing, and arithmetic. The core of the curriculum, however, was theolo-

68 / AMERICAN HISTORY

Jonathan Edwards

tended formal elementary schools, the colonies enjoyed a fairly high literacy rate and, in that respect, compared very favorably with the most advanced nations of Europe.

Colonial Education: Colleges

American colleges in the seventeenth and eighteenth centuries were rather crude institutions. Generally, they had only a few score students and a few professors, all of whom taught a variety of subjects. Greek, Latin, mathematics, logic and rhetoric, and theology constituted the core of the curriculum. Most colleges were intended for the training of ministers; and though astronomy, ancient history, and a smattering of secular studies were offered, religion was the primary preoccupation of the faculty. America's first college, Harvard, was founded in 1636 to train Congregational ministers. William and Mary was established under Anglican auspices in 1693, and it quickly became the intellectual capital of the South. Yale was

gical and provided training in the basic tenets of the Puritan faith. The Massachusetts system was adopted by other New England colonies, but enforcement was haphazard. By the eighteenth century, many smaller towns were not providing the education required of them by law, and many parents were keeping their offspring out of the schools because children's labor was needed to augment family income. Nevertheless, although the New England educational system was not entirely effective, it was important in that it established the precedent for the modern public school system. In the Middle Colonies of New York, New Jersey, and Pennsylvania, there were no public school systems; education was left to the care of the church. Many denominations (especially the Anglicans, Quakers, and Dutch Reformed) maintained parish schools for the education of the congregation's children. In the South, education was in private hands and was generally confined to the children of the well-to-do classes. Many of the larger planters hired tutors to instruct their children, and made the tutors' services available to local neighborhood children. The South, though, was not to have a public school system until after the American Civil War. For the most part, colonial education was conducted in the home. Although only a minority of American children at-

Dr. Wheelock (founder of Dartmouth College) leading his family in a prayer during erection of the college in a forest.

founded in 1701 by orthodox Congregationalists who objected to the radicalism of the Harvard faculty (it was said that Harvard professors refused to believe in the existence of witches!). In 1746, Princeton was opened as a Presbyterian institution; and in 1749, the College of Philadelphia (now the University of Pennsylvania) became the only non-sectarian institution of higher learning in the thirteen colonies. The Anglicans founded King's College (Columbia) in New York City in 1754, and the Baptists established Brown University in 1764. Generally, only sons of the wealthy went to college, and these institutions served an extremely small elitist group.

The Colonial Press

Perhaps the most distinguishing characteristic of colonial society was the number of newspapers and their extensive circulation. America was indeed the land of the newspaper. The first newspaper to appear on a regular basis was John Campbell's Boston *News Letter,* founded in 1704. On the eve of the American Revolution, thirty-seven newspapers were being published regularly, the most important of them being William Bradford's *American Weekly Mercury* (Philadelphia, 1719); *The New England Courant* (Boston, 1721), which afforded young Ben Franklin his first journalistic experience; the mature Franklin's *Pennsylvania Gazette* (Philadelphia, 1729); John Peter Zenger's *New York Weekly Journal* (1733); and the *Virginia Gazette* (Williamsburg, 1736). For the most part, colonial newspapers were published weekly and appeared as four-page tabloids. As was the custom in England, they ran their best-paying advertisements on the front page and relegated the news to the inside pages. They listed the arrival and departure times of ships, announced auctions, ran local news items, and plagiarized with a heavy hand. They borrowed entire columns of news from English papers, and they noted significant events in other colonies.

Until 1735, the colonial press operated under fairly stringent governmental restrictions. However, the John Peter Zenger case of that year became a landmark in the development of American freedom of the press. Zenger was tried for libeling New York's Governor William Cosby in the New York *Weekly Journal* (under British law any public criticism of royal officials was libelous). But, Andrew Hamilton, Zenger's attorney, declared that truth was a complete defense against any charge of libel, and the jury accepted his argument and acquitted Zenger. The colonial press served to unify the American colonies by making the people of one colony aware of what was taking place in other colonies, and it also served as a vehicle for venting popular grievances against the British authorities. The press was a powerful instrument of dissent and played a vital role in the coming of the American Revolution.

Colonial Contributions to Science

Although colonial America was a young land faced with the awesome task of survival in an untamed wilderness, it possessed urban islands of culture, and made some notable contributions to science. *Benjamin Franklin's* (1706-1790) experiments with electricity and his invention of the lightning rod, bifocals, and the Franklin stove are too well known to need elaboration here. Winning a world-wide scientific reputation, Franklin came to symbolize American creative genius. However, there were more like him — the most notable being the following:

(1) **James Logan** (1674-1751) is generally credited with introducing Newton's *Principia Mathematica* to the American colonies.

(2) **Cotton Mather** (1683-1728), son of a distinguished family of Puritan ministers, was an early advocate of innoculation against disease, and his 1721 *Christian Philosophy* reconciled Newtonian thought with Christian theology.

(3) **Cadwallader Colden** (1688-1776) classified the flora of New York; he also developed a valuable supplement to Newtonian physics, arguing that gravity was a property of matter.

(4) **Jared Eliot** (1685-1765) compiled the first American handbook on scientific agriculture.

(5) **David Rittenhouse** (1732-1796), the most famous American astronomer of the age, calculated the transits of Venus and Mercury.

(6) **Ezra Stiles** (1727-1795) was another astronomer. He calculated the transposition of the Sun and the Moon.

In 1743, the *American Philosophical Society*

Numb. II.

THE
New-York Weekly JOURNAL

Containing the freshest Advices, Foreign, and Domestick.

MUNDAY November 12, 1733.

Mr. *Zenger*.

Ncert the following in your next, and you'll oblige your Friend,
CATO.

Mira temporum felicitas ubi sentiri quæ velis, & quæ sentias dicere licit.
Tacit.

THE Liberty of the Press is a Subject of the greatest Importance, and in which every Individual is as much concern'd as he is in any other Part of Liberty: therefore it will not be improper to communicate to the Publick the Sentiments of a late excellent Writer upon this Point. Such is the Elegance and Perspicuity of his Writings, such the inimitable Force of his Reasoning, that it will be difficult to say any Thing new that he has not said, or not to say that much worse which he has said.

There are two Sorts of Monarchies, an absolute and a limited one. In the first, the Liberty of the Press can never be maintained, it is inconsistent with it; for what absolute Monarch would suffer any Subject to animadvert on his Actions, when it is in his Power to declare the Crime, and to nominate the Punishment? This would make it very dangerous to exercise such a Liberty. Besides the Object against which those Pens must be directed, is their Sovereign, the sole supream Magistrate; for there being no Law in those Monarchies, but the Will of the Prince, it makes it necessary for his Ministers to consult his Pleasure, before any Thing can be undertaken: He is therefore properly chargeable with the Grievances of his Subjects, and what the Minister there acts being in Obedience to the Prince, he ought not to incur the Hatred of the People; for it would be hard to impute that to him for a Crime, which is the Fruit of his Allegiance, and for refusing which he might incur the Penalties of Treason. Besides, in an absolute Monarchy, the Will of the Prince being the Law, a Liberty of the Press to complain of Grievances would be complaining against the Law, and the Constitution, to which they have submitted, or have been obliged to submit; and therefore, in one Sense, may be said to deserve Punishment. So that under an absolute Monarchy, I say, such a Liberty is inconsistent with the Constitution, having no proper Subject in Politics, on which it might be exercis'd, and if exercis'd would incur a certain Penalty.

But in a limited Monarchy, as *England* is, our Laws are known, fixed, and established. They are the streight Rule and sure Guide to direct the King, the Ministers, and other his Subjects: And therefore an Offence against the Laws is such an Offence against the Constitution as ought to receive a proper adequate Punishment; the severa Constil

Peter Zenger's appeal to uphold freedom of the press (1733).

was organized to promote and disseminate scientific knowledge in America. Under the guidance of Benjamin Franklin, it became the leading cultural institution of colonial America.

Colonial Literature

Colonial America was not especially renowned for its creative literature, and during the seventeenth century, religion and religious themes dominated the literature of America. *Michael Wigglesworth* (1631-1705) wrote the most popular work — *Day of Doom* (or *Doomsday Book*). Published in 1662, it was a Puritan account of the Last Judgment, and it bemoaned New England's loss of religious zeal. *Samuel Sewall* (1652-1730) indicates in his *Diary* the dilemma of the Puritan living in an age when religion bore less and less relevance to human life. The *Diary* portrays the Yankee business mentality at work. *William Byrd II* (1674-1744) portrays in his *Journal* the life of the Southern planter aristocracy. During the eighteenth century, history was the most notable branch of American literature. Cotton Mather, in 1702, wrote a still-useful *Ecclesiastical History of New England, 1620-1698,* and Cadwallader Colden wrote a classic *History of the Five Indian Nations*. However, the literature of colonial America was, for the most part, a poor imitation of Europe's.

TOWARD THE AMERICAN REVOLUTION

The American Character

By 1763, America had a mature colonial culture. Basically British, it was still sufficiently divergent to constitute a new and separate culture. Americans were a highly individualistic people who had scant patience with such venerable institutions as aristocracy, monarchy, and established churches. Celebrating the inherent worth and dignity of the individual, they did not quickly bend their necks to those who considered themselves their social superiors. They had faith in the ability of the individual to overcome hardship and master nature, were confident that human intellect could unlock the secrets of the universe and refashion the world, and were certain of the inevitability of progress and the perfectibility of man. Optimistic and materialistic, living for the here and now, they were impatient of correctable wrongs and preventable evils. Claiming the rights of Englishmen, they demanded the right to determine their own destiny; and they had abiding faith in the political truths enunciated by John Locke.

Locke and the American Revolution

John Locke's two *Treatises on Civil Government,* written in 1690 to justify the Glorious Revolution, were used to justify the American Revolution as well. Holding that government was the result of a social compact among men which was designed to secure their mutual happiness and benefit, Locke stressed the mutual obligations of both the ruler and the ruled. Government must rest upon the free consent of the governed; it exists to secure and protect the lives, liberty, and property of its subjects; and it may not restrict a subject's liberty except as punishment for unlawful behavior. Nor may it seize property (by taxation) without obtaining the consent of property owners or their chosen representatives. Any government which violates its trust, forfeits its right to rule; and it may justly be overthrown by the people and replaced with such new government as they deem best suited to their needs. King George III, in levying taxes on America without the consent of its people, was acting as a tyrant, destructive of the constitutional guarantees extended to all Englishmen. Resistance to his rule was not rebellion; rather it was a defense of English constitutional liberties.

This is not to say that eighteenth-century Americans were democrats in the modern sense of the word. Both they and John Locke believed that government should represent the people who owned property, that only those with a stake in society could be trusted with the powers of government, and that those who lacked property were a dangerous rabble who could not be trusted to exercise an intelligent franchise. The American Revolution was an essentially middle-class struggle designed to preserve traditional constitutional liberties as they were understood at the time.

REVIEW QUESTIONS FOR CHAPTER 8

1. The highest governing authority of the British Empire was

   (A) the royal governor
   (B) the Board of Trade
   (C) the Privy Council
   (D) the Admiralty

2. The colonial legislature elected the governor in Connecticut and in

   (A) Massachusetts
   (B) Rhode Island
   (C) Pennsylvania
   (D) New York

3. The gentry class consisted of all the following *except*

   (A) Anglican ministers
   (B) Puritan clergymen
   (C) Southern planters
   (D) artisans

4. The largest religious denomination in colonial America was the

   (A) Anglicans
   (B) Baptists
   (C) Presbyterians
   (D) Congregationalists

5. All the following are associated with the Great Awakening *except*

   (A) Jonathan Edwards
   (B) Thomas Paine
   (C) George Whitefield
   (D) Theodore Frelinghuysen

6. The first Anglican college in America was

   (A) Harvard
   (B) Columbia
   (C) Yale
   (D) William and Mary

7. John Peter Zenger is associated with the

   (A) *American Weekly Mercury*
   (B) *Pennsylvania Gazette*
   (C) *New York Weekly Journal*
   (D) *New England Courant*

8. The man who introduced Newton's work to America was

   (A) James Logan
   (B) Cotton Mather
   (C) Cadwallader Colden
   (D) David Rittenhouse

9. The historian of the Five Indian nations was

   (A) Cotton Mather
   (B) Samuel Sewall
   (C) William Byrd II
   (D) Cadwallader Colden

10. The *Day of Doom* was written by

   (A) Michael Wigglesworth
   (B) Benjamin Franklin
   (C) Cotton Mather
   (D) None of the above

Explanatory Answers

1. **(C)** The Privy Council formulated colonial policy in the King's name

2. **(B)** Connecticut and Rhode Island escaped royalization of their governments.

3. **(D)** Artisans were members of the middle class.

4. **(D)** The Congregationalists had 575,000 members.

5. **(B)** Paine was a Deist.

6. **(D)** William and Mary preceded Columbia by over fifty years.

7. **(C)** He was editor of the *New York Weekly Journal*.

8. **(A)** James Logan introduced the *Principia Mathematica* to the colonies.

9. **(D)** Colden's study of the Iroquois is still a classic.

10. **(A)** It was the most popular literary work of early America.

PART TWO:
THE REVOLUTION AND THE YOUNG REPUBLIC, 1763-1828

Chapter 9

THE AMERICAN REVOLUTION, 1763-1783

The American Revolution of 1776–1783 was one of the most crucial events of modern history. It was the first significant revolt against the Old Regime, and it gave birth to modern republicanism. Founded on the propositions that government must rest upon the consent of the governed and that man could shape the course of his destiny, and proclaiming the inherent worth of the individual, the American Revolution was among the most radical of all political movements. It has inspired countless revolutions in the nearly two centuries which have elapsed since its outbreak, and its goals of human equality and dignity are still the standards to which democrats everywhere aspire. However, while the implications of the American Revolution were profoundly radical, the men who led it were basically conservative. The Revolution was a defense of traditional English liberties against a usurping king, and it began as an effort to restore the British Empire as it had existed before 1763. When the struggle began, independence from England was the farthest thing from the minds of the American leaders, and few sought any significant social reform — much less the establishment of anything even remotely resembling a modern democracy. What the leaders wanted was the right to determine their own destinies within the British Empire. They wanted Dominion status; had the modern British Commonwealth existed in 1776, there would have been no American Revolution.

PRELUDE TO REVOLUTION 1763-1773

Britain's New Imperial Policy

With the end of the French and Indian War, England had a huge post-war debt which necessitated heavy domestic taxes, and she was faced with the financial burden of defending her extensive empire. Since the American colonies benefited from British military protection, Lord Bute's ministry was determined to make America pay its fair share of this defense burden; and to that end, it was decided to centralize, as much as possible, the administration of the English colonies. However, the measures adopted by England proved extremely unpopular in America and alienated colonial support of Great Britain. The most important of these new measures follow:

(1) **The Proclamation of 1763.** In the spring of 1763, the Ottawa Indians, under the leadership of Chief Pontiac, attacked Detroit. Resentful of white encroachment on their ancestral lands, numerous Great Lakes tribes joined the rebellion; and the Pennsylvania, Maryland, and Virginia backcountry regions were once again the scene of Indian warfare. Hoping to quiet the fears of the Indians, the Earl of Hillsborough issued a proclamation which forbade white settlement west of the Alleghenies and which ordered settlers in the Ohio Valley to return to the East. In effect, the West was closed to American settlement, and the thirteen colonies were confined to the area between the Atlantic Ocean and the Allegheny Mountains. Not only would this have stunted America's growth, it would also have ruined Ohio Valley land speculators (among whom was George Washington). The proclamation convinced the Americans that England was insensitive to their needs, and they simply ignored it. Britain did not have enough troops to adequately enforce the ban on trans-Allegheny settlement.

(2) **The Sugar Act of 1764.** Far more serious than the Proclamation of 1763 was the proposal by George Grenville (First Lord of the Treasury) to overhaul the mercantile system and make America pay for itself. As the first step in his program, Grenville pushed the Sugar Act through Parliament in 1764. It reduced the foreign molasses tax from six cents a gallon to three cents, but made provision for a stringent enforcement of the act. It also placed higher import duties on sugar, indigo, coffee, pimento, wine, and textiles, and was designed to raise 45,000 British pounds annually. In a companion measure, Grenville established a vice-admiralty court at Halifax, with authority over all thirteen colonies, to try violations of the mercantile laws. The measure placed the burden of proof upon the accused instead of upon the prosecution, and it stiffened bonding procedures for ships to prevent violation of the trade laws. The Sugar Act threatened to ruin the American rum industry, and it appeared to be an unconstitutional attempt to levy taxes without consent.

(3) **The Currency Act of 1764.** Passed at the prompting of English creditors, the Currency Act forbade the American colonies from making their paper currency legal tender. Since America lacked sufficient specie to meet her trade deficit with England, this act, along with higher import duties, threatened to ruin the economies of several colonies. In Boston, merchants agreed not to buy British goods as a protest against the Grenville program, and non-importation agreements quickly spread throughout the colonies.

(4) **The Quartering Act of 1765 and 1766.** Enacted at the request of General Thomas Gage, the Quartering Act required civil authorities and private persons to house and supply British troops at the civilians' own expense. While quite common in England, the requirement that private citizens house and supply British troops appeared tyrannous to the Americans; and a number of colonial assemblies, especially New York's, refused compliance with the law.

(5) **The Stamp Act of 1765.** The first direct tax ever levied by Parliament on the American colonies, the Stamp Act was to go into effect on November 1, 1765, and was expected to raise £60,000 a year. It required tax stamps on all legal documents, insurance policies, ship's papers, newspapers, pamphlets, almanacs, playing cards, and dice. All proceeds were to be used for the defense of America, and all stamp agents (who were to receive a commission for printing the stamps) were to be Americans. (None other than Benjamin Franklin applied as the stamp agent for Pennsylvania.) However, the Stamp Act produced a storm of protest which surprised even the dim-witted British government.

The Stamp Act Crisis

Both the Stamp Act and Grenville's general colonial policy alienated the support of the most influential groups in America: lawyers, printers, merchants, shipowners, and land speculators. Opposition to the act was nearly unanimous and transcended sectional and class barriers. By affecting the economic interests of large numbers of Americans, the British were uniting the disparate American colonies as never before. On June 6, 1765, the Massachusetts Assembly approved James Otis' resolution that an intercolonial conference convene in New York City in the fall to consider the problem of the Stamp Act. Other colonies seconded the proposal.

The Stamp Act Congress
(October 7-25, 1765)

Attended by nine of the thirteen colonies, the Stamp Act Congress accepted James Otis' contention that no taxation could be imposed upon the American colonies except with the colonies' own consent. It also accepted Daniel Dulany's argument that Parliament could legislate for the American colonies in matters of trade and could levy taxes for the purpose of regulating trade, but that it could not impose internal taxes (taxes collected from the colonial population which were not related to the regulation of trade, such as those imposed by the Stamp Act). On October 19, the Congress passed a "Declaration of Rights and Grievances" (the work of John Dickinson) which asserted (1) that Americans enjoyed all the rights and privileges of freeborn Englishmen, (2) that taxes could be imposed upon them only with the consent of their elected representatives, (3) that since America was not represented in the House of Commons, Parliament could not legally tax Americans, and (4) that only their own colonial assemblies had the authority to tax Americans. The Declaration specifically condemned the Stamp Act and the use of vice-admiralty courts as unconstitutional and petitioned the king to repeal both measures. At the same time, hundreds of colonial merchants pledged that they would boycott all British goods until such time as the Stamp Act was repealed. Moreover, the Sons of Liberty (lower-class youths who were often led by men of wealth and high social standing) made certain that the boycott was honored and that no tax stamps were distributed. Often resorting to violence, they intimidated recalcitrant merchants and officials into supporting their campaign; and in Boston, the mob destroyed the home of Chief Justice Thomas Hutchinson.

Repeal of the Stamp Act, 1766

The American boycott soon made its effects felt on the merchants of Great Britain. In January, 1766, merchants from thirty English towns petitioned Parliament to repeal the Stamp Act on the grounds that several bankruptcies had resulted from the American boycott. In March, the Stamp Act was repealed (effective May 1, 1766), and when news of it reached America in April, there was widespread rejoicing. The boycott was immediately ended; but in their joy, the Americans overlooked the fact that Parliament had passed a Declaratory Act which stated that Parliament had the right to legislate for America "in all cases whatsoever." At the same time, Parliament reduced the tax on foreign molasses from three cents a gallon to one cent, which was another victory for the colonial merchants. Since it had cost the Americans a penny a gallon to bribe British customs officers not to enforce the Sugar Act of 1764, the new duty was cheerfully paid, and all friction between America and England seemed to be fading away.

The Townshend Acts of 1767

In August, 1766, Charles Townshend became Chancellor of the Exchequer. Noting the American distinction between internal and external taxes, Townshend proposed to raise revenues solely through external taxes which the Americans conceded were legal and constitutional. In 1767, Parliament passed the Townshend Acts which (1) placed import duties on lead, paint, paper, glass, and tea, (2) authorized the issuance of Writs of Assistance (general search warrants) to help enforce the mercantile laws, and (3) created an American Board of Customs Commissioners (resident in Boston) to enforce the new duties. In addition, all legislative acts of the New York Assembly were invalidated until such time as that colony complied with the Quartering Act.

The Townshend Acts were no more acceptable to the Americans than the Grenville reforms, and once again colonial merchants revived their non-importation policy. John Dickinson enunciated the American attitude toward the Townshend Acts when he stated that while Parliament could regulate trade and could impose taxes incidental to such regulation, it could not impose taxes on trade for the purpose of raising revenue. In other words, Dickinson was calling on Parliament to enact only non-profit taxes! In British eyes, it appeared that the Americans simply did not want to pay taxes of any kind and that they wanted the harried British taxpayer to bear the whole burden of imperial defense. In 1768, Massachusetts, Virginia, and most of the other colonies condemned the Townshend Acts as "taxation without representation" and as unconstitutional measures. The situation in Boston became so ugly that two regiments of British troops were landed in the city in October, 1768, to maintain order.

Non-Importation and the Boston Massacre

Throughout 1768–1769, English goods were boycotted, and imports from Britain, which totaled 2.1 million British pounds in 1768, fell to a mere 1.3 million pounds in 1769. By the time Lord Frederick North became head of the government in January, 1770, it was obvious that the Townshend Acts were a failure and would have to be drastically revised. On March 5 (the very day of the Boston Massacre), Lord North proposed the repeal of all the Townshend duties except for the one on tea; that would be retained as a symbol of Parliament's authority to tax the colonies. In addition, he decided to allow the Quartering Act to expire without renewal. Once again, American economic pressure had been successful in thwarting Parliament, and the American non-importation policy was discontinued.

The conciliatory policy of Lord North's ministry was interrupted only by the Boston Massacre. Ever since British troops had been stationed in Boston, relations between the people and the soldiers had been tense. On March 5, 1770, a Boston mob taunted a group of soldiers, hurling stones, snowballs, and garbage at them and daring them to open fire. One or more of the soldiers apparently panicked and opened fire on the mob. When it was all over, five people had been killed (including one Crispus Attucks, believed to have been a Negro) and six wounded. Indignation swept the city, and the troops had to be confined at Castle Garden for their own protection. Six soldiers were tried for murder by the civil authorities. However, John Adams and Josiah Quincy defended the British troops and succeeded in winning four acquittals, but the two other soldiers were convicted of manslaughter and branded on the hand. Considered as a minor incident at the time, the Boston Massacre was later glorified as the opening round in the struggle for American independence. Despite the incident, there was, nevertheless, a definite thaw in Anglo-American relations between 1770 and 1773. Anti-British agitation died down, trade with England returned to normal, and the unpleasantness of the recent past seemed to have been a ghastly nightmare. However, this improvement in Anglo-American relations did not last.

THE RELUCTANT REVOLUTIONARIES

The Tea Act of 1773

By the spring of 1773, the English East India Company was on the verge of bankruptcy. Many important officials of the English government held stock in the company, and the company, itself, exercised governmental authority over the valuable Indian subcontinent. As the company was too important to be permitted to go bankrupt, Parliament was under a heavy obligation to save the East India Company. In May of 1773, Parliament authorized the East India Company to sell its tea directly to agents or consignees in America. By eliminating the middle man, the company would be able to undersell American tea merchants and recoup its losses. However, the Townshend duty of three cents a pound was retained, and therein lay trouble. The Americans objected to the Tea Act as creating a monopoly (illegal under the common law), and, thereby, ruining American tea merchants. Also, they refused to pay the duty on the tea since to do so would be to acknowledge Parliament's right to levy direct taxes on America. On December 16, 1773, a Boston mob, dressed as Mohawk Indians and apparently under the leadership of Sam Adams, dumped 342 chests of tea into Boston harbor. England's reaction was swift and harsh.

The Coercive (Intolerable) Acts

Between March and June, 1774, Parliament passed a series of measures collectively known as the Coercive Acts. Designed to restore law and order to America, they consisted of the following measures:

(1) **The Boston Port Act.** It prohibited the loading or unloading of any ship in Boston harbor (except for military supplies and cargoes of food and fuel) until such time as the East India Company was compensated for the tea dumped into the harbor.

(2) **The Administration of Justice Act.** The measure provided that British officials charged with crimes while suppressing a riot or collecting customs would be transported back to England for trial. The act applied only to Massachusetts and was based on the supposition that British officials could not receive a fair trial in that colony.

78 / AMERICAN HISTORY

Bostonians paying their taxes by tarring and feathering a British revenue collector.

(3) **The Massachusetts Government Act.** Members of the Governor's Council were no longer to be elected by the Assembly; instead they would be appointed by the Crown and serve at the King's pleasure. Only one town meeting would be held each year, and additional meetings would require the written approval of the governor. Juries were to be selected by the sheriff, rather than elected by the town, and the governor was empowered to remove from office minor judicial officials. The Massachusetts Government Act severely undercut the traditional liberties of the colony, and it appeared to be evidence of England's attempt to place America under despotic rule.

(4) **The Quartering Act.** It applied to all the colonies and restored the provisions of the earlier act which had been allowed to lapse.

(5) **The Quebec Act.** Although not a part of the Coercive package, the Americans regarded it as one of the Intolerable Acts. It extended the boundaries of Quebec to include the Ohio Valley, and it recognized French civil law and the traditional rights of the Catholic church in the province. It aroused opposition in America because Virginia, Massachusetts, and Connecticut all had land claims in the Ohio Valley region.

The First Continental Congress

In order to deal with the crisis created by the Coercive Acts, twelve colonies (Georgia was not represented) sent fifty-five delegates to an intercolonial meeting which convened in Philadelphia in September, 1774. Attended by such outstanding colonial leaders as Patrick Henry, John and Sam Adams, Peyton Randolph, and Joseph Galloway, the Continental Congress dealt with three major proposals. On September 17, it approved the radical Suffolk Resolves which (1) declared the Coercive Acts unconstitutional and called upon the colonies to ignore them, (2) urged Massachusetts to form its own government and to withhold taxes from the royal government until the Coercive Acts were repealed, (3) called upon the people to arm themselves and form a militia, and (4) recommended a strict economic boycott against all British goods until the Coercive Acts were repealed. However, moderate and conservative delegates felt that the Suffolk Resolves were too extreme, and they supported a counter plan proposed by Joseph Galloway.

Galloway's Plan of Union. Hoping to reconcile England and America, Joseph Galloway revived Ben Franklin's 1754 Albany Plan of Union. He proposed to have the King name a president-general for the thirteen colonies, with power to veto acts of the Grand Council. The Grand Council would be elected by the assemblies of the thirteen colonies and would constitute an inferior branch of the British legislature. It would have the authority to veto acts of Parliament that concerned America. Likewise, Parliament would have the right to veto acts passed by the Grand Council. The Galloway Plan did not appear adequate to the task of resolving Anglo-American differences and was rejected by the Congress by a single vote.

Instead, the Congress passed a series of resolutions which condemned as unconstitutional virtually every act of Parliament, passed since 1763, that had bearing on America. The Congress reaffirmed that only the colonial assemblies, and not Parliament, could impose taxes in America, and pledged to continue the boycott against English goods. The Congress agreed to reconvene in May of 1775 if its grievances had still not been redressed. Not once was American independence of England mentioned as a serious possibility. The Americans wanted British military protection, but they also wanted to restore the Empire as it had existed prior to 1763. Such American leaders as James Wilson, John Adams, and Thomas Jefferson enunciated the Dominion theory of the British Empire. They argued that England and the thirteen colonies were united only by their allegiance to a common monarch; in all other respects they were sovereign and independent. In return for England's military protection, the colonies permitted England to regulate imperial trade, but except for that one area, Parliament had no authority over America. Had England accepted this interpretation of the Empire, the American Revolution could have been avoided. England, however, was not yet ready to transform the Empire into a Commonwealth.

From Lexington and Concord to Bunker Hill

With England showing little sign of honoring the American demands for repeal of the Coercive Acts, Massachusetts, early in 1775, prepared for war and began laying up arms and ammunition. In April, General Thomas Gage ordered his troops to proceed to Concord and seize military supplies believed to be stored there. At Lexington (on the

Patrick Henry in the First Continental Congress.

road to Concord), a group of American Minute Men attempted to stop the British advance. A skirmish ensued in which eight Americans were killed and ten wounded. The British proceeded to Concord, but on their return trip, they were continually harassed by American militia men. By the time the British finally returned to camp, they had suffered casualties of 73 killed and 174 wounded, compared to American casualties of 93 men killed, wounded, or missing. April 19, 1775, marks the actual outbreak of the American Revolution, even though independence was not to be declared for another fifteen months. Immediately after the battle at Lexington and Concord, the Americans laid siege to Boston; and on April 23, the Massachusetts legislature authorized the raising of a 13,600-man militia under the command of Artemas Ward.

The Second Continental Congress. When the new Congress convened in Philadelphia in May of 1775, it contained some new faces (Benjamin Franklin, Thomas Jefferson, and John Hancock among others), and revealed a markedly more radical mood. As a result of the recent outbreak of hostilities in Massachusetts, the Congress was challenged to take sterner measures to defend "the rights of Englishmen." Accordingly, it authorized the creation of a Continental army under the command of George Washington. He was selected because of his experience in the French and Indian War and because, as a Virginian, he would symbolize the unity of the American colonies in their support of Massachusetts. The Congress also authorized the issuance of paper currency to finance the war effort. (The paper was eventually to be redeemed by the thirteen colonies in proportion to their population.) Finally, the Congress selected a committee to negotiate alliances with the Indians and with the governments of continental Europe. While independence had not been proclaimed, the thirteen colonies had taken a major step in the creation of an independent American government.

Bunker Hill. Meanwhile, in Boston, the British sought to improve their military position by occupying Dorchester Heights. Learning of the British intent, the Americans, in June of 1775, occupied Breed's Hill (near Bunker Hill, which gave its name to the battle) to prevent the British from taking Dorchester Heights. With 100 of their men killed and 267 wounded, the American defense of Breed's Hill almost turned into a major rout as the militiamen ran out of ammunition. However, the British suffered 1,054 casualties, including a large number of officers, and were so weakened by the battle that they were unable to pursue the retreating Americans. Two weeks later, General Washington arrived in Massachusetts to take command of the American forces.

The Parting of the Ways

Still hoping to avoid an irreparable rupture with England, the Continental Congress, in July, 1775, approved John Dickinson's Olive Branch Petition. Proclaiming its devotion to King George III, the Congress called upon George to end Parliament's unlawful attempt to rule America and held out the hope of reconciliation. In August, King George rejected the American petition and declared the colonies to be in a state of rebellion. From September to November, a disappointed Congress formally rejected Parliament's claim to exercise governmental authority over America. The Congress authorized the establishment of a navy and decided to send representatives to Europe to seek foreign support for the struggle against England. As the year ended, it seemed that England and America would never be able to peacefully resolve their differences.

"Common Sense"

In January, 1776, Thomas Paine published "Common Sense." Ridiculing the idea that Parliament, and not King George, was responsible for the enmity between England and America, he branded the King as a tyrant; and he called upon the American people to proclaim their independence of England. Declaring that America was destined to be a great and free nation which would redeem mankind from despotism, Paine asserted that it was absurd for a small island like England to rule a vast continent. "Common Sense" was a popular tract which enjoyed a wide circulation, and it was instrumental in accommodating the American people to the idea of independence.

The Decision for Independence

By 1776, the hope of peaceful reconciliation with England was quickly fading. George III appeared intent upon repressing the American colonists and had begun to hire Hessian mercenaries for service in America. In March, pinned down

Thomas Paine

The Causes of the American Revolution

The decision for independence probably did not reflect the majority sentiment of the American people. It has often been said that one-third of the American people remained loyal to England (indeed, as many as 50,000 active Loyalists fought with the British), that one-third were indifferent to the political storms raging about them, and that only one-third of the American people supported the Patriot cause. Although it was a minority movement, the revolution enlisted the support of Southern planters, Northern merchants, lawyers, and newspaper editors — those who commanded the economic and political resources of the thirteen colonies. Although it took place nearly two centuries ago, the causes of the American Revolution are still being debated. The major schools of thought follow:

(1) **The Nationalist School.** Best represented by George Bancroft, the Nationalist school dominated nineteenth-century American thought. It viewed the revolution as a Providential act designed to overthrow tyranny and secure the blessing of liberty and popular democracy for all mankind. Simplistic in its approach, it accepted the

in Boston by American militiamen, the British decided to evacuate Massachusetts and establish a new base of operations in New York City. In the same month, France agreed to extend economic and military assistance to the Americans. On June 7, Virginia's Richard Henry Lee introduced a resolution in the Congress calling upon it to proclaim American independence. Nearly a month later, on July 2, 1776, Congress did so; and two days later it approved Thomas Jefferson's draft of a Declaration of Independence. Couched in Lockean terms, the Declaration accused King George of systematically undermining the constitutional liberties of his subjects and charged that he had breached the contract which bound America to his sovereignty. Invoking the right of revolution, the Americans pledged to institute a new government which would safeguard their lives, liberty, and property. At the insistence of the Southern delegates, however, Jefferson's condemnation of the slave trade was stricken from the final version of the Declaration of Independence.

Thomas Jefferson reading the rough draft of the Declaration of Independence to Benjamin Franklin.

Patriot interpretation of the revolution at face value.

(2) **The Whig School.** A product of the late nineteenth century, the Whig school was popularized by the English historian George Otto Trevelyan. It argued that George III was, indeed, a tyrant who was attempting to undermine the English constitution and that in opposing him, the Americans were defending the rights of all Englishmen and were thus fighting England's battle. The American Revolution was seen as preserving the liberty of the English people.

(3) **The Imperial School.** Developed by George Louis Beer, Charles M. Andrews, and Lawrence H. Gipson, the Imperial school was a product of the early twentieth century, and it sought to study the American Revolution within the larger context of the British Empire. Arguing that the mercantile system benefited both America and the Empire as a whole, this school held that the imperial reforms of the post-1763 period were designed to strengthen the entire Empire, and that the Americans should have contributed to the cost of their own defense. The American Revolution was seen as resulting from a selfish and shortsighted effort of the Americans to escape just taxation.

(4) **The Economic Determinists.** A product of the 1920's and 1930's, the economic determinists were led by Charles A. Beard who saw the revolution as an economic conflict between the merchants of England and America. Arguing that mercantilism injured colonial merchants, Beard saw the conflict with England as the effort of American merchants to cast off the restrictions of the mercantile system.

(5) **The Neo-Nationalist School.** The most popular school of thought, the Neo-Nationalist position has developed since World War II, and its leading advocates are Clinton Rossiter and Edmund S. Morgan. Downplaying economic causes, it sees the revolution as an American attempt to preserve English constitutional liberties as the Americans understood them. The centralizing policy of the post-1763 era violated the traditional liberties of the thirteen colonies, and the Americans wanted to restore the empire as it had existed prior to 1763. Stressing the political and constitutional aspects of the revolution, the Neo-Nationalists see it as a basically conservative attempt to restore the *status quo* of the pre-1763 era.

THE WAR OF INDEPENDENCE

The Opposing Forces

On paper, the British enjoyed a marked military advantage, but wars are not fought on paper. Washington seldom commanded more than 16,000 men at any one time, and at Valley Forge, his forces shrunk to less than 2,000 men fit for combat. The states rarely fulfilled their quotas of troops and supplies, which meant that the Patriots were invariably short of men and equipment. On the other hand, Britain had a well-trained, well-equipped army of 60,000 men scattered throughout its far-flung Empire, and she augmented her forces in America with Hessians, Loyalists, and Indians. However, the British troops were 3,000 miles removed from their main base of supply, and they had to defend and occupy a coastline which stretched for more than 1,000 miles. They were unfamiliar with the American interior and were unable to supply themselves once outside the coastal cities. While the British held the coast, the Americans controlled the interior and from that position, constantly harassed the Redcoats.

Victory Through Retreat

In August, 1776, Washington's forces were defeated at the Battle of Long Island (fought in Brooklyn), and the Americans retreated to Manhattan Island. A month later, the British occupied New York City, and Washington fled to Harlem Heights (which was then well outside city limits). Seeking to outflank him, the British landed a force in Westchester; and in October, Washington was defeated at the Battle of White Plains. Retreating across New Jersey, Washington crossed the Delaware River and inflicted a defeat on the surprised Hessian garrison at Trenton on Christmas night. In January, 1777, he inflicted another defeat on the British at Princeton and cleared northern New Jersey of Redcoats. Proceeding to Morristown, Washington took up winter quarters to await the coming of spring. Although Washington cannot be considered a military tactician of the first magnitude, he did realize that as long as the Patriots had an army in the field (no matter how small or how battered), their cause was not lost. Consequently, Washington preferred not to engage superior British forces; instead, he harassed their rear and committed his troops to battle only when certain that he was favored by numbers or terrain — or as in the case of Trenton, by surprise. Fortunately for Washington, the British suffered from incompetent leadership. Neither Lord William Howe nor Sir Henry Clinton possessed the energy and foresight to adequately follow up their military advantage over the Patriots.

1777: A Crucial Year

Initially, General Howe was to have secured New York City in 1776; he then was to move up the Hudson River in the spring of 1777 to link forces with General John Burgoyne, who was to lead his forces down from Canada along the Lake Champlain route. Had this plan been carried out, the British would have controlled the Hudson and Mohawk Valleys and would have severed communications between New England and the South. The British could then have dealt with each region separately. However, stung by Washington at Trenton and Princeton, Howe inexplicably decided to capture the Patriot capital at Philadelphia, rather than joining forces with Burgoyne. In July, 1777, Howe set out for Philadelphia. He was intercepted by Washington at Brandywine, defeated Washington, and entered Philadelphia in September. The Continental Congress fled to the interior. In October, Washington again attacked the British forces, who were now concentrated at Germantown. Again he was defeated, and the remnants of his army took up winter quarters at Valley Forge. The fall of Philadelphia disheartened the Americans, but it did not constitute a major setback. Howe had still not crushed the Patriot army, and he controlled little of the American interior. Meanwhile, Burgoyne had led his forces down from Canada, but he was constantly harassed by the Americans. His Indian allies deserted him, and his lines of supply were critically overextended. At Saratoga, he found himself surrounded by American forces under Horatio Gates. His supplies cut off, and with no prospects of relief from Howe's forces, Burgoyne surrendered his 5,800 man army on October 17. Burgoyne's surrender saved New England from isolation and bolstered American morale. It also convinced the French that the Patriot cause was viable and that they could form an alliance with the Americans with fair prospects of success.

The French Alliance

The Americans had sought an alliance with France for some time, and they had sent Benjamin Franklin to Versailles to enlist the support of King Louis XVI. In February, 1778, France and the Continental Congress concluded a treaty which contained the following:

(1) France pledged to secure the independence of the thirteen United States.

(2) France renounced all territorial claims to the North American mainland.

(3) America was to receive all North American territory won from the British.

(4) France and the United States both pledged not to make a separate peace with England.

(5) The United States was to recognize French sovereignty over France's West Indian possessions.

(6) The United States and France pledged perpetual friendship to each other. France, of course, was more interested in weakening England than in helping America, but the French alliance was, nevertheless, instrumental in enabling America to defeat the British. Without it, the American Revolution may well have failed.

Monmouth Courthouse

In 1778, Sir Henry Clinton succeeded Howe as commander of the British forces and decided to return his headquarters to New York City. In June, Clinton marched his forces across New Jersey and was met at Monmouth Courthouse by Washington. Unfortunately, General Charles Lee failed to follow up Washington's attack, and Clinton's army was allowed to escape the Patriot trap relatively unscathed. The Battle of Monmouth was the last significant battle fought in the North, as the British now turned their attention to the Southern colonies. Late in 1778 and early in 1779, the American George Rogers Clark led an expedition into the Ohio Valley and captured Kaskaskia, Cahokia, and Vincennes. His exploits checked British power in the Ohio Valley and blunted the threat posed by the Indians. However, the operation was largely peripheral.

The Southern Campaign and Yorktown

In December, 1778, a British expeditionary force was landed in Georgia and captured Savannah. In

May, 1780, Clinton captured Charleston, South Carolina; and in August, Cornwallis (his second in command) defeated the Patriots at Camden, giving the British control of South Carolina. In April, 1781, against Clinton's orders (Clinton had returned to New York City), Cornwallis decided to conquer Virginia. Meeting little opposition, Cornwallis established his headquarters at Yorktown near Chesapeake Bay. Washington, who had been planning to attack the British in New York City, turned his attention to Cornwallis. In August, the French Admiral DeGrasse brought his fleet up from the West Indies and met his countryman, Barras, who had sailed south from Newport. The two French squadrons linked up at the mouth of Chesapeake Bay and cut off Cornwallis' access to the sea. Meanwhile, Washington, Rochambeau, and Lafayette attacked Cornwallis overland. On October 19, 1781, surrounded by American and French troops and blockaded at sea, Cornwallis surrendered his 7,000-man army, even as a strong British relief squadron was sailing from New York. Yorktown was the last significant battle of the American Revolution, and Washington's defeat of Cornwallis all but ended the war. In March, 1782, Lord North was forced to resign as prime minister, and a month later, the British indicated that they were willing to enter peace talks.

The Treaty of Paris (September, 1783)

The American treaty with France pledged both powers not to make a separate peace with England. However, in 1779, Spain entered the war against Great Britain, and France bound herself not to make peace with England without the concurrence of Spain. The Spanish would not make peace until they had taken Gibraltar from England; thus the American Revolution was needlessly prolonged. Desperately wanting peace, America entered into secret negotiations with the British, and in November, 1782, reached a preliminary agreement. However, this treaty was not to become operative until France and England concluded a treaty of their own. Finally, in September, 1783, the final agreements were signed in Paris. The treaty provided for the following:

(1) Spain was to receive Florida in lieu of Gibraltar.

(2) Great Britain was to recognize the independence of the United States and relinquish control of the Ohio Valley to the Americans.

(3) The boundary of the United States was to be fixed at the Great Lakes in the North, the Mississippi River in the West, and the thirty-first parallel (Georgia-Florida border) in the South.

(4) The United States would be permitted to retain its fishing rights off the coast of Newfoundland.

(5) Both the United States and Great Britain were to enjoy equal rights of navigation on the Mississippi River.

(6) British subjects would be given the right to sue for the collection of debts unpaid as of 1776.

(7) The Continental Congress was to recommend to the states that confiscated Loyalist property be returned to the owners or their heirs. However, this provision of the treaty was not carried out, as the states refused to return confiscated Loyalist property.

The treaty was highly favorable to the United States, which was given control of the strategic Ohio Valley. Great Britain hoped that a lenient peace would facilitate the resumption of friendly relations with America. She needed American agricultural produce and valued America as a market for her manufactured goods. She was also confident that America's experiment in republican government would fail and that the thirteen colonies would soon be begging to rejoin the British Empire. After all, with the exception of Switzerland, there was not a nation in the civilized world that did not have a king.

REVIEW QUESTIONS FOR CHAPTER 9

1. Parliament's first direct tax on America was the

    (A) Sugar Act of 1764
    (B) Currency Act of 1764
    (C) Stamp Act of 1765
    (D) Townshend Act of 1767

2. The Declaration of Rights and Grievances (1765) was mainly the work of

    (A) James Otis
    (B) John Dickinson
    (C) Daniel Dulany
    (D) Sam Adams

3. The Stamp Act Congress conceded that Parliament had the right to

    (A) regulate colonial trade
    (B) impose taxes on America
    (C) veto acts of the colonial assemblies
    (D) do all of the above

4. Which was *not* one of the Intolerable Acts?

    (A) The Boston Port Act
    (B) The Tea Act
    (C) The Massachusetts Government Act
    (D) The Administration of Justice Act

5. The First Continental Congress did all of the following *except*

    (A) call for a colonial militia
    (B) declare the Coercive Acts unconstitutional
    (C) call for a boycott of English goods
    (D) call for American independence

6. Washington's first significant victory came at

    (A) Long Island
    (B) White Plains
    (C) Trenton
    (D) Princeton

7. France was persuaded to ally with America after

    (A) Burgoyne's surrender at Saratoga
    (B) Washington's victory at Princeton
    (C) Bunker Hill
    (D) Valley Forge

8. George Rogers Clark captured all of the following forts *except*

    (A) Kaskaskia
    (B) Vincennes
    (C) Cahokia
    (D) Detroit

9. All were associated with the Yorktown campaign *except*

    (A) Cornwallis
    (B) Lafayette
    (C) Clinton
    (D) DeGrasse

10. The Treaty of Paris did not give the United States

    (A) the Ohio Valley
    (B) Florida
    (C) Newfoundland fishing rights
    (D) free navigation on the Mississippi

Explanatory Answers

1. **(C)** The Stamp Act taxed legal documents, newspapers, etc., and was designed to raise revenue by taxing items in daily consumer use.

2. **(B)** The Declaration held that Parliament's authority over America was limited to the regulation of its foreign trade.

3. **(A)** The regulation of colonial trade was the only area of legitimate Parliamentary authority over America.

4. **(B)** The Tea Act set in motion the chain of events leading to the Intolerable Acts.

5. **(D)** The Congress still hoped for reconciliation with England.

6. **(C)** Washington defeated the Hessian garrison at Trenton on Christmas night, 1776.

7. **(A)** Burgoyne's defeat showed that the American cause was viable.

8. **(D)** He failed to capture Detroit.

9. **(C)** Clinton, the British commander-in-chief, was in New York City. He advised against Cornwallis' Virginia campaign.

10. **(B)** Florida was returned to Spain.

Chapter 10

THE ARTICLES OF CONFEDERATION AND THE CONSTITUTION, 1783-1789

With the end of the American Revolution and the formal establishment of American independence in 1783, the thirteen new states settled down to the task of creating their own national government. Fearing excessive central authority (it was England's attempt to centralize the Empire which produced the American Revolution), the states had no intention of creating an American George III; and they devised instead an instrument of government which was designed to protect local liberties by severely restricting and limiting the powers of the national government. Unfortunately, the national government which they formed was too weak to adequately deal with the many problems besetting the young American nation. While the 1783-1789 period may not have been as critical as early historians thought, it was certainly a time of crisis and epochal development in the nation's history. Out of the turmoil of the 1780's and the shortcomings of the Articles of Confederation, the Constitution of the United States emerged. Granting the national government the powers which it desperately needed, the Constitution left to the states sufficient authority to safeguard liberty, and it provided the United States with a government strong enough to insure stability, yet flexible enough to permit growth and development.

THE NEW AMERICAN STATES

State Constitutions

When the Second Continental Congress proclaimed America's independence of England, the colonial charters under which the American states had functioned became null and void. Accordingly, Congress called upon the states to draft new instruments of government, and over the next few years, eleven of the thirteen states adopted new constitutions (Rhode Island and Connecticut retained their colonial charters, but deleted all references to the British Crown). Except for Massachusetts, whose constitution was drafted by a specially elected constitutional convention and was ratified by the electorate, the new state constitutions were written by revolutionary state congresses or conventions and were not directly ratified by the electorate. Great importance was attached to these state constitutions, for in Lockean terms, each was the social compact which bound the people into a political commonwealth and which laid down the mutual rights and responsibilities of rulers and subjects. While they all differed in their features, the new state constitutions shared enough common characteristics to permit generalization. Their outstanding provisions were the following:

(1) **Weak Executive Power.** In nine of the thirteen states, the governor was elected for a one-year term, and seven of the thirteen states limited his eligibility for re-election. In nine states, the governor was virtually stripped of his veto power over acts of the legislature, and he had to share his power of appointment with the legislature. Except for New York and Massachusetts, where the governor was elected by the people, he was elected to office by the state legislature. On the whole, the governor's powers were severely clipped, and he was subordinate to the legislature. Since executive powers had been abused by King George III, the American states wanted to make certain that their constitutions would not create any little King Georges. However, they so weakened the governor that he was unable to act as a brake on arbitrary and excessive acts of the legislature.

(2) **Bicameral Legislatures.** Except for Pennsylvania and New Hampshire, the state legislatures had two houses: a lower house, commonly called the assembly, and an upper house, usually called the senate. All tax and money bills had to originate with the lower house, which had the power of the purse. However, each house could generally veto legislative acts of the other. Members of the assembly were usually elected annually (semi-annually in Rhode Island and Connecticut), while members of the upper house were elected for terms of two to four years. In many states, the legislature shared the power of appointment with the governor, and since he lacked a veto, the legislature became the dominant branch of government. Generally, the legislature was given too much power, and after a few years many Americans shared Thomas Jefferson's sentiment when he stated that a hundred tyrants were as bad as one. However, as the legislature was considered closer to the people than the governor, and was answerable to them, it was felt that power vested in the legislature was safer than power vested in the executive.

(3) **Property Qualifications for Office-holding.** Americans of the eighteenth century felt that the men elected to govern them should be "gentlemen of property and standing," and all states imposed minimum property qualifications for elective offices, which escalated with the importance of the office. Members of the assembly were required to own as much as £500 worth of property in Maryland and New Jersey, and senators had to be worth at least £1000.* The property requirement for the governorship went as high as £10,000 in South Carolina. Generally, property requirements tended to be lower, but still substantial, in other states.

(4) **Property Qualifications for Voting.** During the Revolution, property qualifications for voting were substantially lowered, but they were not abolished. It was still the feeling of most Americans that a man should have some stake in society (property ownership) before being permitted to vote. Most states permitted voting upon the payment of a poll tax (which excluded the poorest element of society, while Virginia required the ownership of twenty-five acres of cultivated land). It is believed that a large majority of the American people were able to meet the property qualifications necessary for voting.

(5) **Judicial Tenure during Good Behavior.** Colonial judges had served at the king's pleasure and were therefore under great pressure to decide cases his way. This undermined judicial independence and defeated the impartial administration of justice. To prevent a repetition of this situation, American judges were appointed by the legislature, but enjoyed tenure of office during good behavior. In other words, a judge could be removed from the bench only for cause. He was independent of political pressure and could render impartial justice without fear of political reprisal.

(6) **Bill of Rights.** The state constitutions contained bills of rights which specifically guaranteed the people the traditional "rights of Englishmen." A fair and speedy trial by jury, immunity from cruel or unusual punishments, security of home, property, and person; freedom of speech and of the press, and the right to petition for a redress of grievances were declared the inalienable rights of Americans. In addition, freedom of conscience was protected and religious tests for voting and office holding were usually abolished. Designed to protect individual liberty against the awesome power of the state, the bills of rights have served as the foundation of American civil liberties.

The state constitutions, then, reflected the political lessons of the American Revolution. They

---

* Many American states were still using the British monetary system in the period just after the Revolution.

restricted executive power, protected civil liberties, augmented the powers of the legislature, and secured the independence of the judiciary. They were intended to prevent a recurrence of the grievances which produced the American Revolution and were designed to safeguard the people from the unbridled power of the state.

THE ARTICLES OF CONFEDERATION

The American Fear of Centralized Government

When Richard Henry Lee introduced his resolution of American independence in June, 1776, he also proposed that the thirteen colonies form a perpetual league of friendship. However, the American people were fearful of centralized authority as a threat to liberty and had no intentions of creating a strong central authority which might one day become as oppressive as the British imperial government. Consequently, Lee's resolutions were debated for almost six months. Finally, declaring that government should remain close to the people, and that its powers should be sharply limited, the Continental Congress approved the Articles of Confederation and Perpetual Union in November, 1777, and sent them to the individual states for ratification.

The Western Lands Controversy

Although the Continental Congress acted as though the Articles of Confederation were in force, the government which they created did not become legally effective until March 1, 1781. Led by Maryland, the smaller states refused to ratify the Articles of Confederation until the larger states (Virginia, New York, Massachusetts, and Connecticut) surrendered their western land claims to the national government. Maryland, and her landless sister states, felt that as the American Revolution was the common effort of thirteen states, any western lands acquired as a result of the Revolution should be the joint property of all the states and should be used for the benefit of the whole American people. Furthermore, Maryland feared that western lands would swell the already great influence of the larger states, and that these states would dominate the new American government to the detriment of the smaller states. For over three years this dispute over western lands held up the ratification of the Articles of Confederation. Then, in 1780, New York yielded its western claims to the Congress and was soon followed by Massachusetts and Connecticut. When Virginia gave up its western land claims early in 1781, Maryland promptly ratified the Articles of Confederation, and the new central government became effective.

Powers of the Congress

The Articles of Confederation empowered Congress to:

(1) declare war and make peace

(2) negotiate treaties with foreign nations, and conclude agreements with the Indians

(3) raise and maintain an army and navy

(4) coin money and borrow funds

(5) regulate weights and measures

(6) establish a post office.

The individual states also agreed to recognize citizens of sister states as their own citizens (in other words, a New Yorker in Virginia would enjoy all the rights and privileges of Virginians), and to give full faith and credit to legislative acts passed by their sister states (a New Yorker could not flee to Virginia to escape the judgment of a New York court or to circumvent a New York law). Finally, the states agreed to a perpetual union — the implication being that no state could abrogate the Articles of Confederation without the permission of all the other states. However, the Articles of Confederation contained glaring weaknesses which undermined the effectiveness of the Congress.

Limitations on Congressional Power

The Congress had no power to levy taxes on the states or on citizens of the thirteen states. All it could do was request funds from the states, which the states were under no compulsion to honor. For example, in 1781, Rhode Island refused to approve a 5 per cent customs duty for the support of the Congress, and over the years many other states proved unwilling to shoulder the financial burden of supporting the Congress. As a result, the credit of the national government declined sharply. Moreover, the Congress had no authority to regulate interstate or foreign commerce. On more than one occasion, trade rivalry among the states threatened to erupt into war, and states would often erect tariff barriers against the products of neighboring states. Although the Congress could negotiate treaties with foreign nations, it had no way to force individual states to honor the terms of those treaties, especially if they imposed restrictions upon American trade and commerce. In the absence of a federal court system, the Congress had no way to impose its will upon the states or to make recalcitrant states obey its laws. Indeed, each state retained its sovereignty as an independent nation, exercised all functions not specifically delegated to the national government, maintained its own militia, and controlled its own commerce and taxing powers.

Operations of the Congress

Each state, regardless of its size, population, or wealth, had but a single vote in the Congress. This was resented by the larger states which felt that the small states exercised an influence in the Congress far out of proportion to their actual power. The congressional delegation of each state was selected by the state legislature and consisted of not less than two nor more than seven members. A state's vote in Congress was determined by the majority of its delegation, but it lost its vote whenever its delegation divided evenly on any issue. Legislation had to receive the approval of at least nine of the thirteen states before being adopted, and it was extremely difficult to get three-fourths of the states to agree on any legislation. As a result, Congress was often powerless to act in the face of imminent danger. In addition, proposed amendments to the Articles of Confederation had to receive unanimous consent before adoption, which meant that it was virtually impossible to alter the basic instruments of government. Perhaps the most outstanding weakness of the national government was the lack of strong executive authority. There was no single head of government or head of state. When Congress was not in session, a thirteen-man executive committee (one member from each state) handled affairs of state; and five executive departments (appointed by the Congress) were responsible for foreign affairs, finance, war, the navy, and the post office. Lacking strong executive leadership and handicapped by the refusal of the states to honor its requests, the Congress was doomed to ultimate failure in most of its efforts.

Congress and Western Lands

Despite its many shortcomings, the Congress was notably successful in formulating policy regarding the western territory of the United States; and it established the basic procedures by which new states entered the American union. By the *Ordinance of 1784,* (drafted largely by Thomas Jefferson), the Congress declared its intention of forming new states from its western territories which would eventually enter the union on terms of absolute equality with the thirteen original states. Congress did not want to establish colonies which might harbor grievances against the central government (much as the American colonies did against England), and it decided to make the western states equal members of the Union.

The Land Ordinance of 1785. Again the work of Jefferson, the Land Ordinance of 1785 regulated the disposition of western land. It provided for the sale of land at public auction after a government survey. All western land tracts were to be divided into townships of 6 square miles each. The townships would then be subdivided into 36 sections of 640 acres each. Four sections would be set aside for the use of the national government, one section would be turned over to the local town government for use as a school site, and the remaining 31 sections would be sold in 640-acre units for at least a dollar per acre. It was hoped that the sale of public lands would yield a sufficient revenue to enable the national government to support itself without the necessity of levying taxes. However, the minimum purchase price of $640 was beyond the means of most Americans, so that the act favored land speculators who purchased large blocks of land and then repartitioned them for sale in smaller units to the settlers. Over the next half-century, the national government would make land available in smaller units so that persons of more moderate means could afford to buy land, but the basic pattern of public land distribution would remain the same.

The Northwest Ordinance of 1787. Based, in part, upon Jefferson's 1784 Ordinance, the Northwest Ordinance governed the process by which new states were admitted to the union. It provided that no less than three nor more than five states would be created from the Northwest Territory. The region would be administered by a governor and by magistrates appointed by the Congress. When a territory's population reached 5,000 adult males, a bicameral territorial legislature would be formed and a non-voting representative would be sent to the national Congress. When the population reached 60,000 adult males, the people of the territory could draft a state constitution and apply for admission to the union. Such constitutions would have to provide for freedom of religion, trial by jury, public support of education, and for the prohibition of involuntary servitude — except as punishment for crime. Slavery was specifically barred from the Northwest Territory, as it was hoped (even by Southerners) that slavery would soon disappear as an American institution. With minor exceptions, this process was followed throughout American history as the procedure by which new states were brought into the union.

The Failures of the Congress: Foreign Affairs

The weakness of the national government soon became apparent in the realm of foreign affairs. Citing the failure of the American states to compensate the Loyalists for their seized property (as recommended by the Treaty of Paris), England refused to evacuate Oswego, Niagara, Detroit, and other forts which she was maintaining on American soil, and she closed Canada and the West Indies to American trade. Throughout the period of Confederation, the Congress was unable to secure British evacuation of American soil or to win any significant trade concessions from her. Similarly, in the Southwest, Spain prevented the free passage of American shipping through the mouth of the Mississippi at New Orleans, maintained her claim to territory in what is now Mississippi and Alabama, and instigated her Indian allies to attack American settlements. John Jay was sent to Spain in 1785 to secure America's free navigation of the Mississippi, but his efforts proved futile. Spain's closure of the port of New Orleans threatened the prosperity of the American West, for in the absence of land transportation, the Mississippi River was the only avenue of transportation by which American crops could reach the world market; and for a time, the West threatened to secede from the American union and make a separate accommodation with Spain. The Congress' failure to open the port damaged its prestige, particularly in the West. At the same time, European nations were reluctant to enter into trade agreements with the Congress, since it was powerless to secure state compliance with such measures. The Europeans were uncertain whether they were dealing with one American government or with fourteen.

The Failures of the Congress: Domestic Affairs

The unwillingness of the states to adequately support the national government was compounded by the severe economic depression which struck America from 1784 to 1786. The Congress was unable to service the nation's foreign debt; it could not satisfy domestic creditors and was also unable to meet its financial obligation to veterans of the Continental Army (indeed, angry veterans ran the Congress out of Philadelphia in 1784). Throughout the nation, farmers and debtors demanded currency inflation (through the issuance of paper money) to relieve the severe money shortage, and they asked for stay laws which would ban property foreclosures. When the Massachusetts legislature refused to meet these demands in 1786, a group of debt-ridden farmers, led by Daniel Shays, launched a civil insurrection against the government of the state. It took seven months to suppress the Shaysites, and their radical attack

Shays' mob in possession of a courthouse.

on property frightened conservatives throughout the nation. It was obvious that America needed a stronger national government — one that was able to regulate commerce, levy direct taxes, and enforce its will. The spectre of social revolution raised by Daniel Shays spurred the movement to strengthen the national government.

THE CONSTITUTION OF THE UNITED STATES

Pinckney's Proposals and the Annapolis Convention

Realizing the weaknesses of the Articles of Confederation, South Carolina's Charles Pinckney proposed a series of reforms in August, 1786. His proposals would have amended the Articles to provide for a federal court system to enforce foreign treaties and national laws, would have given the Congress the power to regulate foreign and interstate commerce, and would have required the states to honor congressional tax levies. However, Pinckney's proposals could not even win agreement in the Congress, much less secure the approval of thirteen separate states. One month later, a convention, called by Virginia to discuss problems of interstate commerce, opened at Annapolis. Only delegates from New York, New Jersey, Delaware, Pennsylvania, and Virginia attended. New Hampshire, Massachusetts, Rhode Island, and North Carolina accepted invitations to attend the convention, but their delegates failed to arrive on time; Georgia, South Carolina, Connecticut, and Maryland refused to attend. The delegates realized that with such poor representation any discussions would be fruitless. So instead, the convention adopted Alexander Hamilton's call for the states to send representatives to a new convention to be held in Philadelphia in May, 1787, for the purpose of revising the Articles of Confederation. The Congress gave its blessing to Hamilton's resolution, and every state except Rhode Island agreed to send delegates to the convention.

The Constitutional Convention

After some delay caused by tardy arrivals, the Constitutional Convention finally opened for business on May 25, 1787. Among the fifty-five delegates were such distinguished men as George Washington (who was elected president of the convention), Benjamin Franklin, James Madison,

The signing of the Constitution in 1787.

George Mason, Roger Sherman, Gouverneur Morris, James Wilson, and Alexander Hamilton. Of the fifty-five delegates, twenty-nine were college educated (a very high proportion for that age). More than half of the delegates were lawyers; the others were planters, merchants, physicians, and college professors. It was soon decided to entirely discard the Articles of Confederation and draft a new instrument of government. The major problem facing the delegates was how to create a central government powerful enough to secure effective government, but not so powerful that it would become tyrannical.

The Virginia Plan. On May 29th, Edmund Randolph proposed an organization of government favoring the larger states and known as the Virginia Plan. He called for the following:

(1) A bicameral national legislature in which each state would be represented in proportion to the size of its population.

(2) The lower house would be elected by the people (more precisely, by those people qualified to vote in state elections).

(3) The upper house would be elected by the lower house from lists of nominees supplied by the state legislatures.

(4) A chief executive (with the power to veto acts of the legislature) would be elected by the legislature.

(5) A federal court system would be established to enforce acts of the national government and foreign treaties.

The New Jersey Plan. The Virginia Plan was opposed by the smaller states, who rightfully felt that they would be completely overshadowed by the larger states in the councils of the government. Consequently, New Jersey's William Paterson drew up a counterplan in June which contained the following proposals:

(1) The Articles of Confederation would be retained, and all states would have equal representation in the Congress.

(2) Congress would have the right to levy direct taxes and regulate commerce.

(3) The executive branch of the government would be plural, but would have no veto power.

(4) A federal court would be established to enforce acts of Congress.

The Connecticut Compromise. The New Jersey Plan appeared as unfair to the larger states as the Virginia Plan had appeared to the smaller states, and the convention deadlocked over the issue of proportional representation. It was not until July that Connecticut's Roger Sherman proposed a mutually agreeable compromise solution. His plan called for these measures:

(1) The lower house of the national legislature would be elected by the people and would represent each state in accordance to its population. (In a separate and later agreement, it was decided that representation would be based on the whole number of the white population with Negro slaves counting as three-fifths the number of whites. In other words, for purposes of both taxation and representation five Negroes counted as three whites. This satisfied the South by increasing its representation in Congress, and it satisfied the North by making the South liable to taxation on its slave population.)

(2) The upper house of the national legislature would give equal representation to all states, regardless of their size. Since the upper house could veto acts of the lower house, this would maintain the doctrine of state equality in the councils of the national government.

Acceptance of the Connecticut Compromise cleared the way for the Great Debate of August-September, 1787, in which the final details of the proposed new government were hammered out.

The Structure of Government

As finally worked out, the structure of the new government followed Montesquieu's dictum that only a system of checks and balances could preserve liberty and check the misuse of governmental authority. Consequently, each branch of the national government had clearly defined powers and was responsible to a different constituency. The major institutions of government as finally worked out by the Constitutional Convention are described below.

(1) **The House of Representatives.** The House was to be elected by all those people qualified to vote for members of the lower House of their respective state legislatures, and the size of each

state's congressional delegation would be determined by the numbers of its population. Each representative would be elected for a two-year term, as short terms (necessitating frequent elections) were felt to reflect the popular will more accurately than a long congressional term would. All revenue measures would have to originate in the House, and no bill would become law which failed to receive the House's approval.

(2) **The Senate.** In the Senate, each state would be guaranteed two votes. Senators would be elected for six-year terms, in such manner as each state would deem fit. (Invariably, senators were elected by the state legislature and were expected to represent the interests of their state. The popular election of senators did not come about until 1913.) The Senate would have the power to veto measures passed by the House and was to approve major presidential appointments (advise and consent); it was also to have the responsibility of ratifying treaties made with foreign powers.

(3) **The President.** Selected by the Electoral College (electors chosen by the state legislature or the voters for the express purpose of selecting a president), the President would be elected for a four-year term. He would be commander-in-chief of the nation's armed forces and would conduct foreign policy (though the Senate had to ratify treaties, and only Congress could declare war). He would have power to veto proposed laws (a two-thirds vote of each house of Congress was necessary to override a presidential veto) and he would execute federal law. He would make all major civil and military appointments (subject to Senate approval) and would have authority to pardon persons convicted of federal crimes.

(4) **The Supreme Court.** The Constitution did not fix the size of the Supreme Court (it has had as few as five members), but it did provide that its Justices would be appointed by the President (with Senatorial approval) and would hold life tenure during good behavior. The Supreme Court was to have the power to hear all cases involving a federal question (the allegation that a state was violating federal law for instance, or cases concerning the requirements of the Constitution). It would handle suits involving foreign citizens, would settle disputes among the states, and would have the right to hear appeals from the lower federal courts.

(5) **The Electoral College.** In the Electoral College, the voting strength of each state was equal to the total number of its representatives in the Congress (House and Senate). With no provision made for political parties, the Founding Fathers expected each elector to vote for two men for President, one of whom must be from outside the elector's own state. The man who received an absolute majority of the electoral votes cast would be designated as the President, and the runner-up would be Vice-President. In the event that no one received a majority of the votes cast, the House of Representatives (with each state casting a single vote) would select the President from among the three men receiving the highest number of electoral votes (the House would be under no obligation to select the candidate with the largest plurality). The founders of the Constitution felt that the Presidency was an office of too much power to permit the people to elect its occupant. The Electoral College was supposed to be composed of the most distinguished and capable men of each state, and theoretically, they would elect the most capable man in the country as president.

Powers of the Congress and the States

The Constitution was a federal instrument which divided powers between the states and the national government. The states were forbidden to coin money, impair the obligations of contracts, levy import duties, negotiate with foreign powers, or declare war and make peace. The national government was empowered to regulate foreign and interstate commerce, levy customs duties, and impose direct taxes on the states (so long as it did not discriminate among the states). Moreover, the national government was required to see that each state had a republican form of government. Congress could not grant titles of nobility, tax exports, or impose religious tests for federal office-holding. Finally, federal law was declared to be "the supreme law of the land," and it was binding upon all states. Those powers not specifically delegated to the national government were left to the control and discretion of the states. This latter provision was intended to prevent Congress from usurping power and from becoming tyrannical in its exercise of power. As we shall see, however, the implied powers doctrine was to greatly expand national authority.

Ratification of the Constitution

In September, the Constitution was sent to the Congress with the proviso that it would become operative when ratified by nine states (it would not be binding upon states which withheld ratification). Congress, in turn, sent the Constitution to the separate states, instructing them to summon special ratifying conventions to consider approval or rejection of the new instrument of government. Although the states called special elections to select the members of the ratifying conventions, fully three-fourths of all eligible voters failed to cast votes (which would indicate that the furious political storm which swirled about the Constitution did not disturb the monumental apathy of the American people). Nevertheless, the supporters of the Constitution (the Federalists) and its opponents (the Anti-Federalists) waged a titanic struggle to control the ratifying conventions in New York, Massachusetts, and Virginia.

Table 4

State Ratification of the Constitution

State	Date Approved	Vote in Convention
Delaware	December 7, 1787	Unanimous
Pennsylvania	December 12, 1787	46 (Yes) 23 (No)
New Jersey	December 18, 1787	Unanimous
Georgia	January 2, 1788	Unanimous
Connecticut	January 9, 1788	128 (Yes) 40 (No)
Massachusetts	February 7, 1788	187 (Yes) 168 (No)
Maryland	April 28, 1788	63 (Yes) 11 (No)
South Carolina	May 23, 1788	149 (Yes) 73 (No)
New Hampshire	June 21, 1788	57 (Yes) 46 (No)
Virginia	June 25, 1788	89 (Yes) 79 (No)
New York	July 26, 1788	30 (Yes) 27 (No)
North Carolina	November 21, 1789	195 (Yes) 77 (No)
Rhode Island*	May 29, 1790	34 (Yes) 32 (No)

* Rhode Island had previously rejected the Constitution in a popular referendum.

Federalists vs. Anti-Federalists

Generally speaking, the Federalists drew their support from the large planters and wealthy farmers, the well-to-do merchants and lawyers; while the Anti-Federalists drew their support from poor farmers and artisans. This, however, is a gross oversimplification, for the battle over the Constitution transcended social class and economic standing.* There were wealthy planters and merchants who opposed the Constitution, and there were poor farmers and artisans who supported it. The Anti-Federalists were those who feared centralized authority, those who were fearful that even with a system of checks and balances the national government would still become an oppressive force. Federalists, on the other hand, worried more about the weakness of the present national government than they did about the possible abuse of power by the proposed new government. Waged in the newspapers, broadsides, and in the conventions themselves, the struggle between the Federalists and Anti-Federalists centered in the three crucial states of Massachusetts, New York and Virginia. If any of these states rejected the Constitution, the success of the new government would be doubtful; if all rejected it, it would be doomed.

Massachusetts

When the Massachusetts convention first met, the Anti-Federalists appeared to be in the majority. However, during the course of the debates on the Constitution, it was suggested that civil liberties could be safeguarded by the addition of a Bill of Rights. The promise of a Bill of Rights enabled Sam Adams to throw his support to the Federalists, and he carried enough delegates with him to insure Massachusetts' ratification of the Constitution.

New York

With New Hampshire's ratification on June 21, 1788, the Constitution of the United States became a living document, but New York had still to ratify; if it did not, then New England would

---

* Charles A. Beard's contention (enunciated in *An Economic Interpretation of the Constitution of the United States,* 1913) that the Constitution was a conservative counterrevolution against the democratic idealism of the Declaration of Independence and was designed to safeguard the interests of property holders and creditors is no longer considered valid. The primary purpose of the Constitution was not to protect property interests, but to solve the problem of federalism: that is, how power should be divided between the states and the national government.

be physically cut off from the rest of the union. Governor George Clinton and a large segment of New York's wealthy classes feared that the new government would compromise the prosperity of the state through national control over commerce. However, Alexander Hamilton, James Madison, and John Jay wrote a series of polemical essays, known as the *Federalist Papers,* which were designed to win popular support for the Constitution. While it is hard to judge how many people changed their minds as a result of reading the *Federalist Papers,* it is fair to say that they were instrumental in securing New York's ratification. On July 26, 1788, the New York Convention ratified the Constitution by the slim margin of three votes; New York had decided to give the new government a fair chance to show its worth.

Virginia

One month before New York voted its approval, Virginia had ratified the Constitution by a ten-vote margin. The support of men like George Washington, Thomas Jefferson (who had reservations), and James Madison enabled the Federalists to win the support of lesser-known delegates who were inclined to the opposition. Like Massachusetts, Virginia approved the Constitution on the condition that a bill of rights safeguarding civil liberties be added to it.

On March 4, 1789, the first Congress under the new Constitution assembled in New York City (the temporary capital); and on April 30, 1789, George Washington took the oath of office as the first President of the United States. It remained to be seen whether the new government would vindicate the aspirations of the men who framed the Constitution.

From the Independent Chronicle and Universal Advertiser, Boston, Thursday June 26, 1788.

REVIEW QUESTIONS FOR CHAPTER 10

1. As a general rule, the new state constitutions shared all of the following features *except*

    (A) weak governors
    (B) bicameral legislatures
    (C) universal manhood suffrage
    (D) judicial tenure

2. Under the Articles of Confederation, Congress did *not* have the right to

    (A) establish a post office
    (B) coin money
    (C) declare war
    (D) regulate commerce

3. The survey and sale of western land was provided for in

    (A) the Ordinance of 1784
    (B) the Land Ordinance of 1785
    (C) the Northwest Ordinance
    (D) the Great Compromise

4. The Northwest Ordinance of 1787 provided for all of the following *except*

    (A) the institution of slavery
    (B) public support of education
    (C) freedom of religion
    (D) a governor appointed by Congress

5. The Virginia Plan did not call for

    (A) a federal court system
    (B) state equality in Congress
    (C) a single chief executive
    (D) a bicameral legislature

6. The New Jersey Plan was proposed by

    (A) Edmund Randolph
    (B) Roger Sherman
    (C) James Wilson
    (D) William Paterson

7. Under the Constitution, Congress did not have the power to

    (A) tax exports
    (B) tax imports
    (C) regulate interstate commerce
    (D) levy taxes on the states

8. Who was not an author of the *Federalist Papers?*

    (A) Alexander Hamilton
    (B) James Madison
    (C) Sam Adams
    (D) John Jay

9. Generally, all of the following groups were Federalists *except*

    (A) planters
    (B) merchants
    (C) lawyers
    (D) artisans

10. The last state to ratify the Constitution was

    (A) New York
    (B) Rhode Island
    (C) Virginia
    (D) Massachusetts

Explanatory Answers

1. **(C)** Property requirements for voting were still retained.

2. **(D)** The states retained jurisdiction over their own commerce.

3. **(B)** Land was sold in 640-acre sections at a minimum price of a dollar per acre.

4. **(A)** Slavery was barred from the Northwest Territory.

5. **(B)** States were to be represented in accordance with their population.

6. **(D)** Paterson was a delegate from New Jersey who formulated the views of the smaller states.

7. **(A)** Customs duties apply only to imports, not exports.

8. **(C)** Adams was an Anti-Federalist leader in Massachusetts who supported the Constitution when promised a bill of rights to safeguard individual liberties.

9. **(D)** Artisans tended to be Anti-Federalists.

10. **(B)** Rhode Island did not ratify until 1790.

Chapter 11

THE FEDERALISTS UNDER WASHINGTON AND ADAMS, 1789-1801

In February, 1789, the members of the Electoral College cast their ballots for President of the United States. Receiving all sixty-nine votes, George Washington was unanimously elected President, and John Adams (who had received thirty-four votes) became Vice-President. It was fortunate that Washington was selected, for the new government still had to prove itself. While the President had enormous potential power, the exact boundaries of that power had yet to be defined, and the policies pursued by the President would go far in determining the nature of the presidential office. A weaker man might have failed to live up to the responsibilities of his office, and a more ambitious one might have sought personal aggrandizement. Under Washington's firm leadership, the government of the United States endured its first trials, and emerged from them stronger and more viable. And the Presidency was established as a post for dynamic and vital leadership.

WASHINGTON'S FIRST TERM 1789-1793

Launching the New Government

Obligated by their promises to the Massachusetts and Virginia ratifying conventions, the Federalists had to draft a Bill of Rights to the Constitution. However, they did not want to call a second constitutional convention and run the risk of undoing their previous work, so at the suggestion of James Madison, they decided to offer the Bill of Rights in the form of amendments to the Constitution. Between September 9 and December 22, 1789, the Bill of Rights was adopted as the first ten amendments to the Constitution. Like similar state bills of rights, the amendments guaranteed freedom of worship, speech, and the press; prohibited cruel and unusual punishments; protected the person, home, and property from unlawful search and seizure; barred the self-incrimination of individuals, and left to the states all powers not specifically delegated to the national government.

During the summer and early fall of 1789, Washington named the heads of the executive departments of the government. Thomas Jefferson was named as Secretary of State, Alexander Hamilton became Secretary of the Treasury, Henry Knox became Secretary of War, and Samuel Osgood was named as Postmaster General. It was Washington's policy to consult with his department heads regarding the formulation and implementation of domestic and foreign policies, and from these meetings, the President's Cabinet emerged. The Constitution made no provision for a Cabinet to advise the President, so that Washington's Cabinet

Washington and his Cabinet: (left to right) George Washington; Henry Knox, Sec. of War; Alexander Hamilton, Sec. of the Treasury; Thomas Jefferson, Sec. of State; Edmund Randolph, Attorney General.

was an extralegal device. However, it proved useful in guiding the President's policies, and by the time of John Adams' administration, it was a regular feature of the government.

Also in September, 1789, Congress passed the Federal Judiciary Act, which created a Supreme Court consisting of a Chief Justice and five Associate Justices. Under the Supreme Court, Congress created three circuit courts (when the Supreme Court was not in session, the Justices were expected to "ride the circuit" and preside over the circuit courts), and thirteen district courts. The Act also provided for the office of Attorney General to prosecute violations of federal law. Washington named John Jay as Chief Justice, and selected Edmund Randolph to serve as Attorney General.

Hamilton's First Report on the Public Credit and the Emergence of Political Parties

The Founding Fathers had hoped that America might escape the divisive influence of political parties. They saw political parties as representing special economic or social interests which sought to control the government to their own advantage and to the detriment of the public interest. The founders had hoped that the national government would be run by disinterested statesmen who would put the good of the whole society ahead of personal or factional concerns. However, during Washington's first term, the Federalist - Anti-Federalist schism (which had come into existence during the struggle over ratification of the Constitution) was revived by the policies of Alexander Hamilton.

The fiscal and economic program devised by Alexander Hamilton was the major political issue of Washington's first term. On January 14, 1790, Hamilton proposed that the debt inherited from the Confederation (11.7 million dollars was owed to foreign creditors, and 44.4 million dollars was owed to domestic creditors) be refunded at face value. Thus, holders of depreciated Confederation securities could turn them in for new interest-bearing bonds issued by the national government. He further proposed that the Revolutionary War debt incurred by the states (up to 21.5 million dollars) also be assumed as an obligation of the national government. Hamilton's purpose was to establish and strengthen the credit of the United States, thereby creating foreign and domestic confidence in the government. In addition, he was convinced that the new government would not survive unless the powerful business and commercial interests (who held the domestic debt) were bound to the government by ties of financial interest. There was no better way to create that financial attachment than by making the American business community recipients of new government bonds.

The Opposition to Assumption

There was no question about the national government's obligation to redeem the foreign debt incurred by the Confederation, but the other aspects of Hamilton's program aroused a vehement opposition. Spokesmen for the agrarian interests condemned Hamilton's program as (1) creating a moneyed aristocracy which would dominate the nation in the interests of commerce and to the detriment of agriculture, (2) dangerously enlarging the powers of the national government at the expense of the states, and (3) benefiting speculators who had purchased the depreciated securities of indebted farmers and veterans far below face value and who would now reap a rich reward by receiving the face value of their securities. Moreover, the Southern states (which had largely liquidated their debts) objected to being taxed to pay the debt of Northern states which had defaulted on their obligations. As was to be expected, Thomas Jefferson opposed Hamilton's funding scheme; and James Madison, who had been a strong supporter of the new government, also broke with the Federalists. In April, the House defeated Hamilton's assumption plan by a vote of 31 to 29, and the Republican (or Democratic-Republican) opposition to the Federalists began to crystallize.

The Sectional Compromise

Unwilling to admit defeat, Hamilton kept the assumption issue alive in Congress. In June, Madison arranged a dinner between Hamilton and Jefferson. Hamilton proposed a sectional compromise on the debt issue. He promised to use his influence to have the permanent capital of the national government established in the South along the banks of the Potomac if the Southern agrarians would enact his assumption plan. Jefferson, in particular, was anxious to have the capital located in the South where the agrarian interests could exercise a restraining influence over the policies of the government; and he and Madison agreed to Hamilton's proposal. In July, 1790, Congress established the District of Columbia as the future site of the capital (the capital was to remain in Philadelphia until 1800) and passed Hamilton's assumption plan. The Federalists had scored an initial victory.

The Bank of the United States

On December 13, 1790, Hamilton proposed the creation of a federally chartered Bank of the United States. Under his plan, the national government would own 20 per cent of the Bank's shares (the Bank would be capitalized at $10,000,000), with private investors holding the remaining 80 per cent. The shareholders would elect a twenty-five-man board of directors who would elect the president of the Bank. The Bank would be chartered for a twenty-year period; it would conduct regular commercial banking, issue notes equal to the amount of its capitalization, and serve as a repository of government funds. It was Hamilton's hope that the Bank of the United States would create a sound national currency, strengthen confidence in the financial integrity of the national government, and permit stable economic growth by making needed credit available to the business community. However, Washington was uncertain as to the constitutionality of the bank, and he requested opinions from his Cabinet members.

Jefferson and Strict Construction

Thomas Jefferson argued that the Bank of the United States was unconstitutional since the power to charter a bank was not among the powers granted to Congress under the Constitution. Banking was properly the preserve of the separate states, which retained authority over all functions not specifically entrusted to the Congress. Jefferson believed that the Constitution should be "strictly constructed," and the national government should adopt no measures unless they were specifically related to powers and functions granted by the Constitution. The doctrine of strict construction was to be a rallying cry for Southern agrarians down to the Civil War — and beyond.

Hamilton and Implied Powers

Alexander Hamilton declared that the Bank of the United States was constitutional under the "implied powers" clause, which authorized Congress to make all laws necessary for the effective execution of the powers granted it by the Constitution. Since Congress had the powers to tax, it obviously had the right to create a repository for tax revenues; since it had the power to regulate interstate commerce, it could charter a bank in order to secure a sound national credit system. Under Hamilton's interpretation, Congress had the right to do all things not specifically *prohibited* by the Constitution. Over the next two centuries, this argument would be successfully used to greatly enlarge the powers of the national government. Washington was not entirely convinced by either Jefferson or Hamilton, but he decided to support Hamilton since it was Hamilton's department that was involved with the Bank, and the President signed the Bank's charter on February 25, 1791.

Hamilton's Report on Manufactures

On December 5, 1791, Hamilton issued his classic Report on Manufactures. Wanting to unite the business classes with the national government, he proposed (1) a system of tariffs, bounties, and subsidies to promote the development of both industry and agriculture, and (2) a vast program of federally sponsored public works to facilitate transportation and commercial intercourse. While it was to be the basis for Henry Clay's American System (see page 218), Hamilton's neo-mercantilist program made only a small impression at the time; and it was vigorously opposed by the agrarian interests who wanted to keep federal power to a minimum. By and large, little of substance resulted from the report.

Federalists vs. Republicans

By the spring of 1791, Thomas Jefferson and James Madison were emerging as leaders of the Republican opposition, while Alexander Hamilton and John Adams were spokesmen for the Federalists. (Washington generally inclined toward the Federalist position and came to rely heavily on Hamilton for advice.) As Washington's first term drew to a close, the two factions differed not only on political means, but on political ends as well.

As a group, the Republicans had the following characteristics:

(1) They represented the small farmer and artisan class.

(2) They wanted America to remain a land of small, financially independent freeholders. They feared industrialism, urbanism, and organized finance as destructive to republican government; and they wanted an agrarian America in which there would be no great extremes of wealth or poverty.

(3) They feared centralized government, believed that "that government was best which governed least," and wanted the states to retain preponderant power.

(4) They believed in the essential goodness of man, were sympathetic to the plight of the debtor classes, and were confident that the people could best rule themselves.

The Federalists, on the other hand, shared these characteristics:

(1) They represented the commercial middle class, its professional allies (lawyers, Anglican and Congregational clergymen, doctors, professors, etc.), and the nationalist (as opposed to sectionalist) interests.

(2) They wanted a diversified economy, with government assistance given to industry, commerce, shipping, finance, and agriculture. They welcomed industrialism, urbanism, and organized finance as strengthening the nation; they felt that a strong nation would benefit all social classes.

(3) They wanted a strong national government, under presidential leadership, and generally sought to reduce the power of the states.

(4) They believed that man was inclined toward evil and that a strong government was necessary to restrain him. They sympathized with the wealthy classes, did not feel that the people were competent to rule themselves, and favored the rule of an elite (the natural aristocracy of the talented and the wealthy).

As Washington's first term drew to a close, Jefferson and Hamilton took an intense personal dislike to each other, and only Washington's strong hand kept his Cabinet from breaking up. In the election of 1792, Washington received 132 electoral votes (3 electors abstained from voting) and was reelected President; John Adams was reelected Vice-President with 77 votes over the Anti-Federalist (Republican) George Clinton, who received 50 second-place votes. Washington had survived the domestic storms of his first term, but foreign problems were to plague his second term.

WASHINGTON'S SECOND TERM 1793–1797

The Problem of the French Revolution

When the French Revolution broke out in 1789, almost every American (Federalist or Republican) supported it. Generally, Americans viewed the French Revolution as the struggle of the French people to secure those rights and liberties which the Americans had already secured as a result of their own revolution. However, when the French Revolution took a radical turn in 1792–1793, the Federalists (led by Hamilton) began to oppose it. They now saw the French Revolution (with the execution of the king, the seizure of lands from the church and aristocracy, and the declaration of war against Austria) as an attack against the very foundations of civilized society; and they became strongly pro-British. The Federalists now saw England as the bulwark of social order and stability. The Republicans, on the other hand (led by Jefferson), continued to support the general goals of the French Revolution. They justified its excesses on the grounds that the Old Regime was so repressive that only a violent upheaval could bring about needed reforms; although unfortunate, the violence of the French Revolution was unavoidable. For Americans, however, the problem was that under the terms of the Franco-American treaty of 1778 (which was still in force), the United States was pledged to maintain French sovereignty in the West Indies; and with France at war with England, this clause might well involve the United States in a war against England. Neither Federalists nor Republicans wanted war, but disagreements over the attitude America should take toward France further intensified the Federalist-Republican division and helped give shape to the American two-party system.

The Neutrality Proclamation and Citizen Genêt

In April of 1793, George Washington issued a proclamation of neutrality (which, strangely enough, did not mention the word "neutrality"). The proclamation declared that the United States was at peace with both England and France and wished both nations well; and it warned American citizens to refrain from hostile acts directed against either power. Supported by the leaders of both political factions, the proclamation expressed America's deep desire to remain at peace. Fortunately, France did not wish America's active military assistance — realizing that America had little military power, the French simply preferred to have our friendship. In April, 1793, Citizen Genêt was sent to America by the French revolutionary government to secure a favorable trade agreement. France wanted American produce and naval stores and hoped that neutral American ships could penetrate the British blockade erected against the French. Unfortunately, Genêt, who was given a hero's reception by the American people, exceeded his authority and undermined Franco-American relations.

In South Carolina, Genêt commissioned several American ship captains to act as privateers against the British (a privateer was an auxiliary naval unit authorized by one nation to attack the shipping of a hostile power). But, had American vessels attacked British ships, the English would certainly have considered it a belligerent act of the United States government. Moreover, Genêt was raising military units on American soil for campaigns against neighboring Spanish and English colonies. Had these colonies been attacked from American bases, it would have compromised American neutrality. Washington angrily demanded that Genêt refrain from such activities, and the French minister agreed to do so, but later went back on his promise. In August, 1793, the United States demanded that the French recall Genêt and replace him with a new minister. The Jacobins had since come to power in France, and they also wanted Genêt's return to France, for they planned to put him on trial (he was a member of the ousted Girondist faction). Genêt was permitted to remain in America as a political exile. The upshot of the Citizen Genêt affair was that Washington relied more heavily on Hamilton's advice in foreign relations and veered away from the pursuit of friendship with France. Dismayed at this state of affairs, Jefferson resigned as Secretary of State on July 31, 1793 (his resignation was effective as of December 31, 1793). To ease growing tensions with Great Britain, the Neutrality Act was passed by Congress in June, 1794. It forbade American citizens to engage in hostile acts against any nation at peace with America and outlawed the outfitting of armed foreign vessels in American ports.

The Whisky Insurrection

The mounting crisis over foreign policy was temporarily interrupted by the Whisky Insurrection of July-November, 1794. The farmers of western Pennsylvania objected to the excise tax imposed on their homemade whisky. (In the absence of effective transportation systems, wheat could not easily be hauled to market in bulk form. It was, therefore, processed into whisky which was easier to transport and which brought a better price on the market.) When the farmers prevented federal agents from collecting the tax, Washington (in August) ordered the farmers to cease their interference and return to their homes. The stubborn farmers refused, and Washington (in September) ordered the militia to suppress the insurrection and uphold the authority of federal law. Once the troops were called out, the insurrection quickly collapsed, and its leaders were tried for treason. Two men were sentenced to death, but Washington pardoned them the following year. Although a minor episode, the Whisky Insurrection was still important in that it was the first serious challenge to federal law. Its speedy suppression showed that the national government had the will and the means to enforce its edicts.

Jay's Treaty

The outbreak of war in Europe severely strained Anglo-American relations. As a neutral power, the United States claimed the right to trade in noncontraband goods (items not used for military purposes) with any nation wishing to do business with her. But England, wanting to undermine the economic strength of France, issued her Orders in Council in 1793, which interfered with American neutral trade. Under the so-called Rule of 1756, England maintained that any trade which was illegal in time of peace could not be made legal during time of war. In other words, if French mercantile laws prohibited Americans from engaging in certain types of trade during peacetime, such trade could not be legalized during times of war. The British used this doctrine to justify their seizure of American vessels. They further outraged Americans by the impressment of American sailors. Under British law, sailors who deserted from Brit-

John Jay

ish ships could be re-impressed into the British navy if they were found serving on neutral vessels. Since Britain was short of men, and since it was not always easy to distinguish an American from an Englishman, impressment was much abused. England literally kidnapped American sailors and forced them to serve on British ships (indeed, the British did not recognize American naturalization and maintained that once born an Englishman, one remained English all one's life). As a result, America and England verged on war in 1794. That spring, John Jay was sent to England to secure British evacuation of the Northwest Territory, win recognition of American neutral rights, end impressment, and secure a favorable commercial treaty.* In November, 1794, Jay concluded

---

* Jay's bargaining power was undercut by information given the British by an American secret agent, known as No. 7. This agent told the British how far America was prepared to go before declaring war, so that England made concessions only on the most sensitive issues and refused to concede on the lesser issues. Agent No. 7 was none other than Alexander Hamilton.

his negotiations with the British and agreed to a treaty which provided for the following:

(1) England promised to withdraw from the Northwest Territory by June 1, 1796. This was a major victory for the United States, for it would give America effective control of the lucrative fur trade and would end British-instigated Indian raids against American settlements in the Ohio Valley.

(2) American ships were admitted to British East India ports on a non-discriminatory basis and were admitted to the West Indian ports with restrictions on their cargoes.

(3) The question of pre-Revolutionary debts owed to England and the question of compensation for seized American cargoes were to be referred to a joint commission for settlement.

(4) Finally, American trade with Britain was put on a most-favored nation basis, which meant that America would receive the benefits given by England to her most-favored trading partner.

Opposition to Jay's Treaty

When the terms of Jay's Treaty were released in March, 1795, they pleased few people. New England was angered by the treaty's continued restrictions on trade with the West Indies, and Virginia resented the submission of the debt question (since most of the money was owed by Virginia) to a joint commission. Moreover, the treaty made no mention of the impressment issue, and it failed to secure repeal of the Rule of 1756 and to guarantee recognition of American neutral rights. The Republicans took the lead in organizing the opposition to Jay's Treaty. Even Washington was not entirely satisfied with it, but accepted it as the best that America could get at the time. After prolonged debate, the Senate finally ratified the treaty in June, but it deleted the unacceptable clause relating to the West Indian trade. A stopgap measure, Jay's Treaty failed to resolve the fundamental conflict with England over American neutral rights. It was to take another war to set the matter right. Nevertheless, Jay's Treaty aroused French antagonism. France felt that America had defaulted on its obligations under the Franco-American Treaty of 1778, and the French began to harass American shipping in much the same fashion as the English had done.

Pinckney's Treaty

Having glossed over its differences with England, the United States, in 1795, sought to normalize relations with Spain. In October, Thomas Pinckney negotiated a treaty with Spain which provided for Spanish recognition of the thirty-first parallel as the southern boundary of the United States and of the Mississippi River as the western boundary (in short, the boundaries of the 1783 Treaty of Paris were recognized by Spain). In addition, America was given free navigation rights on the Mississippi, with the right to deposit American produce at New Orleans for three years — Spain reserved the right to renegotiate the deposit privilege. Pinckney's Treaty was instrumental in satisfying Western demands for access to the Gulf of Mexico and helped to repair the loss of prestige resulting from Jay's Treaty.

Washington's Farewell Address

By September of 1796, Washington's second term as President was drawing to a close; and with the aid of Madison and Hamilton, he wrote his classic "Farewell Address" (actually, it was never delivered in public, but was published in a Philadelphia newspaper). It contained four main points:

(1) He would not stand for a third term as President of the United States, as he felt that an extended tenure would not serve the interests of republican government. Washington thus established the tradition (not broken until 1940) that a President should not serve more than two consecutive terms, and he lent his authority to the idea that a periodic change of leadership preserved republican liberties.

(2) He warned against the development of sectional antagonisms (South versus North, West versus East) as undermining the unity of the nation, and he deplored the rise of political factions (or parties) which, he felt, contributed to the intensification of sectional rivalry.

(3) He urged the American people to safeguard and maintain the public credit of the United States.

(4) He cautioned against the United States entering into permanent alliances with foreign

powers. (The word "entangling" was not used by Washington, but was later used by Jefferson and erroneously applied to Washington.) However, Washington did not advise a policy of isolation, and he specifically urged the nation to form temporary alliances to meet and overcome foreign emergencies.

Washington had given shape, direction, and force to the Presidency. He instituted the Cabinet system, established the two-term tradition, and vigorously maintained the authority of federal law. With the aid of Hamilton, he redeemed the public credit and established a sound system of national credit. In foreign affairs, he secured British evacuation of the Northwest Territory, and he gave the nation a much-needed period of peace during which it was able to develop sound political and economic institutions.

The Election of 1796

The removal of Washington's strong hand from the helm of government gave rein to the rapid development of political parties. The election of 1796 was a close contest, and gave evidence of the rising strength of the Democratic-Republican party. In the Electoral College, Federalist John Adams received 71 votes to 68 for the Democratic-Republican Thomas Jefferson. Federalist Thomas Pinckney received 59 votes, and Aaron Burr, another Democratic-Republican, finished last with 30 votes. Although John Adams was elected President, his arch-rival Thomas Jefferson became Vice-President, even though he opposed most of Adams' principles and programs.

THE ADMINISTRATION OF JOHN ADAMS, 1797–1801

"His Rotundity, the President of the United States"

It was John Adams' misfortune to follow George Washington as President — he could not help but suffer by comparison. A recognized authority on political and constitutional theory, Adams was a capable lawyer, but he lacked the stature and charisma of Washington. Short and plump, he was called "His Rotundity" by political detractors. Moreover, he made the mistake of retaining Hamiltonians in his Cabinet (Hamilton had broken with

John Adams.

Adams and had intrigued to elect Thomas Pinckney as President) and they often undermined his programs. Nevertheless, his taking office in March, 1797, marked the first peaceful transfer of power under the United States Constitution and demonstrated that a republican government could achieve the orderly transfer of power from one man to another.

The XYZ Affair

By the time Adams assumed office in March, 1797, France, whose relations with the United States remained strained, had already seized some three hundred American vessels, and the two countries verged on open warfare. That spring, Adams named Charles C. Pinkney, John Marshall, and Elbridge Gerry (of Gerrymander fame) as commissioners to France, with instructions to secure a treaty of friendship and commerce with the French. Arriving in Paris in October, the American commissioners were kept waiting by Talleyrand, France's foreign minister. Finally, three agents of Talleyrand (designated XYZ in the American report of the incident) called on the commissioners and declared that France would open negotiations only if the United States extended France a loan and paid a $250,000 bribe to Talleyrand. The American commissioners stoutly refused Talleyrand's demands, and the negotiations failed. In April, 1798, the XYZ Affair was made known to the American people, who, regardless of political affiliation, turned strongly against France. "Millions for defense, not one cent for tribute" was a cry heard throughout the land, and the Hamiltonians in Adams' Cabinet demanded war against France.

The Undeclared Naval War of 1798-1800

John Adams, however, refused to declare war on France, preferring to follow a peaceful course while strengthening national defense. In the spring and summer of 1798, Congress repealed the 1778 treaty with France and passed twenty measures designed to bolster the army and create a navy. Nevertheless, an undeclared naval war (centered in the Caribbean) broke out between the United States and France. Although the Americans took about a hundred French ships, and sustained comparatively light losses themselves, the results of the conflict were inconclusive; and the hostilities were officially ended by the Convention of 1800. The Convention released the United States from its 1778 treaty with France and recognized the American principle that "neutral ships make neutral goods" and, therefore, are not subject to seizure. However, the French refused to compensate the United States for the Americans' prior losses, and the Convention was vigorously opposed by the Hamiltonians, whose rupture with Adams became irrevocable. Adams, nevertheless, had kept the United States out of war, and had followed Washington's example of avoiding war if at all possible.

The Alien and Sedition Acts

Although Franco-American relations were at a low ebb, many leading members of the Democratic-Republican opposition were European refugees, and it was assumed by some Americans that these refugees would be in sympathy with France. Indeed, many Federalists became convinced that their political opponents were active agents of the French revolutionaries, and were working to undermine the American government and align the United States with France. Capitalizing on the anti-French and anti-foreign sentiment which was sweeping America, the Federalists pushed the Alien and Sedition Acts through Congress. They consisted of the following:

(1) **The Naturalization Act (June, 1798).** It extended from five to fourteen years the period of American residence required for citizenship, and it was designed to give the government more time in which to deport "subversive" aliens. It was repealed in 1802.

(2) **The Alien Act (June, 1798).** This measure empowered the President to deport any alien who was regarded as a threat to the public peace or safety, and it deprived accused aliens of constitutional safeguards. The act was allowed to expire in 1802.

(3) **The Alien Enemies Act (July, 1798).** In time of war, the President was authorized to arrest and deport all aliens who were subjects of the enemy power.

(4) **The Sedition Act (July, 1798).** This act made it a criminal offense for any American citizen or alien to interfere with the execution of federal law or to incite "insurrection, riot, or unlawful assembly" against the government. It also provided for $2,000 fines and two years imprisonment for anyone who published material designed to bring into "disrepute" the United States Government or its officers (the President). However, the Sedition Act was meant to expire with the term of office of the incumbent President; it was a blatant attempt to shield the Adams administration from public criticism by the Democratic-Republican opposition.

Effects of the Sedition Act

The Sedition Act was invoked only against Republican editors, and it was condemned by the Republicans as an arbitrary, despotic, and unconstitutional abridgment of freedom of speech and freedom of the press. By making martyrs of Republican editors, the measure rallied public opinion to the support of the opposition party and severely undermined public confidence in, and support of, the administration of Federalist John Adams. The Sedition Act was a major issue in the election of 1800, and it is considered to be a prime factor in the defeat of the Federalists. It also gave rise to the Kentucky and Virginia Resolutions of 1798 and 1799 respectively.

The Kentucky Resolutions were written by Jefferson and the Virginia Resolutions, by Madison. These measures were passed by their respective state legislatures, and they both set forth the compact theory of the Constitution. The Resolutions held that the national government was formed by the several states, and that whenever the national government exercised powers not specifically delegated to it by the Constitution, each state had the right to judge for itself as to the constitutionality of federal law. The states were thus the final arbiters of constitutionality; and the implication was that if a given state ruled an Act of Congress unconstitutional, that act would be null and void within the boundaries of that state. The Kentucky and Virginia Resolutions were condemned by the Northern states, which held that the federal courts and not the states were the final judges of constitutionality. At this time Kentucky and Virginia made no effort to impede or nullify the enforcement of the Sedition Act, and both proclaimed their loyalty to the Union. However, the doctrine which they set forth would later be picked up by the Southern states to justify both their opposition to federal law and their eventual secession from the Union. The philosophy embodied in the Kentucky and Virginia Resolutions gave rise to a dispute over the nature of the American Union that later was to be settled only by battle — and by the death of more than half a million Americans.

REVIEW QUESTIONS FOR CHAPTER 11

1. The doctrine of implied powers is associated with

    (A) Thomas Jefferson
    (B) James Madison
    (C) George Washington
    (D) Alexander Hamilton

2. The Republicans believed in all of the following *except*

    (A) strong state power
    (B) strong central government
    (C) the agrarian social order
    (D) the political supremacy of the small farmer

3. The Federalists believed in all of the following *except*

    (A) federal aid to industry
    (B) the rule of an elite
    (C) weak central government
    (D) strong presidential leadership

4. Jay's Treaty provided for all of the following *except*

    (A) repeal of the Rule of 1756
    (B) British evacuation of the Northwest Territory
    (C) most-favored nation status for the United States
    (D) limited United States trade with West Indies

5. Pinckney's Treaty did not provide for

    (A) free navigation of the Mississippi
    (B) the United States' right of deposit at New Orleans
    (C) recognition of the 1783 border
    (D) free trade with Latin America

6. In his "Farewell Address," Washington did not advise

    (A) formation of a two-party system
    (B) isolation
    (C) unlimited reelection of the president
    (D) permanent alliances

7. John Adams named all of the following as commissioners to France *except*

    (A) Charles C. Pinckney
    (B) Thomas Pinckney
    (C) John Marshall
    (D) Elbridge Gerry

8. The Hamiltonians opposed the Convention of 1800 because it

    (A) failed to compensate the United States for ship seizures
    (B) failed to repeal the Rule of 1756
    (C) failed to release the United States from the 1778 treaty
    (D) failed to give the United States trade concessions

9. The Sedition Act was aimed against

   (A) aliens
   (B) Hamiltonians
   (C) Republicans
   (D) pro-French radicals

10. The Kentucky Resolutions were written by

    (A) James Madison
    (B) Thomas Jefferson
    (C) John Marshall
    (D) Thomas Pinckney

Explanatory Answers

1. **(D)** The doctrine holds that Congress may do all things not specifically prohibited by the Constitution.

2. **(B)** The Republicans felt that "that government is best which governs least."

3. **(C)** The Federalists favored strong national power.

4. **(A)** England refused to recognize the free trading rights of neutrals.

5. **(D)** Free trade with Latin America was not sought.

6. **(B)** Washington merely warned against entering into permanent alliances.

7. **(B)** Thomas Pinckney negotiated the treaty with Spain.

8. **(A)** France refused to pay for the cargoes it illegally seized.

9. **(C)** The act was designed to stifle Republican criticism of the Adams administration.

10. **(B)** Jefferson enunciated the compact theory of the Constitution.

Chapter 12

JEFFERSONIAN AMERICA, 1801-1809

Thomas Jefferson called the election of 1800 a revolution, and he considered it as second in importance only to the American Revolution itself. Jefferson's estimation, however, was somewhat exaggerated. The Federalists, representing neo-mercantilistic, nationalistic, and elitist interests did lose the election to the Republicans, who stood for a laissez faire policy (no governmental intervention in the economy, either for or against businessmen), states' rights, and the rule of the common farmer. However, the results of the transfer of power were more symbolic than substantive. Jefferson, for example, made no efforts to undo Hamilton's funding program or his policy of assumption of state debts; nor did he attempt to repeal the charter of the Bank of the United States. Moreover, under the pressure of events, Jefferson was forced to abandon much of his strict constructionism in favor of the Hamiltonian concept of implied powers. Indeed, Jefferson had to pursue certain policies which actually tended to increase federal power. Also, like John Adams, Jefferson could not adequately resolve the problem of Anglo-French interference with American seaborne commerce, and he left office with a major portion of the nation disgusted with his foreign policy.

The Election of 1800

By 1800, the American people were disgruntled by the high taxes imposed by the Federalists (to finance defense improvements), and they were angered by the Sedition Act. Nevertheless, the results of state-legislature elections indicated that the presidential election would be quite close (generally, the Electoral College was selected by the state legislatures). Indeed, the election of 1800 was one of the most bitter contests in American history. Federalists accused Thomas Jefferson of being an atheist, a Jacobin who was conspiring with the French, and an indolent pleasure-seeker who had fathered mulatto children. For their part, the Republicans accused John Adams of being an Anglophile with monarchist tendencies, of living like a debauched aristocrat, and of undermining republican liberties. In the Electoral College, Thomas Jefferson and Aaron Burr both received seventy-three votes for President, while John Adams received sixty-five; Charles C. Pinckney received sixty-four votes, and John Jay, one. Since there was no separate ballot for Vice-President, Jefferson and Burr tied for the Presidency, even though the Electors intended Jefferson to be President and Burr to be Vice-President. The election was thrown into the House of Representatives, which would select the President from among the three highest candidates.

In the House, Jefferson had the support of eight states, while Burr was supported by six;

Thomas Jefferson

and two states were evenly divided between them. The Federalists, who could not elect Adams but who could defeat Jefferson, were determined to support Aaron Burr and deny Jefferson the Presidency. For thirty-five ballots, the House was deadlocked, with no faction strong enough to elect its choice. Finally, Alexander Hamilton used his influence to break the deadlock. While he bitterly opposed Jefferson, he realized that Jefferson was a man of character and integrity, whereas he recognized Burr as an unprincipled political opportunist. For the good of the nation, Hamilton threw his support to Jefferson; and on the thirty-sixth ballot, James A. Bayard (Delaware's lone Congressman) voted for Jefferson and thus elected him President. The election had demonstrated the shortcomings of the Electoral College system. To prevent a repetition of the Jefferson-Burr fiasco, the Twelfth Amendment to the Constitution, providing for the separate election of the President and Vice-President, was passed.

Jefferson's Inaugural Address and Gallatin's Financial Policy

In his Inaugural Address (March 4, 1801), Jefferson appealed for the support of all political factions and pledged (1) a government of limited powers, (2) reduction of the national debt and of governmental expenditures, (3) support for the legitimate rights of the states, (4) acceptance of the principle of majority rule, (5) protection of civil liberties (a slap at the Alien and Sedition Acts), and (6) friendship for all nations.

Jefferson's economic policies were brilliantly executed by Albert Gallatin who was Secretary of the Treasury from 1801 to 1814. During Jefferson's two terms, Gallatin reduced the national debt from 83 million to 57 million dollars and repealed internal taxes, including the unpopular whisky tax. However, these economies succeeded at the expense of the army and navy, so that America's ability to meet the threat posed by European powers was compromised. Gallatin, however, did introduce the practice of having Congress vote appropriations for specific purposes — a reform which facilitated the development of modern budgetary techniques. Although Jefferson met with success in his financial policies, he was frustrated in his battle with the Supreme Court.

Jefferson and the Supreme Court

Anticipating increased business before the federal courts, the lame-duck administration of John Adams pushed through the Judiciary Act of 1801 which reorganized the federal court structure and permitted the last-minute appointment of Federalists to the bench. With the federal courts safely in Federalist control, the Republicans concluded that their political opponents were going to use the courts to strike down any Republican-sponsored legislation of which the Federalists did not approve. Jefferson was determined to counterattack. Although he could not remove Federalist judges without cause, he could abolish the courts over which they presided. The Judiciary Act of 1802 did just that, and it restored the federal court structure to the form it had under the Judiciary Act of 1789. However, the battle was just beginning.

Marbury versus Madison

On his last night in office, John Adams had commissioned William Marbury as a justice of the peace for the District of Columbia. However, through some oversight, the signed and sealed commission was not delivered. The next morning, it was still on the desk of the new Secretary of

State, James Madison; and President Jefferson ordered Madison to withhold delivery of Marbury's commission. Marbury brought suit in the Supreme Court, and asked for a Writ of Mandamus (as authorized by Section 13 of the Judiciary Act of 1789) which would force Madison to deliver Marbury's commission. Chief Justice John Marshall was now faced with a dilemma. If he ruled in favor of Marbury, and Jefferson refused to comply with the Court's edict, Marshall would be powerless to enforce compliance and would undermine the prestige of the Court. If he ruled against Marbury, he would give Jefferson an undeserved and partisan victory. Marshall devised a brilliant compromise. He ruled that (1) Marbury was entitled to his commission and castigated Jefferson and Madison for withholding it, but that (2) the Constitution (which defined the jurisdiction of the Supreme Court) did not give the Court original jurisdiction in matters involving Writs of Mandamus, and that (3) Section 13 of the Judiciary Act of 1789, which granted the Court such power, was unconstitutional. In short, Marbury did not get his commission, but Marshall had invalidated an act of Congress (a power not clearly granted the Court by the Constitution) and had established the principle of judicial review. The Court now had a precedent for declaring acts of Congress unconstitutional, and the real losers in Marbury versus Madison were Jefferson and the Republicans.

MAD TOM in A RAGE

Jefferson, in trying to pull down the Federal pillar, is depicted as destroying the Federal Party with the aid of the Devil.

The Impeachment Campaign

Determined to purge the bench of Federalists, Jefferson's congressional supporters hit upon impeachment as an effective method of removing Federalist judges. In 1803, John Pickering, judge of the federal district court in New Hampshire, was impeached (indicted) by the House of Representatives for his subversive political opinions. It so happened that Pickering was an alcoholic and was mentally deranged; and his indictment was, therefore, upheld by the United States Senate, sitting as a court of impeachment. Emboldened by their success against Pickering, the Republicans next moved against their enemy, Samuel Chase, Associate Justice of the Supreme Court. An extreme Federalist, Chase had presided over various sedition trials in which he displayed an open anti-Republican bias; he had even lectured the jury on the evils of democracy. However, the Senate (even though dominated by the Republicans) refused to convict Chase for his political beliefs, and he was acquitted of all charges. Chase's acquittal not only ended the impeachment campaign, but also preserved the judicial independence of the federal courts. Had Chase been convicted, John Marshall undoubtedly would have been the next target for impeachment, and the Supreme Court would have become a puppet of the executive and legislative branches of government.

The Louisiana Purchase

If Jefferson's campaign against the courts was not in the best interests of the nation, his purchase of the vast Louisiana Territory more than made up for it. In October, 1800, Napoleon forced Spain to sign the secret Treaty of San Ildefonso by which Louisiana was returned to France. Napoleon had plans to revive the once vast French empire in America, and in 1801, he sent a 20,000-man army to suppress the Negro insurrection which had broken out on the island of Haiti. After securing Haiti, Napoleon planned to use the island as a base from which to consolidate his control over Louisiana. However, when news of France's acquisition of Louisiana became known, Jefferson reacted strongly. He declared that although France was America's traditional friend, any power which controlled the mouth of the Mississippi (and thus had the power to cut off American access to the Gulf of Mexico) became the natural enemy of the United States. Since France was much stronger than Spain, French control of New Orleans was much more menacing than Spanish control over the city. Accordingly, Jefferson told the French that if they remained at New Orleans, the United States would have to "marry itself to the British fleet and nation." At the same time, Robert R. Livingston, the American minister to Paris, was instructed either to negotiate the irrevocable right of deposit at New Orleans or to purchase the port from France. In January, 1803, James Monroe was sent to Paris and was authorized to offer two million dollars for New Orleans and West Florida.

Meanwhile, Napoleon's army in Haiti had been wiped out by a slave insurrection; and without Haiti, Napoleon could not hold the Louisiana Territory. He, therefore, offered to sell the entire Louisiana Territory (exclusive of Florida) to the United States for fifteen million dollars. Monroe and Livingston jumped at the offer (even though it exceeded their instructions) and signed a treaty of transfer in May, 1803. Their action, however, posed severe constitutional problems for Jefferson. He was a strict constructionist, and the Constitution did not authorize Congress to purchase territory. At first he had wanted to pass a constitutional amendment giving Congress this right, but he realized that Napoleon might not want to wait that long before concluding the deal. Jefferson, therefore, accepted Hamiltonian reasoning and declared that the right to purchase territory was an implied corollary to Congress' power to negotiate treaties with foreign countries. Strict construction, in this instance, was sacrificed to Jefferson's desire to acquire new lands for American farmers; he hoped that the Louisiana Purchase would provide enough virgin land to maintain agrarian supremacy in the United States for centuries to come. The Senate ratified the Louisiana Purchase treaty in October, 1803, and the territory of the United States was doubled.

Problems of the Louisiana Purchase

The acquisition of Louisiana brought with it a number of new problems. First, although the Louisiana Territory stretched from the west bank of the Mississippi to the Rocky Mountains, its precise northern and southwestern boundaries were not defined. The United States claimed part of Texas as being within the Louisiana borders, and there was no indication of where Louisiana ended and Canada began. In order to learn more about the Louisiana Territory and to find a Northwest passage to the Pacific, Jefferson sent Meriwether Lewis and William Clark on an expedition to explore the area. (Actually they were dispatched before the United States acquired Louisiana.) Journeying up the Missouri River, Lewis and Clark entered Yellowstone country, crossed the Rocky Mountains, and descended the Columbia River to the Pacific Coast. While they did not find the hoped-for Northwest passage, they did strengthen America's claim to the Oregon Territory. They returned to Washington, D.C. in 1806. While Lewis and Clark were on their expedition, the army sent Zebulon Pike to seek out the sources of the Mississippi River. In 1806–1807, Pike moved up the Arkansas River into the Rockies and traveled down the Rio Grande River, where he was arrested by the Spaniards. Although these expeditions added to geographical knowledge of the West, they did little to fix the borders of the Louisiana Territory.

Although the Louisiana Purchase pleased the West and the South, it did not please New England. Fearing that New England would decline in importance as new Western states entered the Union, the Federalist Essex Junto (extremely conservative Massachusetts Federalists, led by Timothy Pickering) wanted New England to secede from the United States and form a separate Northern confederacy. The Essex Junto hoped that New York would join their proposed Northern confederacy, but the New York Federalists would have nothing to do with the plan, and most of the New Englanders were not anxious for it either. The only result of the abortive scheme was to further discredit the already-declining Federalist party.

Reform of the Land Law and the Election of 1804

The Land Ordinance of 1785 provided for the sale of public land in units of 640 acres, which was more than the average farmer could afford. In 1800, the Federalists passed a new land law which permitted the sale of half-sections (320 acres) at $2.00 per acre (one-fourth of the money down and the remainder to be paid within four years). This helped to bring public land within the reach of more Americans, and the Jefferson Land Act of 1804 helped even more. It allowed the sale of quarter-sections (160 acres) at $1.64 an acre.

As Jefferson's first term drew to a close, his administration was highly popular. He had doubled the size of the United States and had made land more easily available to people of moderate means. He had reduced the national debt, government expeditures, and the federal tax burden. In the 1804 presidential election, Thomas Jefferson easily defeated the Federalist candidate, Charles C. Pinckney, receiving 162 electoral votes to the 14 for Pinckney. He carried every state except Connecticut and Delaware. Republican George Clinton defeated Rufus King for the Vice-Presidency. However, Jefferson's popularity was to suffer during his second term, as foreign affairs once again plagued the nation.

The Burr Conspiracy

After killing Alexander Hamilton in the famous duel of July, 1804, Aaron Burr fled to the West, where he raised an expedition designed either to detach the West from the United States or to detach Texas (and possibly Mexico) from the Spanish empire. To this day, no one can say for certain what Burr's plans were, although it is fairly obvious that he intended to carve out for himself a sizeable kingdom somewhere. When informed of Burr's activities, Thomas Jefferson was readily convinced that Burr was plotting treason against the United States and he ordered his arrest. Burr was apprehended in Alabama and was brought before the federal court in Virginia, where he was tried for treason. None other than John Marshall presided over the trial, and he (in a classic definition of treason) concluded that the evidence against Burr was not sufficient to merit conviction.* Jefferson, who had ordered Burr's trial, had again been foiled by Marshall; and Burr went into a European exile to avoid prosecution for the murder of Hamilton.

---

* Marshall ruled that there must be two eye-witnesses to an overt act against the United States government for the act to be considered treason.

FOREIGN AFFAIRS

The Tripolitan War (1801-1805)

Along with most European nations, the United States, under Presidents Washington and Adams, had paid tribute to the pirate states of the Barbary Coast (Algiers, Morocco, Tripoli, and Tunis) to insure American merchant ships in the Mediterranean against attack. In 1801, the Pasha of Tripoli increased his tribute demands, and when Thomas Jefferson refused to honor his demand, Tripoli declared war on the United States. Jefferson, despite his pacifist inclinations and his aversion to military spending, outfitted a naval squadron under Commodore Edward Preble and Lieutenant Stephen Decatur in 1803, and ordered it to proceed to the Mediterranean. Through a vigorous blockade and bombardment of Tripoli, Decatur forced the Pasha to capitulate, and in 1805, the Pasha signed a favorable treaty with the United States which reduced the tribute system. The United States, however, continued the usual tribute payments to the other Arab states until 1816. The young American republic had flexed its muscles and had asserted its right to sail the high seas free of piracy. But England and France were more formidable than the Tripoli pirates, and they were again preying on American ships.

Violation of American Neutral Rights

By 1805, the military situation in Europe had stalemated. Napoleon was the master of the European continent, but England still controlled the high seas. As neither was able to deliver the decisive military blow, each of the two nations resorted to the tactics of economic strangulation in order to bring the other to its knees. England placed continental ports under blockade, while Napoleon forced his European satellites to cut off their trade with England and announced a blockade against English ports. And both England and France interfered with American shipping. From 1803 to 1812, England seized 917 American vessels, while France took 558 American ships. England's violations of American neutral rights aroused a stronger reaction than similar actions by France, because the English actions were more systematic and were accompanied by the impressment of American sailors into the British navy. In April, 1806, Congress enacted the *Nicholson*

Non-Importation Act, designed to force British recognition of American neutral rights by prohibiting the importation of those English goods which could be produced in the United States or acquired from other foreign nations. At the request of President Jefferson, the Nicholson Act was suspended in December, 1806, pending the outcome of negotiations with the British government. Unfortunately, the English refused to make any substantive concessions, and Anglo-American relations soon worsened.

The Chesapeake-Leopard Affair

In June, 1807, the *Chesapeake,* a United States Navy ship, was stopped just outside American territorial waters by the British ship, the *Leopard.* The *Leopard* demanded the right to search the *Chesapeake* for British deserters. When the *Chesapeake* refused to comply, the *Leopard* opened fire, killing three American sailors and wounding eighteen others; she then removed four alleged deserters from the *Chesapeake*. A furious Jefferson ordered all British vessels out of American ports and called a special session of Congress to consider action against the English.

The Embargo Act

Resisting the cry for war, Jefferson proposed, and Congress hastily approved, the Embargo Act which was put into effect at the end of December, 1807. The Act prohibited all American trade with foreign lands and, except for the American coastwise trade, confined all American ships to their home ports. Jefferson was confident that Europe was economically dependent upon American foodstuffs and supplies and that Europeans needed our trade far more than Americans needed theirs. He believed that if Europe were denied all American goods, then she would soon be brought to her knees and would agree to recognize the neutral rights of the United States in return for a resumption of normal trade relations. Never had Jefferson so miscalcu-

Cartoon of a Federal merchant trying to smuggle goods out of the country during the Embargo Act (spelled backwards "O grab me"). He is snapped by Federal authorities symbolized in the form of a turtle (government oppression).

lated the effects of his legislation. The Embargo Act disturbed American economic and political life in several ways:

(1) American farm prices declined by about 25 per cent, and the economy became depressed in all its major sectors.

(2) New England, which lived by trade and commerce, was especially hard-hit. The New England merchants vigorously opposed the Embargo Act, for wartime prices were so high that if one in six of their ships ran the blockade, that ship yielded enough profits to cancel the loss of the other five ships. The Embargo Act revived the New England Federalist party and awakened the spirit of secession. It also encouraged widespread American smuggling and evasion of the law.

(3) Ironically, the Embargo Act planted the seeds of the American industrial revolution, which was the last thing Jefferson wanted to do. New England capital, which would normally have been invested in shipping and commerce, began to be invested in textiles; and between 1808 and 1816 the foundations of the American textile industry were laid down. An industrial Northeast was soon to be competing with the agrarian South for control of the nation, and the day of Jefferson's beloved farmer was soon to pass in favor of the age of the industrial worker. The Embargo Act helped to destroy the agrarian republic so dear to Jefferson.

The Non-Intercourse Act (March, 1809)

The Embargo Act was so unpopular that Jefferson, in his final days in office, was forced to acquiesce to the passage of the Non-Intercourse Act. This measure moderated the severe terms of the Embargo Act by reopening American trade with all powers except England and France. It also empowered the President to restore normal trade relations with England and/or France as soon as one or the other of these two powers recognized American neutral rights. The Non-Intercourse Act was a compromise measure which pleased few people. It sought to vindicate the principle of the embargo and to pressure England and France into respecting American rights, while, at the same time, giving a measure of relief to hard-pressed farmers and merchants. Unfortunately, it did neither; and James Madison was to inherit the delicate problem of defending America's rights on the high seas.

During his second term, Thomas Jefferson alienated the support of New England and contributed to the tragic sectional division of the United States. Aside from the abolition of the African slave trade in 1808, his second term could point to few accomplishments. Whether another man could have done a better job is debatable, but his embargo policy was an obvious failure whose deleterious effects might well have been avoided. Jefferson's once firm command of the legislative process seemed, at this time, to elude him; and he left office with much of the nation hostile to his policies.

REVIEW QUESTIONS FOR CHAPTER 12

1. In the House of Representatives, the Federalists supported the candidacy of

   (A) Thomas Jefferson
   (B) Aaron Burr
   (C) John Adams
   (D) Charles C. Pinckney

2. Jefferson's Secretary of the Treasury was

   (A) James Madison
   (B) Albert Gallatin
   (C) James Monroe
   (D) Robert R. Livingston

3. Jefferson tried to, but failed to impeach

   (A) John Pickering
   (B) John Marshall
   (C) William Marbury
   (D) Samuel Chase

4. The Land Law of 1804 provided for the sale of public land in units of

   (A) 640 acres
   (B) 320 acres
   (C) 160 acres
   (D) 80 acres

5. The Federalist candidate for the 1804 Presidential election was

   (A) Charles C. Pinckney
   (B) Rufus King
   (C) John Adams
   (D) George Clinton

6. Stephen Decatur was the hero of the war against

   (A) Algiers
   (B) Morocco
   (C) Tunis
   (D) Tripoli

7. The *Chesapeake-Leopard* affair resulted in the passage of

   (A) the Nicholson Act
   (B) the Embargo Act
   (C) the Non-Intercourse Act
   (D) none of the above

8. The Embargo Act did all of the following *except*

   (A) stimulate industrial development
   (B) depress farm prices
   (C) end impressment
   (D) antagonize New England

9. The Non-Intercourse Act prohibited trade only with

   (A) England
   (B) France
   (C) England and France
   (D) France and her satellites

10. The African slave trade was ended in

    (A) 1805   (C) 1807
    (B) 1806   (D) 1808

Explanatory Answers

1. **(B)** The Federalists wanted to deny Jefferson the Presidency.

2. **(B)** Gallatin significantly reduced the national debt and the tax rate.

3. **(D)** Chase was acquitted by the United States Senate.

4. **(C)** Quarter-sections could now be purchased for $1.64 per acre.

5. **(A)** Pinckney carried only Delaware and Connecticut in losing to Jefferson.

6. **(D)** Decatur bombarded the harbor of Tripoli and forced the Pasha to capitulate.

7. **(B)** The *Leopard* fired on the *Chesapeake* and impressed four American seamen.

8. **(C)** The Act had little impact on British policy-makers.

9. **(C)** Trade with England and France was barred until they recognized American neutral rights.

10. **(D)** Under the Constitution, 1808 was the earliest date for slave-trade abolition.

Chapter 13

THE VIRGINIA DYNASTY AND THE WAR OF 1812

James Madison was no more successful than Thomas Jefferson in winning British respect for American neutral rights, and he reluctantly drifted into war under pressure from young "War Hawks" within his own Republican party. Like the contemporary Vietnam War, the War of 1812 was highly unpopular with many Americans, especially in New England and New York. It was labeled "Mr. Madison's War," and two states and numerous individuals refused to participate in it. Nevertheless, the War of 1812 can rightfully be considered "The Second War of American Independence." Although the United States did not realize its war aims (which included the annexation of Canada and Florida), and although the war failed to win explicit British recognition of American neutral rights, the War of 1812 awakened the latent force of American nationalism and gave rise to the so-called Era of Good Feelings. The young republic had successfully defended its national honor (even though it claimed few military victories) in battle with the world's most powerful state and had consolidated the United States' standing as an independent power. With Jackson's victory at New Orleans, the United States had become a nation conscious of its own identity and confident of its future. If the spirit of sectionalism had not been buried at New Orleans, it had at least been dealt a hard blow; and it was not to become a potent force for another two decades.

The Election of 1808

Maintaining Washington's two-term tradition, Thomas Jefferson declined to stand for reelection in 1808; but he was determined to pick his successor and, thereby, continue the rule of laissez faire, states' rights, and agrarian interests. At Jefferson's urgings, the congressional caucus nominated James Madison (also a Virginian) as the Republican candidate for the Presidency.* (Prior to the 1830's Presidential candidates were nominated in caucus by the congressional members of each political

---

* Jefferson's opponents accused him of perpetuating a Virginia Dynasty in the White House; and the presidencies of Jefferson (1801–1809), Madison (1809–1817), and James Monroe (1817–1825), all of whom were Virginians, is commonly referred to as the Virginia Dynasty.

party or by individual state legislatures. The modern convention system had not yet been developed.) However, Madison was not the unanimous choice of the Republican party. The Southern Old Republicans (extreme agrarians led by John Randolph and John Taylor of Caroline) felt that Jefferson was not sufficiently true to agrarian principles and wanted to nominate James Monroe. However, after flirting with the Old Republicans, Monroe declined to run. Furthermore, the Eastern Republicans, who opposed Jefferson's embargo, nominated New York's George Clinton as their candidate for the Presidency. The Federalists renominated the losing 1804 ticket of Charles C. Pinckney and Rufus King. In the presidential election, Madison won handily, receiving 122 electoral votes to 47 for Pinckney and 6 for Clinton. In the vice-presidential election, George Clinton defeated Rufus King by a vote of 113 to 47. Nevertheless, the Federalists did make some notable gains. In the House, they doubled their number to forty-eight members, although they failed to secure a majority of House seats.

DOMESTIC AFFAIRS UNDER MADISON

The Floridas

Foreign affairs were of such overriding importance during Madison's presidency that it is difficult to make clear-cut distinctions between foreign and domestic affairs. Nevertheless, there were important domestic developments. Jefferson had cast longing eyes on West Florida and had tried to claim it as part of the Louisiana Purchase. In September, 1810, Southern expansionists instigated a local revolt against the Spaniards in West Florida, took control of Baton Rouge, and proclaimed the Republic of West Florida. One month later, James Madison accepted from the rebels possession of the territory in the name of the United States; and with Europe preoccupied by the Napoleonic Wars, there was little that Spain could do to recover the territory. In January, 1811, Congress authorized the annexation of East Florida in the event of a similar "revolution" against Spanish authorities or in the event that a foreign power other than Spain sought to assert authority in East Florida. However, there was no "revolution" in East Florida, and the United States had to wait until 1819 before acquiring the territory. The seizure of West Florida, though, indicated the aggressiveness of Southern agrarianism and revealed its insatiable land hunger.

James Madison

Failure to Recharter the Bank of the United States

Early in 1811, the charter of the Bank of the United States came up before Congress for renewal. Although Secretary of the Treasury Albert Gallatin wanted the Bank rechartered, the Southern Old Republicans opposed the measure as a vestige of Hamiltonianism; and they were successful in blocking the Bank's recharter. Believing that the government should be strictly neutral in all economic matters, the Republicans viewed the Bank of the United States as an unwarranted aid to the business and financial community; and Vice-President Clinton cast the tie-breaking vote in the United States Senate which killed the Bank. Unfortunately, in the absence of a national bank, the United States government was not able to adequately finance the War of 1812, and the war effort was needlessly impeded by poor financing.

Tecumseh

Aided and supplied by the British in Canada, Tecumseh (a leader of Indian tribes in the Northwest Territory) and his brother (a religious leader known as "The Prophet") were determined to preserve their ancestral homeland and stop further

Tecumseh

American penetration of the Northwest Territory. In the summer of 1811, the Indians went to war with the Americans, presenting a formidable threat to the settlers of the Ohio Valley. However, in November, William Henry Harrison broke the back of the Indian resistance when he defeated Tecumseh's forces at the Indian capital on Tippecanoe Creek. Tecumseh's war aroused increased anti-British sentiment along the frontier, for the Americans were convinced that the British were instigating the Indians' attacks on the American settlers. When the War of 1812 began, the Indians of the Northwest became active allies of the British army.

AMERICA GOES TO WAR

Macon's Bill No. 2

Back in 1807, England had passed a new series of Orders in Council designed to cut off all American trade with ports under the control of France. Early in 1809, Madison had been assured by British Ambassador David Erskine that the Orders in Council of 1807 would be repealed (as they applied to the United States) if the United States resumed trade with England. In April, Madison reopened trade with England only to find out that Erskine had exceeded his instructions and that the British ambassador's agreement had been repudiated by the British foreign minister, George Canning. In August, 1809, an indignant Madison reinstituted the Non-Intercourse Act against Britain. However, seeking relief from the economic depression which had fallen on America, Congress enacted Macon's Bill No. 2 in May of 1810. It meekly reopened trade with both England and France, but it empowered the President to restore the Non-Intercourse Act against the enemy of that nation which agreed to respect America's neutral rights. In other words, if either France or England repealed its discriminatory legislation against American trade, the United States would cut off all trade with the other power.

Napoleon, hoping to widen the breach between England and America, decided to take advantage of Macon's Bill No. 2. Late in 1810, he instructed his ambassador to assure the Americans that the Berlin and Milan Decrees (which interdicted trade bound for England) would no longer be enforced against the United States. Actually, Napoleon was practicing a deception, for he had previously ordered the seizure of all American merchant ships in French-controlled ports. Moreover, with England in command of the seas, Napoleon's blockade was largely ineffective; and his suspension of the Berlin and Milan Decrees as they applied to the United States had little real impact. Nevertheless, Madison took the bait. On November 2, 1810, he imposed the Non-Intercourse Act against Britain. England replied by blockading New York harbor and increasing her impressment of American sailors. Relations between the United States and Britain rapidly deteriorated.

Enter the War Hawks

Like Jefferson, Madison was determined to avoid war and gain respect for American rights through diplomacy. However, in the congressional elections of 1810, a group of young and extremely nationalistic representatives complicated Madison's efforts. Termed "War Hawks" by John Randolph, they came from the agrarian frontiers of the South and the West and included Henry Clay, Richard M. Johnson, John C. Calhoun, William Lowndes, Langden Cheves, Felix Grundy, and Peter B. Porter. Henry Clay succeeded in being elected Speaker of the House of Representatives, while Calhoun, Grundy, and Porter won seats on the Foreign Relations Committee, and Langden Cheves became Chairman of the Naval Committee. Together they demanded that Madison be more vigorous in his defense of American neutral rights. They regarded impressment, attacks on American ships, and blockades of American ports as offenses against the national honor which could only be washed away with British blood.

Madison's War Message

Throughout 1811, Madison attempted to persuade the British to modify their Orders in Council. However, as late as April of 1812, the British refused to grant any concessions. Then suddenly, under domestic economic pressure, the British government, in June, 1812, agreed to modify their Orders in Council. But by then it was too late, for on June 1, Madison asked Congress for a declaration of war against Britain. In his message, Madison cited four main reasons for war: (1) continued British impressment of American seamen, (2) British interference with American trade on the high seas and her attacks on American naval vessels in the territorial waters of the United States, (3) systematic British blockade of American ports, and (4) British refusal to revoke the Orders in Council. On June 4, 1812, the House voted approval of a declaration of war by a vote of 79 to 49, and the Senate followed suit on June 18th by a vote of 19 to 13. Interestingly enough, New England (except for Vermont), New York, New Jersey, and Delaware, as well as the Old Republicans opposed the war. Massachusetts and Connecticut went so far as to refuse to permit their militia to participate in the war. The states with the greatest maritime interests vigorously opposed a war whose ostensible purpose was the defense of those very maritime interests. With Europe at war, prices were so high that, even when operating under the handicap of the British Orders in Council, American merchants were still able to make handsome profits. But American involvement in a war would further interfere with maritime trade, result in an even tighter British blockade, and would endanger profits. Therefore, New England and New York preferred an unsatisfactory state of peace to a possibly disastrous state of war. The leaders of the pro-war faction were Westerners and Southerners who were not directly affected by British violations of American neutral rights.

Reasons for War

Among the primary reasons for America's declaration of war against England were the following:

(1) **Depressed Farm Prices.** The American farmer blamed his low farm prices on the British Orders in Council, which, he felt, kept his produce from reaching the markets of Europe. Agrarian interests supported the War of 1812, hoping that it would lead to higher farm prices.

(2) **Southern Expansionism.** The Southerners hoped to use the War of 1812 as a pretext for the acquisition of Florida.

(3) **Indian Threat in the Northwest.** The Westerners wanted to annex Canada and remove the British presence in North America. They felt that the English were stirring up the Indians of the Northwest Territory and that once the English were removed from Canada, the Indian threat would come to a quick end.

(4) **Considerations of National Honor.** Extremely nationalistic and patriotic, the War Hawks were concerned about violations of American neutral rights, even if the maritime states were not. They wanted to gain international respect for American rights; impressment, blockades, and ship seizures offended their sense of national honor. Undoubtedly, the issue of neutral rights was of overriding importance in their decision for war.

The Military Balance Sheet

When the war began in June of 1812, the United States was clearly outmatched. The American army was badly organized, poorly disciplined, and ill-trained; and it was led by officers whose own training was inadequate. Moreover, the war was unpopular in New England and New York; and the lack of a national bank forced the government to rely on loans and inflationary borrowing. The only American asset was its small but highly efficient navy. However, over the long haul, the American navy was no match for the much larger British fleet. On the other hand, England, although it possessed one of the world's finest armies, was preoccupied with the Napoleonic Wars and was handicapped by having to fight in a theater of war far removed from its main bases of supply. On the whole, the War of 1812 was an American military disaster, and by no stretch of the imagination can the Americans be said to have won the war. They were fortunate that England could not devote the time, energy, and resources needed to win the War of 1812; they were lucky that Britain entrusted its forces in America to second-rate officers and that the British were too war-weary to see the war through to a successful conclusion.

Fiascos Follow Debacles

In the summer of 1812, the Americans conceived a bold three-pronged invasion of Canada. William Hull was to invade Canada by way of Detroit; Stephen Van Rensselaer was to attack the British on the Niagara line; and Henry Dearborn was to follow the Lake Champlain route and attack Montreal. In August, 1812, Hull marched his forces into Canada, but he met resistance from local Canadians and promptly retreated back to Detroit. However, he was pursued by British and Indian forces, and he surrendered Detroit and his 2400-man unit to the British without so much as firing a shot. During October and November, Van Rensselaer attacked along the Niagara line but was defeated on the heights when the New York State militia refused to support his forces by fighting outside the territorial borders of New York State. Similarly, Dearborn had to abandon his march on Montreal when the New York militia refused to fight outside their home state.

Redemption on the High Seas

The invasion of Canada had failed, and the Americans were not to pose another serious threat to Canada for the remainder of the war. Fortunately, American military honor was redeemed through the exploits of the navy. In the early stages of the war, the *Constitution* defeated the British *Guerrière* and the *Java,* the *United States* bested the *Macedonian,* and the American *Wasp* took the *Frolic,* the *Hornet,* and the *Peacock*. But although these naval engagements pleased American pride, they were isolated and insignificant events which did not substantially alter the military balance or change the strategic situation of the United States and Britain. England could well afford the loss of a few ships.

The Election of 1812

Popular disaffection with the war was measurable in the presidential election of 1812. The Virginia Dynasty again selected James Madison as its Presidential candidate, while anti-war Eastern Republicans nominated New York's DeWitt Clinton, who was also endorsed by the Federalists. Although Madison was reelected by an electoral vote of 128 to 89, Clinton carried New England and the states north of the Potomac (with the exception of Vermont and Pennsylvania); and the Federalists, winning substantial victories in the Northeast, doubled their strength in Congress. For the Vice-Presidency, Republican Elbridge Gerry defeated Federalist Charles Jared Ingersoll by a vote of 131 to 86. As Madison prepared to begin his second term, new humiliations awaited the United States.

The Campaigns of 1813; the British Blockade and its Effects

As 1813 opened, the British were still the undisputed masters of the sea (despite their embarrassing naval defeats at the hands of the Americans); and they clamped a tight naval blockade on the Chesapeake and Delaware Bays, the mouth of the Mississippi, Long Island Sound, New York Harbor, and the ports of Charleston, Port Royal and Savannah. Only New England was free of blockading British ships. The English hoped that New England would secede from the United States and rejoin the British Empire, but when their hopes failed to materialize, they extended the naval blockade to include New England in 1814. Although the Americans continued to win isolated naval engagements, they were unable to break the highly effective British blockade which reduced American commerce to a trickle. As a result of rapidly declining imports, the United States was denied its most lucrative source of tax revenues (customs duties); and its financial troubles were greatly intensified. Denied imported manufactured goods, the Americans turned to domestic manufacturing; and the direct result of the British blockade was to spur the development of American industry. The War of 1812 gave birth to the industrial revolution in America.

The Creek War

In 1813, the Creek Indians of the Southwest (Alabama and Mississippi), resentful of American expansion, went to war against the United States and threatened American control of West Florida and New Orleans. However, early in 1814, Andrew Jackson, commanding the Tennessee militia, defeated the Creeks at Horseshoe Bend and thus deprived the British of a potentially valuable ally for their proposed attack on American positions along the Gulf of Mexico. By the Treaty of Fort Jackson (August, 1814), the Creeks were forced to cede two-thirds of their tribal lands to the United States, which then became supreme in the Alabama-Mississippi region.

The Battle of Lake Erie

In September, 1813, Captain Oliver Hazard Perry won one of the most crucial battles of the War of 1812. Building a squadron near Erie, Pennsylvania, with materials carried overland from Pittsburgh, Perry defeated a larger British squadron near Put-In Bay and took control of Lake Erie. With Perry supreme on Lake Erie, the British were forced to abandon their lake-front strongholds (including Fort Detroit), and this enabled William Henry Harrison to secure the Northwest Territory for the United States. Harrison followed the British into Canada and defeated them at the Battle of the Thames in October. Although the Battle of the Thames was more a skirmish than a formal battle, it did result in the death of Tecumseh and deprived the Indians of their most capable leader. After the Battle of the Thames, the Indians (noting the shifting fortunes of war) deserted their British allies; and the English did not again pose a serious threat to the Northwest Territory.

Harrison did not pursue the retreating British forces deeper into Canada, but returned to the Northwest Territory. However, during October and November of 1813, the Americans again failed to take Montreal; and they were thwarted in their attempt to win control of Lake Ontario and to penetrate the Niagara line. In retaliation for the American attempt on Montreal, the British seized Fort Niagara, and in December, they burned Buffalo. Although the Americans had scored triumphs on Lake Erie and in the Northwest Territory, they were frustrated in their efforts to invade Canada, and they were powerless to break the British blockade. On the whole, the campaigns of 1813 produced a stalemate. Neither side held a clear advantage; neither side had delivered, or been dealt, a crushing blow.

The British Offensive of 1814

In April of 1814, Paris fell to the victorious allies, and Napoleon abdicated his throne. Britain was now free to turn her full military attention to the United States, and that spring, her strategists conceived a three-pronged drive designed to knock America out of the war. An 11,000-man army under the command of General Sir George Prevost was to march down from Montreal, following the Lake Champlain route, and was to capture the Hudson Valley and possibly New York City as well. Meanwhile, a 4,000-man force under General Robert Ross was to make a diversionary attack in the Chesapeake Bay region and threaten Washington, D.C. and Baltimore. Finally, a third army was to be raised in Jamaica, attack New Orleans, and close the Mississippi to American shipping. Had this campaign been executed according to plan, it might have meant the end of the United States; but fortunately for the Americans, the British were, once again, ineffective.

In August, 1814, the British General Ross's forces landed at the mouth of the Patuxent River in Maryland, just southeast of Washington. At Bladensburg, a village outside Washington, D.C., the British came upon an American force (commanded by General William H. Winder) which was twice the size of the British force. As soon as the British charged, the Americans turned tail and ran. Consequently, the British entered the Capital and burned numerous public buildings, including the White House. In haste and humiliation, James Madison and the officers of the United States government were forced to flee the city. Having destroyed Washington, D.C., the British marched on Baltimore. However, Fort McHenry, guarding the approaches to the city, withstood a furious British attack (it was there that Francis Scott Key composed the "Star Spangled Banner"). After bombarding the Fort through the night of September 13, the English broke off the engagement and returned to their bases in the West Indies, where they prepared to join the attack on New Orleans.

New York Holds

In July, 1814, prior to General Prevost's descent from Montreal, the Americans again tried an invasion of Canada along the Niagara line, but they were repulsed at Lundy's Lane inside the Canadian border. Later that summer, Prevost began his march into New York, and at Plattsburg (on the western shore of Lake Champlain), he encountered stiff American resistance from 3,300 men under the command of General Alexander Macomb. On September 11, Captain Thomas Macdonough defeated the British squadron on Lake Champlain, and Prevost broke off hostilities and returned to Canada, even though he still enjoyed wide numerical superiority over the defending Americans. Prevost's retreat ended the threat to New York and dashed England's hopes of physically cutting America in two.

The Treaty of Ghent

Plattsburg was the last significant battle of the War of 1812, for earlier in the year, England and America had agreed to discuss peace terms at Ghent, Belgium. The discussions began in August, and the United States was represented by a galaxy of its leading political figures. John Quincy Adams was chairman of the American delegation which also included Speaker of the House Henry Clay, former Treasury Secretary Albert Gallatin, former Senator James A. Bayard, and Jonathan Russell, United States minister to Sweden. The British were represented by Lord Gambier, Henry Goulburn, and William Adams, none of whom were of the stature of the American delegates. At the start of the discussions, England demanded that the United States cede its claim to the Northwest Territory in favor of the Indians, who would constitute a buffer state between Canada and the rest of the United States. The British also demanded territory along the Canadian border, and they stoutly refused to make any concessions on impressment and neutral rights. The Americans, for their part, absolutely refused to make any territorial concessions. However, Prevost's defeat at Plattsburg weakened England's bargaining position. Therefore, when the Duke of Wellington advised the British cabinet that territorial concessions by the United States were absurd as long as the Americans controlled the Great Lakes, England settled for the *status quo ante bellum*. On Christmas Eve, 1814, the Treaty of Ghent was signed. It made absolutely no mention of the impressment issue, granted no concessions regarding neutral trading rights, and restored the prewar borders of the United States.

The Hartford Convention

From December, 1814 to January, 1815 (before news of the Treaty of Ghent had time to reach America), the Federalists of New England held secret discussions at Hartford to plan for a convention "to revise the Constitution." As these discussions were called on account of New England's vehement opposition to the War of 1812, it was widely feared that the Federalists would seek to have New England secede from the Union and establish an independent New England Confederacy. However, moderate Federalists prevailed at Hartford, and at the convention, itself, there was no attempt to urge secession. Instead, the convention passed a series of resolutions which declared the following:

(1) The states may decide for themselves the constitutionality of acts of Congress. (New England thus embraced the philosophy of the Kentucky and Virginia Resolutions.)

(2) The three-fifths clause, which favored the slaveholding states at the expense of the North, must be repealed.

(3) There must be a two-thirds vote of Congress before admitting new states to the Union or before war is declared. (This was designed to bolster the sagging congressional influence of New England.)

(4) The President must be limited to a single four-year term.

(5) Congress' authority to restrict trade, through measures such as the Embargo Act, must be severely limited.

(6) Naturalized citizens must be prohibited from holding public office.

The work of the Hartford Convention was cut short by news of the Treaty of Ghent and by Jackson's victory at New Orleans. The Federalists, who had constantly denounced the war, were now scorned as traitors by the American people, who were becoming nationalistic. After 1815, the Federalists ceased to exist as an organized political party, and the Virginia Dynasty was, for the time being, in absolute control of the American political field.

The Battle of New Orleans

The climactic battle of New Orleans was totally unnecessary; it was fought after the War of 1812 had already been ended, and it had no affect on the outcome of the peace negotiations. Late in

George III (across the Ocean) urging the delegates of the New England States, meeting at the Hartford Convention, to secede.

December, 1814, 7,500 British troops under Major General Sir Edward Pakenham landed on the Gulf Coast near New Orleans. On January 8, 1815, Pakenham foolishly ordered a general assault, across open country, on heavily fortified American lines. Andrew Jackson's Tennessee riflemen were lined up in three ranks behind their defenses and kept up a steady rain of fire on the approaching British ranks. After the battle, the British had suffered 2,100 men killed or wounded, and another 500 were taken prisoner. The Americans suffered casualties of 8 men killed and 13 wounded. Although the battle was without military significance, it had enormous repercussions on the American psyche.

The Triumph of American Democracy

In 1815, "democracy" was a word which still bore suspicious and unfavorable connotations, but New Orleans helped to change that. Raw, untrained, and poorly disciplined American farmers had inflicted a crushing defeat on the superbly trained British army — replete with aristocratic officers. In the American imagination, this demonstrated the moral superiority of the American farmer over the sophisticated, cultured, and educated English aristocrat. A belief that became widespread was that the unspoiled and uneducated American farmer possessed an intuitive knowledge of right and wrong that came directly from God, while the civilized and cultured Britisher (or Easterner) lacked this knowledge because he had been corrupted by civilization. Therefore, the common people (who possessed this intuitive moral sense) were better fitted to rule society than the cultured and corrupted upper classes; when the common people spoke, they did so with the voice of God *(vox populi, vox Dei)* — a voice which society could not ignore. In the American mind, dream became confused with substance, and the Battle of New Orleans was seen as the decisive battle of the War of 1812. It was considered the battle which redeemed the honor of America and which demonstrated the superiority of the common man. After 1815, the democratic spirit became an irresistible force in American political life.

As for Andrew Jackson, he was the Hero of New Orleans and the embodiment of the rising American democratic spirit. He was to give his name to an age, and he was to become irrevocably identified with the triumph of American democracy.

REVIEW QUESTIONS FOR CHAPTER 13

1. The candidate of the Old Republicans in 1808 was

   (A) James Madison
   (B) DeWitt Clinton
   (C) James Monroe
   (D) George Clinton

2. West Florida was seized by the United States in

   (A) 1808
   (B) 1809
   (C) 1810
   (D) 1811

3. All of the following opposed the Bank of the United States *except*

   (A) Albert Gallatin
   (B) George Clinton
   (C) John Randolph
   (D) Thomas Jefferson

4. The hero of the battle of Tippecanoe Creek was

   (A) Henry Dearborn
   (B) William Henry Harrison
   (C) David Erskine
   (D) Henry Clay

5. All of the following were War Hawks *except*

   (A) John C. Calhoun
   (B) Peter B. Porter
   (C) Langden Cheves
   (D) John Randolph

6. All of the following were factors in causing the War of 1812 *except*

   (A) the desire to annex Canada
   (B) the desire to annex East Florida
   (C) anger over impressment
   (D) the desire to annex New Orleans

7. The American general who surrendered Detroit to the British was

   (A) Henry Dearborn
   (B) William Hull
   (C) Stephen Van Rensselaer
   (D) William Henry Harrison

8. The victor at Horseshoe Bend was

   (A) William Henry Harrison
   (B) Andrew Jackson
   (C) Oliver Hazard Perry
   (D) the Creek Indians

9. Washington, D.C. was burned by troops under the command of

   (A) George Prevost
   (B) Edward Pakenham
   (C) Robert Ross
   (D) William H. Winder

10. The British invasion of New York State (1814) was stopped at

   (A) Buffalo
   (B) Plattsburg
   (C) Fort Niagara
   (D) Fort Ticonderoga

Explanatory Answers

1. **(C)** Monroe declined to accept the nomination of the extreme agrarians.

2. **(C)** Southerners staged a "revolution" in West Florida in 1810.

3. **(A)** Gallatin was the Secretary of the Treasury under Jefferson and Madison.

4. **(B)** Harrison broke the back of Tecumseh's forces at Tippecanoe.

5. **(D)** Randolph was the one who first coined the term "War Hawk."

6. **(D)** The United States already possessed New Orleans.

7. **(B)** Hull surrendered without firing a single shot.

8. **(B)** Jackson defeated the Creeks at Horseshoe Bend.

9. **(C)** Ross was in command of a diversionary force which was to attack the Chesapeake Bay region.

10. **(B)** Plattsburg was the last battle of military significance of the War of 1812.

Chapter 14

THE ERA OF GOOD FEELINGS AND THE COMING OF JACKSON, 1816-1828

The "Era of Good Feelings" is a term used to designate the Presidency of James Monroe (1817–1825). It implies that during this period the American people became conscious of, and took pride in, their nationality and that as a result of this sense of national unity, partisan and sectional quarrels faded away. While it is true that the Federalist party died after 1815, and that the United States was a one-party nation in this period, the term "Era of Good Feelings" is a gross oversimplification. The Era of Good Feelings was extremely short-lived and really came to an end with the Panic of 1819. Although the Democratic-Republican (Republican for short) party dominated the nation's political life, it became highly factionalized after 1819, with New England, the South, and the West vying for influence and leadership. The Missouri Compromise of 1820 again revived the spirit of sectionalism and made slavery a disruptive political issue. The political maneuvers of the disputed 1824 presidential election dramatically set section against section, and the policies of John Quincy Adams heightened tensions between the agrarian South and the industrializing North and, at the same time, divided the West. The Era of Good Feelings spawned political and sectional antagonisms which led inevitably to the American Civil War.

MADISON'S LAST YEAR

The Republicans Enact the Federalist's Program

If it taught nothing else, the War of 1812 demonstrated that Jefferson's Republican doctrine of governmental *laissez faire* was not in the best interests of the United States. Accordingly, during his last year in office, Madison adopted many Federalist tenets. He agreed to maintain a standing army of 10,000 men (the Republicans had previously condemned standing armies as endangering civil liberties), increased appropriations for the United States military academy at West Point, and approved an eight-million-dollar naval expansion program. While modest by European standards, Madison's program of military expansion by the federal government was a major break with the intellectual premises of Jeffersonian agrarianism. Madison also approved recharter of the Bank of the United States and the passage of America's first protective tariff.

The Second Bank of the United States

The difficulties involved in financing the War of 1812 convinced the most stubborn of Republicans that a national bank was an absolute necessity. In 1816, Congress passed John C. Calhoun's bill calling for the establishment of a Second Bank of the United States. Only state banking interests (whose activities would be subject to regulation by the national bank), the extreme Virginia agrarians, and some bitter Federalist partisans opposed the measure. Henry Clay, in seconding Calhoun's bill, admitted that his earlier opposition to the bank had been a mistake. The organization of the Second Bank followed that of the First Bank, except that its capitalization was increased from 10 million dollars to 35 million. The federal government owned 20 per cent of the Bank's capitalization, and the President named five of the Bank's twenty-five directors. The Bank was to serve as a federal repository. It could issue notes equal to the amount of its capitalization and in return for its twenty-year charter, it paid the government a bonus of 1.5 million dollars. It was hoped that the Second Bank would provide the nation with a sound credit system which would spur economic development. Unfortunately, the Bank was badly mismanaged in its early years and as it was blamed for the Panic of 1819, it forfeited much popular support.

The Tariff of 1816

When the War of 1812 ended, the British flooded the United States with cheap manufactured goods (often sold below cost), hoping to smother the infant American industries which had developed during the war and, thereby, to remove a source of potential competition. To guard against this, Congress enacted the first tariff designed to protect American industries against foreign competition. The Tariff of 1816 imposed a duty of 25 per cent (20 per cent after 1819) on all foreign cotton and woolen goods and a 15 per cent duty on other types of manufactured items. The tariff was enthusiastically supported by the Middle states and the West, but it was opposed by New England shipping and commercial interests (who made their living by foreign trade) and by Southern agrarians. However, a sizeable percentage of Southern congressmen (led by John C. Calhoun) voted in favor of the Tariff of 1816, hoping that its protective features would stimulate the development of industry in the South and end the region's dependency on one-crop agriculture. Unfortunately, the tariff was not high enough to afford sufficient protection for America's infant industries; and when the South failed to industrialize, the Southerners returned to their traditional policy of opposition to tariffs. (Since the South sold its cotton on an unprotected world market, the tariff resulted in higher-priced manufactured goods without increasing the price of Southern cotton. Therefore the tariff worked against the economic interests of the South.)

The Election of 1816

In the Congressional caucus, the Young Republicans (dissatisfied with the Virginia Dynasty) supported William H. Crawford as their candidate for the Presidency. However, Madison retained enough support to secure the nomination of his candidate, James Monroe, by a vote of 65 to 54. The now traditional Virginia-New York coalition was maintained by the nomination of Daniel D. Tompkins as Vice-President. The moribund Federalists nominated Rufus King as their candidate for the Presidency, but in the Electoral College, Monroe defeated King by a vote of 183 to 34 and carried every state except Massachusetts and Connecticut.

MONROE'S FIRST TERM

Industrial America is Born

In his Inaugural Address, James Monroe indicated that the Republican party would support and encourage the development of manufacturing. On his good will tour of much of the United States, from May to September of 1817, he was hailed wherever he went (including Boston); and he saw an America very different from the one the Republicans had known a few short years before — he saw the beginnings of an industrial America. From 1790 to 1820, the population of the United States jumped from 4 million to 9.6 million, and the bulk of this increase was from natural growth, for only 250,000 immigrants entered the country in this period. Moreover, the population of the trans-Appalachian West had grown from 100,000 to 2.2 million in the same period, and the urban population of America stood at about 700,000. It was in the towns and cities

James Monroe

of America that the nation's economic life was being transformed.

The Birth of the Factory

Back in 1790, a young English refugee named Samuel Slater constructed, from memory, a highly complicated machine to spin cotton. He built the loom for the Rhode Island firm of Almy and Brown, and, in doing so, gave birth to the American industrial revolution. In 1800, Eli Whitney succeeded in making rifle parts with such precision that a part from one rifle could be inserted into another without any loss of effectiveness. The technique of interchangeable parts was one of the major developments of the industrial revolution and made possible mass-production industry. However, while the individual states chartered more than three hundred corporations between 1781 and 1801, American industry remained insignificant until the War of 1812, when European manufactured goods were prevented from reaching the United States by the British blockade. Then, in 1813, Francis Cabot Lowell and his Boston associates established a textile factory at Waltham, Massachusetts.

The Lowell System

Lowell hired young, unmarried New England farmgirls to work his looms and paid them an average weekly wage ranging from $2.50 to $3.00 (about half the wages normally paid to adult male workers). They were housed in simple but decent dormitories built by the company, and they were strictly chaperoned. When they were not working, the girls were encouraged to read the Bible, study, and write poetry. Most of the girls worked at the plant in order to raise money for their dowries or to supplement family income, and they generally married after a few years. The Lowell factory was an economic success; and after the end of the war, textile plants sprang up all over Massachusetts and New England. However, as competition increased in the 1820's, working conditions began to deteriorate; and an American proletariat began to develop. The length of the working day was from twelve to fourteen hours, with a six-day work week being the rule. Men tended to average a dollar a day in wages; women made half that, and children earned about twenty-five cents per day. Child labor was a necessary evil for childrens' wages were often needed to supplement family earnings, and their small hands could perform certain tasks on the loom (tying broken strands) which an adult could not do.

Ironically, the industrial revolution revived the dying institution of slavery. Eli Whitney's cotton gin solved the problem of separating the cotton fiber from the seeds, and the demand for cotton to supply the textile mills of England and New England encouraged the widespread planting of the crop. After 1815, the rich black belt of Alabama, Mississippi, and Lousiana was opened to cotton cultivation; and the demand for slave labor to work the new cotton fields made the institution of slavery vital to the economy of the South.

The Transportation Revolution

After 1815, internal improvements (the construction of highways and canals, and, later, railroads) were demanded by Western farmers who

Carding, drawing, and spinning at the Slater cotton mill, first in America (1790).

wanted to get their crops to Eastern markets and by manufacturers who wanted to get their products to Western markets. (Generally, the South, which used its abundant rivers as a natural transportation system, opposed internal improvements at federal expense.) In his last annual message, President Madison urged the passage of a constitutional amendment to permit internal improvements at federal expense; but, nevertheless, he vetoed a congressional bill which would have earmarked the Bank bonus of 1.5 million dollars for internal improvements. Monroe also favored internal improvements in principle, and he urged a constitutional amendment to permit them. But like his predecessor, he vetoed specific bills — in one instance (May, 1822), a proposal to construct a national road through the Cumberland Gap which would have linked the East and the West. With the Federal government dragging its feet, many states instituted their own internal improvements. From 1817 to 1825, the State of New York built the Erie Canal, which made possible direct water communications between New York City and the Ohio Valley. Completion of the canal led to a tremendous commercial boom for New York City, and it touched off a wave of canal-building which quickly got out of hand and helped to bankrupt a number of state governments.

In the 1820's, steamboats came into general use on America's internal waterways and made transportation efficient, cheap, and rapid. Late in that decade, the first railroads were built; and by the 1830's, they linked many areas of the country. The roads, canals, and harbors built by the states and the development of steamboats and railroads spurred the growth of American industry by providing manufacturers with wide and rapidly expanding markets for their wares. By lowering transportation costs, these internal improvements also benefited the Western farmers, who could now get their produce to market quickly and cheaply. Within a generation, the transportation revolution had turned the United States into a rapidly industrializing nation — one that was outgrowing its agrarian heritage.

Foreign Affairs under Monroe: Normalizing Relations with England

After the War of 1812, both England and America were anxious to restore relations and resume their commercial intercourse with one another. In April, 1817, the Rush-Bagot Agreement was concluded, which provided for mutual naval disarmament on the Great Lakes. It marked one of the rare times in human history when disarmament was successfully implemented. One year later, the Convention of 1818 fixed the United States-Canadian border at the forty-ninth parallel, from the Lake of the Woods to the Rocky Mountains. It also provided for joint Anglo-American occupation of the Oregon Territory (Oregon, Washington, Idaho, and British Columbia) for a ten-year period, with citizens of each nation to enjoy equal commercial privileges in the territory. With the Convention of 1818, all serious differences between England and America were resolved; and the two nations enjoyed generally harmonious relations.

Jackson and the Seizure of Florida

During the War of 1812, hostile Seminole Indians (who were joined by runaway Negro slaves) used Spanish Florida as a base for their forays against American settlements in Georgia. In July, 1816, the American army destroyed Fort Apalachicola in East Florida, which was being used as a base of operations by the Seminoles; and in December, 1817, General Andrew Jackson was given command of the Georgia-Florida border area, with instructions to pursue hostile Indians into Florida, if necessary. In January, 1818, Jackson sent a letter to President Monroe (through Congressman J. Rhea), stating that he (Jackson) could take control of Florida within sixty days if it were made known to him that such action was desired. Monroe and his Cabinet made no formal answer to Jackson's Rhea Letter, and Old Hickory interpreted their silence as their tacit approval of his scheme. In April, 1818, he pursued hostile Indians into Florida, but he exceeded his instructions by capturing the Spanish towns of St. Marks and Pensacola and by executing two British traders for allegedly selling supplies to the Seminoles. The execution of the two British traders raised a furor in England (which fortunately subsided without leading to war) and Jackson's conduct touched off a Cabinet crisis in Washington. Both Secretary of War Calhoun and Secretary of the Treasury Crawford wanted Jackson court-martialed, and in 1819, both the House and the Senate censured Jackson's conduct in Florida. However, Secretary of State John Quincy Adams defended Jackson's conduct, and President Monroe took no action to discipline the General. At the time of Jackson's foray into Florida, Adams was conducting negotiations with the Spanish government for the transfer of Florida to the United States, and he used Jackson's actions to good advantage.

Adams pointed out to the Spanish government how weak its hold on Florida was and how easily the United States could seize it; he advised the Spanish to avoid the humiliation of an American seizure by ceding Florida to the United States. In February, 1819, the Adams-Onis treaty was concluded. It contained the following provisions:

(1) Spain was to transfer title to East Florida to the United States and would recognize America's prior annexation of West Florida.

(2) The United States was to assume responsibility for the claims of its citizens against Spain to the extent of 5 million dollars.

(3) The United States was to renounce all territorial claims to Texas arising from the Louisiana Purchase.

(4) The border between Texas and the Louisiana Purchase area was to be fixed at a line running along the Sabine, Red and Arkansas Rivers north to the forty-second parallel and then due west to the Pacific. (Thus, Spain renounced its claims to the Pacific Northwest in favor of the United States.)

Although the Adams–Onis treaty fixed the Southern border of the United States, the Americans were to push their frontiers ever westward and obliterate the Adams–Onis border.

The Panic of 1819 and the Growth of Sectionalism

Depression overtook the United States in 1819. This economic crisis was caused by commodity price inflation, wild land speculation, and overextended investments in manufacturing, as well as mismanagement of the Second Bank of the United States (which resulted in contracted credit) and the collapse of foreign markets for American agricultural produce. The Panic of 1819 was severe and was felt with the greatest impact in the rural South and West. It was largely blamed on the Bank of the United States — commonly called "The Monster" at this time. The Panic intensified Western and Southern distrust of Eastern manufacturing interests and led to renewed antagonism between debtors and creditors. In many states, notably Kentucky and Tennessee, debtors demanded relief against mortgage foreclosures, and they rejected the political leadership of aristocratic planters and merchants. The social tensions spawned by the Panic of 1819 facilitated the rise of democracy (in the 1820's most states granted universal manhood suffrage, abolishing property requirements for voting) and shifted political power to the common man. It also abruptly ended the Era of Good Feelings.

The Missouri Compromise

In 1819, there were twenty-two states in the Union, eleven of them were free states, and eleven were slave states. However, as a result of uneven development, the North enjoyed superiority over the South in the House of Representatives by a margin of 105 to 81. Only in the Senate did the South retain equality with the North, and the South was zealous in its insistence that Senatorial parity must be maintained between the free and slave states. Southerners were convinced that once the South lost that parity, a hostile North would enact laws prejudicial to the South's slave economy.

In 1819, Missouri applied for admission to the Union as a slave state. In February of that year, a New York congressman, James Tallmadge, offered an amendment which would prohibit the further importation of slaves into Missouri and which would emancipate all slaves in the state once they had attained the age of twenty-five years. The House voted approval of the Tallmadge amendment, which would have doomed slavery to eventual extinction in Missouri, but the Senate rejected it. This touched off a raucous debate that tied up all congressional business for a year. Finally, in February, 1820, Illinois' Senator Jesse B. Thomas offered a compromise solution.

As finally enacted by Congress, the Missouri Compromise permitted Missouri to become a state without restrictions on the institution of slavery; at the same time, Maine (which had just separated from Massachusetts) was allowed to enter the Union as a free state. Thus the balance of free and slave states in the Senate was preserved. In addition, in the remainder of the Louisiana Purchase area, slavery was prohibited north of 36°30' latitude, but it was permitted south of that line. The Compromise resolved the Missouri controversy, but not before it had made slavery a major political issue. Slavery was, as Jefferson observed, "a firebell in the night," sure to disturb the peace of the country and to awaken sectional animosities. Shortly after the Missouri Compromise, abolitionism became an organized movement in the Northern states.

Chief Justice Marshall

The Second Missouri Compromise

The furor over Missouri was not quite ended, however. In July, 1820, Missouri submitted its constitution to Congress, and it contained a clause excluding free Negroes from residing as citizens of the state. Congress rejected the constitution, and Missouri's statehood was again delayed. Finally, in March, 1821, a second compromise was worked out in which the Missouri legislature agreed not to invoke the restrictive clause against citizens of the United States. (Whether or not Negroes could be considered citizens was left undetermined at this time.)

The Marshall Court and the Spirit of American Nationalism

As the Federalists had hoped, the United States Supreme Court, under the leadership of Chief Justice John Marshall, became a bulwark of nationalism against the states' rights tendencies of the Republicans. Marshall's major decisions and their implications follow.

(1) **Fletcher versus Peck**, 1810. The Georgia legislature revoked the charter of a land company

that held lands along the Yazoo River after it was learned that its charter had been obtained by fraud. Marshall ruled that the courts could not inquire into the motivations behind a legislative grant, and that unilateral revocation of a charter by a subsequent legislature violated the sanctity of a contract and was unconstitutional under the full-faith clause. The decision was a landmark in freeing private enterprise from legislative and governmental restraints.

(2) **Martin versus Hunter's Lessee,** 1816. In this minor land-title dispute, the Supreme Court ruled that an individual had the right to appeal a decision of a state court to the federal courts when a constitutional question was involved. Marshall affirmed the Supreme Court's appellate jurisdiction over the state courts and established the supremacy of the federal courts over the state courts.

(3) **The Dartmouth College Case,** 1819. Back in 1816, the Republican-controlled New Hampshire legislature revoked the charter of Dartmouth College (a charter dating back to colonial times) and appointed a new board of directors, dominated by Republicans. The old board of directors enlisted the services of Daniel Webster and sought to recover their original charter. Marshall ruled that New Hampshire's unilateral revocation of the college's charter violated the contract clause of the Constitution. The decision hindered the effectiveness of state regulation of public institutions and limited the regulatory power of the state over corporations engaged in public service.

(4) **M'Culloch versus Maryland,** 1819. This case involved the constitutionality of a tax imposed on the transactions of the Bank of the United States by the state of Maryland. Speaking for a unanimous Court, Marshall delivered a sweeping interpretation of the nature of the American Union. He declared that the powers of the federal government were derived from the people of the United States (not from the states) and were operative directly upon the people. Since the states did not grant power to the federal government, they could not very well withdraw power from it. Moreover, the Bank of the United States was constitutional under the implied powers clause of the Constitution (Marshall accepted Hamilton's doctrine of implied powers) since the right to charter a bank was a legitimate function of Congress' expressed power to regulate the national coinage. Since the Bank of the United States was a lawful agency of the national government, its operations could not be interfered with by the states. Maryland's tax on the Bank interfered with the Bank's lawful functions (as Marshall declared "the power to tax is the power to destroy") and was therefore illegal. The decision established the supremacy of federal power over the states; it reaffirmed the doctrine that federal law was supreme throughout the nation and binding upon the states.

(5) **Sturgis versus Crowningshield,** 1819. The ruling on this case invalidated a New York State law (which granted relief to debtors) as an impairment of the contract clause of the Constitution. The decision sustained the rights of property against governmental attempts to restrict them in the interests of social justice.

(6) **Gibbon versus Ogden,** 1824. Marshall struck down as unconstitutional a New York State law granting a monopoly of steamboat transportation between New York and New Jersey to a single company. The Court declared that the federal government had exclusive jurisdiction over interstate commerce and that even in the absence of contrary federal legislation in the area, the states may not exercise any jurisdiction affecting interstate commerce. The decision further reduced state authority in favor of federal power.

The Marshall Court broadly interpreted the powers granted to the national government; it was instrumental in increasing national power, while greatly reducing the scope of state power and limiting the Jeffersonian states' rights doctrine. Finally, Marshall freed American business from the restrictions of state government and facilitated the rise of free-enterprise capitalism in the United States. John Marshall's contributions to the growth of American nationalism were enduring, and he must rank as one of the most important architects of the American nation.

The Presidential Election of 1820

The Federalist party had so deteriorated by 1820 that it offered no opposition to Monroe's 1820 presidential candidacy. All political factions were now contained within the broad confines of the Republican party. Running unopposed, James Monroe received 231 electoral votes and was reelected President (three electors abstained and one unregenerate Federalist voted for John Quincy Adams). Daniel Tompkins was reelected Vice-

President. However, during Monroe's second term, the Republican party factionalized around sectional leaders.

MONROE'S SECOND TERM

Russia and the Pacific Northwest

In 1823, Tsar Alexander of Russia claimed the Pacific Coast of North America as far south as the fifty-first parallel for his nation, and he issued an *ukase* (edict) which closed the Bering Strait to the shipping of foreign nations. American Secretary of State John Quincy Adams vigorously opposed the Russian claim (indeed, the 1823 Monroe Doctrine was as much aimed against Russia as it was against Spain). In April, 1824, Adams concluded an agreement whereby Russia relinquished all territorial claims to North America south of 54°40′ latitude and opened the Bering Strait to international shipping. This removed Russia's claim to the Pacific Northwest coast and left England as the only European power with a territorial claim in the region (Spain had renounced her claims in 1819).

The Monroe Doctrine

In 1821, the United States recognized the independence of Spain's former Latin American colonies and, along with England, began to cultivate trade relations with them. In 1822, at the Congress of Verona, Prince Metternich of Austria pledged the Quadruple Alliance to the recovery of the Latin American republics for Spain. However, England did not want to see Spanish authority restored in Latin America since it would endanger the profitable trade relations which she had developed in that region. Accordingly, George Canning proposed a joint Anglo-American statement warning the European powers not to attempt to recolonize Latin America. Former Presidents Jefferson and Madison both urged Monroe to accept Canning's offer and join with Britain in securing the independence of the Americas. However, John Quincy Adams opposed a joint statement. He did not want it to appear that the United States was allied to, or subservient to, Great Britain; he urged Monroe to issue a statement which would be aimed at all European powers and which would emphasize the neutrality of the United States. Consequently, in December, 1823, President Monroe delivered the now famous Monroe Doctrine (which embodied the ideas of Adams) as a message to Congress. The major points of the message were the following:

(1) America and Europe constituted two separate and distinct political, social, and economic worlds; and, therefore,

(2) the New World was no longer open to colonization by any European power.

(3) Existing European colonies in the Americas would not be interfered with.

(4) However, any attempt to reassert control over former colonies or to establish new ones was to be considered as a threat against the United States and as an act of provocation.

(5) So long as Europe did not interfere in the affairs of America, the United States would not meddle in European affairs and would confine its diplomatic initiatives to the protection of American neutral rights.

Since the Monroe Doctrine was not ratified by the Senate it was merely an expression of one President's foreign policy; and it had no standing in international law. Indeed the European powers did not consider the Monroe Doctrine to be of any consequence (since the United States lacked the military force to adequately implement the Monroe Doctrine) and they generally ignored it. However, England supported the concept of Latin American independence; and as long as the British navy commanded the world's seas, the continental powers of Europe were unable to restore Spanish authority over Latin America. It was England, not the United States, which enforced the Monroe Doctrine.

The Rise of Partisanship and the Growth of Democracy

When James Monroe began his second term in March of 1821, he was a lame-duck President. Almost immediately, a host of presidential aspirants began jockeying for position in the 1824 race. In Monroe's Cabinet, John C. Calhoun and William H. Crawford (both presidential aspirants) argued so violently and with such partisan intensity that they disrupted the normal functions of government. In addition, there was widespread dissatisfaction with the congressional caucus system as the means by which presidential candidates were nominated; the people wanted a greater say in the election of future Presidents. In the early 1820's most states provided for the popular election of presidential electors (instead of having them chosen by the state legislatures), and property qualifications for voting were irrevocably being abolished in favor of universal manhood suffrage. Indiana permitted all white males to vote in 1816, and Illinois and Connecticut did the same in 1818. The next states to follow suit were Alabama (1819), Maine (1820), and Massachusetts and New York (1821). With electors chosen by the people and with more people qualified to vote, the Presidency was becoming an institution subject to popular control.

Leading Presidential Candidates and Their Programs

William Henry Crawford. The last candidate of the congressional caucus, Georgia's William Henry Crawford was the choice of the Virginia Dynasty (Jefferson, Madison, and Monroe) and represented the traditional policies of the agrarian-dominated Republican party. Unfortunately, a paralytic stroke, suffered in September, 1823, all but eliminated Crawford as a serious presidential candidate.

Henry Clay. Nominated for the Presidency by his native Kentucky, Clay was the voice of Western nationalism. In March, 1824, he enunciated the American System, calling for a vast federal program of internal improvements to be financed by revenues from a tariff. The tariff would promote American industry and create new urban markets for Western produce, while internal improvements would permit the free exchange of Eastern manufactured goods and Western farm products.

Andrew Jackson. A national hero, Jackson was nominated by local Tennessee politicians who hoped to use his candidacy as a vehicle for their own advancement. They did not expect their candidate to become a serious contestant. Jackson attacked "King Caucus" and urged greater popular participation in the selection of the President. As for Clay's American System, he neither endorsed it nor rejected it, although he indicated approval of the tariff.

John C. Calhoun. A nationalist during the Era of Good Feelings, Calhoun grew conservative in

John C. Calhoun

the 1820's and began to emerge as a spokesman for the sectional interests of the slave-owning South. He opposed the protective tariff since it increased the price of manufactured goods (which the South had to buy), while affording no protection to cotton. Hostile to the American System, Calhoun sought to increase the political influence of the slave states in the Union. When it became obvious that his candidacy was attracting no enthusiasm outside of his native South Carolina, he withdrew as a presidential nominee to run as Vice-President on the tickets of both Andrew Jackson and John Quincy Adams.

John Quincy Adams. The candidate of New England, Adams was nominated at a popular rally in Boston. An ardent nationalist, he achieved a brilliant record in international diplomacy and enthusiastically supported Henry Clay's American System. Unfortunately, he lacked a personal political following and failed to cultivate one.

The Election of 1824

Running well in the West and the South, Andrew Jackson secured a plurality of the popular and electoral vote but failed to secure a majority of the electoral vote, thus throwing the presidential election into the House of Representatives. The results of the election follows:

Jackson 153,544 (99)* carried La., Miss., Ala., S.C., N.C., Tenn., Ill., Ind., Penn., N.J., Md.
Adams 108,740 (84) carried Me., Vt., N.H., Mass., R.I., Conn., N.Y.
Clay 47,136 (37) carried Mo., Ken., Ohio.
Crawford 46,618 (41) carried Ga., Va., Del.

It was fairly obvious that Henry Clay (not himself eligible for the Presidency since he did not finish among the top three in the Electoral vote) would be instrumental in determining the next President; and as Speaker of the House, he was in a good position to influence the voting in the House. Jackson's supporters claimed that Old Hickory deserved to win the Presidency since he was the most popular choice; however, he was also Clay's rival for the affections of the West, and his attitude toward the American System left something to be desired. Accordingly, Clay announced that he was supporting John Quincy Adams for the Presidency. As Adams was a strong supporter of internal improvements and did not have any appreciable following in the West, Clay's choice was logical (though it was to have unfortunate repercussions for him). In the House, Missouri, Kentucky, and Ohio (all of which had gone for Clay) switched over to the Adams column, along with Louisiana, Illinois, and Maryland (Jackson states). Receiving the support of thirteen states (to seven for Jackson and four for Crawford), John Quincy Adams became the sixth President of the United States. Wishing to continue the broadbased coalitions which had marked the administrations of Madison and Monroe, Adams offered Cabinet posts to both Clay and Jackson. Jackson declined, but Clay accepted the post of Secretary of State (which was, at the time, the route to the White House). Later, Jackson's followers

* In lists of election results used in this text, numbers in parentheses refer to Electoral College votes.

John Quincy Adams

were to charge that Adams had been elected President as the result of a corrupt bargain with Henry Clay, and the charge was to follow Clay for the rest of his life. Actually, Clay had not asked for, nor had Adams promised, any office in return for his support; Adams simply felt that Clay was the most experienced Westerner available for the State Department. However, the corrupt-bargain charge was potent political propaganda which discredited Adams and drew support away from Clay.

THE ADAMS ADMINISTRATION

The Re-Emergence of Political Parties

John Quincy Adams was one of the most capable and experienced men ever to hold the office of President; unfortunately, he was not a politician, and his administration was largely unproductive. He stoutly refused to employ his patronage powers (the right to appoint and dismiss federal office holders) to build a political following personally loyal to himself. He felt that men should be appointed to office on the basis of merit and that they should be dismissed only for poor performance of duty, not for their political convictions.

As a result, Adams removed only twelve men from office during his four-year term; he permitted followers of Jackson, Calhoun, and Crawford to retain their posts, and he rewarded neither the supporters of Clay (his principal ally) nor his own supporters. During his administration, the Jackson-Calhoun-Crawford wing of the Republican party became known as Democratic-Republicans (Democrats for short) and claimed to be the true heirs of the Jeffersonian tradition. The Adams-Clay wing became known as National Republicans (in the 1830's they were to take the name "Whig"), and the Democrats accused them of being Hamiltonian Federalists in disguise. During Adams' term of office, Congress was controlled by the Jackson-Calhoun-Crawford wing (Jackson, himself, serving as a Senator) which opposed most of the administration's legislative program and which spent its time actively preparing for the election of 1828.

Adams Seeks to Implement the American System

In December, 1825, John Quincy Adams proposed to Congress a bold and visionary program to spur national development. He called for (1) an extensive federal program of internal improvements, (2) a national university to promote American cultural development, (3) astronomical observatories ("light houses in the sky") to promote scientific knowledge, (4) standardized weights and measures, (5) exploration of the United States interior and the Pacific Northwest, (6) subsidies and bounties to promote agriculture, commerce, and manufacturing, and (7) federal support to encourage the arts, sciences, and literature. Unfortunately, except for the appropriations of 2.3 million dollars for internal improvements (mainly in the form of federal highways), Congress failed to act on Adams' program. In general, Congress felt that art, science, and culture were aristocratic trappings which the democratic United States neither needed nor wanted.

The Panama Congress Fiasco

In 1826, the United States was invited to send representatives to the Panama Congress (called by Simon Bolivar to discuss Latin American problems and to seek some form of political unity or cooperation). Henry Clay, seeking to cultivate good relations with the Latin American states and hoping to see the United States assume leadership in the Americas, urged acceptance of the invitation; and President Adams sought a congressional appropriation to permit the sending of an American delegation. While approval was eventually voted, the Panama Debate was among the most bitter congressional fights of the Adams administration. Jacksonians were fearful that the Panama Congress would condemn slavery (black delegates were in attendance at Panama) and would violate America's traditional neutrality by committing the United States to participation in a super-governmental organization of the American states. Of the two American delegates named to represent the United States at the Congress, one died on the way, and the other did not arrive until the Congress had ended.

The Tariff of Abominations

As previously noted, the Tariff of 1816 did not have duties high enough to sufficiently protect American industry from European competition. In 1824, a new tariff act was passed, which increased duties on textiles from 20 per cent to 33⅓ per cent and which raised duties on iron, lead, glass, and hemp. Supported by the West and the Middle states, the Tariff of 1824 was opposed by the South and by the commercial interests of New England (though it was supported by the manufacturing interests). However, the Tariff of 1824 did not meet the expectations of the manufacturing interests of the Middle states, and they emphatically demanded even higher tariffs. In the spring of 1828, the Jacksonians (who controlled Congress) concocted a tariff package which was designed to fail and which would, thereby, discredit Adams. They reasoned that no matter what Congress did or did not do, the South and much of the West was going to vote for Jackson in the 1828 presidential election, while New England would be equally solid for Adams. The election would, therefore, hinge on the votes of New York and Pennsylvania. The Tariff of 1828 (the Tariff of Abominations) placed duties as high as 50 per cent on raw wool, pig and bar iron, hemp, and whisky. It was highly beneficial to the Middle states, but discriminated against New England since it increased the cost of products which the region consumed. The Jacksonians were confident that Adams would veto the measure and, consequently, alienate the Middle states. Adams, however, signed the measure (the Middle states, nevertheless, still went for Jackson in 1828), and the South howled with anger.

In December, 1828, John C. Calhoun penned (although he did not publicly admit authorship) the *South Carolina Exposition and Protest,* in which he reaffirmed the compact theory of the Constitution first expressed in the Kentucky and Virginia Resolutions. He also expressed the doctrine of state nullification, holding that when a state decided that an act of Congress was unconstitutional, it had the right to nullify the operation of that act within the confines of its own borders. Calhoun further declared that minority rights (those of the agrarian, slaveholding South) could not wantonly be violated by the opposing economic interests that enjoyed a numerical majority; he asserted that a republican government should equitably represent the interests of all economic and sectional interests. Calhoun's statement was the first major exposition of the extreme states' rights doctrine. Although the doctrine was aimed against the Tariff of Abominations, it would be broadly applied in the generation ahead and would lead to civil war.

The Election of 1828

Basically a replay of the 1824 contest, the election of 1828 pitted Andrew Jackson and John C. Calhoun (Democratic-Republicans) against John Quincy Adams and Richard Rush (National Republicans). The Jacksonians had been preparing for the election for four years, and they were well-organized. They had a string of newspapers, edited by young Westerners, which drummed up popular support for Old Hickory; and the Democrats had developed well-oiled, professional political machines in many key states. In New York, the Albany Regency, headed by Martin Van Buren, was the forerunner of the modern political machine (that is, it used patronage and state contracts to develop a potent political following), and it succeeded in securing Andrew Jackson the bulk of that state's electoral vote. Outside of New England, Adams had little popular support and virtually no political organization to speak of. The results of the election follow:

Jackson   647,231 (178)

Adams   509,097 (83)

Adams carried only New England (with Maine dividing its vote between Adams and Jackson) and New Jersey; the New York vote was divided with Jackson. Old Hickory won the South, the West, and the crucial state of Pennsylvania. Jacksonian Democracy was about to burst upon the American scene.

REVIEW QUESTIONS FOR CHAPTER 14

1. In his last year of office, Madison approved all of the following *except*

    (A) a standing army
    (B) a national bank
    (C) a tariff for revenue only
    (D) an expanded navy

2. The Rush-Bagot Agreement

    (A) fixed the United States-Canadian border
    (B) demilitarized the Great Lakes
    (C) gave Florida to the United States
    (D) settled the Oregon dispute

3. Jackson's seizure of St. Marks and Pensacola was defended by

    (A) John Quincy Adams
    (B) John C. Calhoun
    (C) William Henry Crawford
    (D) James Monroe

4. The Adams-Onis Treaty provided for all of the following *except*

    (A) the ceding of Florida to the United States
    (B) the definition of the Louisiana boundary
    (C) the United States' acquisition of Texas
    (D) Spain's surrender of land claims north of the forty-second parallel

5. The quarrel over Missouri was touched off by the

    (A) Tallmadge amendment
    (B) Thomas amendment
    (C) Clay amendment
    (D) Adams amendment

6. The Missouri Compromise did all of the following *except*

    (A) bar slavery north of 36°30′ latitude
    (B) allow slavery in Missouri
    (C) bar slavery south of 36°30′ latitude
    (D) admit Maine as a free state

7. The constitutionality of the Second Bank of the United States was affirmed in

    (A) Fletcher versus Peck
    (B) M'Culloch versus Maryland
    (C) Gibbon versus Ogden
    (D) Martin versus Hunter's Lessee

8. The Monroe Doctrine embodied the ideas of

    (A) John Quincy Adams
    (B) Henry Clay
    (C) George Canning
    (D) Andrew Jackson

9. In 1824, the candidate of the congressional caucus was

   (A) John Quincy Adams (C) Henry Clay
   (B) William Henry Crawford (D) John C. Calhoun

10. The author of the American System was

    (A) Andrew Jackson (C) John C. Calhoun
    (B) John Quincy Adams (D) Henry Clay

Explanatory Answers

1. **(C)** Madison supported the protectionist Tariff of 1816.

2. **(B)** The Agreement provided for mutual naval disarmament.

3. **(A)** Adams used it to pressure Spain into ceding Florida to the United States.

4. **(C)** The United States renounced all claims to Texas.

5. **(A)** The Tallmadge Amendment would have barred importation of slaves into Missouri and would have emancipated all slaves once they had reached age twenty-five.

6. **(C)** The Compromise permitted slavery south of that line.

7. **(B)** A Maryland tax on the Bank's transactions was struck down.

8. **(A)** The Doctrine, embodying Adams' ideas, was aimed at Russia as well as at Spain and sought to establish the diplomatic independence of the United States from Great Britain.

9. **(B)** Crawford was the last candidate of the caucus system.

10. **(D)** The American System called for high tariffs and internal improvements.

PART THREE:
THE MIDDLE PERIOD, 1828-1877

Chapter 15

THE ERA OF JACKSONIAN DEMOCRACY, 1828-1844

The period between 1820 and 1850 (commonly called the "Age of Jackson") was one of great social ferment and reform. Jackson and his followers by no means approved of, or supported, the myriad of reform movements which sprang up during this period, but the reform spirit of the 1820's was instrumental in bringing Jackson to power. Jacksonians were not initiators of the mid-nineteenth century reform spirit; but they were its beneficiaries. Historians credit evangelist Charles G. Finney's Great Revival (which began in New York State in 1824) with producing the reform impulse in America. The Great Revival lasted for a full generation and gave new life to American Protestantism (it especially benefited Methodism, Baptism, and similar evangelical sects). Like the earlier Great Awakening, it stressed the possibility of universal salvation through faith in Christ and acceptance of His love. Emphasizing direct communion between man and God, the Great Revival urged men to prepare the way of the Lord by working for the improvement of their society. It gave religious justification to attempts at social improvement and gave birth to numerous moral and social causes. Movements for temperance (prohibition or limitation of the use of alcoholic beverages) arose during this period; and movements for the abolition of imprisonment for debt, for improved prison conditions, and for better treatment of the insane, the orphaned, and of the chronically ill were all in evidence, as were calls for expanded systems of public education. Furthermore, the abolitionist cause (discussed in the next chapter) gained impetus from the reform spirit. Demands for equal rights for women and for recognition of the rights of workingmen to organize and to strike for better wages and working conditions were also being voiced. The spirit engendered by the Great Revival also led to the demands for political reform that helped the Jacksonians achieve power.

THE NATURE OF JACKSONIAN DEMOCRACY

Andrew Jackson: All Things to All Men

The term Jacksonian Democracy was not used by contemporaries, but is, rather, a twentieth-century interpolation. It does not describe a definite or concrete program of reform; instead, it symbolizes a spirit or political attitude. Jacksonian Democracy embraced men of widely divergent and often contradictory views. They were held together primarily by the personality of Andrew Jackson and not by any formal body of ideological belief. Historians are still in vigorous disagreement as to precisely what Jacksonian Democracy was. The major schools of thought follow:

(1) **The Frontier Interpretation.** According to Frederick Jackson Turner (who was among the first to use the term), Jacksonian Democracy represented the triumph of the Western frontier over the conservative and aristocratic East. It was based on the proposition that all men were equal and that the people as a whole (excluding women and Negroes, of course), rather than a social elite, should control and run their government. With the triumph of Jackson in 1828, democracy as we know it today was born in America. The age of Jackson, as Carl R. Fish observed, was the age of the common man.

(2) **The Eastern Workingman Thesis.** According to Arthur M. Schlesinger, Jr., the intellectual heart of Jacksonian Democracy was not on the Western frontier but in the Eastern cities of America. He saw the Jacksonian movement as led by spokesmen for the Eastern working class which sought to tame the economic power of the rising capitalist order in the interest of social justice. Jacksonian Democracy was thus seen as the intellectual forerunner of the New Deal. However, in the quarter-century since the publication of Schlesinger's *Age of Jackson,* the Eastern Workingman thesis has been pretty well demolished.

(3) **The Entrepreneurial Interpretation.** In the view of Richard Hofstadter, Jacksonian Democracy was neither a Western democratic movement nor an Eastern working-class movement; rather, it was middle class and pro-capitalist in nature. It was a movement designed to end economic monopoly and smash the power of the old mercantile elite, thus permitting middle-class entrepreneurs to dominate the American economic order. Jacksonian Democracy, according to Hofstadter, sought to make the middle class dominant in America so that this class could effectively exploit the economic resources of the nation.

(4) **The Neo-Jeffersonian Interpretation.** The most satisfying interpretation of Jacksonian Democracy was offered by Marvin Meyers. He saw the movement as a Neo-Jeffersonian attempt to reconcile the traditional agrarian values of America with the new realities of a rising industrial order. It sought to preserve individualism and personal liberty in a society which demanded ever-increasing degrees of standardization and regimentation. The contribution of the Jacksonians was to preserve agrarian values in an industrializing society.

However one interprets Jacksonian Democracy, there can be little doubt that Jackson's elevation to the Presidency marked a new departure in American political history. Power had definitely shifted from the East to the West, from the old mercantile aristocracy to the rising middle class, from the Yankee-Protestant elite to the common man. The shift was also one of style rather than substance, of mood rather than actuality. The prime achievement of the Jacksonian age, aside from the acceptance of political democracy itself, was the rise of the organized political party and the beginnings of the political machine.

JACKSON'S FIRST TERM 1829-1833

Washington, D. C. Had Never Seen Their Likes Before

On March 4, 1829, Andrew Jackson took the oath of office as seventh President of the United States. His inaugural address, promising economy in government, respect for states' rights, a just Indian policy, and "reform" of the federal civil service, could well have been delivered by Thomas Jefferson. On the major issues of the day — the tariff, the bank, internal improvements, and the currency — the new President was silent. In keeping with the new democratic spirit, Jackson's inaugural ball was opened to the public; and his enthusiastic followers almost trampled him to death and almost demolished the White House. Washington society had never before seen so many common people acting as though they ran the government; and the realization that they might well do so, proved disconcerting. So did the new President's policies.

The Kitchen Cabinet and the Spoils System

Selecting his Cabinet officers to satisfy sectional and factional demands, Jackson did not place his confidence in his Cabinet. Rather, he relied upon the advice and counsel of Western newspaper editors and politicians, such as Amos Kendall,

Isaac Hill, William B. Lewis, Andrew J. Donelson, and Duff Green. Given minor federal appointments, these men constituted an informal Kitchen Cabinet which met with Jackson socially and provided him with the counsel he needed. The Kitchen Cabinet was at the height of its influence from 1829 to 1831; after that date, a reorganized Cabinet largely supplanted the Kitchen Cabinet's advisory function.

Jackson gave Martin Van Buren (the astute head of the Albany Regency — one of the first effective political machines) control of the federal patronage. While the spoils system (the replacement of incumbent federal officeholders with the political friends of the new administration) dated back to Jefferson's presidency, Jackson glorified it as an agency of democracy. The argument was that frequent rotation in office (the wholesale firing of political opponents) made the government more responsive to the people's will and prevented the development of a dangerous bureaucratic aristocracy which might endanger popular liberties. Furthermore, it was argued, the duties of public office were so manifestly simple that any normally intelligent citizen could perform them. No special skills were needed, and as many citizens as possible should be encouraged to serve their government for brief periods of time and then return to private life. Of course, Van Buren used federal offices to reward Jackson's followers, and Van Buren's patronage policy consolidated Jackson's hold over the party and made the party a powerful engine for the achievement of Jackson's political ambitions. On the whole, though, the use of patronage was moderate: only 9 per cent of the federal bureaucracy was replaced during Jackson's first year in office, and only some 20 per cent was replaced between 1829 and 1837. Not until much later would the spoils system become infamous; but in retrospect, Jackson was given the blame for initiating it. Although the old Federalist aristocracy was hard hit by Jackson's patronage policy (and accordingly took an intense dislike toward Old Hickory), the spoils system was not abused by the Jacksonians.

The Growth of Sectional Hostility: the Webster-Hayne Debate

The growth of abolitionism (discussed in the next chapter) aroused sectional animosities between the North and the South and complicated Jackson's presidency. In January, 1830, the Senate began a debate on public-land policy. Thomas Hart Benton of Missouri accused the East of wanting to stifle the development of the West in order to insure a large supply of cheap labor for Eastern factories. Robert Y. Hayne of South Carolina, seeing an opportunity to drive a wedge between the West and the East, vigorously defended the West, hoping to cement a West-South alliance and to isolate the East. During the course of his remarks, Hayne enunciated the compact theory of the Constitution (the idea that the federal government was formed by the states and that the states remained supreme in the Union and could secede at will). Daniel Webster, hoping to kill the possibility of a West-South alliance, concentrated on Hayne's constitutional theories (seeking to show Hayne up as a man more concerned with the immediate welfare of his state than with the good of the nation as a whole). The debate soon became one devoted to the nature of the federal Union. Webster held that the Union was created by the people of the United States, not by the separate states, and that the Union operated directly upon the people and could not be dissolved by the states. He concluded his remarks with the famous statement, "Liberty *and* Union, now and forever, one and inseparable!" The speech electrified the nation, and the constitutional theory advanced by Daniel Webster was to be hallowed by the ordeal of Civil War.

The response to Webster's remarks pleased Martin Van Buren, who was anxious to weaken the influence of John C. Calhoun (his major opponent for leadership of the Democratic party). It also pleased Andrew Jackson. The President, although a states' rights advocate, was, above all else, a strong Unionist; and he was becoming disenchanted with Calhoun's sectionalism. In April, 1830, Jackson and Calhoun met head-on at a Jefferson Day Dinner. In order to drive home his strong nationalism, Jackson proposed a toast, asserting, "Our Union: It must be preserved!" The imperturbable Calhoun responded, "The Union, next to our liberty, most dear." It was the beginning of the break between the two men, who would shortly come to the edge of violence.

The Jackson-Calhoun Split

The break between Jackson and Calhoun was intensely personal as well as ideological. The President had always assumed that Calhoun had defended Jackson's 1818 incursion into Florida.

THE ERA OF JACKSONIAN DEMOCRACY / 149

Cartoon commenting on the resignation of Jackson's Cabinet in the course of the Peggy O'Neale affair.

During the spring of 1830, Jackson was shocked to learn that Calhoun had actually demanded his arrest and court-martial. The Eaton affair, however, made the estrangement between Jackson and Calhoun complete. John H. Eaton, Jackson's Secretary of War, had married Peggy O'Neale, a beautiful Washington widow of questionable morals. Mrs. Calhoun refused to accept her presence in Washington society and led a social boycott against her. Jackson, remembering the similar torment suffered by his own wife, became incensed at the treatment Mrs. Eaton was receiving.* He blamed this cruelty on Calhoun (whom he also accused of fomenting divisiveness in his Cabinet). The only one to champion Mrs. Eaton was the widower, Martin Van Buren, who rapidly rose in the esteem of the President. In April, 1831, Van Buren and Eaton resigned from the Cabinet (making it customary for other cabinet officers to tender their resignations as a courtesy) so that Jackson could reorganize it and exclude Calhoun's followers from the administration.

Van Buren was named as Minister to England and Eaton became military governor of Florida. (Calhoun, however, had his revenge, when as Presiding Officer of the Senate, he cast the tie-breaking vote against Van Buren's confirmation. He had broken a Minister, but he had unknowingly created a future Vice-President.) The new Cabinet, which enjoyed Jackson's confidence, included Levi Woodbury (New Hampshire) as Secretary of the Navy, Edward Livingston (Louisiana) as Secretary of State, Roger B. Taney (Maryland) as Attorney General, Lewis Cass (Ohio) as Secretary of War, and Louis McLane (Delaware) as Secretary of the Treasury. The only member of the original Cabinet who was retained was William T. Barry, the Postmaster General. The Cabinet reorganization isolated the Calhoun faction, and the South Carolinian resigned as Vice-President to take a seat in the United States Senate, where he would be at liberty to actively oppose the administration.

The Nullification Crisis

The South, and particularly South Carolina, had assumed that Jackson opposed the protective tariff, and they expected him to give them relief from the 1828 Tariff of Abominations. Jackson, however, was not especially interested in the tariff question, and he was reluctant to reduce customs duties since this would cut federal revenues and delay the liquidation of the national debt. In the summer of 1832, Henry Clay introduced a new tariff schedule in Congress. While eliminating the more objectionable features of the Tariff of Abominations, the 1832 measure was still clearly protectionist and retained high duties on textiles and iron. That October, John C. Calhoun led the nullifiers (as they were to be known) to victory in the state elections in South Carolina. In November, 1832, the nullifiers called a convention which, citing the compact theory of the Constitution, declared that the Tariffs of 1828 and 1832 were null and void within the state of South Carolina. This Ordinance of Nullification forbade collection of the customs within the borders of South Carolina after February 1, 1833, and forbade citizens of the state from aiding federal authorities in customs collections. It also declared that if the federal government employed force in an effort to enforce

---

* Rachel Jackson had been formerly married; when she married Jackson, she thought that she had been divorced from her previous husband. Jackson's political opponents discovered that her divorce had not been valid, and they used this information as political ammunition against Jackson, causing Rachel great mental torment.

the tariff, then South Carolina would be justified in seceding from the Union and resuming its independent existence as a sovereign state.

South Carolina's Ordinance of Nullification was a direct challenge to federal authority and to the supremacy of federal law. It was a challenge which Jackson was determined to meet. On December 10, 1832, Jackson issued a Proclamation to the People of South Carolina in which he asserted that no state could unilaterally nullify a federal law or secede from the Union. Declaring that he was duty bound to uphold federal law, Jackson vowed to do so, and he warned that nullification was disunion and that disunion accompanied by armed force was treason. He appealed to the people of South Carolina to abide by federal law. However, in case South Carolina failed to heed his appeal, Jackson asked for passage of a Force Bill, which would give him the authority to use federal troops to enforce federal law in the state. Meanwhile, South Carolina's Governor Hayne recruited 2,000 "Minute Men" to oppose federal attempts to forcibly collect the tariff. As February 1, 1833 approached, tensions between the federal government and South Carolina deepened.

Fortunately, South Carolina found itself politically isolated. The states of the North and the West condemned nullification as treason, and the states of the deep South also opposed South Carolina's actions, declaring that nullification was constitutionally unsound and dangerous in practice. In the Senate, Henry Clay proposed a compromise which Calhoun (isolated as he was) agreed to accept. By the Compromise Tariff of 1833, customs duties were leveled down; and it was agreed to reduce all tariffs to a uniform 20 percent duty within ten years and to end protection for items which were not vital to the nation's defense. Upon learning that a compromise was in the works, South Carolina suspended the implementation of its Ordinance of Nullification on January 21, 1833. On March 2, Jackson signed the compromise tariff; and later that month, South Carolina repealed its Ordinance of Nullification. As a last gesture of defiance, however, South Carolina nullified Jackson's Force Bill and declared it to be inoperative within the state. Jackson had successfully upheld federal authority, but South Carolina had again nullified a federal law; and the issue remained unsettled. Nullification was by no means a dead issue; and on his deathbed, Andrew Jackson regretted that he had not hanged John C. Calhoun.

Internal Improvements

If Jackson's attitude on the tariff disappointed South Carolina, his stand on internal improvements alienated much of the West. Rich in agricultural produce, the West needed a vast system of interstate roads, canals, and river improvements in order to get its produce to Eastern markets. Internal improvements were essential to the growth and development of the West, and it was hoped that Jackson, as a Westerner, would favor a policy of federal internal improvements. In 1830, a proposal was made to have the United States government purchase the stock of a corporation chartered to build a road between Maysville and Lexington in Kentucky. Although the road would lie within the boundaries of a single state, it was to be part of a projected interstate highway; and Jackson's Western supporters urged him to support the measure. However, Martin Van Buren argued against the bill and he carried Jackson with him. In May, the President vetoed the Maysville Road bill, declaring that (1) the proposed road lay within the boundaries of a single state and did not qualify as an interstate project and that (2) internal improvements at federal expense were constitutionally questionable and politically unwise. The veto marked the death of a federal program of internal improvements (although federal funds continued to be appropriated for river and harbor improvements), and revealed Jackson as a true disciple of Thomas Jefferson.

Jackson and Cherokees

Back in 1791, the United States Government signed a treaty with the Cherokee Indians of Georgia which recognized them as an independent society within the territory of the United States and which pledged the federal government to defend Cherokee territorial rights in Georgia. The Cherokees were a highly developed agricultural tribe which was adopting some of the ways of white civilization. Having developed their own written language, they established their own educational system, published their own books and newspapers, and had adapted to their white neighbors. Unfortunately, in 1828, gold was discovered on the Cherokees' land, and the state of Georgia coveted the land belonging to the Indians. The

Georgia legislature passed a law stating that after June 1, 1830, all Cherokee laws would be null and void and that the Georgia state government would assume authority over the Indian lands within its territory. This was a direct challenge to federal authority since a United States treaty guaranteed the tenure of the Cherokee nation. But Andrew Jackson, who did not feel that Indians had any right to impede the progress of white settlement, took no action to enforce federal supremacy. However, a white missionary challenged Georgia's authority over the Cherokee nation in the federal courts, and in 1832, the United States Supreme Court (John Marshall delivering the opinion) held that the federal government had exclusive jurisdiction over Cherokee lands in Georgia and that Georgia laws affecting the Cherokees were null and void. Andrew Jackson, upon hearing the verdict, is alleged to have said "John Marshall has made his decision, now let him enforce it." With the President refusing to implement the decision of the Court, there was nothing to stop Georgia from taking over Cherokee lands. In 1835, the Cherokee nation ceded their lands east of the Mississippi to the United States for 5 million dollars and began the trek to a special Indian reservation that was created for them in the midst of the "American desert" in present-day Oklahoma. One-quarter of the Cherokee nation perished on the long trek to Oklahoma, and the land in the reservation was so barren that the Indians who went there were condemned to a slow and agonizing death.

Jackson's policy was to remove all Indian tribes east of the Mississippi to the new reservation in Oklahoma. Those tribes which refused to leave their ancestral lands were slaughtered. Under Jackson, the United States was a land of freedom and opportunity for whites; it was a land of death for the Indians. "These are crying sins," John Quincy Adams observed, "for which we are answerable before a higher jurisdiction."

The Bank War

The major political issue of Jackson's first term was undoubtedly the struggle over the Second Bank of the United States. Chartered back in 1816, the Bank of the United States had been mismanaged in its early years and was widely blamed for causing the Panic of 1819. However under the guidance of Nicholas Biddle, the Bank was, at this time, doing an effective job in providing the United States with a sound credit system and in checking dangerous inflationary pressures from locally controlled Western and Eastern state banks. The Bank enjoyed the support of the conservative classes, of nationalists such as Henry Clay and Daniel Webster, and of old Jeffersonians like Madison and Gallatin. It also had powerful enemies.

The Bank was opposed by Western agrarians who demanded cheap money to finance their land speculation and who resented the Bank's efforts to achieve a sound (and therefore dear) credit system. Likewise, Eastern workingmen opposed the Bank because it had established a system of paper currency which they erroneously believed created a moneyed aristocracy. This moneyed aristocracy, they felt, was responsible for widening social inequality in American society by artificially concentrating wealth in a single non-productive economic class. They looked upon the Bank as a subversive influence undermining republicanism and democracy and tending to the creation of an aristocratic despotism in the United States. In addition, the Bank of the United States was opposed by state and local banking interests which resented the national bank's restrictions on their credit issues. (The Bank would collect the notes of state banks and present them for payment as a means of making certain that the state banks did not overextend their resources. Any bank which could not honor its notes would be forced to close its doors, and this checked their inflationary tendencies). Furthermore, the Bank was opposed by the rising group of middle-class entrepreneurs who needed easy credit to finance their business ventures. Finally, Andrew Jackson was a passionate bank-hater. He blamed the banks for his own personal financial difficulties during the Panic of 1819, and he would have liked an America without banks. As the largest bank of all, the Bank of the United States personified for Jackson the evils of banking and became his favorite whipping boy. In his 1829 message to Congress, Jackson questioned the Bank's constitutionality, but he made no attempt to kill it by revoking its charter. Indeed, it is doubtful that the Bank would have been a political issue at all in 1832, if it had not been for Henry Clay.

Nominated for the Presidency by the National Republicans, Henry Clay needed a winning issue for the 1832 campaign. Although the charter of the Bank of the United States was not scheduled to expire until 1836, Henry Clay decided to sponsor a recharter bill in 1832. Confident that Jackson would veto it (as a result of pressures from within his own party), Clay could then turn the recharter issue into a winning political issue since the conservative business community would rally to his candidacy. It was one of Clay's most grievous political blunders.

Jackson Vetoes the Bank Recharter Bill

On July 10, 1832, Andrew Jackson vetoed the bank bill in a message which has since become an American political classic. Jackson's veto message rested upon the following grounds.

(1) The Bank of the United States was an economic monopoly chartered by the federal government for the benefit of a small class of moneyed aristocrats. While the general revenues of the government helped support the Bank, it benefited only the aristocratic stockholders of the Bank, many of whom were European bankers and aristocrats.

(2) As a corporation enjoying exclusive privileges granted by the government, the Bank of the United States denied others the right to conduct banking business and denied the equality of economic opportunity to which all Americans were entitled. The government had no right to grant special economic privileges to one group while denying them to others, for to do so was to unite wealth and power in a fashion most destructive to liberty.

(3) The Bank of the United States, because of its vast wealth and political influence, was a potential and actual threat to American republicanism and democracy — a threat which could not be tolerated. The Bank should be destroyed in the interest of representative government.

The Presidential Election of 1832

For the first time in American history, the candidates for the 1832 presidential election were nominated by national conventions chosen by the party rank-and-file. The practice of nominating presidential candidates through the congressional caucus or the state legislature was a thing of the past. From now on, the party faithful would determine their party's standard-bearer. The National Republicans named Henry Clay and Pennsylvania's John Sergeant as its presidential and vice-presidential candidates. Clay campaigned almost solely on the Bank issue (and Nicholas Biddle sought to help his candidacy by tightening credit and inducing economic distress, which, it was hoped, would redound to Jackson's disadvantage). Clay accused Jackson of seeking to ruin the American economy and working to impose economic suffering upon all social classes. The Democrats renominated Jackson for the Presidency and named Martin Van Buren as Vice-President. Parrying Clay's charges, the Jacksonians turned the Bank issue into a question of democracy versus aristocracy, and they ran on the personality and image of the Hero of New Orleans. Finally, the Anti-Masonic party (the first third party in American history) nominated William Wirt of Maryland and Amos Ellmaker of Pennsylvania as its candidates. The Anti-Masonic party was a curious phenomenon. Supported by clergymen, democrats, and newspaper editors, it was a democratic reaction against secret societies which began in the 1820's, when one William Morgan was allegedly murdered by Masons (members of a secret fraternal order) to prevent him from revealing their secrets. The Anti-Masonic party opposed all secret societies as subversive of republican liberties. In the election, Jackson won an overwhelming victory, receiving 687,502 popular votes to Clay's 530,189. In the Electoral College, Jackson had 219 votes, Clay 49, and Wirt 7 (he carried only Maryland). The Bank issue had failed, and "King Andrew" was reelected President.

JACKSON'S SECOND TERM 1833-1837

The "Monster" is Dead

Interpreting his electoral triumph as a mandate from the people to destroy the Bank of the United States (the "Monster," as he called it), Jackson decided to cripple the Bank before Biddle could bring pressure to bear for another recharter attempt. Biddle was deliberately tightening the credit, inducing numerous bankruptcies and widespread economic distress, in an effort to put pressure on Congress to override the President's veto. However, Biddle overplayed his hand, and his credit contraction backfired. On October 1, 1833, the Treasury Department began placing its deposits in local state banks (the so-called "pet banks") rather than in the Bank of the United States. Twenty-three state banks, run by friends of the administration, were designated as federal depositories. However, the policy of placing federal funds in state banks proved disastrous. The local banks used the federal funds as assets to back up their note issues, but they greatly overextended their note issues. The result was a severe inflation which benefited Western farmers and Eastern entrepreneurs (for the moment at least), but which eventually led to a ruinous depression that hurt everyone. In killing the Bank of the United States, Andrew Jackson performed his greatest disservice to the nation, for its destruction played havoc with America's monetary system and led to economic chaos.

The Birth of the Whig Party

The Whig party, which dated back to the election of 1832, came into formal existence in 1834, as a coalition built around opposition to the personality and policies of Andrew Jackson. Basically, it was a continuation of the old Adams-Clay National Republican faction; the Whigs drew support from the Southern followers of John C. Calhoun, the Western supporters of Henry Clay, and the Eastern backers of Daniel Webster. They adopted as the foundation of their program the American system of Henry Clay (protective tariff, internal improvements, and subsidies to business and agriculture), which made their alliance with the Calhounites tenuous and uneasy. Nevertheless, their insistence that Congress must exercise the preponderant power in the national government and that the President must faithfully execute congressional policies, rather than shape his own independent programs, appealed to the Southerners. Jackson, in sharp contrast, believed that the President should be the "tribune" of the people, actively defending and championing their interests, even if that meant opposing the Congress. Where Jackson believed in a strong President and a neutral government (one which did not actively aid or hinder any economic group or interest), the Whigs advocated a weak President and a strong, positive national government, one which actively promoted all manner of economic growth. The Whigs, as such, were a rather loose coalition of Western and Eastern nationalists and Southern states' rights agrarians; and the party did not really coalesce until the election of 1840.

Texas

In comparison with the titanic struggles over nullification and the Bank of the United States, Jackson's second term appeared quiet and anticlimactic. However, Texas was one of the major second-term issues. Back in 1821, Moses Austin obtained a charter from New Spain (later confirmed by an independent Mexico) to settle American colonists in the area which is now Texas. Upon the death of Moses Austin, his son Stephen took over the charter; and in 1824, Texas was organized as a constituent state within the Mexican republic. A year later, it was thrown open to colonization. In return for being permitted to settle Texas, the Americans agreed (1) to recognize Mexican law, (2) to prohibit slavery, and (3) to adopt the Roman Catholic faith. The Americans, however, reneged on their pledges; and in 1830, the Mexican authorities outlawed the institution of slavery and prohibited further American colonization of Texas. With the rise to power of General Santa Anna in Mexico, an attempt was made to bring Texas under central authority and put an end to its autonomy. This led to open revolution by the American settlers in 1835, and Santa Anna invaded Texas. The American resistance at the Alamo (in February and March of 1836) inspired the Texans to maintain their struggle for independence, and at the Battle of San Jacinto (April 21, 1836) Santa Anna was captured by the forces commanded by Sam Houston. Santa Anna was forced to sign a treaty recognizing Texan independence; and although the Mexican government repudiated Santa Anna's treaty, Texan independence was an accomplished fact.

As soon as they achieved their independence, the Texans sought annexation by the United States. While Jackson would have liked to annex Texas, he feared to do so for several reasons. First, the United States had renounced all claims to Texas in the Adams-Onis treaty of 1819, and Jackson feared a possible war with Mexico if Texas were annexed. Secondly, Texas was a slave society, and by 1836, slavery had become a sore point in American politics. If Texas became a slave state, Jackson feared that the Democratic party would be destroyed in the ensuing storm over the slavery issue. Therefore, Jackson did not even extend diplomatic recognition to Texas until his last day in office; and in August, 1837, the new administration formally rejected Texas' annexation. In the 1840's the Texas issue would be revived. As Jackson feared, it was also to arouse the slavery issue, which would eventually lead to the break-up of the Democratic party.

The Presidential Election of 1836

In 1836, Jackson succeeded in having Martin Van Buren nominated as the Democratic candidate for President. As Vice-President, the Democrats picked Richard Mentor Johnson of Kentucky, an eccentric politician who claimed to have killed the great Indian leader Tecumseh. Van Buren ran on Jackson's coattails, promising to continue his policies. The Whigs were unable to agree on a single candidate and nominated three sectional candidates, hoping to deadlock the election and throw it into the House of Representatives. Daniel Webster was the Whig standard-bearer in New England; Hugh L. White, a popular anti-Jackson politician in Tennessee, was the Western and Southern candidate; while William Henry Harrison, the hero of the battle at Tippecanoe Creek, was the Whig candidate in the old Northwest as well as the presidential candidate of the Anti-Masonic party. The Whigs were united only in their passionate dislike of Andrew Jackson, although they generally favored a national bank, internal improvements, and tariff protection. However, their electoral machinery could not compare with the Democrats, and they tended to view the masses with suspicion. The election was a clear triumph for Van Buren. The voting results were as follows:

Van Buren	761,549	(170)
Harrison	549,567	(73)
White	145,396	(26)
Webster	41,287	(14)

Webster carried only his native Massachusetts, while White took Georgia and his own state of Tennessee. Harrison made a surprisingly strong showing, considering that he had no political experience. He carried Indiana, Ohio, Kentucky, Maryland, Delaware, New Jersey, and Vermont. His campaign testified to the political popularity of war heroes, and it was a lesson which was not lost upon the Whigs.

On the day he left office, before retiring to his Tennessee plantation, Jackson gave his farewell address. Urging loyalty to the Union, he condemned sectionalism, paper currency, banks, monopolies, and speculations. He also left his successor a depression which Jackson, himself, was instrumental in creating.

THE VAN BUREN PRESIDENCY
1837-1841

The Panic of 1837

Far more severe than the Panic of 1819, the depression which began in 1837 lasted through 1842-1843 in the West and the South (the East recovered sooner). At its height, the price of Southern cotton fell 50 per cent, and Western wheat was equally hard hit. In the East, workers rioted in many major cities, demanding lower food prices, work (at government expense if necessary), and relief from burdensome financial obligations. The depression resulted from dangerous land speculation in the West and South, from the reckless overextension of credit by state banks to finance this wild land speculation, from crop failures during 1835-1836, and from the collapse of European markets for American produce. The immediate cause of the depression was Andrew Jackson's Specie Circular (July, 1836), a presidential directive which required that all payments for federal lands be made in specie (gold and silver), rather than with the often depreciated paper notes of state banks. This requirement produced a rapid loss of confidence in state bank-note issues which led to the failure of many banks. Furthermore, as credit became tighter, numerous farmers were unable to meet their obligations and lost their lands. Although the Specie Circular was the immediate cause of the depression, the Panic of 1837 had its roots in long-term weaknesses in the American economy; and a crisis would have developed sooner or later even without the Specie Circular. Unfortunately, Americans in the mid-nineteenth century lacked the economic knowledge to adequately deal with economic depressions.

In September, 1837, Martin Van Buren blamed the depression on the runaway speculation of the state-chartered banks. He called for a specie currency to replace the bank-note system. (This was a counterproductive measure since an inflated currency is needed to spur economic production during times of depression, and a specie currency actually contracts the money supply and makes credit more expensive.) Van Buren also called for an independent treasury to house federal revenues so that local banks would not use federal assets to back up their speculative note issues. However, the independent treasury was not implemented until July, 1840; and the following year, the victorious Whigs repealed the act which created the treasury. Aside from the independent treasury, Van Buren could only urge cutbacks in federal expenditures as a way of combating the depression (another counterproductive move) and wait until an economic reversal, arising from the natural working of economic law, brought prosperity back to America. Van Buren, who lacked the charisma of Jackson and who would have suffered by comparison with Old Hickory even in the best of circumstances, was hurt by the depression and lost much of his political following.

The Gag Rule

It was Van Buren's misfortune to inherit a depression and to reap the bitter harvest of the slavery controversy. Van Buren's presidency marks the emergence of slavery as a divisive issue in American political life — an issue which would shatter the unity of both major parties. By 1836, abolitionists and anti-slavery partisans were flooding Congress with petitions demanding the abolition of both slavery and the slave trade in the District of Columbia. These petitions were referred to the District of Columbia Committee and were consistently denied. However, they slowed congressional business and aroused the vehement hostility of Southern congressmen. In May, 1836, South Carolina's Henry L. Pinckney proposed that the House of Representatives automatically table (without bothering to read, much less consider) all abolitionist petitions it received. Hoping to expedite its business, the House voted approval of the Pinkney resolution. However, John Quincy Adams (who had returned to the House after serving as President) led a one-man crusade against this Gag Rule.

As a House rule, the Gag resolution had to be approved by each separate session of Congress (it was invoked by every Congress from 1836 to 1844, when it was ended) and was, consequently, kept alive as a political issue. Adams argued that his constituents had a constitutional right to petition Congress for a redress of grievances; and as the Gag Rule denied them that right, it was unconstitutional. He insisted upon presenting and hearing petitions sent by his constituents, and he was soon joined by a small group of fellow congressmen who had anti-slavery sentiments or who shared his constitutional view. Adams' defense of the right of petition earned him the title of "Old Man Eloquent" and succeeded in arousing widespread public sympathy for his stand. His crusade focused public attention on the slavery problem and gave the abolitionists a concrete issue on which to appeal to the American people. It made the South appear as the enemy of free speech, and it helped turn Northern public opinion against the Southern cause.

The struggle over the Gag Rule soon spilled over into the Senate, when Vermont's Benjamin Swift introduced a resolution calling upon Congress not to admit any new slave states to the Union. John C. Calhoun immediately accepted the challenge and, in 1837, introduced a series of counterresolutions which reaffirmed the compact theory of the Constitution. Calhoun declared that Congress had no right to interfere with the domestic institutions of any state, that it could not interfere with the interstate slave traffic, and that it was obligated to prevent states from attacking the social institutions of their sister states. Although Calhoun won the contest in the Senate, the slavery issue was by no means dead. In 1839, the Liberty party, led by James G. Birney, was formed to oppose the westward expansion of slavery and to maintain free soil for free men in the Western territories.

Relations with England

Between 1837 and 1842 Anglo-American tensions along the United States-Canadian border were high. In December, 1837, Canadian militiamen burned the *Caroline* (an American steamboat which had been supplying Canadian rebels against the British on Navy Island) on the American side of the Niagara River and killed an American seaman named Amos Durfee. War fever mounted in the United States, but fortunately it subsided. However, in 1838, tensions again rose as a result of a boundary dispute in the Maine-New Brunswick area. The treaties which defined the United States-Canadian border were vague as to the precise determination of the Maine-New Brunswick border, and several previous attempts to fix the border through international arbitration had failed. During the so-called Aroostook War of 1838-1839, Canadian and American lumberjacks (joined on both sides by militiamen) fought each other to control logging sites in the disputed border area, and Winfield Scott was placed in command of American forces along the Canadian border. Fortunately, a truce was arranged and no blood was shed. Both sides agreed to settle their territorial claims through diplomatic negotiations. The Webster-Ashburton Treaty (August, 1842) finally resolved the border dispute by giving the United States 7,000 square miles of land and by assigning the remaining 5,000 square miles of the Aroostook region to Canada. Lastly, in 1841, New York State authorities arrested Alexander McLeod, a Canadian deputy sheriff, and charged him with the murder of Amos Durfee. The British angrily demanded McLeod's release, but the United States asserted that it had no jurisdiction to interfere in a state criminal proceeding. Fortunately, a New York jury freed McLeod for lack of evidence (New York's Governor Seward had been prepared to pardon McLeod, in the event of a guilty verdict, in order to avoid international complications). With the acquittal of McLeod, Anglo-American relations improved, and the Webster-Ashburton Agreement left the region of Oregon as the only substantial territorial dispute still existing between the two nations.

The Taney Court

It was Andrew Jackson's good fortune to be able to appoint seven new members to the United States Supreme Court, among whom was Roger B. Taney, named as Chief Justice to replace the late John Marshall. All of Jackson's appointees were agrarian, states' rights Democrats, and for twenty-eight years the Jacksonians dominated the Supreme Court, just as the Federalists had dominated the Marshall court. The Taney court, however, did not break sharply with the nationalism of the Marshall court; rather, it changed the emphasis of the Supreme Court. The new court recognized the rights of the states to regulate private property and to restrict the activities of business for the general welfare of society. It ruled that states could regulate interstate commerce in the absence of contrary federal laws as long as they did not interpose state authority against that of the federal government (hence, the states could act concurrently with the national government in regulating business and commerce). While allowing the states a greater measure of authority, the Taney court never adopted the extreme states' rights views of the Calhounites, and it upheld the Unionist views of Andrew Jackson. The Taney court was most active in the late 1830's and 1840's and placed its seal of approval on the doctrine that government must serve the best interests of the general society even if that means restricting the freedom of vested economic interests.

Chief Justice Taney

The Presidential Election of 1840

The 1840 presidential campaign marked a turning point in American political history. It was the first election campaign to be fought with the instruments of modern political democracy. Mass rallies, torchlight parades, newspaper advertisements, billboards, broadsides, and campaign buttons and posters were all employed in the effort to get out the vote. The technique was highly successful, for a higher percentage of the electorate voted in the 1840 election than had ever voted in any previous election. Jacksonian Democracy came of age in 1840, but it was the Whigs, not the Democrats, who profited from the maturation of the democratic process.

The Whigs, noting the popular appeal of Tippecanoe, bypassed the better-known Henry Clay (who had too many political enemies) in favor of the elderly William Henry Harrison. For Vice-President, the Whigs selected John Tyler, a Virginia states' rights Democrat who had broken with Andrew Jackson. Unwilling to antagonize anyone, the Whigs declined to adopt a platform and centered their campaign on a personal attack on Van Buren ("Van, Van, the used up man," the Whig crowds shouted at their rallies), charging that he was living like an English aristocrat while the common people suffered from the effects of the depression. The Democrats renominated Martin Van Buren, but they were so divided that they could not agree on a vice-presidential candidate and did not name a running mate for Van Buren.

THE ERA OF JACKSONIAN DEMOCRACY / 157

Poster used in Harrison and Tyler campaign.

The Democrats swore opposition to a national bank and to internal improvements; they promised strict construction of the Constitution and declared that Congress did not have the right to interfere with the institution of slavery.

Log Cabins and Hard Cider

The campaign took on distinctive coloration when the Whigs pounced upon the statement of a Democratic newspaper which asserted that Harrison would gladly leave politics for a pension that would enable him to sit on the front porch of his log cabin and sip hard cider. Realizing the implications of the charge, the Whigs proudly announced that their candidate was a man of the people (born in a log cabin and enjoying the delights of hard cider), who rose from humble origins and who enjoyed the simple republican pleasures of life. Indeed, even Daniel Webster sang the praises of the log cabin and regretted that he had not been born in one. In contrast, Van Buren was portrayed as a luxury-loving aristocrat. Embracing the techniques of political democracy and playing up to the masses, the Whigs rolled up a decisive victory. Harrison polled 1,275,017 votes to Van Buren's 1,128,702, and he captured the Electoral College by a vote of 234 to 60. In addition, the Whigs took control of Congress.

And Tyler Too

Delivering his inaugural address in inclement weather, President Harrison promised to be a weak chief executive and to defer to the superior authority of Congress. Unfortunately, the weather brought on a serious illness which resulted in the President's death on April 4, 1841. John Tyler was now President, and his states' rights and agrarian bias soon became apparent. In August and September, 1841, Tyler vetoed bills passed by the Whigs which called for a new national bank. He also came out against federal internal improvements, aid to industry, and virtually every major Whig plank. In protest, Tyler's entire Cabinet (except for Webster) resigned, and his relations with the Whigs in Congress deteriorated to such an extent that he became a President without a party. Forced into an alliance with the Democrats, Tyler was largely ineffective (he failed, for example, to secure a treaty of annexation with Texas). He was the first President to be denied renomination by his own party, and his presidency was as inglorious as it was brief.

REVIEW QUESTIONS FOR CHAPTER 15

1. All were members of the Kitchen Cabinet *except*

   (A) Amos Kendall
   (B) Duff Green
   (C) Andrew J. Donelson
   (D) Martin Van Buren

2. All were factors in the Jackson-Calhoun split *except*

   (A) the Indian removal policy
   (B) nullification
   (C) the Peggy O'Neale affair
   (D) the 1818 Florida campaign

3. The Nullification crisis was ended by

   (A) the Force Bill
   (B) the Tariff of 1833
   (C) the Tariff of 1832
   (D) Jackson's Declaration to the People of South Carolina

4. The Bank of the United States was opposed by all of the following groups *except*

   (A) the state banking interests
   (B) the Western farmers
   (C) the Whigs
   (D) the rising middle class

5. Jackson was opposed for the presidency in 1832 by

   (A) William Henry Harrison
   (B) Daniel Webster
   (C) Hugh L. White
   (D) Henry Clay

6. The Whigs supported all of the following propositions *except*

   (A) a national bank
   (B) a strong President
   (C) internal improvements
   (D) tariff protection

7. The Panic of 1837 resulted from all of the following *except*

   (A) land speculation
   (B) the Specie Circular
   (C) overextension of credit
   (D) lack of confidence in Van Buren

8. Opposition to the Gag Rule was led by

   (A) John Quincy Adams
   (B) Daniel Webster
   (C) Henry Clay
   (D) John C. Calhoun

9. The Webster-Ashburton Treaty settled

   (A) the *Caroline* affair
   (B) the Oregon boundary dispute
   (C) the Maine-New Brunswick border dispute
   (D) the McLeod case

10. Tyler broke with his own party over a bill to

    (A) annex Texas
    (B) recharter a national bank
    (C) return Indian lands
    (D) occupy Oregon

Explanatory Answers

1. **(D)** Van Buren was a member of the regular Cabinet and a close advisor to Jackson.

2. **(A)** Calhoun, like Jackson, had small regard for Indian rights.

3. **(B)** The Tariff of 1833 lowered tariff rates to a uniform 20 per cent after ten years.

4. **(C)** The Whigs favored the Bank as an instrument of sound credit.

5. **(D)** Clay opposed him primarily on the Bank issue.

6. **(B)** They felt that the President should be subordinate to Congress.

7. **(D)** Lack of confidence in Van Buren was not a causative factor in the Panic of 1837.

8. **(A)** Adams felt that the Gag Rule deprived his constituents of their rights to petition for a redress of grievances.

9. **(C)** It divided the Aroostook region between the United States and Canada.

10. **(B)** Tyler opposed the measures of his own party and was the first President to be denied renomination.

Chapter 16

AMERICAN ROMANTICISM AND THE GROWTH OF SOUTHERN CIVILIZATION

The American character matured in the years from 1815 to 1860 and took on its classic form. Foreign observers (such as Alexis de Tocqueville, Charles Dickens, and Harriet Martineau) and American writers, alike, agreed that the American was a new man, whose like had not been seen before. He was passionately materialistic and acquisitive. Believing in the virtues of hard work, thrift, and sobriety, he expected to grow wealthy; and he devoutly believed that poverty was a providential punishment for laziness, indolence, and sloth. A firm believer in progress, the American optimistically expected his society to improve constantly and rapidly, and he was impatient with social evils and abuses which he felt were remediable. His religion celebrated the glory of the individual man and stressed the wonders which the self-reliant man could perform in the world. Rejecting the claims of aristocratic superiority, the American prized egalitarianism as an ideal, even if his society fell far short of realizing it in practice. He knew that democracy was the only just and workable system of government in the world, and he felt that eventually all mankind would follow in the political footsteps of the American nation. The American, however, was not doctrinaire. Rather, he was a pragmatist who bent his ideological preconceptions to fit the realities of an imperfect world. Tough, yet sentimental, he sang the praises of family life and deferred to women, even if his personal life denied his professions of family devotion.

On the other hand, the American was also tolerant of corruption in business and government, and he displayed ugly racial prejudices. Too many Americans believed that "the only good Indian was a dead Indian," and too many were willing to believe that the African slave was something less than a man. Observers of the American scene were shocked by the American's propensity for physical violence; he seemed ready to settle every dispute, no matter how trifling, with the knife or the gun. Observers were also disturbed by the hard drinking which seemed to permeate all social classes, and by the American's disdain for culture as something emasculating. At the same time, Americans south of the Mason-Dixon line were developing their own subculture.

> *Wedded to the institution of human slavery, they built their society around the romantic illusions of medieval chivalry; and the Southerners were left behind as the rest of the nation marched into the industrial age. When it came time to adapt to changing conditions, the South was unable to leave the dream world it had created, and it fought a desperate struggle to preserve an illusion.*

AMERICA IN THE ROMANTIC AGE*

The Revolution in America Education

Until 1840, America could scarcely be said to have had a system of public primary education. Most children received their elementary education in church-supported schools, private academies, or from private tutors or members of their own families. Such "public" schools as did exist were intended for the children of paupers, and a humiliating pauper's oath was required from the parents before the child would be accepted by the school. The level of American education was low, with religion (the Protestant variety) and Yankee morality forming the core of the curriculum. However, in the 1830's a widespread movement for a true system of public education arose. It was supported by working-class families, who wanted a better life for their children, and by educational reformers, such as Horace Mann and Henry Barnard, who realized that illiteracy was not compatible with democracy.

In 1837, Horace Mann became State Superintendent of Education in Massachusetts; and shortly thereafter, Henry Barnard helped to reorganize the school systems in Rhode Island and Connecticut. Placing education under state control, these two men succeeded in establishing uniform and mandatory state curriculums which raised the quality of public education, lengthened the school year to six months, and sought to enforce compulsory attendance. Barnard and Mann also increased teachers' salaries, and established Normal schools for the training of teachers. Finally, they enriched the curriculum, adding practical business subjects and American history to the traditional course offerings. Mann won widespread business support for his reforms by convincing businessmen that compulsory public school education would produce trained and disciplined workers who would be more efficient and productive than poorly educated workers. In the 1840's most states adopted some form of compulsory, tax-supported public education, although enforcement of the education laws tended to be lax. In 1860, only 5 per cent of adult whites were illiterate, even though only one white child in six attended a public school.

The public schools, though, did help to shape a common American culture. Virtually all schools used texts prepared by William Holmes McGuffey, and these books inculcated traditional Protestant virtues of thrift, hardwork, and sobriety. Extremely patriotic in content, McGuffy's readers helped to develop a unifying historical mythology, and their literary selections helped mold the development of American literature.

Secondary, Higher, and Adult Education

In 1821, Boston opened the first public high school in America. Accepting only the better students, the high school was designed to offer advanced training in liberal arts and business subjects. Often called "the poor man's college," it fitted young men for careers in industry and public service. By the time of the Civil War, there were some 320 public high schools in the United States (most of them were concentrated in the Northeast, and virtually none had been established in the South). In this same period some eighty new colleges opened their doors, including the state universities of Indiana, Michigan, Wisconsin, Virginia, Alabama, Tennessee, and Missouri. Although most colleges continued to be church affiliated, they modernized their curriculums and offered instruction in the physical sciences, history, modern languages, literature, and the humanities. The typical college had only a hundred or so students, and was housed in one or two small buildings. It had a handful of faculty members who each taught a variety of subjects, and it had inadequate laboratories and libraries, when it had them at all. However, important innovations were begun in this period. The first professional schools

---

* Romanticism was a literary and artistic movement which flourished in Europe and America in the generation after 1815. It stressed emotion over reason, glorified nature while denigrating industry, and sought a mystical understanding of, and union with, God.

Group of young men of the sophomore class at Harvard engaged in dueling and card playing.

for the training of medical doctors, dentists, and lawyers were created, and institutions such as Mount Holyoke, Rockford Seminary, and Elmira College pioneered in the higher education of women.

The Lyceum movement started in Massachusetts in 1826, and it rapidly spread across the nation. Lyceums were voluntary organizations designed to improve cultural awareness and broaden the intellectual horizons of adults. They acquired libraries (circulating the books among the membership), held philosophical and literary discussions, and encouraged members to cultivate their literary and artistic talents. They also sponsored public lectures, inviting well-known scientists, authors, and artists to speak. The Lyceums enjoyed wide popularity and enabled Americans to see and hear men like Charles Dickens, Ralph Waldo Emerson, and Louis Agassiz, and they undoubtedly raised the general educational level of the American people.

Newspapers and Magazines

In the 1830's, no fewer than fourteen hundred newspapers were being regularly published in the United States; and in the 1840's, they were joined by some six hundred magazines. Americans devoured newspapers and magazines on a massive scale and were among the best-informed people in the world. In 1833, Benjamin F. Day began selling the *New York Sun* for a penny a copy, bringing it within the financial reach of the average workingman. Seeking to cultivate a working-class market, James Gordon Bennett's *New York Herald* (1835) specialized in the reporting of crimes and scandals, while Horace Greeley's *New York Tribune* (1841) championed a host of reforms designed to appeal to the workingman. The American newspaper vigorously attacked or defended the nation's politicians (depending upon the personal bias of the publisher) and contributed to a healthy and democratically sound political life. The development of the American newspaper and the American democratic order are one and inseparable.

Nile's Weekly Register (1811) and the *North American Review* (1815) were the only general-interest magazines to enjoy a national circulation, most magazines being regional or local in their circulation. These two magazines covered topical events and published essays on the American scene and on current problems and prospects. *The Southern Literary Messenger* (1834), which Edgar Allan Poe edited for a time, *Harper's Magazine* (1850), and the *Atlantic Monthly* (1857) published the best in contemporary American literature. Unfortunately, much of American literature was directed at a feminine audience; and it tended to be highly emotional, sentimental, syrupy, and moralistic in content. American men associated literature with these "soap operas" and tended to reject culture as effeminate. *Godey's Lady's Book* (1837) was the leading magazine directed at the female audience, and it was an influential arbiter of fashion and social taste. *De Bow's Review* served the commercial interests of the South, while *Hunt's Merchants Magazine* performed a similar function for Northern business interests. Together, the newspapers and magazines of America contributed to the cultural diversity of America.

The Golden Age of American Literature

In the period from 1815 to 1860, America had a galaxy of writers, poets, and historians whose like would scarcely be seen again. Washington

Irving, the first American author to win European recognition, immortalized the Dutch folklore of New York in *Knickerbocker's History of New York* (1809) and in *The Sketch Book* (1819-1820). James Fenimore Cooper, of Cooperstown, New York, wrote more than thirty novels, most of which concerned the adventures and perils of life on the American frontier. His "Leatherstocking" tales, which included *The Last of the Mohicans* (1826) and *The Deerslayer* (1841), portrayed such stock characters as the noble Indian, the resourceful frontiersman, the virtuous American maid, and the villainous Englishmen, and his tales have become a part of our frontier mythology. Herman Melville, master of symbolism, filled his novels with philosophical and psychological insights as he explored the innate evil residing in the human soul. *Moby Dick* (1851), his best-known work, registered his sharp dissent from the optimistic assumption of the Transcendentalists that man was inherently good. A nay-sayer in a land where yes was the key to success, Melville was rejected in his own time; and his literary genius was not recognized until the twentieth century. Similarly, Nathaniel Hawthorne stressed the reality of sin and the psychology of evil in the *Twice-Told Tales* (1837) and in the *Scarlet Letter* (1850). Writing of America's Puritan past, he cautioned the optimists that their unshakable faith in man was unwarranted.

In poetry, the American genius excelled. Edgar Allan Poe wrote poetry revealing the terrors of the mind, while Walt Whitman celebrated the glories of American democracy. John Greenleaf Whittier found his inspiration in rural New England, while William Cullen Bryant and Henry Wadsworth Longfellow found their material in the history and folk legends of America. James Russell Lowell and Oliver Wendell Holmes used poetry and criticism as vehicles to attack slavery and to proclaim their belief in the dignity of man.

In history, George Bancroft (from 1834 to 1882) wrote a classic ten-volume *History of the United States* which declared that God had brought America forth to redeem humanity from despotism. John Lothrop Motley chronicled the history of the Dutch Republic; William H. Prescott recounted the conquest of the Aztec and Incan Empires; and Francis Parkman produced both great literature and great history in his account of the French-English struggle for the American continent. Richard Hildreth advanced an economic interpretation of American history which both Beardians and Marxists were to rediscover in the twentieth century, and Jared Sparks collected the writings of, and wrote a biography of George Washington.

Ralph Waldo Emerson was the master of the essay as well as one of the most profound intellects of his age. His disciple, Henry David Thoreau, glorified a life lived close to nature in *Walden* (1854) and laid the intellectual foundations for the doctrine of civil disobedience in his *Resistance to Civil Government* (1849). Arguing that conscience must be served above all else, Thoreau urged his fellow citizens to withhold their support (by refusing to pay taxes, serve in the army, etc.) of unjust or evil policies pursued by the government.

American Art

The art of mid-nineteenth-century America has been unjustly denigrated and underrated. Charles Wilson Peale, Gilbert Stuart, John Trumbull, and Samuel F. B. Morse were excellent portrait painters, while Asher B. Durand and the "Hudson River School" revealed the majesty of the American landscape. Although America made no contributions to serious music, Stephen C. Foster, John Howard Payne, and Lowell Mason wrote ballads, hymns, songs, and tunes which captured the American imagination and which have become an integral part of America's musical heritage. In sculpture, Hiram Powers won fame with "The Greek Slave," which focused attention on the plight of American slaves as well. Finally, P. T. Barnum became the master showman of his age, appealing to the mass audience and becoming a show-business legend.

Science and Technology

America's contributions to science and technology were substantial, if unheralded. Asa Gray did important work in studying plant distribution and was an early champion of Charles Darwin's evolutionary theories (indeed, Darwin used Gray's work in arriving at his own conclusions). Louis Agassiz was a leading zoologist; John J. Audobon classified the birds of America; and Benjamin Silliman worked to advance the study of chemistry and minerology in the United States. Joseph Henry made pioneering discoveries in electromagnetism; Crawford W. Long was a leader in anesthetics research; and Benjamin Pierce made important contributions to mathematics. In technology, Cyrus McCormick revolutionized agriculture with his mechanical reapers and harvesters, and Charles Goodyear succeeded in vulcanizing rubber in 1844. Two years later, Elias Howe revolutionized the textile industry when he invented the sewing machine. During the same period, Samuel Colt developed the handgun, or revolver, and Samuel F. B. Morse made possible instantaneous communications with the perfection of the telegraph. By the time of the Civil War, America was well on its way to becoming the technological leader of the Western world.

Transcendentalism

Although the Americans were an intensely practical people, they were not devoid of the instinct for speculation and philosophy. The most important philosophical concept to emerge from mid-nineteenth-century American society was the Transcendental movement. Primarily a New England movement, it won a wide following among Unitarians; and its leading advocates were Ralph Waldo Emerson, George Ripley, and Henry David Thoreau. According to the Transcendentalists, the universe is ruled by an all-pervasive intelligence known as the Over-Soul (or God, in more conventional terms). As an intelligent being, man possesses a portion of the divine Over-Soul within his own being and is, therefore, divine. Man, the Transcendentalists believed, was in the process of realizing his own divinity and would shortly become the actual lord of creation. Extremely optimistic, the Transcendentalists believed in the inevitability of progress; and they sought to use their knowledge to speed the emancipation of mankind from the evils of poverty, ignorance, and social injustice. As they worked to improve their society, they would enable man to more readily realize his divinity and, thus, bring man into the golden age. Transcendentalism spurred the New England intellectuals to become active reformers; and increasingly, they were attracted to abolitionism as the ultimate reform. Slavery, they felt, was not merely an affront to man; it was also a denial of his divinity and an affront to the Over-Soul. Slavery must be destroyed in order to enable man to achieve the full measure of his greatness.

The Abolitionist Crusade

Although abolitionism eventually commanded the energies of most reformers, it was never a mass movement; and even on the eve of the Civil War, it was rejected by a majority of the American people. With slavery protected by state laws, as well as federal constitutional restraints, the institution could be overthrown only by revolution or by a Southern acknowledgment that slavery was an evil. However, as the abolitionists became more shrill in their denunciation of slavery, the Southerners became more extreme in their defense of the institution. As abolitionism was generally equated with disunion and civil strife, moderate Americans shunned it. But the moral appeal of the abolitionists could not long go unanswered.

In 1817, the American Colonization Society was organized to send free Negroes back to Africa and to encourage slaveholders to emancipate their slaves and return them to Africa. Extremely paternalistic, the American Colonization Society (which enjoyed the support of Abraham Lincoln) did not believe that blacks and whites could ever live together on terms of equality, and it favored African resettlement as the only way of solving America's race problem. However, few Negroes were willing to return to Africa, and the society was a failure.

Shortly after the Missouri Compromise of 1820, Benjamin Lundy, a Quaker, brought out the *Genius of Universal Emancipation* (an abolitionist newspaper) which sought to appeal to the moral sense of Southern slaveholders and to persuade them to voluntarily free their slaves. However, the gradualism of Lundy was not to the liking of his young assistant, William Lloyd Garrison. In 1831, Garrison began the *Liberator,* a newspaper which demanded the immediate abolition of slavery by whatever means were necessary. At the same time, he organized the New England Anti-Slavery Society to work for the implementation of his goals, and he began the American Anti-Slavery Society in 1833. However, Garrison was so extreme that he alienated the more moderate abolitionists who were willing to achieve emancipation gradually by appealing to the better instincts of the Southerners. Finally, in 1840, Garrison split his own movement when he demanded that women be permitted to participate in the society on an equal footing with men. Many male abolitionists were willing to emancipate the slaves, but were unwilling to emancipate their wives; and the quarrel further reduced Garrison's effectiveness.

More effective than Garrison was the Midwesterner Theodore Dwight Weld who used the high-

Facsimile of "The Liberator," edited by William Lloyd Garrison.

ly emotional techniques of the evangelist to convince his audiences of the evils of slavery and of the necessity for emancipation. Nevertheless, abolitionism, led by such men as William Ellery Channing, Theodore Parker, and Wendell Phillips, grew slowly. By 1850, there were some two hundred local abolitionist societies in the North, claiming a combined membership of 200,000 (less than one per cent of the general population). Often advocating complete social equality between blacks and whites and civil rights for free Northern Negroes, the abolitionists aroused the hatred of lower-class whites who feared Negro competition. Abolitionist meetings were frequently broken up by white mobs; and the leaders of the meetings were manhandled and, in some cases, murdered. While few Americans were willing to embrace abolitionism and the idea that blacks should be accorded equal treatment with whites, many Americans freely admitted that slavery was a moral pollution; and they were determined to keep it from spreading into the Western territories. With the establishment of James G. Birney's Liberty party in 1839, the anti-slavery movement became a political reality. Arguing that slavery must be confined to the Southern states, the movement did not urge abolition; but it did insist that the West be preserved exclusively for white settlement and that slavery not be permitted to establish roots there. By the 1850's anti-slavery would be a prime political issue and would be instrumental in bringing on the Civil War. While the abolitionists failed to win the support of their fellow citizens, they did publicize the slavery issue, and they turned it into a moral issue which could not indefinitely be ignored.

Utopias in the Wilderness

While abolitionism became the leading reform

cause in the generation between 1820 and 1850, it was by no means the only reform movement in America. Religious and social ferment was everywhere. It was in this period that America gave birth to Mormonism (which claimed to have received God's final revelation), to Millennairianism (which predicted the imminent Final Judgment of the World), and to the Rappites, who renounced marriage and sex and lived together in primitive communistic communities. Scores of reformers sought to prove that they knew the secret of social harmony by establishing utopian communities which would implement their social theories. Countless backwoods utopias were created to show the world how life really should be lived. Most of them disappeared as soon as they were organized; a few endured for a time, but all of them ultimately failed. The Transcendentalists established Brook Farm in Massachusetts as a religious experiment to combine intellectual pursuits with physical labor; Robert Owen founded New Harmony in Indiana to show that capitalism could be humane and that it need not exploit the working class; the Sylvania Phalanx community sought to implement the socialistic theories of Charles Fourier; John Humphrey Noyes' Oneida Community combined manufacturing and group marriage to produce the ideal society. The Amana Community implemented the communism of the New Testament; while Fanny Wright's Nashoba Community sought to train free Negroes for a place in society. Some utopian communities were frivolous, others were noble in their intentions; but all gave evidence of the widespread interest in reform and social improvement which characterized America in the generation before the Civil War.

THE GROWTH OF SOUTHERN CIVILIZATION

The Contrast with the North

Between 1815 and 1860, the industrial revolution transformed the North, bringing it unprecedented prosperity and widespread population growth. The growth of the free states gave control of the House of Representatives to the North, threatened both the South's parity in the Senate and its hold over the national government, and made the wealth of the South seem puny in comparison with that of the North. The South remained agricultural in an age of rapid industrialization, and it clung to the institution of human slavery at a time when the conscience of the Western world demanded its abolition. Forced to justify its "peculiar institution," the South began to construct an elaborate mythology which set it apart from the rest of the American nation and turned the region into a nation within a nation. At the heart of Southernism, was the institution of Negro slavery.

Table 5

The Distribution of Slavery in 1850

Number of Slaves	Number of Owners
1-9	255,268
10-49	84,328
50-199	7,675
200-499	243
500 and up	11

347,525 slave owners out of a population of more than 6,000,000 free whites.

The Southern Defense of Slavery

Goaded by the abolitionists, the South (which had its own abolitionist movement until the 1830's) was forced to justify slavery and suppress all forms of internal dissent. The South, fearing that abolitionists were stirring up slave revolts, stifled every Southern voice which protested against slavery; Southern states sought to keep abolitionist newspapers out of the mails and to prevent Congress from receiving anti-slavery petitions, and they made it a criminal offense to teach a slave how to read (for fear that he would come upon abolitionist propaganda). Under the hammer blows of the abolitionists, the South became a closed society, monolithic in its defense of slavery and determined to preserve its way of life at all costs. It defended slavery on the following grounds:

(1) **The Biblical Argument.** The South pointed out that slavery was sanctioned by the Old Testament, that the ancient Hebrews were slaveholders, and that the Bible defined the mutual rights and responsibilities of slave and master. Furthermore, the New Testament also acknowl-

edged the legitimacy of slavery, and St. Paul specifically counseled slaves to be obedient to their masters and not to rebel against their authority. Far from being an affront to God (as the abolitionists charged), slavery was permitted by divine law.

(2) **The School of Civilization Argument.** Slavery, the South argued, was in the best interests of the Negro race. Slavery took the Negro out of the savage African jungle where he had lived like a beast. It converted him to Christianity and saved his soul from eternal damnation, and it introduced him to the blessings of a superior Western civilization. Slavery was the school in which the savage learned the ways of civilization; it was the institution which would ultimately redeem the black race from the savagery of Africa.

(3) **The New Athens Argument.** Southerners, like George Fitzhugh, pointed out that every civilization known to man had rested upon slavery, and they argued that slavery was the price which man paid for civilization. In order to produce great art, literature, music, philosophy, and science, some men had to be freed from the necessity of physical labor, which meant that others must be forced to produce enough wealth to support a leisure class. Civilization, by its very nature, rested upon the exploitation of the masses so that the elite few could exercise their genius. The South, they would argue, unlike the materialistic and uncultured North, was producing a great culture (even if there was little concrete evidence of it) and was the cultural successor of Greek civilization. The South would be a new Athens; and slavery was a small price to pay for cultural greatness. Furthermore, while the Northern wage-slave lacked security against disease and the infirmities of old age, the happy, contented slave was fed, housed, and cared for in sickness and in health, in infancy and in old age. The Negro slave, it was argued, was infinitely better off than the exploited and oppressed Northern wage earner.

(4) **The Inferior Race Argument.** Finally, Southerners proclaimed the Negro to be inherently inferior to the white man (some Southerners denied that the Negro had a soul, while others denied that he was a member of the human species) and proclaimed slavery to be the Negro's natural state. Southerners warned that if slavery were abolished, then the fabric of Southern society would deteriorate; rapacious blacks would run rampant — looting and stealing. In such an event, race war would be inevitable; and the blacks would be exterminated. Slavery, then, was the only condition under which the Negro could live in Western society; to leave him in Africa would only condemn him to primordial savagery.

Although the Southern apologists for slavery won few Northern converts, they did succeed in convincing themselves that slavery was the integral foundation of their own cherished way of life. Ever since the Civil War, historians have debated the question of whether or not slavery, as an institution, was profitable. One argument asserted that if slavery had been unprofitable, then it would have been only a matter of time before the South abolished it, and consequently the Civil War would have been needless. However, this argument misses the main point of Southern slavery. It was not so much an economic institution (although the modern consensus is that slavery, as a whole, did yield a profit) as it was a social institution. The strongest supporters of slavery were poor whites who owned no slaves but who enjoyed the psychological benefits of belonging to the master race. The abolition of slavery would ultimately challenge white supremacy, and it was this that Southern whites could not abide. Anything which endangered their privileged social position was anathema; they could never accept Negro equality, and therefore they could never permit the abolition of slavery — no matter how inefficient or unprofitable the system might have been.

The Structure of Southern Society

Southern society can be divided into at least six classes. At the apex of Southern society stood the plantation aristocracy. The large planters owned at least 800 acres of land and worked 40 or more slaves. Large planters numbered only 8,000 people in a society of more than 6,000,000 whites but they dominated the political, economic, and social life of the South; and they were the ideal to which all Southerners aspired. Beneath the great planters were the more numerous medium and small planters. They owned 200 acres of land or less (generally less), and had less than 40 slaves (two-thirds of all Southerners who owned slaves owned less than 10). They numbered in excess of 80,000 people but still constituted an infinitesimal proportion of the total Southern white population. They did not enjoy the wealth or the social prestige of the great planters, but they were closely linked with the plantation aristocracy and followed their social lead. Next in importance was

Cotton plantation on the Mississippi.

a small professional class (ministers, lawyers, doctors, professors) who, together with the larger merchants, served the needs of the planters, represented their interests, and constituted their social satellites.

The overwhelming majority of the Southern white population made their living as small independent farmers. While the more prosperous farmers might own one or two slaves, 75 per cent of all Southern families were not slaveholders. Generally, these small farmers worked between 50 and 100 acres of land. Having little capital reserve, they rarely hired outside help and, instead, relied upon the labor of their wives and children to plant and harvest their crops. Most were living close to the subsistence level and had only a small cash income. On the same social level as the farmers were the small merchants of the towns and villages, who constituted a small Southern middle class. Finally, at the bottom of white society stood the highlanders (or hillbillies), who attempted to eke out a living from marginally productive lands. Often despising physical labor, they tended to be a lazy, indolent group addicted to criminality and physical violence. Looked down upon as white trash, they were fiercely anti-Negro and took pride in their skin color as their only claim to social prestige or standing.

The Negro

The four million Negroes living in the South on the eve of the Civil War made up the great underbelly of Southern society. However, they can also be differentiated into distinct groups. At the top of black society were some quarter-million free Negroes who resided in the larger towns and cities of the South. These were the people who had been emancipated by their owners or who had been allowed (because of their special skills) to work for wages and purchase their own freedom. They tended to earn their livelihood as barbers, carpenters, masons, blacksmiths, domestics, and tradesmen. A very few achieved some measure of prosperity, and a handful became slaveholders themselves (though most Negroes who owned slaves owned members of their own families whom they purchased from their former owners). At least one Mississippi black became a planter.

Over three and one-half million Negroes lived out their lives as slaves. A small percentage of them lived in the plantation house and served the planter as domestics — butlers, cooks, maids. Living with the planter's family, they often developed close and intimate relations with the master and his family and identified with his interests. They tended to despise the field hands, as well as the poor whites, and often betrayed incipient insurrections against the master. Their servitude was not oppresive, and they are regarded as the aristocrats of the slave population. Another small privileged group of slaves were the few black overseers (or slave drivers) and the plantation artisans (carpenters, masons, smiths, etc.) who were able to avoid the rigors of the field. However, the vast majority of slaves were field hands.

The Field Hand

On the eve of the Civil War, an adult male field hand was worth anywhere from $1200 to $1500, a female in her prime was worth about a $1000, and a child was worth at least $200 as an investment. These high prices (the highest they had ever been) testify to the profitability of the slave system, but tell little about the life of the average slave. Like everyone else in an agrarian society, the field hands worked from dawn to dusk; but their labor was notoriously inefficient, and they had to constantly be spurred on with the whip and the lash. Although it is dangerous to generalize about the treatment of the average slave (not every master was a Simon Legree), a certain amount of physical coercion was considered necessary in order to get the slaves to work, although the high price of slaves tended to militate against gross maltreatment (a multilated or crippled slave had no market value). Undoubtedly, there were sadists (among masters and overseers) who took delight in brutalizing their slaves; but, for the most part, harsh physical punishment was reserved for chronic shirkers, troublemakers, and runaways.

The master provided his slaves with housing (generally crude, windowless huts with earthen flooring which provided scant protection against the cold of winter), clothing (two suits of clothing a year, made of the coarsest and cheapest material possible), and meat (mostly pork, with chickens and turkeys given out on special occasions and holidays). Medical care was generally quite poor. The mistress of the plantation treated most illnesses, and doctors were called only in the event of a dire emergency. An unofficial code of honor required slaveholders to care for slaves too old to work and those incapacitated by accident or disease. The extent to which a master honored this code depended upon his own moral sense, but social pressures tended to make certain that masters did not flagrantly violate their obligations.

Legally, a master was not permitted to willfully murder a slave, although if a slave died as a result of moderate correction, the master was not liable to the penalty of the law. It was impossible to enforce this law against murder, however, since slaves were not permitted to testify against whites; and a slave was not likely to denounce his master for fear of reprisals. Generally, conditions for slaves tended to be best on small plantations where there were few hands and where the master developed close personal ties with his slaves. The larger the plantation and the more remote the master, the worse conditions became. In addition, slavery in the Upper South (where slaves could more readily flee North) was less harsh than slavery in the deep South, where there was small likelihood of successful flight.

Each slave family was expected to maintain its own vegetable patch and, except for meat supplied by the master, was expected to grow all its own food. Legally, slave marriages and family relationships had no standing. A master was free to sell his slaves at will — either individually or in family groups; and he could mate his slaves as he chose. In the upper South, especially, slaves were bred for export to the lower South; and a conscious attempt was made to produce strong, healthy slaves through selective breeding. Again, though, like everything else about slavery, the existence and stability of slave families depended solely upon the moral sense of the master. For the most part, Southern slaves were a sullen and resentful lot, ready to rebel when conditions became unbearable. The master and his family lived in constant fear of slave insurrection.

Slave Rebellions

Historians have identified some two hundred to three hundred slave insurrections during the three centuries that slavery existed in America. However, most of these insurrections were local affairs, confined to a single plantation, and were brought on by a long train of abuses. Only a small number of insurrections erupted on a larger scale, and no slave insurrection ever posed a serious threat to the existence of slavery in the Southern states. Nevertheless, they were frightening. In 1822, a plot devised by Denmark Vesey (a free Negro in Charleston, South Carolina), and supported by fellow black artisans, was betrayed to the authorities. Vesey, influenced by abolitionist tracts, had planned to forcibly overthrow slavery by inspiring armed insurrection among local slaves. Nine years later, a slave insurrection led by the Negro religious visionary, Nat Turner, claimed the lives of fifty-seven whites in Southampton County, Virginia. Local whites were also convinced that Turner had been influenced by abolitionist propaganda. In Southern eyes, the abolitionists were not merely attacking an abstract evil, they were fomenting slave insurrection and endangering the lives of every Southern white. When the Southerners condemned abolitionism and demanded the suppression of abolitionist literature, they felt they were acting in defense of their homes and families. Northern refusal to curb the abolitionists convinced Southerners that the North was hostile to the Southern way of life, and the South's fear and resentment manifested itself in an irrational and dogmatic defense of slavery. The more they were attacked, the more determined the South became to safeguard slavery as the indispensable bulwark of Southern civilization.

The planters, themselves, slept with their doors and windows bolted and with guns under their pillows. To guard against slave insurrections and plots, they organized night patrols to make certain that no Negroes were lurking about (slaves could not move about after dark except with the express permission of their owners). Masters observed the slaves' religious meetings and forced slave pastors to emphasize that obedience to the master was obedience to God; and the slaveholders made it a crime to teach a slave to read or write.

Unwilling to accept Negro equality, the South could do nothing else but maintain the institution of human slavery. To do so, it had to defy the conscience of the Western world and justify that which could not be justified. As a result, the South became intellectually, morally, socially, economically, and politically estranged from the rest of the United States. By 1845, the South had become a nation within a nation. Its efforts to secure independence will be related in the chapters which follow.

REVIEW QUESTIONS FOR CHAPTER 16

1. Horace Mann implemented his educational reforms in

   (A) Connecticut
   (B) Massachusetts
   (C) Rhode Island
   (D) New York

2. The first penny paper in the United States was the

   (A) *New York Herald*
   (B) *New York Tribune*
   (C) *New York Sun*
   (D) *New York Times*

3. The first American author to win European acclaim was

   (A) Washington Irving
   (B) James Fenimore Cooper
   (C) Herman Melville
   (D) Nathaniel Hawthorne

4. The historian of the Dutch Republic was

   (A) George Bancroft
   (B) William H. Prescott
   (C) Francis Parkman
   (D) John Lothrop Motley

5. *The Genius of Universal Emancipation* was published by

   (A) William Lloyd Garrison
   (B) Theodore Dwight Weld
   (C) Benjamin Lundy
   (D) Theodore Parker

6. Robert Owen founded a utopian community at

   (A) New Harmony
   (B) Oneida
   (C) Nashoba
   (D) Brook Farm

7. Two-thirds of all slaveholders held less than _____ slaves

   (A) 10
   (B) 20
   (C) 30
   (D) 40

8. Slaveholders constituted _____ percent of the Southern population

   (A) 10
   (B) 25
   (C) 40
   (D) 50

9. On the eve of the Civil War, the slave population numbered roughly

   (A) 3 million
   (B) 3½ million
   (C) 4 million
   (D) 4½ million

10. On the eve of the Civil War, field hands were worth between

(A) $ 900 and $1200
(B) $1200 and $1500
(C) $1500 and $1800
(D) $1800 and $2000

Explanatory Answers

1. **(B)** Mann became Superintendent of Education in Massachusetts in 1837.

2. **(C)** The *New York Sun* became a penny paper in 1833.

3. **(A)** Washington Irving received European recognition for his recreation of New York's Dutch legends.

4. **(D)** John Lothrop Motley wrote a classic account of the rise and fall of the Dutch Republic.

5. **(C)** It was begun by Benjamin Lundy in 1821.

6. **(A)** New Harmony was designed to show that capitalism could be made humane.

7. **(A)** Over 250,000 slaveholders held less than ten slaves.

8. **(B)** One Southern family in four owned slaves.

9. **(B)** 3½ million Southern Negroes were slaves and ¼ million were free.

10. **(B)** A field hand sold for $1200 to $1500, the highest price ever.

Chapter 17

MANIFEST DESTINY AND THE MEXICAN WAR, 1844-1848

Although the term, itself, was not coined until the summer of 1845, when John O'Sullivan used it in an editorial in the United States Magazine and Democratic Review, *the spirit of Manifest Destiny dates back to the American Revolution. As popularized in the 1840's the concept of Manifest Destiny held that God had predestined the United States of America to extend from the Atlantic Ocean to the Pacific Ocean and from the Gulf of Mexico to the Arctic Ocean. Thus, the expansion of the United States into areas occupied by foreign nations was not aggression but, rather, obedience to the will of God (the fact that other nations opposed our God-given right of expansion only went to prove that they were unworthy of consideration by either the United States or God). Once having achieved its Manifest Destiny, the United States would then realize its Providential mission in the world — the creation of an empire of liberty which would serve as a beacon for all the oppressed peoples of the world. Having conquered the New World, the spirit of American democracy would redeem the Old World by banishing despotism and by making freedom the birthright of every human being. The fact that America was denying freedom to millions of Negroes was a minor embarrassment which did not negate the nobility of the American dream. In the 1840's virtually every American shared (to a greater or lesser extent) belief in the concept of Manifest Destiny. Although extreme advocates of this concept envisioned the eventual annexation of Canada and the conquest of Latin America (thereby making the United States the undisputed master of the entire Western Hemisphere), the immediate targets of American expansionism in the 1840's were Oregon and Texas. Oregon was acquired peacefully; but the realization of America's Manifest Destiny in Texas led to war with Mexico.*

THE OREGON DISPUTE

Rival British and American Claims to Oregon

The Oregon Territory (modern Idaho, Washington, Oregon, and British Columbia) was claimed by both the United States and Great Britain, with each power having an equally strong legal case. The United States' claim was based on the following:

(1) The discovery of, and navigation of, the mouth of the Columbia River by Captain Robert Gray in 1792.

(2) The explorations of Lewis and Clark from 1804 to 1806.

(3) The transfer to the United States of Spain's territorial claims north of the forty-second parallel in the Adams-Onis treaty of 1819; and Russia's 1823-1824 surrender to the United States of its claim to territory south of 54°40′ latitude.

(4) The activities (since 1811) of the Astor Fur Trading Company in the region.

(5) Actual occupation of the Willamette Valley by American settlers.

Britain's claims had the following bases:

(1) The Nootka Sound treaty (1790) with Spain, recognizing England's rights in that region.

(2) The exploratory voyages of Captain Cook (1778), Captain George Vancouver (1792), and Sir Alexander Mackenzie (1793).

(3) The commercial activities of the Hudson's Bay Company.

(4) The establishment (1805) of Fort McLeod.

Early Efforts to Settle the Dispute

During the administration of John Quincy Adams, the United States proposed that the Oregon Territory be divided between America and England at the forty-ninth parallel (thus, extending to the Pacific Ocean the boundary between the Louisiana Purchase and Canada). However, Britain rejected this offer since it would have given the United States control of the valuable Columbia River Basin and of Puget Sound. Indeed, the Columbia River Basin and Puget Sound were at the crux of the Oregon dispute. Both powers recognized the justice of partition, but each wanted the commercially and strategically valuable Columbia River Basin. In August, 1827, the Convention of 1818 (which provided for joint Anglo-American occupation of Oregon with equal rights of settlement for citizens of both nations) was renewed for an indefinite period, with the stipulation that the agreement could be unilaterally terminated by either power upon one year's advance notice. This, however, merely postponed the day of reckoning. As more and more Americans were attracted to Oregon by the fertile land of the Willamette Valley, demands for American jurisdiction over Oregon increased. In 1843, American settlers in Oregon organized a constitutional convention and requested the United States to assume governmental authority over them. The United States took no action on the request, and, for the moment, the *status quo* was continued.

THE TEXAS DISPUTE

Texas Annexation Rejected

Texas, because of the slavery issue, was a far more vexing problem than Oregon, and it was one which complicated the domestic politics of the United States. After it became apparent that anti-slavery Northerners would block United States annexation of Texas, the Texans withdrew their offer of annexation (October, 1838) and resigned themselves to an independent existence—at least temporarily. Under President Mirabeau B. Lamar, the Republic of Texas pursued an independent foreign policy that was designed to secure its continued existence in the face of intense Mexican hostility. In 1839-1840, Texas concluded favorable treaties with France, Holland, Belgium, and Great Britain. France and England, in particular, saw Texas as a valuable buffer state which would block the expansion of the United States in the Southwest, and which would provide them with cotton, while absorbing their manufactured products. Hoping to keep Texas independent of the United States, the European powers promised economic and commercial aid to Texas and sought to improve the republic's relations with Mexico. When the Mexicans invaded Texas in 1842, in order to reassert their authority over their former province, it was England and France that arranged a truce. These events were not lost upon the United States, which feared that Texas might become a satellite of England and France. If this happened, the Monroe Doctrine would be impaired and American expansionism in the Southwest would be frustrated. To forestall this possibility of satellization, the Tyler administration resumed negotiations with Texas on the possibility of annexation, only to receive a stern warning from Mexico's General Santa Anna that American annexation of Texas would mean war with Mexico. Nevertheless, a preliminary treaty of annexation was agreed upon in April, 1844.

Texas and the Presidential Election of 1844

The slaveholding South desperately longed for the annexation of Texas. Since slavery was already established in Texas, the acquisition of this large area would provide a vast new frontier for the expansion of slavery and might help restore the sectional balance between the North and South (especially if the huge state were subdivided). On the other hand, Northern Whigs and anti-slavery Democrats opposed the annexation of Texas for the very same reasons that the South favored it. In June, 1844, after publication of Secretary of State John C. Calhoun's vigorous defense of slavery in Texas, the Senate rejected the treaty of annexation by a vote of 35 to 16. Many Northerners became convinced that the movement for the annexation of Texas was part of a slaveholders' conspiracy to seize control of the national government by creating enough new slave states to permit the South to control the Senate and the Presidency.

Van Buren and Clay are Impaled on the Horns of a Dilemma

In 1844, Martin Van Buren was the leading presidential candidate of the Democratic party, while Henry Clay was favored to win the nomination of the Whig party. In April, Van Buren and Clay met and agreed to keep the question of the annexation of Texas out of the presidential campaign. Unfortunately, neither was able to do so. If Van Buren or Clay came out in favor of Texas annexation, they would lose the support of the Northern wings of their parties; but, if they oppose annexation, they would forfeit support of their Southern followers. Consequently, both men issued separate statements declaring that while they favored the ultimate annexation of Texas, they opposed its immediate annexation because of the divisive question of slavery. Both men also asserted their hope that the slave issue would eventually be resolved. While their statements generally satisfied the North, Van Buren's opposition to Texas annexation infuriated Andrew Jackson, who broke with his former protégé and threw his support to James Knox Polk, another Democratic contender for the presidency.

The Presidential Campaign of 1844

As a result of Southern opposition, Van Buren was unable to get the two-thirds support necessary for nomination, and the Democratic convention deadlocked. On the ninth ballot, the convention turned to dark-horse candidate James Knox Polk of Tennessee, whose credentials as a Jacksonian were good, but who was also obscure enough not to have made any powerful enemies. As Vice-President, the convention named New York's Silas Wright, a Van Burenite and anti-slavery man. Wright, however, refused the nomination, and George M. Dallas of Pennsylvania was chosen to replace him on the ticket. Boldly embracing the tenets of Manifest Destiny, the Democratic platform called for "the reoccupation of Oregon and the reannexation of Texas." There was a tacit understanding that the South would support the acquisition of Oregon in return for Western support of the annexation of Texas as a slave state, and the phrase "54°40′ or fight" became the Democratic campaign slogan. The Whigs, as expected, nominated Henry Clay and New Jersey's Theodore Frelinghuysen as their standard-bearers; and the party adopted a platform which made no mention of Texas, but which called for a single term for President. The fledgling Liberty party named James G. Birney and Thomas Morris as its candidates for President and Vice-President, respectively, on a platform of total opposition to the expansion of slavery. President Tyler, denied renomination by the Whigs or Democrats, had planned to run as an independent, but he withdrew in favor of Polk when the Democrats came out in favor of Texas annexation. Henry Clay, hoping to gain Southern support, qualified his opposition to Texas annexation during the campaign, only to alienate Northern support. The results of the election were as follows:

Polk	1,337,243	(170)
Clay	1,299,068	(105)
Birney	62,300	(0)

Clay lost the election because Birney drew enough votes away from him in upstate New York to give that state to Polk. Had Clay not equivocated on Texas, he probably would have carried New York's thirty-six electoral votes and won the election.

Texas is Annexed

The elections of 1844 demonstrated strong sup-

Ceremony to mark the end of the Republic of Texas and the beginning of Texas statehood.

port for American expansion, and the lame-duck administration of President Tyler again pressed for Texas annexation — this time by joint resolution of Congress rather than ratification of a treaty of annexation. On March 1, 1845, Congress approved such a joint resolution, declaring that Texas (if it wished) could divide into as many as five states (thereby giving the slaveholders ten votes in the Senate). Hoping to prevent annexation, Great Britain (in May, 1845) persuaded Mexico to agree to recognize the independence of Texas, but by then it was too late. In October, the people of Texas accepted the terms of the joint resolution, and in December, 1845, Texas was formally admitted to the Union as a state. On March 28, 1846, Mexico broke diplomatic relations with the United States.

THE OREGON DISPUTE IS SETTLED

Oregon is Partitioned

In December, 1845, President Polk, in his annual message to Congress, called for the abrogation of the Convention of 1818 and for the establishment of American sovereignty over the entire Oregon Territory. Polk's stand was extremely popular in the states of the old Northwest Territory; and on May 21, 1846, the United States informed Great Britain that it intended to terminate the Convention of 1818. England was not in an especially heroic mood and did not want to go to war over Oregon. Accordingly, Britain's Richard Packenham proposed that the United States and England submit their dispute to binding international arbitration. Polk rejected the British offer, and tensions mounted. However, in June, 1846, Great Britain told Mexico that it had no intention of intervening in Mexico's dispute with the United States over Texas. As tensions between the United States and Mexico were mounting rapidly, England's decision to maintain its neutrality was well-received in the United States (Mexico had been counting on war between America and England and had hoped to take advantage of the hostilities by reconquering Texas). Moreover, England had recently repealed her Corn Laws (which had imposed discriminatory duties on foreign wheat and grain), and the United States was anticipating profitable new trade relations with Great Britain. All this served to moderate the American stand on Oregon. In June, Polk made it known that the United States would accept a compromise on Oregon, provided that England took the initiative in offering it.

Having publicly committed himself to "54°40' or fight," Polk found it politically embarrassing to accept anything less than the whole of the Oregon territory. Therefore, he took the extraordinary step of laying the British compromise proposal directly before the Senate of the United States, declaring that he would abide by the Senate's recommendation. In this way, Polk was able to save face by placing responsibility for the compromise on the Senate. The Senate approved the British proposal that (1) the present United States-Canadian boundary (the forty-ninth parallel) be extended to the Pacific Ocean, that (2) both nations enjoy free navigation through the Juan de Fuca Strait, and that (3) Britain retain control of Vancouver Island and retain navigation rights on the Columbia River south of the forty-ninth parallel. The agreement was highly favorable to the United States, giving it the Columbia River Basin and Puget Sound. America could now devote its full attentions to Mexico.

THE MEXICAN WAR
The Crux of the Dispute

Having recognized Texas' independence in May, 1845, Mexico could no longer claim jurisdiction over her former province. However, Mexico insisted that the southern boundary of Texas was the Nueces River, while Texas and the United States government were equally insistent that the Rio Grande River was the southern boundary of the state. In June, 1845, General Zachary Taylor was ordered to take up a position in the vicinity of the disputed area; and in August, John Slidell was sent to Mexico City to negotiate a settlement with the Mexican government. Slidell was authorized to offer as much as 40 million dollars for the Rio Grande border and for Mexico's cession of California and New Mexico to the United States. Hostile public opinion, however, prevented the Mexican government from acting on Slidell's offer, and his diplomatic mission collapsed. When news of Slidell's failure reached Washington in January, 1846, Taylor was ordered to advance to the Rio Grande River; and he did so in March.

President Polk's orders to Taylor constituted a technical violation of international law, for the movement of troops into a disputed territorial zone is a provocation. On April 2, 1846, General Pedro de Ampudia demanded that Taylor evacuate the disputed area and return to the Nueces River. Receiving no satisfactory reply from the Americans, General Mariano Arista notified Taylor (on April 24, 1846) that a state of hostilities existed between the two nations; and the next day eleven Americans were killed and five wounded in a skirmish with Mexican forces near Matamoros (on the Mexican side of the Rio Grande). During the night of April 30-May 1, 1846, Mexican forces crossed the Rio Grande River in force — war had begun.

The American People and the Mexican War

On May 11, 1846, President Polk went before Congress to ask for a declaration of war against

"This is the House that Polk built."
Cartoon ca. 1846 against the Mexican War and Polk.

Mexico, declaring that "Mexico has shed American blood upon the American soil." That same day, the House of Representatives voted approval of the war message by a vote of 179 to 14; and the next day, the Senate followed suit by a vote of 40 to 2, with 3 abstentions. The war was highly popular in the South, for Southerners anticipated the acquisition from Mexico of vast stretches of territory which could be organized as slave states. Indeed, there were many Southerners who favored the annexation of all Mexico (as well as a vigorous American expansion in the Caribbean area) as a way of keeping pace with the growth of the Northern free states. The West, caught up in the emotional frenzy of nationalism, also supported the Mexican War, feeling that any gains acquired by the South would be offset by the acquisition of Oregon. In the Northeast, however, there was widespread opposition to the war. It was opposed by abolitionists and antislavery Whigs who both viewed the war as a slaveholders' conspiracy to expand slavery and to dominate the Union. Moreover, many Northerners felt that America's conduct in the Rio Grande dispute had not been above reproach; they felt that America was as guilty as Mexico in provoking the war. Nevertheless, despite the opposition of Northern Whigs and abolitionists, the Mexican War was supported by most Americans.

Comparative Advantages and Disadvantages

Mexico entered the war with a standing army of 32,000 men, trained by European officers along European military lines. Moreover, she enjoyed the advantage of fighting on her own territory, close to her bases of supply; and she could employ interior lines of communications to good military advantage. On the other hand, the Mexican officers were appointed for political reasons, not merit, and as a group, were incompetent; furthermore, the army's equipment was antiquated. The Mexican army was a parade, not a fighting force; and the peasant soldiery lacked motivation. The American army consisted of only 7,365 men, and the United States had to rely on untrained, ill-disciplined, and erratic short-term volunteers to fill its troop quotas. The Americans were fighting on foreign terrain, far from their bases of supply, and their communications system was inadequate. Moreover, Generals Zachary Taylor and Winfield Scott were both Whigs and were distrusted by the Democratic Polk, who rightfully felt that they would use their military exploits for political advancement. In addition, Taylor and Scott were both jealous of each other's success. Cooperation between the two was difficult, for each represented to the other a potential rival for political office. European observers favored Mexico to win the war, but the Americans came prepared to fight.

Early Fighting and American Strategy

Even before the formal declaration of war, Taylor was active along the Rio Grande. On May 8, 1846, Taylor's 2,300-man force engaged a Mexican force of 6,000 men at Palo Alto, Texas. Losing only nine men, the Americans routed the Mexicans, who lost 300 to 400 men and retreated to Matamoros on the Mexican side of the Rio Grande. Continuing his pursuit, Taylor defeated the Mexicans at the Battle of Resaca de la Palma the next day; and all Mexican resistance on the American side of the Rio Grande collapsed. A week later, the Mexicans evacuated Matamoros; and Taylor, crossing the Rio Grande, occupied the town on May 18. The American battle plan called for Colonel Stephen Kearny, commander at Fort Leavenworth, Kansas, to proceed overland to Santa Fe, New Mexico, and secure it from the Mexican authorities. From Santa Fe, Kearny was to go on to California, where Commodore John D. Sloat was to seize San Francisco Bay and blockade the Mexican ports on the Pacific Coast. Meanwhile Commodore David Conner was to blockade Mexico's Gulf ports while Taylor subdued Northern Mexico. Lastly, General Winfield Scott was to lead a joint army-navy expedition against Vera Cruz and proceed overland to the capital at Mexico City. The capture of Mexico City would end the war — it was hoped.

The Santa Anna Episode

In July, 1846, American agents contacted General Santa Anna, who was living in exile in Cuba. Santa Anna, in return for being allowed to pass through the American blockade and return to Mexico (where he would hopefully assume power), agreed to sign a treaty with the United States which would give America the Rio Grande boundary and San Francisco Bay. Once back in Mexico, Santa Anna reneged on his pledge to the United States and led the Mexican war effort against America. Ironically, the United States needlessly prolonged the Mexican War by giving the enemy's leading general safe passage to the war front.

The Conquest of California

In anticipation of war with Mexico, General John C. Frémont had been sent into California (which had a small American population) on a geographical and surveying mission. When war finally came, it is believed that Frémont instigated the American rebellion (June–July, 1846) against Spanish rule which resulted in the establishment of the Bear Flag Republic (an independent California state). In July, 1846, Commodore Sloat landed at and captured Monterey, from which he seized San Francisco and Sonoma. A month later, Commodore Robert F. Stockton took command in California, captured the area around Los Angeles, and named himself Governor of a new American territory. The Mexican majority, however, rebelled against the Americans in September, 1846, and succeeded in driving the Americans out of Los Angeles, Santa Barbara, and San Diego. By the end of the year, all of California south of San Louis Obispo was in Mexican control.

Enter Kearny

Fortunately for the American war effort, Colonel Stephen Kearny was on schedule. Leaving Kansas upon the outbreak of the war, Kearny's forces entered Las Vegas on August 15, 1846, and took control of Santa Fe three days later. Surprisingly, Kearny met almost no opposition from the Mexicans (the remoteness of the sparsely settled New Mexican territory may account for the lack of resistance), and he was able to leave for California toward the end of September. (In the winter of 1846-1847, the New Mexicans rebelled against the American occupation forces, but the rebellion was suppressed.) In January, 1847, Kearny arrived in California, and operating under orders from Commodore Stockton, he suppressed the Mexican revolt in southern California. Although Kearny and Stockton later quarreled over the extent of their respective authority in California, Kearny's arrival ended resistance; and by early 1847, New Mexico and California were safely in American hands.

The Campaigns in Northern Mexico

On August 19, 1846, Taylor marched out of Matamoros to attack the Mexicans at Monterey (in Mexico). Although Mexican resistance, by this time, had stiffened, Taylor was able to take Monterey after a four-day battle (September 20–24). Having fought a hard engagement, Taylor and the Mexican commander both agreed to an eight-week suspension of hostilities. This somewhat unusual armistice produced the expected reaction in Washington. President Polk was furious and countermanded Taylor's truce agreement, ordering him to take the offensive. Meanwhile, General Scott had been given authority to proceed with his attack on Vera Cruz, and large contingents of troops were detached from Taylor's command and transferred to Scott's. Taylor, himself, was ordered to conduct only a holding operation in the North, while Scott directed the main battles out of Vera Cruz. This infuriated Taylor; he was convinced that Washington was plotting against him in order to diminish his presidential chances by allowing his rival (Scott) to win military glory in Vera Cruz and, thereby, capture the popular imagination. Determined to add to his military laurels, Taylor violated his orders and conducted a major assault on Buena Vista in late February, 1847. Faced with heavy enemy resistance and greatly outnumbered by the Mexicans, Taylor's forces nevertheless inflicted a severe defeat on the troops commanded by General Santa Anna. Santa Anna withdrew from northern Mexico and returned to Mexico City, where he prepared to oppose Scott.

A week after Taylor's victory at Buena Vista, Alexander W. Doniphan, proceeding south from Santa Fe, encountered and defeated the Mexicans at the Battle of the Sacramento (River) and captured the provincial Mexican capital at Chihuahua. Buena Vista and Sacramento were the last major battles fought in northern Mexico. For Taylor, the war was over; and all he could do was sit back in idleness and watch Scott win the battles which, Taylor felt, should have been his.

Vera Cruz and the End of the War

In March, 1847, General Winfield Scott and some ten thousand men landed at Vera Cruz. Meeting only light resistance, Scott soon had the city in American hands; and he began to consolidate his position for the march to Mexico City. Although the distance between Vera Cruz and Mexico City was short, the route went through rugged mountain terrain, and in this area, Mexican resistance was the stiffest of the war. On April 8, Scott left

Vera Cruz and met Santa Anna at Cerro Gordo, on the road to Mexico City; here he defeated the Mexican general on April 18. From April to August, 1847, fighting subsided, as Nicholas P. Trist attempted to negotiate a settlement with Mexico. However, Trist's efforts were hindered not only by the stubbornness of the Mexicans, but by Scott (who felt that Trist was attempting to undercut his authority for political reasons and who therefore constantly quarreled with Trist). In August, heavy fighting resumed, and Scott defeated the Mexicans at Contreras and at Churubusco in some of the heaviest fighting of the war; and the road to Mexico City lay open.

With the final collapse of the Trist mission, Scott began the final drive on Mexico City on September 8. After six days, the city fell to the Americans; Santa Anna was toppled from power, and a new Mexican government was established to negotiate the peace. Mexico was completely at the mercy of the United States, its ability to continue the war having been completely destroyed. It remained only for the United States to dictate the final terms of peace.

The Treaty of Guadalupe Hidalgo (February 2, 1848)

The United States rejected Southern suggestions to annex all of Mexico (primarily because the country would have to absorb too many Mexicans who could not be readily assimilated into the general American population) and decided instead to annex those areas of Mexico which contained the fewest Mexicans. The treaty contained the following provisions:

(1) The southern boundary of Texas was to be the Rio Grande River.

(2) Mexico ceded to the United States, California and New Mexico (comprising present-day Arizona, New Mexico, California, Nevada, Utah, and parts of Colorado and Wyoming).

(3) In return for New Mexico and California, the United States paid Mexico 15 million dollars and assumed the claims of American citizens against Mexico up to a maximum of 3¼ million dollars.

The Wilmot Proviso and the Slavery Question

In the midst of the Mexican War, Pennsylvania's Congressman David Wilmot (on August 8, 1846) appended a resolution to an army appropriations bill. The Wilmot Proviso, introduced at the behest of the anti-slavery (Van Buren) wing of the Democratic party, would have excluded slavery from any and all territory acquired from Mexico. (The Proviso would not have applied to Texas, which was not considered a part of Mexico.) Despite vigorous Southern opposition, the Wilmot Proviso passed the House (where superior Northern numbers proved decisive) and was sent on to the Senate. In the Senate, however, the Southerners succeeded in killing the Wilmot Proviso. When Congress reconvened the next winter, the Wilmot Proviso was reintroduced in the House and again won House approval. In February, 1847, the Senate, once more, killed the measure, and the legislative career of the Wilmot Proviso came to an end. However, the debate which it spawned did not die; and the issue which it raised dominated American politics in the 1850's. To counter the Wilmot Proviso, John C. Calhoun (the voice of the slaveholding South) introduced in the Senate a series of resolutions which declared that the Western territories were the common property of the whole nation (belonging to the South as well as the North), that Congress had no constitutional right to bar any specific form of property from the territories, and that Congress was obligated to protect the security of all lawful property (including slavery) in the Western territories.

Calhoun did not obtain complete satisfaction, and the issue remained alive. As James K. Polk completed his first term of office (he had pledged to serve only a single term), he could take his place as one of the most successful Presidents in American history. Pledged to reannex Texas and reoccupy Oregon, he had done both; and he had acquired vast new territories in the American Southwest as well. Polk had achieved his campaign goals; and judging by that standard, he was among the most effective Presidents in the nation's history. As a result of Polk's successes, anti-slavery emerged as a viable political issue. Over the next twelve years the anti-slavery movement would grow, and the emotional crusade to safeguard the West from the taint of slavery would lead to civil war. The Mexican War was instrumental in producing the political crisis over slavery which brought on the American Civil War.

AMERICAN FOREIGN POLICY AFTER THE MEXICAN WAR

The Young America Movement

Although the slavery controversy dominated American politics in the 1850's, foreign affairs were not entirely neglected. Formally organized in 1852, the Young America movement typified the continuing interest in world affairs. Enjoying the support of prominent politicians, such as Stephen A. Douglas, the movement urged a policy of continued American expansion in the Caribbean, and of aid to republican movements in Europe (Americans were deeply stirred by the revolutionary movements which swept Germany and Austria in 1848, and they wanted to lend aid and encouragement to the European republicans). In addition, the movement urged the establishment of free trade among the nations of the world. The Young America movement was short-lived, however, for the charge that Southerners sought Caribbean expansion to promote slavery helped to tear the movement apart.

The United States in Latin America

Hoping one day to build a canal across Central America (which would link the Atlantic and Pacific Oceans and which would shave thousands of miles off the sailing distance between California and America's East Coast), the United States concluded the Clayton-Bulwer Treaty with England in 1850. Since England held territory along the Mosquito Coast (British Honduras) and was also interested in an Isthmian canal, it was important that the United States and England come to an agreement on the construction of a Central American canal. The Clayton-Bulwer Treaty contained the following provisions:

(1) Neither England nor the United States would seek exclusive control over an Isthmian canal, nor would either power seek to fortify such a canal.

(2) Both powers pledged not to further colonize Central America.

(3) The neutrality and security of an Isthmian canal was guaranteed by both powers.

(4) Finally, both powers were assured of equal access to any future Isthmian canal (thus, no discriminatory duties would be levied by one nation against the other).

(5) The treaty left both powers free to construct an Isthmian canal if they so chose.

The Ostend Manifesto

Written in October, 1854, by Pierre Soulé, John Y. Mason, and James Buchanan (all American diplomats at the time), the Ostend Manifiesto was occasioned by the seizure of an American ship by Spanish authorities in Cuba. It was an unfortunate statement. Declaring that American acquisition of Cuba was essential to the security of slavery (Cuba was often envisioned as an additional slave state by Southern expansionists), the above-mentioned diplomats urged the United States government to purchase the island from Spain or (if Spain were unwilling to sell) to wrest it from Spain by force of arms. Not only did the Ostend Manifesto cause the United States political embarrassment in Europe, it was also seized upon by the anti-slavery forces in America as evidence of a slaveholders' conspiracy to seize control of the national government. Disavowed by the Franklin Pierce administration, the Ostend Manifesto was soon forgotten — but not before it had done its damage to North-South relations.

The Walker Filibuster

The contention that the slavocracy was conspiring to expand American power in the Caribbean was given added impetus in 1855, when William Walker, an American adventurer, launched a filibustering expedition against Nicaragua. Taking advantage of the political chaos caused by a recent revolution, Walker was able to seize control of the country and to name himself President of Nicaragua. While Walker enjoyed some support in Washington, his introduction of slavery into Nicaragua aroused intense Northern opposition to his seizure of power. In 1857, Walker was overthrown by a coalition of neighboring Central American states organized by Cornelius Vanderbilt, another American who had extensive business interests in the area. When Walker attempted to regain power later that year, he was executed, ending a curious episode in American history.

Cartoon circulated in the presidential campaign when James Buchanan was the Democratic nominee. The tramps are using the language of the Ostend Manifesto while they rob Buchanan.

The United States and the Opening of Japan

The expansion of American maritime interests in the Pacific in the mid-nineteenth century made it imperative that Japan's seclusion be ended and that the Japanese be brought into the community of nations. Not only were Japanese ports needed as coaling and supply stations for international shipping, but American whalers who were shipwrecked along the Japanese coast were often mistreated by the suspicious Japanese authorities. In November, 1852, President Millard Fillmore dispatched Commodore Matthew C. Perry on a voyage to Japan, with instructions to secure both a commercial treaty and humane treatment for shipwrecked American sailors. Sailing into Tokyo Bay in July, 1853, Perry delivered Fillmore's message to the Japanese and announced that he would return for their answer later. Reentering Japanese waters in February, 1854, with a fleet of seven ships, Perry cowed the Japanese into signing the Treaty of Kanagawa (March, 1854), which opened the ports of Shimoda and Hakodate to American trade and provided for the humane treatment and safe return of shipwrecked sailors. The United States had succeeded in ending two centuries of Japanese seclusion and had unknowingly awakened a slumbering giant.

Salving America's Conscience: the Gadsden Purchase

In 1853, the United States government paid Mexico 10 million dollars for 29,640 square miles of desert waste at the southern tip of Arizona and New Mexico. The ostensible reason for the Gadsden Purchase was the acquisition of a site for a proposed southern railroad to the Pacific. However, the Gadsden Purchase is generally viewed as an additional compensation for the American seizure of California and the Southwest from Mexico, and as an effort to ease a guilty American conscience. Be that as it may, the Gadsden Purchase rounded out the borders of the continental United States and was the last American acquisition in the territory of the traditional forty-eight states.

The Mormon Trek to Deseret

Among the epic migrations in American history was the Mormon settlement of the Salt Lake Valley in present-day Utah. Back in 1823, Joseph Smith claimed to have been visited by the Angel of the Lord who led him to the final revelations of the Lord. With the aid of the Angel, Joseph Smith translated the Book of Mormon into English, and in 1830, he established the Church of Jesus Christ of the Latter-Day Saints (Mormons for short). Predicting the imminent return of the Saviour, Smith advised his growing band of followers to lead a righteous and polygamous life, and he organized them into a communal and theocratic society. However, the Mormon practice of polygamy aroused the violent antagonism (or perhaps jealousy) of their Gentile neighbors. Persecuted by their neighbors and harassed by local authorities, the Mormons were driven out of upstate New York and took refuge in Kirtland, Ohio. From Ohio, they were driven to the Missouri frontier, and then to Nauvoo, Illinois. For a time, they found peace in Nauvoo; but in 1844, an internal Mormon quarrel produced mob violence in which Joseph Smith and his brother were killed. The death of Joseph Smith threatened to destroy the Mormon church, but a capable leader was found to succeed him. Brigham Young decided that the Mormons would find peace only if they left the territorial United States and settled in a remote wilderness where they would be free to live in accordance with their conscience.

In the winter of 1846, the Mormons left for what was then the New Mexico territory; and they arrived in the Salt Lake Valley in June, 1847. Establishing the state of Deseret, the Mormons elected Brigham Young as their governor, began an extensive irrigation system to water the desert lands, and established a communal and theocratic society in which economic activities were strictly regulated. Lying along the route to California, Deseret prospered during the 1848–1849 gold rush, and it became a leading commercial center for the Southwest. Unfortunately, the Americans seemed to follow the Mormons wherever they went; and in 1850, Deseret became part of the newly organized Utah Territory. For a time, war between the Mormons and the United States appeared imminent, as the Mormons refused to abandon polygamy in accordance with American law. Cooler heads prevailed, however, and the Mormons agreed to observe the spirit, if not the substance, of American law; and the threat of war subsided.

REVIEW QUESTIONS FOR CHAPTER 17

1. The American claim to Oregon was based on all of the following *except*

    (A) the Lewis and Clark expedition
    (B) the Adams-Onis Treaty
    (C) the Nootka Sound Treaty
    (D) the settlement of Willamette Valley

2. James Polk won the 1844 election because Henry Clay lost the anti-slavery vote in

    (A) New York
    (B) Massachusetts
    (C) Pennsylvania
    (D) Ohio

3. The partition of Oregon gave the United States all of the following *except*

    (A) The Columbia River Basin
    (B) Vancouver Island
    (C) Puget Sound
    (D) Juan de Fuca Strait

4. Mexico insisted that the southern border of Texas was

    (A) the Rio Grande
    (B) the Red River
    (C) the Nueces River
    (D) the Arkansas River

5. The Mexican War was unpopular in the

    (A) South
    (B) West
    (C) Northeast
    (D) Northwest

6. The decisive battle of the war in northern Mexico was fought at

    (A) Cerro Gordo
    (B) Buena Vista
    (C) Matamoros
    (D) Monterey

7. The Vera Cruz expedition was led by

    (A) Winfield Scott
    (B) Zachary Taylor
    (C) Stephen Kearny
    (D) John C. Frémont

8. The Ostend Manifesto was directed against

    (A) Mexico
    (B) Nicaragua
    (C) California
    (D) Cuba

9. The Mormon Church was founded by

    (A) Brigham Young
    (B) Joseph Smith
    (C) William Walker
    (D) David Wilmot

10. The Clayton-Bulwer Treaty gave the United States

   (A) Oregon
   (B) New Mexico
   (C) the right to build an Isthmian canal
   (D) the Gadsden strip

Explanatory Answers

1. **(C)** The Nootka Sound treaty was made between England and Spain.

2. **(A)** Birney took enough votes away from Clay to give New York to Polk.

3. **(B)** Vancouver Island remained British.

4. **(C)** The Nueces River was the southern limit of the original Texas concession.

5. **(C)** Anti-slavery partisans saw the Mexican War as a slaveholders' conspiracy to acquire territory.

6. **(B)** At Buena Vista, Taylor defeated Santa Anna, who withdrew to Mexico City.

7. **(A)** Scott's expedition was designed to capture Mexico City via Vera Cruz.

8. **(D)** The Ostend Manifesto declared Cuba vital to the welfare of slavery in America.

9. **(B)** Smith claimed to have translated the Book of Mormon — God's final revelation.

10. **(C)** The Treaty provided for a demilitarized canal, open to all nations.

Chapter 18

THE HOUSE BEGINS TO DIVIDE, 1848-1860

Viewed by many Northerners as a Southern slaveholders' conspiracy to expand slave territory and to dominate the national goverment, the Mexican War intensified sectional hostility and made slavery the leading political issue of the 1850's. But slavery was a moral, not a political, issue; it could not be resolved by means of ordinary parliamentary compromise. Questions of good and evil are not subject to compromise; and, as Abraham Lincoln pointed out, America had to be either all free or all slave. Slavery and freedom could not indefinitely coexist — one or the other must triumph. The dispute over slavery was, indeed, an "irrepressible conflict" which could only be resolved by means of the sword. In the dozen years between the end of the Mexican War and the election of Abraham Lincoln as President of the United States, the American people were forced to choose sides; and the resulting polarization in favor of liberty or slavery inevitably led to the American Civil War.

THE LAST GREAT COMPROMISE

The Presidential Election of 1848

The ghost of the Wilmot Proviso, with its demand that slavery be kept out of the Western territories, was the major issue in the election of 1848. The Democrats nominated Michigan's General Lewis Cass (Polk had pledged that he would serve only a single term as President) for President, with General William O. Butler (of Kentucky) selected for the Vice-Presidency. A heavy and slow man, Cass was the originator of the doctrine of "squatter sovereignty" (leaving to local residents the determination of the status of slavery in the territories) which, he hoped, would remove slavery as a divisive issue in American political life. The Democratic platform decried the raising of the slavery issue and affirmed its belief that Congress had no right to interfere with the institution of slavery in the states. The Whigs, recognizing that they were a minority party, searched for a popular candidate with unpublicized views, for the party hesitated to take a stand on the great issues facing the nation. Therefore, the Whigs bypassed Henry Clay (who had too many political enemies) in favor of General Zachary Taylor (the hero of the Mexican War). Taylor was a Louisiana slaveholder, but he was known to be a nationalist; and as a political unknown, he had acquired no formidable enemies. As his running mate, the Whigs selected New York's Millard Fillmore, and they adjourned their convention without adopting a platform. Northern Whigs portrayed Taylor as a supporter of the Wilmot Proviso, while Southern Whigs took pride in the fact that he was a fellow slaveholder. Meanwhile, antislavery Democrats and Whigs, joined by old Liberty party members and moderate abolitionists,

Taylor and the Problem of California

Sectional antagonisms had prevented the organization of the vast territories acquired from Mexico in 1848; and in March, 1849, Zachary Taylor inherited the vexing problem. Back in January, 1849, leading Southerners had signed John C. Calhoun's "Address of the Southern Delegates," which condemned the exclusion of slavery from the Western territories, opposed impediments to the return of runaway slaves, and called upon the North to honor the constitutional rights of the Southern states. It was obvious that the South would continue to oppose any attempt to organize the Mexican cession as slave-free territories. In any event, the discovery of gold in California resulted in a huge influx of new settlers; and by the end of 1849, California had more than enough residents to qualify for statehood. President Taylor supported California's immediate admission as a state, without regard to the issue of slavery. At his behest, California (in October, 1849) adopted a constitution, elected state officials, and applied for admission to the Union as a free state. In December, 1849, Taylor urged favorable congressional action on California's statehood. However, there were, at this time, fifteen slave states and fifteen free states already in the Union. California would shatter the sectional balance and would permit the free states, which controlled the House, to dominate the Senate as well. With the South prevented from expanding slavery into the territories, the South would soon become a helpless minority, subject to the legislative dictates of the majority free states. The Southerners dug in for a long, hard fight.

General Zachary Taylor, the Whig presidential candidate in 1848, depicted by his opponents as resting on a heap of skulls.

met at Buffalo, New York in August 1848, to form the Free Soil party.* Pledged to support the Wilmot Proviso, free homesteads for Western settlers, and federal internal improvements, the Free Soilers nominated former President Martin Van Buren and Charles Francis Adams as their standard-bearers. The results of the election follow:

    Taylor   1,360,101   (163)
    Carried 8 slaves states, 7 free states
    Cass   1,220,544   (127)
    Carried 8 free states, 7 slave states
    Van Buren   291,263   (0)
        Carried no states

Although Zachary Taylor won the Presidency, he owed his election to Martin Van Buren, who took enough votes away from Cass in New York to give that state's 36 electoral votes to Taylor.

---

* Abolitionism and anti-slavery were two separate concepts. The first sought the immediate end of slavery wherever it existed, while the latter merely sought to exclude slavery from the Western territories of the United States and to confine it to those states where it already existed.

The Compromise of 1850

The debate over the admission of California lasted from January through September of 1850. Jefferson Davis of Mississippi (emerging as a leading spokesman for the South) declared that the sectional crisis was the work of greedy Northern politicians who wanted to dominate the Union in order to impose upon it the economic doctrines of the Hamiltonian Whigs. The South, he declared, would fight, if need be, to secure equal access to the Western territories and equal protection of its economic interests. The dying John C. Calhoun made his final appearance on the Senate floor, but he was too weak to read his own address, and a colleague delivered it for him. Declaring that the

Calhoun's last appearance in the Senate.

South was being endangered by the growing imbalance between the sections, he demanded a constitutional amendment to secure equal weight for the South in the councils of government. In an essay published after his death, Calhoun enunciated the doctrine of the concurrent majority — considered one of the most brilliant political analyses ever proposed by an American thinker. According to this "Marx of the Master Class," government existed to perpetuate the interests of the dominant economic classes within the society. The rapid development of industry in the North had threatened the security of Southern slaveholders, and the old sectional balance between North and South had to be restored. This could be done, according to Calhoun, by having two presidents (one from the industrial North, one from the slave South), each having the right to veto acts of Congress. In this way, Congress would be unable to pass measures which endangered the interests of either the North or the South. While theoretically incisive, the concurrent majority concept had small chance of actual implementation.

In order to resolve the Congressional deadlock over California, Henry Clay engineered his last great legislative compromise. Supported by Daniel Webster (who forfeited the support of the New England abolitionists by his stand) and by Stephen A. Douglas of Illinois, Clay proposed an eight-part package containing the following provisions:

(1) California would be admitted to the Union as a free state.

(2) The rest of the Mexican cession would be organized without regard to slavery.

(3) The Texas-New Mexico boundary would be adjusted so as to exclude all of the Mexican cession from the territory of Texas.

(4) Texas would be compensated for the loss of New Mexican territory by having the United States assume the debt contracted by Texas while Texas was still an independent Republic.

(5) The slave trade would be abolished in the District of Columbia.

(6) Slavery in the District of Columbia would be protected, however, and would be abolished only if approved by the people of the District and by the state of Maryland, and only if the owners were compensated for the loss of their slaves.

(7) An effective fugitive slave law would be enacted to return runaway slaves to their owners.

(8) A declaration that Congress had no right to interfere in the interstate slave trade would be provided.

Taylor and the Compromise of 1850

Clay's program faced opposition from several powerful quarters. President Taylor and the overwhelming majority of Northern Whigs opposed the Compromise of 1850, feeling that California should be admitted to the Union on its own merits, with no reference to slavery. Moreover, many Whigs agreed with William Henry Seward that slavery (while it might be protected by the laws of man) violated the higher law of God, and that no compromise should be made (the proposed fugitive slave law, for example) with an institution that was morally evil, and which must, inevitably, be destroyed. On the other hand, Southern fire-eaters (such as Calhoun, Robert Barnwell Rhett of South Carolina, and William L. Yancey of Alabama) also opposed the Compromise, demanding, instead, explicit recognition of slavery in the Western territories. Convinced that slavery must expand or die, Southerners demanded equal access to the West, or secession from the Union. However, the death of Calhoun, and the sudden death (from cholera) of President Taylor in July, 1850, permitted more moderate voices to prevail. Millard Fillmore endorsed Clay's package; and most Northerners accepted Daniel Webster's compromise contention that the laws of nature excluded slavery from the Mexican cession and that the North could be generous in appeasing the demands of the South. Even the South grew moderate. In June, the Nashville Convention rejected the idea of secession and, instead, called for the extension of the Missouri Compromise line of 1820 to the Pacific, with slavery permitted south of 36°30′ latitude. Soon Georgia, Virginia, and Louisiana came around to the support of the Compromise of 1850; and in September, it was successfully enacted into law.

The Fugitive Slave Act (September, 1850)

The hope that the Compromise of 1850 would finally lay the slavery issue to rest and heal the wounds of sectionalism proved abortive. One aspect of the Compromise of 1850 proved highly unpopular in the North, strengthened anti-slavery and abolitionist sentiment, and worked against the long-range interests of the South. This was the Fugitive Slave Act, which provided that Negroes accused of being runaway slaves were to have a hearing before a federal commissioner. The Act did not, however, entitle the accused Negroes to a jury trial to establish their guilt or innocence; nor were they permitted to testify on their own behalf. The alleged owner merely had to prove to the satisfaction of the commissioner that the accused Negro was his slave, and on this *one-sided* testimony, the commissioner would turn the accused over to his alleged master. The procedure struck many Northerners as violating the basic civil rights to which all men were entitled. Moreover, if the commissioner ruled the Negro to be a runaway slave, he received a $10.00 fee; whereas, if he ruled him to be a free man, he was paid a $5.00 fee. This appeared to be an incentive for guilty verdicts, and Northerners were furious that the South thought it could buy a Yankee soul for $5.00. The act also provided for fines of $1,000 and/or six months imprisonment for anyone attempting to interfere with the operation of the Fugitive Slave Act.

Northern abolitionists and anti-slavery zealots simply refused to obey the law. Throughout the North, abolitionist-led mobs broke into jails to release accused runaways and to prevent their return to the South. Public opinion forced the passage of personal liberty laws (which, in effect,

Placard distributed by the anti-slavery Vigilance Committee of Boston.

nullified the Fugitive Slave Act and required jury trials to determine the status of accused Negroes) in New England, Pennsylvania, Ohio, Indiana, Michigan, and Wisconsin. The Fugitive Slave Act was a major tactical error for the South, for the number of runaways (one thousand out of three million) was miniscule, while the number of new anti-slavery zealots grew enormously. In the elections of 1850, those Northern Whigs (such as Daniel Webster) who supported the Compromise of 1850 went down to defeat and were replaced by extreme anti-slavery partisans, such as Charles Sumner and Ben Wade.

The Presidential Election of 1852

The Compromise of 1850 had severely split both major parties. Northern anti-slavery Whigs distrusted the influence of Southern Whigs, while Southern Democrats and Free-Soil Democrats both distrusted the leadership of the national Democratic party. And yet there was (in both the North and

South) a large popular groundswell in favor of conciliation and a willingness to give the Compromise of 1850 a fair chance of survival. In 1852, the Democrats named Franklin Pierce (New Hampshire) and William R. King (Alabama) as their candidates for President and Vice-President, and the party adopted a platform endorsing the Compromise of 1850 and the sentiments of the Kentucky and Virginia Resolutions. The Whigs chose General Winfield Scott and William A. Graham (North Carolina) as their standard-bearers; and they also endorsed the Compromise of 1850, while condemning continued agitation over the slavery question. Finally the Free Soil party nominated John P. Hale (New Hampshire) and George W. Julian (Indiana) on a platform which condemned the Compromise of 1850 and denounced the institution of slavery. The results of the election were as follows:

Pierce	1,601,474	(254)
	Carried 27 states	
Scott	1,386,578	(42)
	Carried 4 states	
Hale	156,149	(0)
	Carried no states	

The election demonstrated that the Whig party was dying as a national institution; large numbers of Northern "Conscience" Whigs could not support the Compromise of 1850 and would not cooperate with Southern Whigs. Moreover, the Free Soil party was no longer a viable political movement. Its program was too narrow, and the American people wanted to bury slavery as a divisive political issue. The Democratic party, however, emerged as the only moderate unifying force left in the nation. Southern moderates, realizing that they had no where else to go, returned to the Democratic party, considering it the only vehicle capable of giving them power in the national government. And most anti-slavery Democrats were willing to give the national party another chance to bind up the nation's sectional wounds. As Pierce succeeded Fillmore, the Democratic party became a coalition of Southern slaveholders and Northern moderates, in which the Southerners were the dominant power. If the Democratic coalition could not survive, the nation itself might not survive; yet forces were at work which would soon destroy the Democratic party.

THE BLOOD OF KANSAS NOURISHES THE REPUBLICAN PARTY

Stephen A. Douglas and the Kansas-Nebraska Act

For reasons that are still subject to debate, Stephen A. Douglas (the Democratic senator from Illinois) shattered the frail unity of the Democratic party and revived the Free Soil movement in a form more potent than ever before. In 1854, he proposed to organize the Kansas-Nebraska area into two territories. However, under the Missouri Compromise of 1820, slavery was barred from the area; and the Southerners would not permit Kansas-Nebraska to be organized into territories so long as slavery was excluded from them. Accordingly, Douglas proposed that the Missouri Compromise be repealed, and that Kansas-Nebraska be organized on the basis of popular sovereignty (that is, the people of each territory would decide for themselves whether to enter the Union as a free or a slave state). Douglas hoped that this proposal would remove slavery as a national issue, once and for all time, and would let local residents determine their own status, free of outside pressure. In proposing the Kansas-Nebraska Act, Douglas was seeking (1) a Northern route for a proposed transcontinental railroad, and (2) Southern support for his future presidential candidacy. The South and President Pierce both favored a transcontinental railroad which would link St. Louis and California through Texas and New Mexico (which had already been organized as a territory and was, at least, partially settled). Douglas realized that his stature would be enormously enhanced if he could secure the eastern terminus of the transcontinental railroad for Chicago instead of St. Louis. However, in order to attract interest in a Chicago terminus, Kansas and Nebraska (through which the road would run) would have to be organized and settled in numbers sufficient to make the route economically feasible. This was the primary reason for Douglas' Kansas-Nebraska Act. The South expected to gain from the Douglas proposal. Since Kansas was adjacent to Missouri (a slave state), the first settlers of the new region were likely to come from Missouri and would, therefore, vote to open the Kansas Territory to slavery. Northern congressmen voted against the Douglas plan by a margin of 26 to 13. However, with Southern support, the measure was passed.

Political Realignment in the Wake of Kansas-Nebraska

The Kansas-Nebraska Act revolutionized American politics and had fateful results for the nation. Southern Whigs, grateful for Douglas' defense of Southern rights in the Western territories, went over to the Democratic party, giving it an even stronger Southern flavor. In July, 1854, Northern Whigs, Free Soilers, and Democrats (such as Charles Sumner and Salmon P. Chase), all of whom were opposed to the Kansas-Nebraska Act, met at Ripon, Wisconsin to form a new political party — the Republican party.* The new party was not abolitionist (although it did have an abolitionist element in it), for it did not call for the end of slavery where it already existed. But it was firmly anti-slavery in its insistence that the Western territories must remain free soil — untainted by the pollution of slavery — and the exclusive domain of the small, independent farmer. Like the defunct Whig party, the Republicans assumed a national stance which favored internal improvements to link the West with the East, protective tariffs to encourage the development of industry, and Western homesteads which would be given free to actual settlers. Not having to worry about Southern support, the Republicans were able to appeal to Northeastern capitalists, small farmers wanting free land in the West, and anti-slavery idealists. The party appealed to both genuine humanitarians and to political opportunists. In October, 1854, an obscure Illinois politician, who had never before denounced slavery, condemned the institution in a speech at Peoria. Now that anti-slavery was a popular cause, Abraham Lincoln was quick to embrace the new Republican party; he was anxious to climb to power on the back of a noble cause which he had only just embraced.

In the November elections, the Democratic party lost some 350,000 votes and carried only two Northern states. The anti-Nebraska forces had scored significant victories in New England, New York, Pennsylvania, and the states of the Ohio Valley. Stephen A. Douglas' presidential ambitions had been dealt a severe blow; and the Democratic party, the last unifying force in America, had been gravely weakened.

Bleeding Kansas

In April, 1854 (one month after the passage of the Kansas-Nebraska Act), New England abolitionists and anti-slavery partisans organized the New England Emigrant Aid Company, whose purpose was to settle Kansas with anti-slavery residents and thereby secure the territory as a free state. To this end, the company sent some two thousand settlers to Kansas. Pro-slavery forces, based in neighboring Missouri, were equally determined to secure Kansas for slavery; and they began to import pro-slavery settlers and border ruffians (Missourians who sought to impose their pro-slavery sentiments on Kansas). In 1855, most Kansas settlers were anti-slavery Northern farmers, who were concentrated in the Topeka and the Lawrence areas. The Southern minority remained along the Missouri River, around Atchison and Leavenworth. When Territorial Governor Andrew H. Reeder called for legislative elections, voter turnout exceeded everyone's fondest expectations. Six thousand votes were cast; and a pro-Southern legislature was elected which quickly established slavery in Kansas (even though there were only two actual slaves in the territory). The difficulty was that Kansas had only 1,500 eligible voters, and it became obvious to everyone that the pro-slavery triumph was brought about by widespread fraud and by the use of border ruffians from Missouri. In anger, the anti-slavery forces called a constitutional convention at Topeka, organized a separate territorial government, and banished slavery from Kansas. Thus, by late 1855, Kansas had two separate governments; each selected by questionable methods, each claiming to be legitimate. It was now up to President Pierce to decide which government was legal. The situation was critical; for from November to December, 1855, there was an outbreak of open fighting between pro- and anti-slavery Kansans (the Wakarusa War). Pierce's final decision on Kansas was as urgent as it was difficult.

Pierce made a purely political decision. The Democratic party was led by its Southern wing, and the Southerners applied massive pressure on Pierce to persuade him to recognize the pro-slavery government. In 1856, Pierce refused to inquire

---

* For a time after the Compromise of 1850, many Northern Whigs joined the Know-Nothing party, which enjoyed a boom in the early 1850's. The Know-Nothings (native Americans) opposed Roman Catholic immigration, alien land ownership, and the right of Catholics to hold public office. The Northern Whigs saw the Know-Nothings as a conservative refuge, but quickly abandoned them when the Republican party was organized. The Know-Nothings rapidly declined; and, eventually, the nativist anti-Catholics also joined the Republican party.

Senator Sumner being attacked by Congressman Brooks.

into the substance of Kansas politics; following the form of the electoral process, he recognized the pro-slavery government and condemned the anti-slavery Topeka constitution as illegal and invalid. The decision further polarized the Democratic party, for the Northern Douglas wing could not, in good conscience, accept the legality of the pro-slavery Kansas legislature. In Kansas, the decision touched off a civil war. In May, 1856, a federal marshal attempted to arrest the free-territory leaders at Lawrence, Kansas. He gathered a posse and invaded the town. A number of buildings, shops, and homes were destroyed, and two Southerners were killed. The Northern press played up and exaggerated the "Sack of Lawrence," and the Republicans used the incident to portray the inhuman savagery of the Southern slaveholders. In retaliation for the Lawrence incident, John Brown and his sons murdered five pro-slavery settlers at Pottawatomie Creek. From May to September, 1856, Kansas settled into a sporadic civil war which claimed the lives of some two hundred people and caused property damage estimated at two million dollars.

"The Crime Against Kansas"

Hoping to improve his declining popularity in Massachusetts, Senator Charles Sumner delivered his famous "Crime Against Kansas" speech on May 19, 1856. Condemning the South for its murder, plunder, and robbery in Kansas, he launched into a personal and bitter attack on the aged senator from South Carolina, Andrew Pickens Butler. Preston S. Brooks, a congressman from South Carolina who was related to Senator Butler, was determined to avenge his family's honor and punish Sumner for his attack on the South. On May 22, he entered the Senate chamber, approached Senator Sumner and proceeded to beat him into unconsciousness with a walking cane. Sumner, pinned at his desk, was unable to ward off the blows. To the North, Sumner had become a martyr — the fearless champion of human liberty struck down by a brutal Southern barbarian in a cowardly and inexcusable attack. Sumner never fully recovered from the Brooks attack; and for several years, he was physically unable to attend the Senate. His chair was purposely left vacant as a reminder of Southern brutality, and Northern public opinion became galvanized into opposition to the slavocracy. Southerners praised Brooks' defense of family and region and prevented his expulsion from the House of Representatives. In Southern eyes, Sumner had gotten the treatment he deserved.

The Presidential Election of 1856

The new Republican party, attempting its first presidential race, demanded the immediate admission of Kansas as a free state and the construction of a federally subsidized transcontinental railroad. The party avoided extreme anti-slavery partisans and nominated John C. Frémont (the Pathfinder) as its presidential candidate. A professional soldier and explorer, Frémont had no political experience (and no political enemies) and was a moderate on the slavery issue. To round out the ticket, New York's William L. Dayton was selected as Vice-President. The Democrats adopted a platform supporting the Kansas-Nebraska Act; but as a gesture of nationalism and conservatism, they nominated Pennsylvania's James Buchanan for President and Kentucky's John C. Breckinridge for Vice-President. By 1856, the Whig party had ceased to exist as a national organization; but the American (Know-Nothing) party named Millard Fillmore and Andrew J. Donelson as its standard-bearers. The Know-Nothings endorsed the Kansas-Nebraska Act, losing the support of their Northern members, who went over to the Republicans. The Know-Nothings were supported primarily by Southern Whigs who could not bring themselves to support the Jeffersonian and states' rights Democratic party; the anti-Catholicism of the Know-Nothings limited their Northern appeal. The results of the election were as follows:

Buchanan   1,838,169 (174)
Carried 14 slave states,
5 free states

Frémont   1,335,264 (114)
Carried 11 free states

Fillmore   874,534 (8)
Carried Maryland

The Republicans carried all of New England, New York, and most of the Middle West. It revealed its strength among Northern farmers, and it captured those states which were growing most rapidly in wealth and population. The Republican party emerged as a major political coalition of the East and West. The Democrats, while they held Pennsylvania (Buchanan's home state), New Jersey, Indiana, Illinois, and California, did so only as the result of support given by conservatives who had not yet joined the Republican party. More than ever, the Democratic party was the representative of the sectional interests of the slaveholding South, and it was rapidly losing its Northern following. American politics was fragmenting along sectional lines.

THE HOUSE DIVIDES AND COLLAPSES

The Dred Scott Decision

Back in 1834, Dred Scott, a Missouri slave, had been taken by his owner (army surgeon Dr. John Emerson) from St. Louis to Rock Island, Illinois and then to Fort Snelling, Wisconsin, where the doctor was stationed. In 1846, Scott was returned to Missouri, and Dr. Emerson's widow eventually married John F. A. Sanford, a New York abolitionist. With Sanford's permission and connivance, Scott brought suit in a Missouri state court, claiming that his temporary residence in a free state (which outlawed slavery) made him a free man. The lower court accepted Scott's contention and declared him to be a free man, but the Missouri Supreme Court reversed the lower-court decision. At this point, the case was brought into federal court on the grounds that the Northwest Ordinance of 1787 had banned slavery in the Ohio Valley and that Scott had become free as soon as he entered the territory. In 1856, the case was argued before the Supreme Court, headed by Chief Justice Roger B. Taney of Maryland (the Court contained five Southern Democrats). The South hoped that the case would resolve the question of slavery in the territories and confidently assumed that the Supreme Court's decision would be accepted by the Northerners as the law of the land.

The majority decision (actually each justice made his own statement, but Taney's is considered the consensus view) was delivered in 1857 by Chief Justice Taney, who went far beyond the immediate issue in question and handed down an essentially political judgment. Taney ruled as follows:

(1) As a slave, Dred Scott was not a citizen of the United States or of any state, and, therefore, he was not entitled to bring suit in federal court. At this point, Taney could have merely dismissed the case and ended the matter. But, he went further:

(2) Slaves were property. Indeed, they constituted a form of property distinctly and explicitly recognized by the Constitution of the United States.

(3) Since the Constitution guaranteed citizens against the loss of life, liberty, or property (except by due process of law), and since slaves were legal property, Congress had no constitutional right to bar slavery from the Western territories. Congress could no more prevent a Missourian from taking his slave to Wisconsin than it could prevent him from taking his horse there.

(4) Moreover, Congress was obligated to protect slave property in the territories to the same extent that it was obligated to protect other forms of property. Consequently, the Missouri Compromise of 1820 was unconstitutional.

Effects of the Dred Scott Decision

Only Justices John McLean and Benjamin Robbins Curtis dissented from the Taney decision, holding that Congress could indeed bar slavery from the Western territories. However, instead of laying the slavery issue to rest, the Dred Scott decision further inflamed sectional animosities. The Republicans, as a party, condemned the decision since it declared the main plank of their platform (the exclusion of slavery from the Western territories) to be unconstitutional. The Douglas wing of the Democratic party also rejected the decision as an infringement on the doctrine of popular sovereignty. Douglas held that the people of a territory could vote to exclude slavery; the Taney decision would force Congress to protect slavery in the territories. Thus, the Democratic party was further fragmented, with Southern Democrats demanding the protection of slavery in the West, even though natural conditions operated to exclude plantation slavery from the region (the land and climate were best suited to a non-slave agricultural system of small farms).

Kansas Again

In 1857, James Buchanan was anxious to resolve the Kansas issue by bringing the territory into the Union as a state, thereby depriving the Republican party of a potent campaign weapon. Accordingly, he sent Robert J. Walker (a Democratic political leader) to Kansas to arrange for a constitutional convention. Because of the extremely complex political situation in Kansas, most Northern emigrants to Kansas were so disgusted with politics and politicians that they did not vote for delegates to the constitutional convention at Lecompton. As a result, the convention was controlled by pro-slavery Southerners, who drafted a constitution which protected property in slaves. This constitution was to be submitted to the people for ratification, and the people were to decide whether the *further* introduction of slavery into Kansas was to be permitted. Walker, however, rejected the constitution drafted at Lecompton since it did not give the voters a real choice as to whether Kansas would enter the Union as a free state or a slave state.

President Buchanan, under extreme Southern pressure, overruled Walker and submitted the Lecompton constitution to the Kansas voters for approval or rejection. As a result of a boycott by the anti-slavery forces, the Lecompton constitution was approved; and in 1858, Buchanan recommended Kansas' admission to the Union as a slave state. However, at this point, Stephen A. Douglas broke with the administration and opposed the Lecompton constitution as a mockery of popular sovereignty. With Douglas in the opposition, the Lecompton constitution had no chance to pass Congress, and the Buchanan forces agreed to a compromise. According to the English Bill (named for Indiana's William H. English), the Lecompton constitution was to be resubmitted to the Kansas voters. If they approved it, Kansas was to achieve statehood and a sizeable federal land grant; if they rejected it, Kansas would have to wait until its population reached the minimum required for a congressional seat before being admitted as a state. In August, 1858, the pro-slavery Lecompton constitution was overhelmingly voted down; and Kansas did not enter the Union until 1861, when it joined as a free state. Douglas' rejection of the Taney decision and the Lecompton constitution hopelessly estranged the Southern Democrats from the national Democratic party, and it greatly weakened the unifying force previously exercised by the Democratic organization.

The Lincoln-Douglas Debates

In 1858, Abraham Lincoln (who had served one term in Congress) challenged Stephen A. Douglas for the Illinois senatorship, and he engaged in a series of classic debates with Douglas. At this time, Lincoln was an unknown and largely unsuccessful politician (although he had won distinction as a corporation lawyer). An old-line Whig of conservative instincts, Lincoln had failed to gain the support of the Illinois electorate, and he was now hoping to capitalize on the slavery issue and gain office. Debating with Stephen A. Douglas (the leading spokesman of the Northern Democratic party) immediately increased Lincoln's political stature and provided him with a national audience for the expression of his views. Although Douglas won the senate seat, Lincoln gained a national reputation as an attractive and rising political leader. The debate also provided him with the opportunity for a comprehensive and public airing of his attitude on slavery. His main points follow:

(1) The institution of slavery is morally wrong. However, it is protected by the United States Constitution and cannot be interfered with in those states in which it already exists. Lincoln, thus, rejected abolitionism and refused to abolish slavery where it was already established.

(2) Since slavery is morally evil, the institution should be confined to those areas where it already exists, and should *not* be permitted to expand into the West. Lincoln was confident that if slavery were not permitted to expand, it would gradually die out. Although Lincoln did not say how this death would occur, he believed that it would be a natural and evolutionary process of undetermined length.

(3) Congress had the power to exclude slavery from the Western territories under the gen-

eral welfare clause of the Constitution. The West, Lincoln declared, should be reserved for the exclusive use of free *white* farmers. Since free labor could not successfully compete against slave labor, slavery should be barred in the interest of the general social welfare.

(4) On the race issue, Lincoln declared that he was a white supremacist. He did not believe that the Negro race was the social, moral, or intellectual equal of the white race; and that that being the case, equality between the two races was impossible. As long as blacks and whites inhabited the same area, one had to be inferior and the other superior; and Lincoln wanted his race to be dominant. However, free Negroes were entitled to enjoy the fruits of their labor just as whites were, and therefore he favored equal economic opportunity for both races.

(5) Finally, Lincoln declared that a house divided against itself could not stand; he thought the United States would become all free or all slave. That being the case, the North must see to it that slavery was placed in a position where it would inevitably die out. This, he felt, could be accomplished without resort to violence, and he did not expect to see the Union break up because of the slavery issue.

Lincoln emerged from the debate as the voice of the moderate wing of the Republican party. Unlike William Henry Seward, who predicted an "irrepressible conflict" between freedom and slavery, Lincoln was not an abolitionist; and he did not favor the violent extermination of slavery (although he later flirted with a plan to compensate owners who emancipated their slaves).

John Brown's Raid

Aided and encouraged by prominent abolitionist leaders (such as Theodore Parker, Thomas W. Higginson, and Gerrit Smith), John Brown and eighteen followers (including five Negroes) seized the federal arsenal at Harpers Ferry, Virginia in October, 1859, and held a number of local residents as hostages. It was Brown's aim to instigate a slave insurrection in Virginia, establish a free state in the Appalachian mountains, and use this free state as a base of operations for a slave revolt which, he envisioned, would end slavery throughout the South. After the seizure of Harper's Ferry, however, no slaves heeded Brown's call for rebellion; and two days later, he and his remaining men were taken prisoner by United States Marines commanded by Colonel Robert E. Lee. Brown was immediately tried for treason and sentenced to death. He was executed on December 2, 1859.

Although Brown was an unbalanced fanatic, Northern abolitionists made a hero of him; and they used his death as a rallying point for the struggle against the brutal slavocracy. In the South, however, John Brown's raid was considered a terrifying event. It appeared that the Northerners, backed by public opinion, were intent upon waging their own private war against the South and its institutions. The raid helped convince many Southerners that the Northern people were irrevocably hostile to the South and were bent upon destroying the South's cherished way of life. It gave credence to the pleas of the fire-eaters that the South must secede from the hostile North and establish a nation of its own which would expand slavery by absorbing the islands and lands of the Caribbean.

The Davis Resolutions

Motivated by the John Brown raid, by Northern opposition to the Dred Scott decision, and by the refusal to recognize slavery in Kansas, Jefferson Davis (the leader of the Southern extremists) introduced six resolutions in the Senate in February, 1860. They were designed to guarantee the rights of the South, and to head off the threat of secession. Davis declared the following:

(1) No state can interfere in the domestic institutions of its sister states (an obvious reference to the Brown raid).

(2) Any attack on slavery within a slave state is in violation of the Constitution and should be dealt with accordingly.

(3) The Senate must actively oppose legislation discriminating against slave property in the territories.

(4) Congress cannot bar slavery from the Western territories and must protect the institution from local attack (legislative or physical) in the territories.

(5) No state may impede the return of fugitive slaves.

(6) A territory cannot decide to bar slavery until it is admitted to the Union as a state.

The Davis Resolutions were not passed, but they did touch off a heated debate on the rights of the South. That winter, talk of secession swept the lower South (South Carolina, Mississippi, Alabama); and many leaders vowed to leave the Union if a black (abolitionist) Republican were elected President in 1860.

The Presidential Election of 1860

In April, the Democratic National Convention opened in Charleston, South Carolina. Northern Democrats demanded a platform endorsing popular sovereignty in the territories, whereas the Southerners demanded a statement that neither Congress nor the territories, themselves, could exclude slavery from the West. When it became obvious that the Southerners would not carry the convention, delegates from eight slave states walked out. After fifty-seven ballots, Douglas was unable to get the two-thirds vote needed for nomination (because of the Southern walk-out), and the convention was adjourned until June. When the Democratic convention reconvened, it did so in Baltimore. Once again, the Southerners staged a walk-out, but this time the Northern Democrats went ahead and nominated Stephen A. Douglas for President and Herschel V. Johnson (Georgia) for Vice-President; and the party adopted a platform supporting the principle of popular sovereignty. The angry Southerners held their own convention in Baltimore later that month. They nominated John C. Breckinridge (Kentucky) for President and Joseph Lane (Oregon) for Vice-President, and they adopted a platform calling for federal protection of slavery in the Western territories. The Democratic party, the last national institution in the United States, had finally split into a Northern and Southern wing. The bonds of Union were fast breaking.

While the Democrats were splitting, the remnants of the Whig and Know-Nothing parties convened in Baltimore (in May) and reorganized as the Constitutional Union party. Condemning secession and the continued agitation over slavery, the party proclaimed its loyalty to the Union, the Constitution, and the laws of the land (including the Dred Scott decision); and it pledged to enforce federal law. Tennessee's John Bell and Massachusetts' Edward Everett were selected as the party's presidential and vice-presidential candidates.

The Republicans met in Chicago in May, and viewing the disruption of the Democratic party, they were confident of victory. To win, the Republicans had to carry both Pennsylvania and Illinois or Indiana, and their platform and candidates were shrewdly designed to do both. The convention bypassed front-runner William Henry Seward (New York) because he was considered too extreme on the slavery issue (he enunciated the idea of the "irrepressible conflict"), and the Republicans wanted to appeal to moderate Northern sentiment. Similarly, the candidacy of Salmon P. Chase (Ohio) was also rejected, for he was even more radical than Seward; and Missouri's Edward Bates was bypassed because his association with the Know-Nothings would prove an insurmountable handicap among Catholic and immigrant voters. Consequently, on the third ballot, the Republican convention nominated dark-horse Abraham Lincoln, who had the advantage of coming from the crucial state of Illinois and who lacked a political past which might antagonize key voter blocs. As he was strongly backed by Illinois and Indiana, it was hoped that he could bring those states to the Republican side. For Vice-President, the Republicans nominated Hannibal Hamlin of Maine. The party's platform called for a protective tariff (designed to win Pennsylvania), free homesteads (an appeal for farmer support) and protection for the rights of immigrants (an appeal for the support of the German, Irish, and Catholic blocs). It also condemned the doctrine of secession, called for the exclusion of slavery from the West, and for the maintenance of the Union at all costs.

The campaign developed into two separate contests for the same office. In the North, the Presidency was a race between Douglas and Lincoln; in the South, it was a contest between Breckinridge and Bell. The results of the election follow:

Lincoln   1,866,352 (180)
Carried 18 free states

Douglas   1,375,157 (12)
Carried Missouri and 3 New Jersey votes

Breckinridge   847,953 (72)
Carried 11 slave states

Bell   589,581 (39)
Carried 3 slave states

Lincoln received only 39.9 per cent of the

popular vote (which means that 60 per cent of the American people rejected him and the platform of his party), and ran very poorly in the Northern cities (with the exception of Boston). In the entire South, he received only 26,000 popular votes and no electoral votes. He carried California by a mere 643 votes (out of a total cast of 119,000) and Oregon by only 264 votes (out of 13,000). His election was made possible solely by the votes of Northern farmers who responded to the promise of free homesteads; and his victory represented a sectional triumph. However, it is doubtful if more than a small minority of those who did vote Republican shared the party's antislavery sentiments.

For the South, the unthinkable had come to pass. A party hostile to the South's economic, social, and cultural interests had come to power in the nation; and a renewed attack on Southern institutions appeared to be only a matter of time. To many Southerners, secession was now a necessity if Southern civilization were to be preserved.

REVIEW QUESTIONS FOR CHAPTER 18

1. The Democratic presidential candidate in 1848 was

   (A) Franklin Pierce
   (B) Lewis Cass
   (C) Stephen A. Douglas
   (D) Millard Fillmore

2. The Compromise of 1850 did *not* provide for

   (A) California's admission as a free state
   (B) the Fugitive Slave Law
   (C) the extension of the Missouri Compromise line to the Pacific
   (D) slavery in Washington, D.C.

3. The Compromise of 1850 was *not* supported by

   (A) Zachary Taylor
   (B) Daniel Webster
   (C) Millard Fillmore
   (D) Stephen A. Douglas

4. The Higher Law doctrine is associated with

   (A) Abraham Lincoln
   (B) Stephen A. Douglas
   (C) Daniel Webster
   (D) William Henry Seward

5. Personal liberty laws were directed against the

   (A) Compromise of 1850
   (B) Fugitive Slave Act
   (C) Dred Scott Decision
   (D) Kansas-Nebraska Act

6. The Republican party was organized out of opposition to the

   (A) Compromise of 1850
   (B) Kansas-Nebraska Act
   (C) Dred Scott Decision
   (D) Missouri Compromise

7. The "Crime Against Kansas" speech was delivered by

   (A) Charles Sumner
   (B) Abraham Lincoln
   (C) William Henry Seward
   (D) Salmon P. Chase

8. Which one was not a presidential candidate in 1856?

   (A) James Buchanan
   (B) John C. Frémont
   (C) Millard Fillmore
   (D) Stephen A. Douglas

9. Lincoln favored all of the following *except*

   (A) white supremacy
   (B) abolition
   (C) a ban on slavery's expansion
   (D) free homesteads

10. In 1860, the Republican party did *not* support

(A) free homesteads
(B) popular sovereignty
(C) a protective tariff
(D) protection for the rights of immigrants

Explanatory Answers

1. **(B)** Cass originated the doctrine of squatter sovereignty.

2. **(C)** The Mexican cession was organized without reference to slavery.

3. **(A)** Taylor's death in July, 1850, permitted the Compromise to pass Congress.

4. **(D)** The doctrine held that slavery violated the law of God, if not of man.

5. **(B)** The personal liberty laws granted accused slaves jury trials.

6. **(B)** The Kansas-Nebraska Act repealed the Missouri Compromise's ban against slavery in that region.

7. **(A)** The speech resulted in Sumner's being assaulted by Preston Brooks of South Carolina.

8. **(D)** Douglas ran in 1860.

9. **(B)** Lincoln did not oppose slavery where it already existed.

10. **(B)** The Republican party opposed the Western extension of slavery.

Chapter 19

THE CIVIL WAR AND RECONSTRUCTION UNDER LINCOLN, 1860-1865

Historians are still in disagreement over the causes of the American Civil War. Late nineteenth and early twentieth-century historians, such as James Ford Rhodes and John W. Burgess, saw the war as springing primarily from the moral and constitutional issues raised by slavery. In the 1930's, followers of Charles A. Beard argued that the Civil War constituted the Second American Revolution, in which Northern capitalists seized control of the national government from Southern agrarians. The Civil War was a struggle between capitalism and agrarianism; and the slavery issue was used as a cover to justify a war fought for economic purposes. In the 1940's, historians, such as Charles Randall and Avery Craven, argued that the Civil War was a needless conflict which resulted from the selfish, incompetent, and knavish behavior of American politicians, North and South. The implication was that the Civil War could have been avoided had the American people enjoyed political leadership of a higher quality. However, in the last few decades, historians have again stressed the overriding importance of the slavery question in provoking the Civil War. A moral issue, not subject to normal political compromise, slavery was a question which could only be resolved by force of arms. While other factors were certainly at work in dividing the North and the South, slavery was the single issue which possessed the emotional impact sufficient to sustain pro-war sentiment.

LINCOLN AND THE SECESSION CRISIS

South Carolina Leads the Exodus

Lincoln's election as President of the United States in November, 1860, convinced the Southern militants that the national government would soon be in the hands of men who were hostile to the South and who were determined to destroy its social institutions. In December, 1860, a special convention was held in South Carolina to consider that state's future relation to the Union. Citing the compact theory of the Constitution (which held that the federal government was a creation of the states, and that individual states could withdraw from the Union at will), and pointing to Northern exclusion of slavery from the Western territories as evidence of hostility to the social institutions of the South, the South Carolinians held that they were entitled to resume their independent existence as a national entity. On December 20, 1860, the state proclaimed its independence of the United States of America. Over the next month, similar conventions were held throughout the lower South; and six sister states joined South Carolina in secession (Mississippi, January 9; Florida, January 10; Alabama, January 11; Georgia, January 19; Louisiana, January 26; and Texas, February 1). The upper South (Virginia, Arkansas, Tennessee, and North Carolina) declined to secede from the Union, but they made it clear that they would leave the Union if the federal government made any attempt forcibly to bring the states of the lower South back into the Union. Of the states which had seceded, only Texas submitted the issue to popular referendum (Virginia and Tennessee were to do so later); in the other states, secession was decided by conventions specially elected for that purpose.

Buchanan and the Secession Crisis

Although the secession of the lower South was a direct challenge to federal authority, the Northern people were by no means united on the question of how the challenge should be met. While Lincoln (and the bulk of the Republican party) argued that the individual states could not unilaterally secede from the Union and that federal authority must be upheld, peacefully if possible, forcibly if necessary, large segments of the Democratic Party and the Northern public were of a different opinion. President James Buchanan, in his annual message to Congress, declared that although the Southern secession was deplorable, the federal government had no authority to coerce seceding states back into the Union or to hold any states in the Union against their will. Consequently, when the seceding states seized federal forts, arsenals, post offices, court houses, and other installations in December, 1860 and January, 1861, the Buchanan administration made no attempt to resist the state take-overs and maintain federal authority in the lower South. Indeed, a number of Buchanan's Southern Cabinet officers actively aided the Southern states in the acquisition of federal properties and military supplies. Moreover, many Northerners shared Horace Greeley's opinion that the "erring sisters" (states of the lower South) should be permitted to leave the Union in peace. Those who held this view were confident that the Southern States would soon realize the error of secession and would return to the Union. As the winter of 1860-1861 progressed, secession was an accomplished fact; and men of goodwill desperately searched for a peaceful resolution of the secession crisis.

The Crittenden Proposal

Hoping to head off the imminent secession of the Southern states, Kentucky's Senator John J. Crittenden, in December, 1860, introduced a resolution which would have permitted slavery in the Western territories south of 36°30′ latitude. This attempt to revive the old Missouri Compromise line would have permitted slavery in at least a portion of the Western territories, and it was hoped that this gesture of conciliation would persuade the South to call off its secession. However, Lincoln refused to give his endorsement to the Crittenden Proposal (feeling that it was a direct violation of the Republican party's platform plank opposing the Western extension of slavery), and it came to nothing. In this instance, Lincoln was acting irresponsibly, for his election was the triumph of a minority party which could hardly be said to have had a mandate from the American people (indeed, 60 per cent of the electorate rejected Lincoln and his party). Desperately searching for a way to avoid war, the peace forces were without the active support of the President-elect.

The Washington Peace Convention

On February 4, 1861, a group of prominent American leaders (Northerners as well as Southerners) met in Washington, D.C. in a final effort to reconcile the North and the South. Chaired by former President John Tyler, the peace convention was called at the behest of the Virginia legislature, which hoped that it could formulate a political solution to the slavery issue. Unfortunately, the delegates of the convention were unable to agree among themselves, and they failed to produce any compromise plan. The failure of the convention indicated the bankruptcy of America's political leadership.

The Montgomery Convention

On the same day that the Peace Convention convened in Washington, the representatives of the seceded states met at Montgomery, Alabama to organize a new federal government. Four days later (February 8, 1861), a constitution for the Confederate States of America was adopted. Following the United States Constitution in most respects, the Confederate constitution specifically recognized the compact theory and was careful to safeguard states' rights (it did such a good job in this respect that the Confederate war effort was often hindered by state reluctance to obey the war-time edicts of the central government). In addition, it gave positive recognition to slavery, proclaiming servitude to be the natural condition of the Negro race. On February 9, 1861, the provisional Confederate government elected Jefferson Davis President and Alexander H. Stephens Vice-President of the Confederacy. Before Lincoln had even taken office, the lower South had established its own independent federal government — their secession was a reality; and the prospects of peaceful reunion were remote.

Lincoln Takes Office

Two days after the election of Jefferson Davis as President of the Confederate States of America, Abraham Lincoln left Springfield, Illinois for Washington, D.C. Making numerous stops along the route to Washington, Lincoln was careful to speak only in generalities, and he gave no hint of what his policy would be toward the seceded states. Unfortunately, Lincoln's journey to Washington ended badly. On the night of February 22, it was learned that Southern sympathizers in Baltimore planned to assassinate the President-elect; and Lincoln was hastily and secretly brought into Washington in his night clothes. When the story was made public, Lincoln was pilloried in the press and portrayed as a cowardly figure who moved only under cover of darkness. Finally, inauguration day came. In his March 4, 1861 inaugural address, Lincoln was conciliatory. He told the Southern states that he had neither the right nor the desire to interfere with slavery where it was already established. However, he went on to declare that the American Union was indivisible, that no state or combination of states could unilaterally dissolve the Union, and that secession was therefore illegal. He promised to uphold federal authority in the South (maintain postal service, collect customs, retain federal installations, etc.) and declared that the issue of war or peace was in the hands of the South. Vowing not to impinge upon Southern rights, he warned the South not to interfere with the lawful operations of the federal government.

The Fort Sumter Crisis

By the time Lincoln became President in March, 1861, Fort Sumter (located in Charleston harbor) was one of the last remaining federally controlled installations within the area of the Confederacy. Sumter soon became a symbol of critical importance to both sides. If the Confederacy was to make good its claim to independence, it would have to remove the remaining vestiges of federal authority from its territory. Similarly, if Lincoln were to maintain federal authority in the South (short of actual war), he would have to hold on to all federal structures still remaining under national control. The loss of Sumter would damage federal prestige, while its retention by the Union would be an embarrassment to the Confederacy. On April 6, 1861, Lincoln notified the South Carolina authorities that he intended to reprovision Fort Sumter. However, he declared that no attempt would be made to supply it with military goods and that only food and medicine would be brought in. The Confederates could not permit Fort Sumter to be reprovisioned and still maintain the Confederate claim to independence. Accordingly, General Pierre G. T. Beauregard was instructed to demand Sumter's surrender and to reduce the fort if it was refused. On the night of April 12, 1861, the Confederates began their bombardment, and the fort surrendered the next day. Federal property had been attacked; and on April 15, Lincoln proclaimed a state of insurrection in the South and called for 75,000 ninety-day volunteers to suppress the rebellion.

The attack on Sumter galvanized the Northern public into support for the Union. Many Northerners who did not feel that the federal government had the right to coerce the Southern states back into the Union now trooped to the colors. Their nation had been attacked, and they were ready to defend its honor and preserve its unity. Indeed, Southern historians have accused Lincoln of deliberately provoking the attack on Fort Sumter in order to rally public opinion for a war which it otherwise would not have supported. This charge, however, is unfair. Lincoln's policy was to uphold federal authority, peacefully if possible, forcibly if necessary. In any event, on April 17, Virginia left the Union and joined the Confederacy; and in May, 1861, Arkansas, Tennessee, and North Carolina followed Virginia into the Confederacy. However, in June, the mountainous counties of West Virginia seceded from Virginia and remained loyal to the Union (West Virginia was admitted to the

Bombardment of Fort Sumter.

Union as a state in 1863). The border states of Missouri, Kentucky, Maryland, and Delaware (all of which were slave states) declined to secede (in Maryland and Missouri federal troops were employed to make certain that they would not secede), but they proclaimed their official neutrality in the Civil War. (Before the implementation of the federal draft in 1863, troops were raised by the individual states; and a state's official neutrality merely indicated that it would not raise troops for either side. However, tens of thousands of individual citizens from the border states did participate in the war and could be found fighting on both sides). With the secession of Virginia, however, the Confederacy had won a major victory; and the Confederate capital was quickly moved from Montgomery to Richmond.

THE CIVIL WAR: FROM FIRST BULL RUN TO ANTIETAM

Union and Confederate Strengths and Goals

In material terms, the North enjoyed overwhelming superiority over the South. The twenty-three states which comprised the Union contained twenty-two million people and continued to enjoy a steady influx of European immigrants even during the war years. The Union had a balanced economy: it was agriculturally self-sufficient and continued to export wheat throughout the war; it had extensive industries capable of producing all the arms and war material needed to supply its armies; and it possessed an efficient and extensive railroad and transportation system which could rapidly move men and supplies from one theater of war to another. Moreover, the bulk of the Navy remained in Union hands, and its shipbuilding facilities guaranteed that the North would maintain naval superiority over the South. On the other hand, the eleven states of the Confederacy had a population of nine million (of whom three and one-half million were Negro slaves) and attracted no immigrants. The Confederacy's economy was overwhelmingly agrarian, but the South concentrated on commercial crops such as cotton and tobacco and was often unable to adequately satisfy its own food requirements. It had little in the way of industry and found it difficult to meet its military requirements. Lastly, its railroads were inadequate, and its transportation could not compare with that

Jefferson Davis and his Cabinet. Davis is sitting to the left of General Robert E. Lee (standing in center).

of the North. However, the South had a martial spirit (military virtues were prized, and its people were familiar with the use of firearms), and its generals tended to be superior to those of the North (many distinguished Union officers resigned their commissions to join the Confederacy). Moreover, the South was fighting on its own soil in defense of its way of life; it enjoyed the advantages of interior lines of communications and was familiar with the terrain. In many cases, Southern soldiers were more highly motivated than Union troops and were more resolute in battle. It was only because of Southern determination and courage that the war lasted as long as it did.

Northern military strategy consisted of three goals: (1) to blockade and starve the Confederacy, (2) to seize the Confederate capital at Richmond, Virginia, and (3) to capture the Mississippi River, thereby dividing the Confederacy into two isolated parts so that each segment could then be reduced separately. The North, in 1861, was fighting the Civil War, not to abolish slavery (Lincoln was careful to repeat that he would not interfere with slavery where it was established), but to preserve the Union and to maintain the integrity of the federal government. The Confederacy sought to capture Washington, D.C., and to seize central Pennsylvania and divide the Northeast from the Northwest. It sought nothing less than Union recognition of its independent existence as a sovereign nation. To bolster its claim to independence, the Confederacy was to seek diplomatic recognition by the European powers (particularly France and England). But although the European upper classes sympathized with the South, no European government recognized the Confederacy. European powers did, however, acknowledge the South's belligerent rights (hence its rights to wage war and to seek to purchase arms and supplies in neutral countries).

1861: Union Defeats at Bull Run and Ball's Bluff

By July, 1861, the Confederate coastline was under tight and relatively effective Union naval blockade. However, the Union march on Richmond did not go well. Under political pressure to get on with the war, Lincoln ordered General Irwin McDowell to advance from Washington into

Virginia with the ultimate objective being the capture of Richmond. McDowell's forces were to engage Beauregard's troops at Manassas Junction, while a second Union contingent was to engage General Joseph E. Johnston in the Shenandoah Valley and prevent him from joining forces with Beauregard. Unfortunately, Johnston eluded the Union troops and successfully linked up with Beauregard. Meanwhile, at Manassas Junction (Bull Run) McDowell appeared to have won the day. But a determined stand by Confederate forces under Thomas J. "Stonewall" Jackson stopped the Union advance and turned a Confederate defeat into a victory. Stopped by Jackson, McDowell ordered a retreat, which swiftly degenerated into a disorderly rout as green Union soldiers ran for their lives. The federal rout at Bull Run left Washington exposed to Confederate attack. However, the Confederates were as disorganized as the Union troops were raw, and they failed to follow up their initial advantage; therefore, First Bull Run had no long-range military significance.

After the disaster at Manassas Junction, Lincoln removed McDowell from command and replaced him with George Brinton McClellan. It was the first of many military shake-ups initiated by Lincoln as he desperately searched for a competent Union general to lead his armies against the Confederates. The overly cautious McClellan (who always imagined that huge Confederate armies were lying in wait beyond the next bend in the road) also proved a disappointment. Only when Ulysses S. Grant was given command did Lincoln find a competent general. The Eastern front remained relatively quiet until October, when the Confederates defeated the Union forces at Ball's Bluff just outside Washington. Once more there was fear for the safety of the Federal capital; but again the Confederates did not follow up their advantage. The defeat at Ball's Bluff, however, resulted in the formation of the Joint Committee on the Conduct of the War to investigate the administration's handling of the war effort. Dominated by leaders of the Republican party's radical faction (Ben Wade, Zachariah Chandler, and Thaddeus Stevens), the Committee demanded a more vigorous prosecution of the war as well as the abolition of slavery. The Committee on the Conduct of the War constantly pressed Lincoln for more radical measures and acted as a spur, driving the conservative Lincoln ever further to the left in his attitude toward slavery.

1862: Union Victories in the West

When the Civil War began, the neutral border state of Kentucky was invaded by Confederate forces. In January, 1862, George H. Thomas defeated the Confederates at the Battle of Mill Spring and established Union supremacy over Kentucky. A month later, General Grant won a decisive Union victory when he defeated Albert S. Johnston's Confederates at Fort Donelson, which commanded the approaches to the strategically important city of Nashville, Tennessee. The loss of Fort Donelson forced the Confederates to yield Nashville to federal troops on February 25, 1862, and gave the Union an important Mississippi Valley stronghold. Pushing through Tennessee, Grant engaged the armies of Johnston, Beauregard (who had been transferred to the West) and Polk at Shiloh on April 6-7, 1862. The bloodiest engagement of the war to date, Shiloh almost resulted in a disastrous Union defeat. But just in time, Grant received sufficient reinforcements from Generals Carlos Buell and Lew Wallace (the author of *Ben-Hur*) to enable him to stem the tide of battle. At Shiloh, Union forces suffered 13,000 casualties out of a total force of 63,000 men, while the Confederates endured 11,000 casualties (including the death of General Johnston) out of 40,000 men. The Confederates retreated to Corinth, giving up Tennessee, and giving Grant a reputation as one of the better Union generals. After Shiloh, Grant made ready for the decisive campaign for the Mississippi Valley.

Finally, on April 26, 1862, a joint army-navy expedition captured New Orleans, at the mouth of the Mississippi, and General Benjamin F. Butler was put in command of the occupied city. While the Union had made significant gains in the West, the Virginia theater continued to be a major disappointment.

1862: Stalemate in the East

On March 9, 1862, a new chapter in military history was begun when the *Monitor* met the *Merrimac* off Hampton Roads, Virginia. The Confederates had clad the *Merrimac* with iron plate and had rechristened her the *Virginia*. Her tough iron hull made her a formidable weapon, and she had played havoc with Northern ships. The *Monitor*, a prototype of the later submarine, was also an ironclad; lying low in the water, it was derisively referred to as a cheesebox on a raft. Towed to the scene of battle by the *Seth Low,* the *Monitor* engaged the *Merrimac* in a duel lasting several hours which ended when the *Merrimac* retreated back into its port. The battle not only ended the career of the *Merrimac,* it also ended the era of wooden ships and gave birth to the era of steel battleships. However, the Union did not fare so well on dry land.

In March, 1862, Lincoln, upset by McClellan's dilatory tactics, removed him from overall command of the army; but he left him in charge of the Army of the Potomac. In April, McClellan decided to take Richmond, not by a direct march from Washington, but, rather, by landing his more than 100,000-man army at Fort Monroe on the Virginia peninsula between the York and the James Rivers (the operation is known as the Peninsula Campaign). McClellan argued that he could use the superior Union naval forces to supply his troops while they made the short overland march to Richmond. Unfortunately, he wasted a valuable month in capturing Yorktown by formal siege. Having taken Yorktown by May 4, McClellan was on the outskirts of Richmond by the end of May. But then the Confederates struck.

After the fall of Yorktown, Lincoln agreed to let McDowell's 30,000-man corps reinforce McClellan's right wing. In order to prevent McDowell from joining McClellan, "Stonewall" Jackson, operating out of the Shenandoah Valley, conducted a brilliant drive (the classic Valley Campaign of May 4 – June 9) which resulted in the defeat of two separate Union armies, one under John C. Frémont and the other under Nathaniel P. Banks. As Washington was now threatened, McDowell's corps had to be recalled to the defense of the capital. Jackson's 18,000 men succeeded in tying down about 45,000 Union troops, whose services were thereby lost to McClellan. Meanwhile, at Fair Oaks, just outside the Confederate capital, Joseph E. Johnston engaged McClellan's forces (May 31-June 1, 1862). The battle was a stalemate; but a gravely wounded Johnston relinquished his command to Robert E. Lee, and a new phase of the war began.

On June 25, Lee began the Battle of the Seven Days, in which he used his full strength to attack McClellan's weak right flank (north of the Chickahominy River), hoping to completely destroy it. (To do this, he had to boldly expose Richmond to McClellan's strong left flank.) Lee successfully drove the Union army across the peninsula, but he failed to destroy McClellan's forces. McClellan retreated to the safety of Harrison's Landing (on the James) where Union naval support prevented Lee from pouncing on the federal forces. From Harrison's Landing, McClellan's forces were evacuated by sea in order to join John Pope's army on the Washington-Richmond overland route. Anticipating the Union strategy, Lee struck first. On August 29-30, Lee's general, James G. Longstreet, smashed Pope's army at Manassas Junction (Second Bull Run), sending the Union forces reeling back to Washington. Early in September, Lee crossed over into western Maryland. He hoped to bolster Confederate prestige by a victorious campaign on Union soil and to threaten Washington from yet another direction. Only McClellan could stop him.

Antietam

On September 17, 1862, at Antietam Creek (near Sharpsburg, Md.) McClellan attacked Lee's 50,000 men with an 87,000-man force. By the day's end, McClellan was on the point of smashing Lee's army when Jackson arrived to bolster the Confederate line. McClellan, who could have driven through had he pressed the offensive, broke off engagements and permitted Lee to withdraw to Virginia. The battle had important repercussions. Lincoln, disgusted with McClellan's lack of nerve, finally discharged him and placed Ambrose E. Burnside in command of the army (Burnside did not last long either). France and England, whose governments had flirted with recognition of the Confederacy, decided against it when Lee was stopped at Antietam. Finally, although the battle was technically a draw, the Union claimed it as a victory (since Lee withdrew); and Lincoln took advantage of this victory by issuing the Emancipation Proclamation. In the West, General Rosecrans defeated the Confederate's Braxton Bragg at Murfreesboro, thereby forcing the Southerners out of central Tennessee. The Confederates were losing their grip on the Mississippi Valley.

Burnside, in December, attempted to cross the Rappahannock at Fredericksburg and march into Richmond. Throwing his men at Lee's fixed defenses, Burnside suffered 12,000 casualties after a single day's fighting. Retreating across the river, he resigned his command. And a dismal year ended on the Eastern front. The Confederates had repulsed the Union armies, but they had not been able to launch an offensive against Northern territory. A war of attrition favored the Union, with its superiority in manpower and material.

LINCOLN AND THE PROBLEM OF SLAVERY

Early Measures

Seeking to retain the loyalty of the border slave states, Lincoln had followed a cautious, conservative policy on the question of slavery. There was, moreover, deep-seated Northern hostility towards Negroes; and many who were fighting to preserve the Union would not have fought a war to free the slaves. However, Lincoln was under extreme pressure from the radical wing of his own party to abolish slavery; and he was gradually moved to the left on the slavery issue. In May, 1861, General Benjamin F. Butler, commanding Fortress Monroe, Virginia, declared that he would consider all escaped slaves who reached his lines as "contraband of war" and would not return them to their owners. Eventually, Lincoln adopted Butler's position as official army policy, for runaway slaves were valuable sources of labor for the army, and denial of slave services to the enemy would also weaken the Confederacy.

The First Confiscation Act

In August, 1861, Congress enacted its first major legislation affecting slavery. The First Confiscation Act provided that all slaves employed in arms or labor (digging trenches, working in commissaries, etc.) against the United States were to be freed. The measure had little immediate effect because slaves working for the Confederate army were beyond the reach of federal law. But the act was a small step in the direction of eventual emancipation. Later that month, John C. Frémont, commanding federal troops in Missouri, ordered the emancipation of all slaves owned by Missourians who were engaged in rebellion against the United States. Fearing the political impact of Frémont's order on the border states, Lincoln modified the order to conform to existing federal law (First Confiscation Act).

Other Measures

Lincoln hoped that the border states would adopt measures to provide for the gradual emancipation of slaves with compensation given to the owners; he also hoped that such a system could be enacted by all the slave states once the war ended. Accordingly, Lincoln approved a measure (April, 1862) which provided for the compensated

Lincoln liberating the slaves.

emancipation of slaves in the District of Columbia. However, the idea of compensated emancipation did not gain widespread approval. Lincoln's innate conservatism on the slavery issue was demonstrated when, in May, 1862, he countermanded General David Hunter's order that all slaves in Hunter's military department (which included portions of Florida, Georgia, and South Carolina) were to be emancipated. Nevertheless, the Radicals in Congress kept the issue of emancipation alive. In June, slavery was abolished in the Western territories of the United States without any compensation being paid to the owners. Since few were affected by this law, it aroused little opposition. Finally, in July, 1862, the Second Confiscation Act freed the slaves of all persons engaged in rebellion against the United States. But, again, the Act had little practical effect. That summer, pressed by Horace Greeley to enunciate his position, Lincoln declared that his prime objective in the war was the preservation of the Union, not the emancipation of the slaves: if he could preserve the Union without freeing a single slave, he would do so; if he had to free every slave to save the Union, then he would do that. The fate of the slave was clearly incidental in Lincoln's considerations.

Hanging and burning a Negro in New York during the draft riots of 1863.

The Emancipation Proclamation

After Antietam, Lincoln issued the preliminary draft of the famous Emancipation Proclamation, which was scheduled to go into effect on January 1, 1863. The proclamation declared that all slaves in areas in rebellion against the United States would be freed. However, the border states of Missouri, Kentucky, Maryland, and Delaware were specifically exempted from the Emancipation Proclamation, as were those areas of the Confederacy under federal occupation on New Year's Day of 1863. It was further provided that any Confederate state which laid down its arms and returned to the Union before January 1 would also be exempted from the Emancipation Proclamation. In short, Lincoln freed all of Jefferson Davis's slaves (which were not his to free) while leaving the slaves in Union-occupied areas in shackles. The proclamation did not free a single slave although it was a definite move in the direction of general emancipation. In issuing the Emancipation Proclamation, Lincoln was influenced by these basic considerations: (1) the need to rally the anti-slavery masses in England to the support of the Union by showing them that the Civil War was a crusade to abolish slavery (it was hoped that such support would neutralize the pro-Confederate sympathies of the British upper classes) and (2) the hope that the proclamation would stir up slave insurrections in the Confederacy (it did not) and thereby weaken the military effectiveness of the Confederate armed forces. Lincoln also hoped that the Emancipation Proclamation would satisfy the demands of the growing Radical Republican faction and would unite the home front politically.

The New York City Draft Riots

Northern unity, however, was ephemeral. In March, 1863, Congress passed the First Conscription Act, which made all men between the ages of twenty and forty-five subject to the military draft. However, the act permitted the wealthy to escape military service by providing a paid substitute in their place or by paying the government $300. The measure was extremely unpopular among working people, especially among the Irish of New York City. When the draft went into effect in July, 1863, the Irish of New York revolted. For four days (July 13–16) Irish mobs burned, looted, and murdered. Free Negroes were especially singled out for attack. Many of them were burned alive, tortured to death, and mutilated by Irish mobs. Federal troops had to be sent into the city to restore order; and, for a time, it was feared that the Union might have to endure a full-scale domestic insurrection in its most important city.

1863: THE CRUCIAL YEAR

Chancellorsville (May 2-4, 1863)

"Fighting Joe" Hooker, the latest Union commander, crossed far up the Rappahannock River with some 130,000 men in an effort to turn Lee's flank and march into Richmond. With a force of less than 60,000 men, Lee defied conventional military tactics by dividing his outnumbered troops. Sending "Stonewall" Jackson through the Wilderness to roll up Hooker's right flank, Lee attacked Hooker's center and left. Hooker, badly mauled, retreated back across the Rappahannock. Lee, however, had won a victory as costly as it was brilliant. His more than 1600 dead included "Stonewall" Jackson — his ablest officer. While the Confederates were holding their ground in Virginia, they were doing poorly in the West.

The Vicksburg Campaign

Vicksburg, Mississippi was the strongest fortified port on the great Mississippi River, and it kept open the lines of communication between the eastern and western portions of the Confederacy. Beginning in December, 1862, General Grant began the campaign to capture Vicksburg and, with it, control the Mississippi River. Landing his forces opposite Vicksburg (on the western, or Louisiana, side), he made several unsuccessful attempts to penetrate its defenses during the winter months of 1863. Finally, Grant despaired of ever capturing Vicksburg from the west. In May, he marched his men down the Louisiana side of the Mississippi, crossed over to the east bank, and marched on Vicksburg from the rear. After failing to break through its defenses, Grant began a formal siege on May 22, 1863. After a six-week struggle, the exhausted 30,000-man Confederate garrison, led by John C. Pemberton, surrendered Vicksburg on July 4. Five days later, General Banks, coming north from New Orleans, captured Port Hudson, the final Confederate strongpoint on the Louisiana side of the Mississippi. The entire Mississippi River was now in the hands of the Union, and a prime Northern objective had been achieved. The eastern Confederacy was cut off from its western half — each segment could now be reduced separately.

Gettysburg: Lee's Last Northern Offensive

In order to relieve Union pressure on Vicksburg and the Mississippi and to demoralize the North, Lee again invaded Northern territory — this time crossing into Pennsylvania. He was hopeful that a great victory on Northern soil would strengthen the peace advocates in the North, initiate the intervention (or at least the mediation) of France and England, and induce the Union to recognize the independence of the Confederate States of America. Crossing the Potomac on June 17, Lee marched into Pennsylvania, taking Carlisle and York on June 27 and 28, and advancing to within ten miles of Harrisburg. George C. Meade (who had recently replaced "Fighting Joe" Hooker) dug in at Gettysburg, a strong defensive point on the line of Lee's march, and waited for the Confederates to either attack or retreat. On July 1, Lee felt out Meade's defenses and occupied Seminary Ridge which was opposite the Union line; federal forces were stretched out for three miles along Cemetery Ridge.

The decisive battles were fought on July 2 and 3. On July 2, Longstreet attacked the federals' left flank on Cemetery Ridge. Although the outer Union lines fell, General Gouverneur Kemble Warren managed to rally the federal forces and hold Little Round Top, thereby repulsing the Confederate charge. The next day, Lee tried a massive frontal assault designed to crack the federal line. Fifteen thousand men (Pickett's Charge) raced across open country under withering federal fire; two-thirds of them were cut down before they even reached Cemetery Ridge, and the 5,000 valiant men who reached the Union line were not enough to crack it. On July 4 (the same day that Vicksburg fell), Lee left the field of battle and withdrew into Virginia. The Union had lost 3,155 dead and some 20,000 wounded or missing, while the Confederates sustained 3,900 dead and some 24,000 wounded or missing. However, the timid Meade failed to pursue Lee and allowed him to slip back

Confederate Gen. Robert E. Lee (left) and Lt. Gen. Thomas J. (Stonewall) Jackson discuss strategy for the Battle of Chancellorsville.

into Virginia virtually unopposed. Had Meade been more aggressive, the Civil War might have ended on the fields at Gettysburg. Lee, however, had been gravely weakened. He would not again take the offensive, and he would fight a defensive war on his own soil for the remainder of the conflict.

More Western Setbacks

In September, 1863, Bragg evacuated Chattanooga, Tennessee to Union troops commanded by General Rosecrans, hoping to lure Rosecrans into a pursuit over open country. Rosecrans followed Bragg's army over the Georgia border and met him at Chickamauga (September, 19-20). Reinforced by units from Lee's command, Bragg inflicted a severe defeat on Rosecrans and forced the Union army to fall back to Chattanooga. Grant was sent to bolster the Union lines at Chattanooga; and in late November, Hooker, Sherman, and Thomas drove Bragg off Missionary Ridge, defeated him at Lookout Mountain, and thus won the battle of Chattanooga. The Confederates had been ousted from eastern Tennessee, and the entire Tennessee River was now in Union hands. General Sherman would soon use Tennessee as a base from which to trisect the South.

After Vicksburg, Gettysburg, and Chattanooga, only a miracle could enable the South to win the war and establish its independence. The South could only hope to wear down the North and wait until Northern public opinion grew tired of the fight and demanded peace.

THE CLOSING BATTLES OF THE WAR

Grant Takes Command

In March, 1864, as a reward for his successful campaigns against Vicksburg and Chattanooga, Ulysses S. Grant was made supreme commander of the Union army. Lincoln had finally found a competent general. Grant was a new type of general — one who understood the implications of modern warfare. Realizing that the war would end only when the Confederate armies were destroyed (the mere occupation of territory would not end the war), Grant was willing to accept frightful losses by hurling his numerically superior forces directly at the Confederate lines in order to destroy the Southern armies. For the spring of 1864, Grant proposed to engage Lee in Northern Virginia (hopefully forcing him to fight a decisive battle), while William T. Sherman was to invade Georgia from Tennessee, destroy Joseph E. Johnston's army, and capture the economically vital city of Atlanta. At the same time, General Banks was to invade Mississippi and Alabama from New Orleans, capture Montgomery, and join forces with Sherman. Banks, however, was soundly trounced at the Battle of the Sabine Crossroads, and never completed his part of the spring campaign. The other two campaigns began in May.

The Campaigns in Northern Virginia

Seeking to turn Lee's right flank, Grant and Meade crossed the Rappahannock and Rapidan Rivers; and when they did so, Lee struck their right flank through the Wilderness. In the Battle of the Wilderness (May 5–6, 1864), Lee inflicted 18,000 casualties on the Union army, while sustaining 10,000 casualties of his own. Lee demonstrated his tactical genius; he was a much more skilled commander than the heavy-handed Grant, but he could not overcome the huge numerical superiority of Grant (Lee had 65,000 men to Grant's 115,000). Unlike his predecessors, however, Grant did not withdraw after the Battle of the Wilderness to regroup his forces; instead, he pressed on to Spotsylvania Court House in an attempt to turn Lee's flank. Lee moved along with Grant, and at Spotsylvania (May 8–12), Grant lost another 12,000 men. Continuing to move left, Grant made another effort to break Lee's lines and attacked his well-entrenched forces at Cold Harbor (June 1–3). The battle was a slaughter. On a single day, Grant lost 12,000 men. After a month of inconclusive fighting, Grant suffered 60,000 casualties to Lee's 25,000-30,000. However, Grant's extravagant use of manpower was wearing down Lee's outnumbered forces.

Petersburg and the Shenandoah Valley

Petersburg, a small town south of Richmond, was a railroad juncture serving the Confederate capital. In June, Grant decided to make a strike for it, hoping to cut off communications with Richmond and to force Lee to commit his forces to open battle. Petersburg was defended by a small unit (under Beauregard) which managed to repulse Grant's attack (with a loss of another 8,000 men) until Lee could send reinforcements. By mid-June, Grant had failed to capture the city, and began a nine-month siege. In an effort to cut rail lines, Grant resorted to the new tactic of digging trenches to outflank the Confederates. Lee met him trench line for trench line, and the world had a foretaste of the trench warfare made famous by World War I. On July 2, 1864, Jubal A. Early crossed into Maryland and threatened Washington. However, he was engaged and defeated by Union troops under Philip H. Sheridan; and with the defeat of Early, Sheridan proceeded to scorch and destroy the Shenandoah Valley. Grant's Virginia campaign had been inconclusive, and Lee's army, although worn down and battered, was still intact. Further to the South, Sherman was meeting with more success.

Sherman's March

On May 7, 1864, General Sherman left Chattanooga, Tennessee with 90,000 men, seeking to destroy Johnston's army and to take Atlanta, Georgia. Like Lee, Johnston preferred not to engage the Union army in open battle unless absolutely necessary, and he waged a defensive operation designed to slow Sherman down while gradually picking him apart. Accordingly, Johnston checked Sherman at the Battles of Resaca and New Hope Church in May, and at Kennesaw Mountain in June. Sherman, however, continued to advance upon Atlanta; and Jefferson Davis, wanting the Confederates to assume the offensive, replaced Johnston with John B. Hood. Hood attacked Sherman twice — each time without success — and finally retreated into Atlanta. Sherman began a formal siege operation but decided to strike behind the city and seize the rail line, thus threatening Hood with starvation. This forced Hood to evacuate Atlanta, which fell to Sherman on September 2.

Having evacuated Atlanta, Hood's forces were relatively intact; and he decided to strike at Sherman's overextended lines of communications and attack Tennessee. Hood (with little more than 40,000 men) hoped that Sherman would follow him into Tennessee; there, Hood hoped to defeat him in the mountains and then drive for the Ohio River and invade the Middle West. But Hood's desperate campaign was a disaster. On November 30, he ordered his men across two miles of open country for an attack on the federal lines at Franklin, Tennessee. With no artillery support, Hood's men were cut to ribbons (6,000 men and eleven generals fell), and he finally withdrew to the mountains south of Nashville. On December 15-16, General Thomas engaged Hood's army at the Battle of Nashville and smashed it to pieces. As Hood's mangled forces retreated toward Mississippi, the federal cavalry pursued them and wiped them out. Hood's army had ceased to exist. Meanwhile, in mid-November, Sherman decided to march from Atlanta to Savannah (Georgia's seaport). It was a 300-mile march; seeking to destroy the Confederate will to fight, Sherman's men systematically destroyed everything in their path on a front sixty miles wide. It was the first time that war had been systematically waged against a civilian and noncombatant population. To the South, it was an example of Northern barbarism; to Sherman, it was a way of bringing home to the Southern people the hell of war; it was a means of dispelling their romantic illusions about the glory of the martial arts. On December 22, 1864, Savannah fell to Sherman. The South had been trisected.

Sherman and the Presidential Election of 1864

For the presidential campaign of 1864, the Republicans renominated Abraham Lincoln for President (even though the Radicals would have liked to dump him in favor of a more militant candidate); and, in a gesture of national unity, Lincoln selected Andrew Johnson, a Tennessee unionist and Democrat, as his vice-presidential candidate. The Democrats, dominated by the pro-Southern Copperheads, adopted a platform calling for the immediate end of hostilities and the restoration of the Union on federal lines (with strong states' rights provisions). The Democrats nominated General George B. McClellan for President and George H. Pendleton for Vice-President and hoped to capitalize on Northern resentment toward the war. However, news of Sherman's capture of Atlanta galvanized Northern public opinion in support of Lincoln and his war policies, and he won an easy victory. In his March, 1865 inaugural address, Lincoln called for a generous peace to bind up the nation's wounds and heal the Union.

The War Ends

In January, 1865, Sherman struck into South Carolina. The Confederates hastily organized a 30,000-man army under Joseph E. Johnston to check Sherman's newest march. Johnston, however, was powerless to stop Sherman, who quickly moved up into North Carolina. Meanwhile, Lee's weakening army was being bled white by Grant in the Petersburg-Richmond theater. When Grant finally succeeded in cutting the rail lines to Richmond, Lee evacuated Richmond and Petersburg on April 2, 1865. Lee now hoped to join Johnston in North Carolina and make a last desperate stand against the federal stranglehold. Grant, however, seized the rail lines to North Carolina, cutting off Lee's retreat. Seeing that his situation was hopeless, Lee surrendered his 25,000-man army to Grant at Appomatox Court House on April 9, 1865. Five days later, Abraham Lincoln was assassinated at Ford's Theatre by John Wilkes Booth. On April 18, Johnston surrendered to Sherman at Durham, North Carolina; and Richard Taylor surrendered the Confederate forces in Mississippi and Alabama on May 4. With the surrender of Kirby Smith at Shreveport, Louisiana on May 2, 1865, the American Civil War formally came to an end. The Union lost nearly 360,000 men; the Confederacy, a little over 275,000 men. The Civil War, in terms of lives lost, remains the most costly war in the nation's history. After the ordeal of the Civil War, there came the agony of Reconstruction.

LINCOLN'S PLAN OF RECONSTRUCTION

The Ten Percent Plan

Since secession was considered illegal, the Confederate states, in Lincoln's view, had never actually left the Union and were merely in a state of insurrection against federal authority. As Commander-in-Chief, it was Lincoln's responsibility to suppress the Southern rebellion and restore normal relations between the seceded states and the Union. Accordingly, in 1862, Lincoln appointed provisional military governors for those portions of Louisiana, Tennessee, and North Carolina which were under federal control. Finally, on December 8, 1863, Lincoln announced his formula for Reconstruction, which provided for the following:

(1) All Southerners (except for the Confederacy's top leaders) who took an oath of loyalty to the Union would receive executive amnesty for their crimes against the nation.

(2) When 10 per cent of the registered voters of each Southern state (as of the 1860 census) had taken the oath of loyalty to the Union, a constitutional convention could be elected to write a new fundamental code for the state.

(3) As soon as the constitutional convention abolished slavery, rejected the doctrine of secession, and repudiated the Confederate debt, the new state government could receive executive recognition and resume its normal relations with the Union.

On balance, Lincoln's proposals were moderate and promised to produce a speedy and magnanimous restoration of the Union. In 1864, Arkansas and Louisiana met Lincoln's requirements and were restored to the Union. However, Congress refused to seat their representatives and insisted that only it could readmit the Confederate states to the Union.

The Wade-Davis Bill (July 4, 1864)

The Radical Republicans, who were rapidly becoming dominant in Congress, considered Lincoln's plan too lenient. They feared that once the South was restored to the Union, the Democratic party would return to power and end Republican control of the national government. In addition, the Radicals wanted to safeguard the civil rights of the Negro and protect him from exploitation by his former master. Consequently, the Radicals offered their own plan of reconstruction in the Wade-Davis bill, which followed Lincoln's plan in most respects except that it required a majority of the Southern electorate to swear an oath of past, as well as future, loyalty to the Union. Obviously, it would have been extremely difficult for a majority of the Southern electorate to affirm that they had not engaged in rebellion against the Union, and the Wade-Davis bill would have served to keep the Confederate states out of Congress. Lincoln pocket-vetoed the measure, and he alienated much of the Radical wing of his party. However, he did finally endorse the Thirteenth Amendment to the Constitution (ratified December, 1865), which abolished slavery throughout the Union (including those areas and states not covered by the Emancipation Proclamation). Differences between the President and Congress over Reconstruction policies would persist, however. But that story belongs to the next chapter.

REVIEW QUESTIONS FOR CHAPTER 19

1. Between December 1860 and February, 1861, all of the following states seceded *except*

    (A) Florida
    (B) Tennessee
    (C) Georgia
    (D) Texas

2. The offer to extend the Missouri Compromise line to the Pacific was part of the

    (A) Crittenden Proposal
    (B) Montgomery Convention
    (C) Washington Peace Convention
    (D) Buchanan program

3. In his first inaugural address, Lincoln did not

    (A) promise to uphold federal authority
    (B) declare secession illegal
    (C) call for the abolition of slavery
    (D) warn the South against interference with federal functions

4. After Sumter all of the following states seceded *except*

    (A) Virginia
    (B) North Carolina
    (C) Arkansas
    (D) Missouri

5. Union troops at First Bull Run were commanded by

    (A) George B. McClellan
    (B) Irwin McDowell
    (C) Ambrose Burnside
    (D) Joseph Hooker

6. Grant's first major victory came at

    (A) Fort Donelson
    (B) Nashville
    (C) Shiloh
    (D) Vicksburg

7. The Shenandoah Valley campaign (1862) was conducted by

    (A) Robert E. Lee
    (B) "Stonewall" Jackson
    (C) Joseph E. Johnston
    (D) John B. Hood

8. Lincoln issued the Emancipation Proclamation after the Battle of

    (A) Gettysburg
    (B) Antietam
    (C) Vicksburg
    (D) the Wilderness

9. Lee was opposed at Gettysburg by

    (A) Hooker
    (B) Meade
    (C) Grant
    (D) McClellan

10. Hood's army was destroyed at the Battle of

    (A) Nashville
    (B) Atlanta
    (C) Savannah
    (D) Durham

Explanatory Answers

1. **(B)** Tennessee seceded after the attack on Fort Sumter.

2. **(A)** The Crittenden Proposal was a last-ditch attempt to preserve the Union by peaceful means.

3. **(C)** Lincoln said that he had no right to interfere with slavery where it existed.

4. **(D)** Missouri, a slave state, remained in the Union.

5. **(B)** First Bull Run was the first major Union defeat of the war.

6. **(A)** Fort Donelson controlled the approaches to Nashville.

7. **(B)** The Shenandoah Valley was a classic campaign in which Jackson tied down two and one-half times as many Union troops as were under his command.

8. **(B)** Antietam was Lee's first defeat on Northern soil.

9. **(B)** Meade had just replaced Hooker as Union commander.

10. **(A)** Hood had hoped to destroy Sherman's lines of communications.

Chapter 20

RADICAL RECONSTRUCTION, 1865-1877

The era of Reconstruction (1865–1877) is among the most important and the most disputed periods in American history, for the problems which it failed to resolve are with us today. Traditionally, Reconstruction (particularly Radical Reconstruction) has been viewed as a tragic mistake, during which a vindictive group of grasping Northern politicians put the vanquished and helpless South to the torture of Negro rule. Citing the gross corruption of the carpetbaggers (Northern adventurers who ruled the South during Radical Reconstruction and who exploited its resources), the enfranchisement of illiterate freedmen, and the systematic exclusion of former Confederates from public life, the traditionalists (known collectively as the Dunning school) have argued that Reconstruction represented the following: (1) an attempt to perpetuate the Republican party's control of the national government by excluding the Democratic South from Congress, (2) an effort to build a Southern Republican party by enfranchising illiterate Negroes (whose votes could easily be controlled by the carpetbaggers), and (3) an attempt to exploit the South for the advantage of Northern capitalists and to reconstruct the South along capitalist, rather than agrarian, lines.

In recent years, there has been a sharp reaction against the traditional interpretation of Reconstruction. Revisionist historians argue that the Radical Republicans were sincere humanitarians and idealists who were seeking to resolve the nation's race problem by granting the Negro civil and political equality with whites. These historians have dismissed the corruption of the carpetbaggers by pointing to the corruption which simultaneously plagued the Northern states (concluding that America as a whole had entered an age of corruption), and they emphasized the positive aspects of Reconstruction (the establishment of public school systems, social welfare advances, and economic rehabilitation). However, the Revisionists have been unduly influenced by the contemporary civil-rights struggle (they view Reconstruction as a lost opportunity for the establishment of racial justice), and their analysis is influenced too much by their own liberal biases. If Reconstruction was not the nightmare which the traditionalists have described, the Radical Republicans were, nevertheless, far from the crusading knights for racial justice which the revisionists have made them out to be. The Radicals were, above all else, practical politicians; and their programs were designed for maximum political advantage, not moral purity. While their ultimate goals may well have been noble, their methods were often deplorable and counterproductive.

PRESIDENT JOHNSON AND THE BREAK WITH THE RADICALS

Johnson Continues Lincoln's Plan of Reconstruction

A Tennessee Unionist of humble origins, Andrew Johnson found himself President of the United States in mid-April of 1865. A man of strong prejudices, he intensely disliked the planter aristocracy of the South, and he repeatedly declared that "treason must be made odious." When he became President, the Radical Republicans had high hopes that he would repudiate Lincoln's "lenient" program of reconstruction and adopt one which was more severe and more to the liking of the Radicals. Johnson, however, decided that Lincoln's plan of reconstruction was in the best interests of the nation as a whole, and he pledged to implement it. While Congress was in recess, over the summer of 1865, President Johnson recognized the loyal governments set up by Lincoln in Arkansas, Louisiana, Tennessee, and Virginia. From May 29 to July 13, 1865, Johnson issued a series of reconstruction proclamations which granted amnesty to Confederates who took the oath of loyalty to the Union,* established provisional governments for the seven Confederate states not yet reconstructed, and authorized the convening of constitutional conventions (elected by loyal voters) to draft new state constitutions. As soon as a state had rejected the doctrine of secession, repudiated the Confederate debt, and abolished slavery, it was eligible for readmission to the Union. By December, 1865, all the Confederate states except Texas had met these requirements, and Johnson announced that the Union had been restored. However, he reckoned without Congress.

---

* Curiously, Confederates owning property worth more than $20,000 had to personally petition President Johnson for pardon. Johnson seemed to relish the idea of aristocratic planters asking him (a poor Tennessee tailor) for pardon, and he granted pardons liberally.

The Theory of Radical Reconstruction

According to the Lincoln-Johnson interpretation, secession was illegal; and the South had never actually left the Union. The Confederate states were in rebellion against the United States; and as Commander-in-Chief, it was the President's responsibility to restore the Southern states to their proper relationship with the other states of the Union. That being the case, Congress had no role in reconstruction, for it was properly the domain of the executive branch of the government. However, having taken a back seat to the President during four long years of war, the Congress was anxious to reassert its authority and power and show the President that the executive branch was not all powerful. It is likely that had Lincoln lived, he would have faced the same difficulties with Congress as Johnson faced; and while he might have handled the situation better, it is doubtful that he could have excluded Congress from a say in the determination of Reconstruction policy.

According to Radical Republican Senator Charles Sumner, the Southern states, in seceding committed something very much like political suicide. Their state governments had to be reconstructed; and since Congress was charged with the constitutional duty of providing a republican form of government for the states, reconstruction was a congressional, not an executive, responsibility. Similarly, Thaddeus Stevens (Radical leader in the House) argued that the Southern states were "conquered provinces," by virtue of their rebellion, and had forfeited all their political rights. Since Congress had the responsibility for admitting states to the Union, it had to formulate the procedures by which the Confederate states were to be reconstructed. In any event, Congress, in December, 1865, established the Joint Committee of Fifteen (headed by Thaddeus Stevens) to study the problems of reconstruction and formulate policy. Dominated by the Radicals, the Committee insisted that the Southern states safeguard the rights of the Negro before being readmitted to the Union. When Congress reassembled for its 1865-1866 legislative session, it refused to seat the representatives of the states which Johnson had declared to be reconstructed. Over the next few months, the President and the Congress would become increasingly antagonistic over Reconstruction policy.

Johnson Vetoes the Freedmen's Bureau Bill

Just after the end of the Civil War, many former Confederate states (especially in the deep South) enacted a series of measures known as the "Black Codes." Ostensibly designed to protect the Negro from exploitation, they were actually designed to bind the Negro to the land and reduce him to serfdom (or peonage). They permitted state authorities to arrest Negro vagrants and lease their labor to private contractors, to impose restrictions and curfews on the movement of freedmen, and to regulate their wages, hours of labor, and conditions of employment and apprenticeship. The "Black Codes" convinced the Radicals that the South was unregenerate in its attitude toward the Negro, and they became ever more determined to protect the civil liberties of the hapless black population. In February, 1866, Congress enacted a measure to greatly enlarge the scope and authority of the Freedmen's Bureau (the Bureau was originally established to provide educational and welfare services for the newly freed Negroes). The Bureau would have the authority to try anyone accused of violating the civil rights of the Negro, and it could invalidate any labor contract which exploited the freedmen. President Johnson, however, vetoed the measure on the grounds (which were legitimate) that military trials of civilians during times of peace violated the Constitution. The veto alienated the Radical Republicans, who began to look upon Johnson as an obstructive apologist for the Southerners. On July 16, 1866, Congress overrode the presidential veto and enacted the Freedmen's Bureau Bill.

Johnson Vetoes the Civil Rights Bill

In April, 1866, Congress approved the nation's first civil rights act, which reversed the Supreme Court's ruling in the Dred Scott Case that Negroes were not citizens of the United States. Besides conferring citizenship on the Negro, the act also guaranteed equal civil rights for the Negro and forbade the states from violating the civil liberties of United States citizens. Johnson, however, vetoed the Civil Rights Act, arguing that is was an unconstitutional infringement of states' rights. As a life-long Democrat, he had never been a strong advocate of centralized authority, and his veto was entirely consistent with his long-standing political philosophy. It did nothing, however, to improve his relations with Congress.

The Fourteenth Amendment and the Congressional Elections of 1866

Formulated by the Joint Committee on Reconstruction, the Fourteenth Amendment to the Constitution of the United States was approved by the Congress in June, 1866, and was presented to the states for ratification. The Radicals declared that ratification of the Fourteenth Amendment by the former Confederate states was a prerequisite for their restoration to the Union. The Amendment declared the following:

(1) All persons born in the territorial United States (except Indians, who were not taxed) were citizens of the United States (thus, the Amendment restated the definition of citizenship contained in the Civil Rights Act).

(2) No citizen could be denied life, liberty, or property except by "due process of law." This made the constitutional protection of the Bill of Rights (the first ten amendments to the Constitution) binding upon the states and applicable in state court proceedings.

(3) Any state which denied the suffrage to any group of adult males because or race, color, or previous condition of servitude would have its congressional representation reduced proportionally. While this section of the Fourteenth Amendment did not require the Southern states to enfranchise their Negro population, it allowed the federal government to reduce the congressional representation of those states which barred Negroes from voting. (This provision has never been invoked against any state.)

(4) Confederate officeholders, even though pardoned by the President, were declared ineligible for future public office.

(5) Payment of the Union war debt was guaranteed, while the Confederate debt was specifically repudiated.

President Andrew Johnson on tour, endeavoring to enlighten the people.

Except for Tennessee, which ratified the Fourteenth Amendment on July, 19, 1866, and was promptly readmitted to the Union, the Southern states balked at ratification; and they looked to President Johnson for leadership and advice. Johnson told the South to reject the Fourteenth Amendment, for he counted on the November congressional elections to unseat the Radical Republicans and give the moderates control of Congress.

In August, 1866, Johnson organized the National Union party (a coalition of Northern Democrats, and moderate and conservative Republicans) in an effort to isolate the Radicals and end their control over Congress. Between August 28 and September 15, 1866, Johnson made a speaking tour of the North, seeking to win support for his new coalition. Unfortunately, the often inebriated Johnson made a series of intemperate speeches in which he attacked the character and motivations of the Radical leaders. The tour was counterproductive and succeeded only in arousing public sympathy for the attacked Radicals. For their part, the Radicals were much better campaigners. They waved the "bloody shirt"; Johnson and his supporters, they declared were controlled by the Democratic party — the party of treason and disunion. (Thus the Radicals labeled all Democrats Copperheads — pro-Southern and anti-Union partisans who had opposed the Northern war effort.) The Radicals called upon the people to complete the struggle for human freedom begun by the Civil War, and they urged the people not to permit the Democrats to undo the work for which half a million men died. They warned Northeastern capitalists that a Democratic triumph would threaten the protective tariff, and they told federal bondholders that the Democrats would seek to pay off the national war debt with depreciated paper currency. Finally, the outbreak of severe race riots in New Orleans and Memphis (during the summer of 1866) helped the Radical cause, for the riots convinced the North that the South was determined to keep the Negro in an inferior status. In the congressional elections, Radical candidates won overwhelming victories; and the faction of Sumner and Stevens controlled two-thirds of each house of Congress — enough to override any presidential veto and to render Johnson a mere cipher. In seeking to exclude Congress from a voice in determining Reconstruction policies, Johnson had made a disastrous political mistake. Had he been more open to congressional advice, he might have been able to moderate the demands of the Radicals (much as Lincoln had done), and he might have avoided an open break with Congress. Reconstruction might have been less traumatic for the South, and the status of the Negro (the ostensible concern of the Radicals) might have improved had the South been less hostile.

RADICAL RECONSTRUCTION

The Condition of the South

For four years, the South had been a battleground. Rival armies had fought and died to possess its soil, and the region had been looted, burned, and devastated. Virtually without exception, the railroads of the South had been ripped apart; its roads had been torn up and its harbors closed; its rivers were clogged with sunken and partially destroyed river boats. Bridges had been knocked out, canals were in disrepair, and factories remained only as burnt out shells. Confederate currency was now worthless, and Confederate bondholders had lost their total investment in the Stars and Bars. Two billion dollars invested in slave property had been wiped out with the stroke of a pen, and the land lay waste — desolate and unplowed. Land which had been worth from twenty to thirty dollars an acre in 1860, was now worth only three to five dollars in acre, and in parts of the South 40 per cent and more of all livestock had been destroyed. Pre-Civil War levels of agricultural output were not reached again until the end of the nineteenth century. Furthermore, although land values had plummeted and agricultural output had declined by as much as 50 percent, the Southern states were forced to raise taxes drastically in order to repair the damage of the war and move the economy off dead center. This sharp increase in tax rates, in the face of a depressed economy, caused widespread hardship and suffering among all elements of the Southern population, and helped ruin many farmers not already ruined by the war. In addition to the economic distress of the post-war South, there was the humiliation of Radical Reconstruction. Blaming their economic troubles on the Radicals, the Southerners formed a hatred of Reconstruction which has not been dispelled to this day, and which has continuously embittered Negro-white relations.

The First Reconstruction Act (March, 1867)

As soon as the new Congress convened, the war against President Johnson was resumed. Overriding the President's veto, Congress passed the First Reconstruction Act, which disbanded the Southern state governments established by Johnson and placed the South under martial law, dividing it into five military districts. Military commanders were empowered to hold new constitutional conventions which would be elected by universal manhood suffrage (excluding ex-Confederates). As soon as the Southern states ratified the Fourteenth Amendment and guaranteed Negro suffrage (while denying it to former Confederates), they would be eligible for readmission to the Union. The provision for Negro suffrage, however, met with widespread Southern opposition, for many whites did not feel that the former slaves had the experience or the education to qualify as voters. In addition, many Southerners felt that any move toward civil equality for the Negro would inevitably lead to social equality and the amalgamation of the races. Believing that the Negro was inferior to the white man, these Southerners were determined to replace slavery with white supremacy. They considered this to be the only way of maintaining satisfactory black-white relations, and they resisted implementation of the Radical program.

Supplementary Reconstruction Acts

In March and July, 1867, and in March, 1868, Congress (overriding Johnson's veto) enacted three supplements to the First Reconstruction Act. These measures authorized military commanders to seek out and enroll potential voters and also declared that a majority of those votes cast (rather than a majority of those qualified to vote) would be sufficient to put a new state constitution into effect. This latter provision would enable a small minority of voters to implement a program of Radical Reconstruction, despite an election boycott by resisting Southerners. As a result of these measures, the post-war South had 703,000 registered Negro voters and only 627,000 qualified white voters. In the black-belt states of Alabama, Mississippi, Louisiana, South Carolina, and Florida, Negro voters outnumbered whites; and the carpetbaggers had a fertile field for their work.

Clipping Johnson's Power

In order to prevent President Johnson from interfering with their reconstruction program, the

A carpetbagger bribing Negroes to get their votes.

Radicals enacted two measures in 1867, designed to limit his executive powers. The Tenure of Office Act prohibited the President from dismissing any Cabinet officer or civilian officer whose appointment was subject to Senatorial confirmation without the approval of the Senate. The act was designed to protect Secretary of War Edwin Stanton, who was cooperating with the Radicals in their reconstruction program. The second measure, The Command of the Army Act, limited Johnson's powers as Commander-in-Chief by requiring him to transmit all his military orders through General of the Army, Ulysses S. Grant (who was also inclined toward the Radicals). Of course, if Grant balked at implementing Johnson's orders, he could (theoretically) be replaced as General of the Army; but the act nevertheless weakened the effectiveness of the President's control over the army.

The Descent of the Carpetbaggers

With the South under military rule, Northerners (who were known to carry their belongings in large carpetbags) followed the army into the vanquished South or came down to work for the Freedmen's Bureau. A mixed parcel, the carpetbaggers were a curious blend of grasping adventurers seeking their fortunes and genuine humanitarians desiring to help the Negro and to aid the South in its return to normality. Working in cooperation with the Scalawags (a term used to describe Southern whites, mainly old Whigs, who cooperated with the Radical Republicans), the carpetbaggers organized the freedmen into effective political machines which permitted the carpetbaggers to control the reconstructed governments. Dominating the constitutional conventions elected in 1867 and 1868, the carpetbaggers wrote the new constitutions of the Southern states; and because of white disenfranchisement, they were able to control the congressional delegations and state governments of the South. Contrary to popular opinion, the era of Radical rule was not one of Negro rule. In no case did a Negro serve as governor of a Southern state, and only in South Carolina did Negroes constitute a majority of the state legislature. Generally, Negroes held lesser state offices (except for two who served in the United States Senate and a handful who sat in the House of Representatives), while Northern carpetbaggers held the higher offices.

Carpetbag Rule: The Balance Sheet

The carpetbaggers introduced many needed and long-overdue reforms. They drafted constitutions which proclaimed the equality of the Negro and the white races, guaranteed Negroes the right to vote, and protected their civil rights. They instituted the first public school system (open to black and white alike) in the South's history, modernized the court system and made the penal code more humane, provided for poor relief and the establishment of public hospitals and charitable institutions, redistributed the tax burden according to ability to pay (even though tax rates were increased at all levels), and made state government more responsive to the popular will. Finally, they appropriated funds for the rebuilding of roads, bridges, and public buildings, and for river and harbor improvements.

Despite the great amount of good work performed by the carpetbaggers, they are remembered for their gross corruption. Throughout the South, the carpetbaggers fleeced the resources of the states. In South Carolina, a state legislator introduced a bill to compensate him for his losses at the race track. It passed. In Louisiana, the governor received 1.5 million dollars for publishing public notices in his newspaper (a ridiculously exorbitant figure), and in the same state, a single session of the state legislature cost one million dollars — ten times the normal prewar cost. In too many instances, public funds appropriated for public construction found their way into private pockets. Roads were paid for which were never built, and those which were built cost the taxpayers far more than was necessary. Never had corruption in the South been so pervasive and extensive as during Reconstruction; and, while the North was equally corrupt, the corruption of the Radical governments alienated and enraged the Southern whites. It was the Negro who finally paid the bill for the excesses of the carpetbaggers.

The Omnibus Act

Under Radical control, the states of Arkansas, Alabama, Florida, Georgia, Louisiana, North Carolina, and South Carolina ratified the Fourteenth Amendment and provided for Negro suffrage. They were restored to the Union (still ruled by the Radicals) by the Omnibus Act of June, 1868. However, Mississippi, Texas, and Virginia still resisted the demands of the Radicals and, consequently, were excluded from Congress. They were finally readmitted to the rights of statehood in 1870, after ratifying the Fifteenth Amendment (proposed February, 1869 and proclaimed effective as of March, 1870) which prohibited the states from denying United States citizens the right to vote on account of race, color, or previous condition of servitude. The Fifteenth Amendment was the last major legislative proposal of the Radicals, for with the failure to impeach Andrew Johnson, their power began to wane.

THE DECLINE OF RADICAL REPUBLICANISM

The Impeachment of Andrew Johnson

Many Radicals were convinced that their program of reconstruction could never be fully implemented as long as Andrew Johnson remained as President and was charged with executing acts of Congress. Although Congress had the power to propose legislation, it was still the responsibility of the President to carry it out. Fortunately for the Radicals, Johnson, in February, 1868, provided his congressional enemies with the excuse they needed to bring impeachment charges against him. Determined to test the constitutionality of the Tenure of Office Act, Johnson attempted to remove Edwin Stanton as Secretary of War and replace him with General Grant. In the House, the Radicals drew up an eleven-count indictment charging Johnson with "high crimes and misdemeanors" in violating the Tenure of Office Act and in seeking to bring Congress into disrepute and public contempt. Approved by a vote of 126 to 47, Johnson went on trial before the United States Senate in March, 1868; the trial lasted two months. The House prosecution was led by Benjamin F. Butler, while William M. Evarts and Benjamin Robbins Curtis defended the President. Since the charges against Johnson were obviously politically motivated, it was apparent that the Democrats would vote, as a unit, for acquittal and that the Radicals would have to win the votes of moderate Republicans in order to get the two-thirds vote needed for conviction. On May 16, 1868, a vote was taken on what the House managers regarded as the strongest of the eleven articles of indictment, and despite enormous political pressure, seven Republican Senators joined twelve Democrats in voting for Johnson's acquittal. The final vote of 35 for impeachment and 19 against was one vote shy of the two-thirds necessary for conviction. Johnson was permitted to serve out his final months in office, but he remained virtually stripped of powers by a hostile Congress. Nevertheless, the Presidency had been redeemed as an independent agency of government. Had Johnson's impeachment been carried, the President would have become a virtual puppet of the Congress; and the separation of powers and the system of checks and balances would have been undermined, to the great detriment of American democracy.

The Presidential Election of 1868

The 1868 Presidential election was a national referendum on Reconstruction and postwar economic problems. Meeting in Chicago shortly after the failure to impeach Johnson, the Republicans selected as their presidential candidate the politically inexperienced and pliable Ulysses S. Grant. The hero of the Civil War, Grant possessed the popular following which the Republican party desperately needed, and he had no strong political convictions at variance with the Radical viewpoint. For Vice-President, the convention named the Radical Schuyler Colfax of Indiana. The party adopted a platform strongly endorsing Radical Reconstruction (although it hedged on the issue of Negro suffrage because of the opposition of many Northern states which had denied free Negroes the right to vote); it also endorsed the payment of the national debt in gold. Lower taxes, continued tariff protection, encouragement of European immigration, and pensions for war veterans (Union not Confederate) were also pledged. Finally, the Republicans appealed to the patriotism of the American people, asking them to stay with the party that had saved the Union and to reject the overtures of the party of "treason and disunion."

The Democrats, for their part, nominated New York's Horatio Seymour for President and Missouri's Francis P. Blair for Vice-President. Strongly condemning Radical Reconstruction and Negro suffrage, the Democrats accused the Republicans of subjecting the South to military tyranny and Negro rule. Seeking to gain the support of Western farmers suffering from low farm prices and tight credit, the Democrats called for tariff reduction and also for currency inflation (which would result in higher farm prices) by paying off the war debt with Greenbacks (the Ohio Idea) instead of with gold. As currency was cheapened, prices would increase; and debtor farmers would

Cartoon depicting 1868 presidential campaign with candidates Horatio Seymour, "the man of words" (left), and Ulysses S. Grant, "the man of deeds" (right).

be able to pay off their debts more easily. In the election, however, Grant carried 26 out of 34 states (6 Southern states were under Radical control and 3 Southern states did not vote in the election) and won the Electoral College by 214 to 80 votes. The General carried the popular vote by only 306,000 ballots out of 5.7 million cast, and he owed his popular majority to the votes of the more than 500,000 Negroes who participated in the election. More than ever before, it was apparent that Radical ascendancy depended upon the Negro vote. If the Negro were prevented from voting, the Republican party would be in serious trouble (it was this consideration which motivated the Fifteenth Amendment), for the Democrats were still a national power; and the return of white supremacy to the South might well return the party of "treason and disunion" to power.

The South is Redeemed

Radical rule proved to be short-lived in the South. Between 1869 and 1871, Georgia, North Carolina, Tennessee, and Virginia overthrew the Radicals and returned the conservative Bourbons (a term borrowed from French history to indicate those who forget nothing of the past and who learn nothing from it) to power. In 1874-1875, Radical rule was ended in Alabama, Arkansas, Mississippi, and Texas; and by the time of the Presidential election of 1876, only Florida, Louisiana, and South Carolina remained under the control of the Radical Republicans. The Bourbons achieved power as a result of the following factors:

(1) The physical intimidation of Negro voters by organizations such as the Ku Klux Klan, organized in Tennessee, in 1866, and headed by General Nathan Bedford Forrest. Although it was formally disbanded in 1869, the Klan (and similar organizations) continued to function clandestinely. It employed whippings, mutilations, and torture to drive out the carpetbaggers and to scare Negroes away from the voting booths.

(2) The restoration of civil rights to former Confederates through various acts of amnesty, and the coming of age of a new generation of white voters who were disenchanted with the corruption of the carpetbaggers, fearful of Negro equality, and anxious to restore white supremacy to the South.

(3) The growing weariness of the Northern public with the goals of Radical Reconstruction and with reform, in general. The

RADICAL RECONSTRUCTION, 1865–1877 / 225

Two members of the Ku Klux Klan in their typical garb.

American people could not sustain the emotional idealism of the war years; they were anxious to get on with the business of building up the nation, and they wanted to restore good relations between the North and South in order to develop the nation's economy. Their concern over the plight of the Negro declined with their waning desire for reform; and when the South began to systematically strip the Negro of his civil rights, the unconcerned North made no protest and no effort to enforce the federal laws protecting Negro civil rights.

Once in power, the Bourbons provided relatively honest and efficient government. Unfortunately, in their efforts to reduce state expeditures, balance state budgets, and liquidate state indebtedness (brought about as a result of Radical misgovernment), they cut back on the financial support given to public education, welfare services, and public health facilities. Many of the progressive social welfare reforms of the Radical Republicans were thrown out with the carpetbaggers; and within a few years, the South had again become a backward region in an otherwise progressive America.

THE ESTABLISHMENT OF WHITE SUPREMACY IN THE SOUTH

The Last Gasp of Radical Republicanism

By the time the presidential election of 1872 came around, the Republican party was no longer united in its reconstruction policies. Disgusted with the corruption of the Grant administration and the Southern Radical regimes, a Liberal Republican faction (including such luminaries as Carl Schurz, Charles Francis Adams, and E. L. Godkin) refused to accept the candidates of the regular (Stalwart) Republican organization. Demanding an end to military rule in the South and reconciliation with the former Confederate states, the Liberal Republicans called for a more moderate tariff, and for federal civil service reform to remove partisan politics from the administration of government. Joining with the Democrats, the Liberal Republicans nominated Horace Greeley for President and B. Gratz Brown for Vice-President. The Republicans renominated Grant for President, and selected Radical Henry Wilson for Vice-President. Defending Radical Reconstruction, they accused the Liberal Republicans and Democrats of willingness to sacrifice, for political advantage, the civil rights of the freedmen — of willingness to return the Negro to the none-too-tender mercies of the white Southerners. Although Grant won re-election with a landslide victory (a popular majority of 763,000 votes and 286 electoral votes to 66 for Greeley), the Liberal Republican revolt was the first major breach in Republican ranks, and it boded ill for the future of the party. A direct result of Liberal Republican pressure in Congress was the Amnesty Act of 1872, which restored civil rights to all but the highest Confederate leaders. The Amnesty Act was instrumental in helping the Bourbons supplant Radical rule in the South.

The Panic of 1873 and the Civil Rights Act of 1875

America's investors and businessmen, in their quest for quick and painless fortunes, had greatly overextended their financial resources. In September, 1873, the failure of Jay Cooke (of the Northern Pacific Railroad) was enough to produce a financial panic which ended in a severe depression that lasted five years. Blaming the depression on the party in power, the American people gave the Democrats control of the House of Representatives in the 1874 elections and reduced to a narrow margin the Republican party's control of the Senate. In rejecting the Republicans, the American people were also rejecting Radical Reconstruction, for the Democrats who were now coming to Congress were committed to the restoration of Bourbon rule in the South. Moreover, by the 1870's the leaders of the Radical faction (men like Thaddeus Stevens, Charles Sumner, and Ben Wade) were either being retired by their constituents or were dying of old age. The young Northern politicians who were replacing them were not reform-minded and were little concerned over the fate of the Negro.

On March 1, 1875 (just as the old Radical-controlled Congress was about to give way to the new Congress elected in 1874), the Radicals mustered the strength to pass another Civil Rights Act (the last act of Radical Reconstruction) as a tribute to the memory of Charles Sumner. The Civil Rights Act of 1875 forbade racial discrimination in public places or in businesses engaged in the public service, and it outlawed the systematic exclusion of Negroes from jury service. The Act, however, was largely ineffectual and was struck down as unconstitutional by the Supreme Court in 1883.

The "Stolen" Presidential Election of 1876

Delighted with their showing in the 1874 congressional elections, the Democrats anticipated victory in 1876, hoping to capitalize on the corruption of the Grant administration and on the depressed state of the economy. As their presidential candidate, they selected the elderly Samuel Jones Tilden of New York. Having good reform credentials (he exposed the corruption of the Tweed ring and sent "Boss" Tweed to the penitentiary), Tilden was also a distinguished corporation lawyer with good connections with the business community. He was, in every respect, the ideal Democratic candidate. Thomas A. Hendricks of Indiana was chosen by the Democrats for the Vice-Presidency. The Republican Stalwarts (regulars) would have liked to renominate President Grant for a third term, but they were not strong enough to defy the two-term tradition. The leading Republican candidate was Maine's James G. Blaine (leader of the "Half-Breed" faction), who was totally unacceptable to the Stalwarts. When the convention deadlocked, Ohio's reform governor, Rutherford B. Hayes, was brought forth as a compromise candidate and was given the presidential nomination. William A. Wheeler of New York was selected as Vice-President.

During the campaign, the Democrats promised to reduce the tariff, end military rule in those Southern states still under Radical control, and reform the national bureaucracy. The Republicans again waved the "bloody shirt," calling the Democrats the party of treason and urging the American people to rally to the party which preserved the Union. In the election, Tilden received 250,000 more votes than Hayes and carried Connecticut, New York, New Jersey, and Indiana, as well as the former Confederate states. However, the voting in Louisiana, South Carolina, and Florida (the states still under Radical rule) was so corrupt that both sides claimed victory (in addition, one electoral vote in Oregon was in dispute). Excluding all disputed electoral votes, Tilden had 184 unchallenged votes, while Hayes had 166 unchallenged votes; 19 votes were in dispute. In order to be elected, a candidate needed 185 electoral votes. Tilden needed one more vote for victory, and Hayes needed all 19 of the disputed votes if he were to defeat Tilden. In December, 1876, Republican and Democratic electors met in the respective capitals of the contested states and sent two conflicting sets of returns to Washington. It was now up to Congress to determine who was entitled to the 19 disputed electoral votes.

The Compromise of 1877

Congress established a 15-man Electoral Commission (5 members from each House of Congress plus 5 Supreme Court Justices) to determine the disposition of the 19 disputed votes. Originally the Commission was to consist of 7 Democrats and 7 Republicans, with independent Justice David Davis serving as the fifteenth member. However, when Davis declined to serve (having been elected to the Senate), the fifteenth seat went to the Republicans. Voting along straight party lines, the Commission awarded all 19 disputed votes to Hayes, thereby giving him the Presidency. The Democrats were outraged, and talk of renewed civil war swept the country. However, the South endorsed the findings of the Electoral Commission, and the crisis subsided. The Southern Bourbons had made a deal with the Republicans. In return for Bourbon support of Hayes, the Republicans agreed to the following:

RADICAL RECONSTRUCTION, 1865–1877 / 227

Cartoon showing the freedom of the Negro voter in the South (1876).

(1) Military rule was to be ended in Louisiana, South Carolina, and Florida; and the South was to have home rule over its Negro population (in other words, the North would acquiesce in white supremacy and make no effort to enforce the fourteenth and fifteenth amendments or the various civil rights acts).

(2) The South was to be provided with federal subsidies to finance railroad construction and other internal improvement projects.

(3) A Cabinet post was to be given to a Southerner, and a fair share of federal patronage was to be distributed to the South.

The Compromise of 1877 formally ended Reconstruction.

Toward Jim Crow

In the generation after 1877, the South gradually, but systematically, stripped the Negro of his civil rights. Literacy tests, poll taxes, grandfather clauses (which denied an individual the right to vote if his grandfather was not a registered voter), and physical intimidation kept the Negro away from the polls and gave undisputed political control to the whites. Gradually, separate schools (given inferior financial support) were established for Negro children; and segregation was introduced in public places (theaters, parks, railroads stations, etc.) and in public services. Finally, the sharecrop system condemned the Negro to unending poverty. In lieu of a money rent, Negro farmers paid their white landlords between one-third and one-half of the annual crop. With the portion of the crop which the tenants retained, they had to pay for seeds, farm tools, clothes, food, and all their other necessities. In cooperation with local landlords, neighborhood retail merchants extended "generous" credit terms to the Negroes (at substantial rates of interest, of course), hoping to keep the sharecroppers in perpetual debt and, thereby, dependent upon the largesse of the landlords. A man who is financially dependent upon another cannot very well assert his claim to political and civil equality. The crushing indebtedness of the Negro kept him passive and permitted the whites to maintain their undisputed control over Southern society.

The white Southerners transferred their hatred and resentment of Radical Reconstruction to the Negro, who bore the brunt of white anger and frustration. By embittering the South, Radical Reconstruction did the Negro a disservice. Failing to bring about racial equality, Radical Reconstruction only postponed the struggle for racial justice to a later age.

REVIEW QUESTIONS FOR CHAPTER 20

1. The "conquered provinces" theory of Reconstruction was advanced by

    (A) Abraham Lincoln
    (B) Thaddeus Stevens
    (S) Andrew Johnson
    (D) Charles Sumner

2. The Fourteenth Amendment did not

    (A) define United States citizenship
    (B) make the "Bill of Rights" binding on the states
    (C) require Negro suffrage
    (D) protect the Union war debt

3. Johnson's National Union party included all of the following *except*

    (A) Northern Democrats
    (B) moderate Republicans
    (C) Radical Republicans
    (D) conservative Republicans

4. The First Reconstruction Act provided for all of the following *except*

    (A) abolition of the Johnson state governments
    (B) martial law
    (C) constitutional conventions elected by universal manhood suffrage
    (D) enforced ratification of the Thirteenth Amendment

5. The attempted impeachment of Johnson was for violation of the

    (A) Tenure of Office Act
    (B) Command of the Army Act
    (C) First Reconstruction Act
    (D) Civil Rights Act of 1866

6. The Omnibus Act of 1868 did *not* restore to the Union

    (A) Alabama
    (B) Texas
    (C) Georgia
    (D) Florida

7. The Democratic presidential candidate in 1868 was

    (A) Horace Greeley
    (B) Horatio Seymour
    (C) Samuel Jones Tilden
    (D) None of the above

8. From 1869–1871 all of the following Southern states were redeemed *except*

    (A) South Carolina
    (B) North Carolina
    (C) Virginia
    (D) Tennessee

9. All were factors in the decline of Radical Republicanism *except*

   (A) the Panic of 1873
   (B) the waning of Northern reform zeal
   (C) the death of the Radical leaders in the 1870's
   (D) the excesses of the carpetbaggers

10. The Electoral votes of all the following states were contested in the Presidential election of 1876 *except*

   (A) South Carolina
   (B) Louisiana
   (C) Georgia
   (D) Florida

Explanatory Answers

1. **(B)** The theory held that the Southern states forfeited their political rights as a result of their rebellion.

2. **(C)** It merely provided for loss of representation for those states which discriminated against voters because of race.

3. **(C)** The National Union party sought to isolate the Radicals.

4. **(D)** The Thirteenth Amendment was already in effect.

5. **(A)** Johnson attempted to remove Edwin Stanton as Secretary of War.

6. **(B)** Texas was not restored until 1870.

7. **(B)** Seymour had been governor of New York.

8. **(A)** South Carolina was not redeemed until the Compromise of 1877.

9. **(D)** Carpetbagger excesses had little impact on Northern public opinion.

10. **(C)** Georgia had already been redeemed.

INDEX

Abolitionism, 164-165
Adams, John, Administration of, 107-109
Adams, John Quincy, 140-141
    Administration of, 141-143
    and Gag Rule, 155
Adams-Onis Treaty, 136
Administration of Justice Act, 77
Alamo, The, 153
Albany Plan of Union, 59
Alien Enemies Act, 108
Alien and Sedition Acts, 108
American Art (19th century), 163
American Colonization Society, 164
American Independence, decision for, 81-82
American Indian Civilization, 8-10
    American Indian, Social Organization of the, 9
    American Indian, Ways of Life, 8-9
American Literature (19th century), 162-163
American Revolution, 74-85
    Causes of, 82-83
American System, 140, 142
Amnesty Act, 225
Andros, Sir Edmund, 41-42, 46
Anglo-Dutch Wars, 21
Annapolis Convention, 93
Anti-Masonic Party, 152
Antietam, Battle of, 206
Appomatox, Surrender at, 213
Aroostook War, 155-156
Articles of Confederation, 90-93
    Congress and Western Lands, 91-92
    Domestic Affairs under, 92-93
    Foreign Affairs under, 92
    Limits on Powers of the Congress, 90-91
    Operation of the Congress, 91
    Powers of the Congress, 90
    Western Lands Controversy, 90
Austin, Moses & Stephen, 153
Aztecs, Conquest of the, 10

Bacon's Rebellion, 29
Bancroft, George, 163
Bank of the United States, First, 102
    Failure to Recharter, 122
    Second Bank of the U.S., 133
Bank War, 151-152
Barnard, Henry, 161
Bennett, James Gordon, 162
Biddle, Nicholas, 150
Black Codes, 218
Bleeding Kansas, 191-192, 194
Board of Trade, 56
Boston Massacre, 77
Boston Port Act, 77
Bradford, William, 36
Brown, John, Raid on Harpers Ferry, 195
Buchanan, James, and Kansas, 194
    and Secession Crisis, 201
Bull Run (Manassas Junction),
    First Battle of, 204-205
    Second Battle of, 206
Bunker Hill, 81
Burgesses, House of, 27

Burr, Aaron and the Election of 1800, 112-113
Burr Conspiracy, 116
Byrd, William II, 71

Calhoun, John C., 140
    and Concurrent Majority, 188
    and Andrew Jackson, 148-149
    and *South Carolina Exposition*, 143
California, Conquest of, 179
Calvert, Cecil (Lord Baltimore), 29-30
Cambridge Agreement, 37
Carolina Proprietary, 31
Caroline Affair, 155
Carpetbaggers, 222
    Carpetbag Rule, 222
Cartier, Jacques, 17
Champlain, Samuel de, 17
Chancellorsville, Battle of, 209
Chase, Samuel, 114
Chattanooga, Battle of, 211
Cherokee Indians, 150-151
Chesapeake-Leopard Affair, 117
Citizen Genêt, 104-105
Civil Rights Act of 1866, 218
    of 1875, 226
Civil War, Causes of, 200
    Union & Confederate Strength and Goals, 203-204
    First Bull Run, 204-205
    Ball's Bluff, 205
    Western Campaigns, 1861-1862, 205
    Monitor and *Merrimac*, 205-206
    Peninsula Campaign, 206
    Shenandoah Valley Campaign, 206
    Battle of Fair Oaks, 206
    Battle of the Seven Days, 206
    Second Bull Run, 206
    Antietam, 206
    Battle of Fredericksburg, 206
    Battle of Chancellorsville, 209
    Siege of Vicksburg, 209
    Battle of Gettysburg, 209-211
    Battle of Chattanooga, 211
    Battle of the Wilderness, 211
    Spotsylvania Court House, 211
    Cold Harbor, 211
    Petersburg Campaign, 211-212
    Sherman's March, 212
    Battle of Nashville, 212
    Appomatox, 213
Clay, Henry, 140
    and Bank War, 151-152
    and Texas Annexation, 175
Clayton-Bulwer Treaty, 181
Coercive (Intolerable) Acts, 77-78
Colden, Cadwallader, 69, 71
Cold Harbor, 211
Colonial America, Class Structure of, 66
    Education in, 67-69
    Literature of, 71
    Press in, 69
    Religion in, 66-67
    Science in, 69-71
    Suffrage in, 65-66

Colonial Government, 64-65
    Assembly, 65
    Governor, 64-65
    Governor's Council, 65
    Imperial Authority, 64
Columbus, Christopher, Voyages of, 4-5
Command of the Army Act, 222
"Common Sense," 81
Compromise of 1850, 187-189
    of 1877, 226-227
Confiscation Act, First and Second, 207
Congress, Powers of, 95
Connecticut, 40
Connecticut Compromise, 94
Conscription Act, First, 208-209
Continental Congress, the First, 79
    Second, 81
Cortés, Hernando, 10
Constitution of the United States, 93-97
    Ratification of the, 95-97
Constitutional Convention, 93-96
Convention of 1800, 108
    of 1818, 135-136
Cooper, James Fenimore, 163
Crawford, William Henry, 140
Creek War, 125-126
Crittenden Proposal, 201
Culpeper's Rebellion, 31
Currency Act of 1764, 75

da Gama, Vasco, 2
Dale's Laws, 26-27
Dartmouth College Case, 138
Davis Resolutions, 195-196
Day, Benjamin F., 162
Declaration of Independence, 82
Declaratory Act, 76
Deism, 66-67
Deseret, 183
Dias, Bartolomeu, 2
Dongan, Thomas, 46
Douglas, Stephen A., and Kansas-Nebraska Act, 190-191
    Debates with Lincoln, 194-195
Dred Scott Decision, 193-194
Dunning School, 212
Dutch in America, 18-21
    Explorations of, 18-19

Education (19th century), growth of, 161
    Secondary, 161
    Higher, 161
    Adult, 162
Edwards, Jonathan, 67
Election of 1800, 112-113
    of 1808, 121-122
    of 1824, 141
    of 1828, 143
    of 1836, 154
    of 1840, 156-157
    of 1844, 175
    of 1848, 186-187
    of 1852, 189-190
    of 1856, 192-193
    of 1860, 196-197
    of 1868, 223-224
    of 1872, 225
    of 1876, 226

Electoral College, 95
Eliot, Jared, 69
Emancipation Proclamation, 208
Embargo Act, 117-118
Emerson, Ralph Waldo, 163
Encomienda System, 11
English Explorations in America, 24
    Early Settlements, 24
Era of Good Feelings, 132
Eric the Red, 1
Ericson, Leif and Thorvald, 1
Lake Erie, Battle of, 126
Erie Canal, 135
Essex Junto, 115
European Age of Discovery,
    Reasons for, 2
European Rivalry for America, 5
Fair Oaks, Battle of, 206
Federalist Papers, 97
Federalists and Anti-Federalists, 96
Federalists and Republicans, 103-104
Fifteenth Amendment, 223
Fillmore, Millard and the
    Compromise of 1850, 188-189
Finney, Charles G., 146
Fitzhugh, George, 167
Fletcher Vs. Peck, 137-138
Florida, Acquisition of West, 122
    Seizure of, 136
Force Bill, 150
Fort Sumter Crisis, 202-203
Fourteenth Amendment, 218-219
Franklin, Benjamin, 69
Freedmen's Bureau Bill, 218
French Alliance, 84
French Colonies, 16-18
    Explorations, 16-17, 18
French and Indian War, 59-61
French Revolution and American
    Politics, 104
Fugitive Slave Act, 189

Gadsden Purchase, 182
Gag Rule, 155
Gallatin, Albert, Financial
    Policies of, 113
Galloway Plan of Union, 79
Garrison, William Lloyd, 164
Georgia, 31
Gettysburg, Battle of, 209-211
Ghent, Treaty of, 127
Gibbon Vs. Ogden, 138
Grant, Ulysses S., 205
    Union Commander, 211
Great Awakening, 67
Great Revival, 146
Greeley, Horace, 162
Guadalupe-Hidalgo, Treaty of, 180

Half-Way Covenant, 38
Hamilton, Alexander, First Report
    on Public Credit, 101-102
    and Bank of the United
        States, 102
    and Implied Powers, 103
    and Report on Manufactures,
        103
Harrison, William Henry and
    Tippecanoe, 123
Hartford Convention, 127
Hat Act of 1732, 57
Hawthorne, Nathaniel, 163
Hayes, Rutherford B., 226
Headright System, 27
Hooker, Thomas and Connecticut, 40
House of Representatives, 94-95

Houston, Sam, 153
Hutchinson, Anne, 39

Immigration to Colonial
    America, 50-51
Implied Powers, 103
Incas, Conquest of the, 10
Indentured Servitude, 28
Industrial Revolution in America,
    133-135
Iron Acts of 1750 & 1757, 57
Irving, Washington, 163

Jackson, Andrew, 140
    and Florida, 136
    First Term as President,
        147-152
        Kitchen Cabinet, 147-148
        Spoils System, 148
        Break with Calhoun,
            148-149
        Nullification Crisis,
            149-150
        Internal Improvements, 150
        and Cherokees, 151-152
        Bank War, 151-152
    Second Term as President,
        152-154
        Removal of Bank Deposits,
            152-153
        Texas Annexation, 153-154
        Concept of Presidency, 153
Jacksonian Democracy, Nature
    of, 146-147
Jamestown Colony, 25-26
Japan, Opening of, 182
Jay's Treaty, 105-106
    Opposition to, 106
Jefferson Land Act of 1804, 116
Jefferson, Thomas, Resigns as
    Secretary of State, 104
    and Strict Construction, 102
    and Election of 1800, 112-113
    as President, 113-118
        Financial Policy, 113
        Supreme Court, 113-114
        Louisiana Purchase, 114-115
        Burr Conspiracy, 116
        Tripolitan War, 116
        Relations with England
            and France, 116-118
        Embargo, 117-118
Jim Crow, 227-228
Johnson, Andrew, Reconstruction
    Policies, 217
    Freedmen's Bureau Veto, 218
    Civil Rights Veto, 218
    14th Amendment, 218-219
    Congressional Elections of
        1866, 219
    Impeachment of, 223
Joint Committee on the Conduct
    of the War, 205
Joint Committee of Fifteen, 217-218
Judiciary Act of 1789, 101
    of 1801, 113
    of 1802, 113

Kansas-Nebraska Act, 190-191
Kentucky and Virginia
    Resolutions, 109
King George's War, 59
King Philip's War, 41
King William's War, 58
Kitchen Cabinet, 147-148
Ku Klux Klan, 224

Land Ordinance of 1785, 91
Lee, Robert E., 206
Leisler's Rebellion, 46-47
Lewis and Clark, 115
Lexington and Concord 79-81
Liberal Republicans, 225
Liberty Party, 165
Lincoln, Abraham, Runs for Illinois
    Senate, 194-195
    Debates with Douglas, 194-195
    Runs for President, 196-197
    Secession Crisis, 200-203
    Assumes Presidency, 202
    and Slavery, 207-208
    and Confiscation Acts, 207
    and Emancipation Proclamation,
        208
    and Reconstruction, 213
Locke, John, and American
    Revolution, 71
Log Cabin and Hard Cider, 157
Logan, James, 69
Long Island, Battle of, 83
Lords of Trade, 56
Louisiana Purchase, 114-115
Lowell System, 134
Lundy, Benjamin, 164
Lyceum Movement, 162

Macon's Bill #2, 123
Madison, James, Domestic
    Affairs under, 122-123
    War Message, 124
    Last Year as President, 132-133
Maine, 40
Manifest Destiny, 173
Mann, Horace, 161
Marbury Vs. Madison, 113-114
Marshall Court, 137-138
Martin Vs. Hunter's Lessee, 138
Maryland, 29-31
    Founding of, 29-30
    Manorial System, 30
    Protestant-Catholic Rivalry,
        30-31
    Toleration Act, 30
Massachusetts Bay Colony, 36-39
    Cambridge Agreement, 37
    Growth of Representative
        Government, 37-38
    Watertown Protest, 38
    Half-Way Covenant, 38
    Town Government, 38
Massachusetts Government Act, 79
Mather, Cotton, 69, 71
Mayans, 9-10
Mayflower Compact, 35
M'Culloch Vs. Maryland, 138
McClellan, George Brinton, 205
McGuffey, William Holmes, 161
Melville, Herman, 163
Mercantilism, 54-58
Mexican War, 177-180
    American People and, 177-178
    Early Fighting, 178
    American Strategy, 178
    Santa Anna Episode, 178-179
    Conquest of California, 179
    Campaigns in Northern
        Mexico, 179
    Vera Cruz Expedition, 179-180
Middle Colonies, Economy of the,
    49-50
Missouri Compromise, 137
Molasses Act of 1733, 57
Monitor and the *Merrimac,* 205-206

Monmouth Courthouse, Battle of, 84
Monroe Doctrine, 139
Monroe, James, First Term as President, 133-138
    Second Term, 139-141
Montgomery Convention, 201-202
Mormons, 183

Nashville, Battle of, 212
National Union Party, 219
Naturalization Act, 108
Navigation Act of 1651, 55
    of 1660, 55
    of 1663 (Staple Act), 55
    of 1673 (Plantation Duties Act), 56
    of 1696, 56
Negro Slavery in Spanish America, 12 (see also Slavery)
    in Virginia, 28
Neutrality Proclamation, 104-105
New England Confederation, 40-41
New England, Dominion of, 41-42
    Economy of, 42
New France, Government and Problems of, 18
New Hampshire, 40
New Haven, 40
New Jersey, 47-48
    Quakers in, 48
New Jersey Plan, 74
New Netherland, Founding of, 19
    Immigration and Land Policies, 20
    Political History of, 20-21
    Economic Development of, 21
New Orleans, Battle of, 127-128
New York, 45-47
    Conquest of New Netherland, 45
    Duke's Laws, 45-46
    Anglo-Dutch Wars, 46
    Struggle for a Legislature, 46
    Charter of Liberties, 46
    Leisler's Rebellion, 46-47
New York City Draft Riots, 208-209
Newspapers and Magazines (in 19th century), 162
Nicholson Non-Importation Acts, 116-117
Non-Importation, 77
Non-Intercourse Act, 118
Northwest Ordinance of 1787, 91-92
Nullification Crisis, 149-150

Oglethorpe, James, 31
Olive Branch Petition, 81
Omnibus Act, 222-223
Ordinance of 1784, 91
Oregon Dispute, 173-174
    Partitioned, 176-177
Ostend Manifesto, 181

Panama Congress, 142
Panic of 1819, 136-137
    of 1837, 154-155
    of 1873, 225-226
Paris, Treaty of (1783), 85
Parkman, Francis, 163
Peninsula Campaign, 206
Penn, William, 48-49
Pennsylvania, 48-49
    Charter, 48-49
    Penn's Frame of Government, 49
    Indian Relations, 49
    Land Grants, 49
    Immigration Policy, 49
    Charter of Liberties, 49

Pequot War, 41
Perry, Matthew C., 182
Perry, Oliver Hazard, 126
Pet Banks, 152-153
Petersburg Campaign, 211-212
Pickering, John, 114
Pickett's Charge, 209
Pierce, Franklin and Kansas, 191-192
Pinckney's Proposals, 93
Pinckney's Treaty, 106
Pike, Zebulon, 115
Pizarro, Francisco, 10
Plymouth Colony, 34-36
    Pilgrims in Holland, 34-35
    Mayflower Compact, 35
    Government of, 36
Poe, Edgar Allan, 163
Polk, James Knox, 175
    and Oregon, 176
    and Mexican War, 177-178
Portuguese Explorations, 2
Prescott, William H., 163
The President, 95
Prince Henry the Navigator, 2
Princeton, Battle of, 83
Proclamation of 1763, 75

Quakerism, 48
Quartering Act, 75, 79
Quebec Act, 79
Queen Anne's War, 58

Radical Reconstruction, Theory of, 212-218
    Dunning School, 216
    Revisionists, 216-217
    Johnson and Reconstruction, 217
    Joint Committee of Fifteen, 217-218
    Freedmen's Bureau Bill, 218
    Civil Rights Act, 218
    14th Amendment, 218-219
    Congressional Elections of 1866, 219
    First Reconstruction Acts, 220
    Supplementary Reconstruction Acts, 220
    Carpetbag Rule, 222
    Omnibus Act, 222-223
    15th Amendment, 223
    Impeachment of Johnson, 223
    Redemption of South, 224-225
    Civil Rights Act of 1875, 226
    Compromise of 1877, 226-227
Reconstruction Act, First, 220
Reconstruction, Lincoln's Plan of, 213
    Wade-Davis Bill, 213
Republican Party, Founded, 191
Republicans and Federalists, 103-104
Rhea Letter, 136
Rhode Island, 39-40
Rittenhouse, David, 69
Rolfe, John, 27
Romanticism, 161-166
Rush-Bagot Agreement, 135
Russia and the Pacific Northwest, 139

San Jacinto, Battle of, 153
Sandys, Sir Edwin, Reforms of, 27
Saratoga, Battle of, 84
Science and Technology (19th century), 163-164
Secession Crisis, 200-203

The Senate, 95
Seven Days, Battle of the, 206
Shays Rebellion, 92-93
Shenandoah Valley Campaign, 206
Sherman's March, 212
Shiloh, 205
Slavery, Description of, 168-169
    Justification of, 166-167
    Rebellions, 169-170
Smith, Captain John, 25-26
Smith, Joseph, 183
Southern Civilization, Growth of, 166-170
Southern Redeemers, 224-225
Southern Society, Structure of, 167-168
Spanish America, Failure of, 13
    Government of, 12
    Society of, 13
Spanish Colonies, 10-13
Spanish Explorations in America, 10, 11
Spanish Indian Policy, 11
Spanish Mercantilism, 12-13
Specie Circular, 154
Spoils System, 148
Spotsylvania Courthouse, 211
Stamp Act, 75
    Crisis, 75-76
    Congress, 76
    Repeal of, 76
State Constitutions (post-Revolutionary), 88-90
Stevens, Thaddeus and Reconstruction, 217-218
Stiles, Ezra, 69
Strict Construction, 102
Sturgis Vs. Crowningshield, 138
Stuyvesant, Peter, 21
Suffolk Resolves, 79
Sugar Act of 1764, 75
Sumner, Charles, and "Crime Against Kansas," 192
    and Reconstruction, 217
Supreme Court, 95

Taney Court, 156
Tariff of Abominations, 142-143
    of 1816, 133
    of 1824, 142
    of 1832, 149
    of 1833, 150
Taylor, Zachary, Presidency of, 187-188
    and California, 187
    and Compromise of 1850, 187-189
Tea Act of 1773, 77
Tecumseh, Revolt of, 122-123
Tenure of Office Act, 222
Texas Annexation, 174-176
    and Presidential Election of 1844, 175
    and Van Buren, 175
    and Clay, 175
Texas Rebellion, 153-154
Thirteenth Amendment, 213
Thoreau, Henry David, 163
Tilden, Samuel Jones, 226
Tobacco Contract, 28
Toleration Act (1649), 30
Townshend Acts, 76
Transcendentalism, 164
Transportation Revolution, 134-135
Trenton, Battle of, 83
Tripolitan War, 116
Turner, Nat, 170
Tyler, John, Presidency of, 157

Undeclared Naval War of 1798-1800, 108
Utopianism, 165-166

Valley Forge, 84
Van Buren, Martin, 148
    and Jackson-Calhoun Rupture, 149
    as President, 154-156
        Panic of 1837, 154-155
        Gag Rule, 155
        Relations with England, 155-156
    and Texas Annexation, 175
Vesey, Denmark, 169-170
Vice Admiralty Courts, 56
Vicksburg, Siege of, 209
Vikings, American Explorations and Settlements of the, 1-2
Virginia, 24-29
    Jamestown, 25-26
    Starving Time, 26
    Dale's Laws, 26-27
    Tobacco Cultivation, 27
    Sandys, Reforms of, 27
    House of Burgesses, 27
    Headright System, 27
    Slavery and Indentured Servitude, 28
    Tobacco Contract, 28
    Royalization of, 28
    during Puritan Revolution, 29
    Bacon's Rebellion, 29
Virginia Company, 24-25
    Charter of 1609, 26
Virginia Plan, 94

Wade-Davis Bill, 213
Walker Filibuster, 181
War of Independence, 83-85
War of 1812, 123-129
    War Hawks, 123-124
    Madison's War Message, 124
    Reasons for War, 124
    Campaigns of 1812, 125
    Activities on the High Seas, 125
    British Blockade, 125
    Battle of Lake Erie, 126
    British Offensives of 1814, 126
    Treaty of Ghent, 127
    Battle of New Orleans, 127-128
War Hawks, 123-124
Wars of Empire, 58-61
Washington, Burning of, 126
Washington George, First Term as President, 100-104
    Cabinet, 100-101
    Second Term, 104-107
    Neutrality and Citizen Genêt, 104-105
    Farewell Address, 106-107
Washington Peace Conference, 201
Watertown Protest, 38
Webster-Ashburton Treaty, 156
Webster-Hayne Debate, 148
Weld, Theodore Dwight, 164-165
Western Lands Controversy, 90
Whig Party, 153
Whisky Insurrection, 105
White Supremacy, 225
Whitefield, George, 67
Whitney, Eli, 134
Wigglesworth, Michael, 71
Wilderness, Battle of the, 211
Williams, Roger and Rhode Island, 39-40
Wilmot Proviso, 180-181
Winthrop, John, 37
Writs of Assistance, 56

XYZ Affair, 107-108

Yorktown, 84-85
Young America Movement, 181
Young, Brigham, 183

Zenger, John Peter, 69